FROM CAVE TO CATHEDRAL

FROM CAVE TO CATHEDRAL

TEMPLES AND SHRINES OF PREHISTORIC
CLASSICAL AND EARLY CHRISTIAN TIMES

E. O. JAMES

London
THAMES AND HUDSON

© THAMES AND HUDSON 1965
TEXT PRINTED IN GREAT BRITAIN BY
WESTERN PRINTING SERVICES LTD BRISTOL

CONTENTS

Contents

Contents

Contents

Contents

Contents

PREFACE

THE SETTING APART FOR SACRED PURPOSES OF PARTICULAR AREAS, buildings, groves and enclosures has been a characteristic feature in the history of religion from prehistoric times to the present day. So far as the sacred places in antiquity are concerned, this is most apparent in the great temples which were constructed in Egypt, Babylonia, Assyria, Jerusalem and India, and which reached their zenith in Greece and finally in Rome, after the earlier precinct, or *sacellum*, had become a *templum* under the influence of the Etruscan and Hellenic prototypes. The designation *templum*, however, being a derivative of the Greek τέμενος signified a sanctuary (ἱερὸν) or precinct (περίβολος), indicating a sacred area consecrated to the worship and service of the god whose altar, statue or shrine it enclosed. Thus, behind the architectural temple lay a long history, going back to the simpler primitive type of cavern sanctuaries and megalithic structures of the Upper Palaeolithic and Neolithic periods respectively, to the remarkable Maltese temples, the henge monuments and the 'high places' on hill-tops, and later the Indian cave-temples and the Minoan-Mycenaean *temenos* with its altar and shrine.

Similarly, in later history the colonnaded oblong basilicas used as courts and places of public assembly in Rome and Pompeii, though not the pagan prototypes of Christian churches as has been widely supposed, nevertheless had considerable influence on the ecclesiastical architecture in and after the fourth century A.D., since they were found to be adaptable to the purposes of corporate worship. And even the basilica seems to have had simpler beginnings, having been derived from the Roman house, just as Christian worship began in private dwellings in apostolic times. The house design in fact remained influential in the construction of oratories and churches until in Byzantium, Sancta Sophia introduced a new type of architecture. With the rise and diffusion of Islam, when churches frequently were transformed into mosques, they underwent some modifications, though the nave, transepts and aisles often survived with additional colonnades, pointed arches and changes in orientation. The Byzantine decoration and plan was generally retained except in the completely new mosques, like that of Ibn Tulun in Cairo in 878, which were essentially Muslim creations displaying the primitive plan and design inherited from Medina. But the tendency has been for local traditions and conditions to be strongly felt in Islamic ecclesiastic architectural styles.

Most of the current literature in this field of inquiry is concerned almost exclusively with either the structure, development of style and decoration of the buildings, or with the rites and liturgies performed in them, and is usually confined to one particular region or faith. Invaluable as these descriptions are and quite indispensable for basic data in the production of a volume such as this, more is required for a full understanding of the religious purposes and functions of sacred places. The fundamental question is raised: why, under what circumstances, and for what purposes have these places come into being?

Without some very urgent reason and compelling cause, men would not have penetrated into the almost inaccessible depths of eery cavern-sanctuaries and painted magico-religious animal designs, often in very difficult and even perilous positions, and performed rites in connexion with them. Nor would they have created the vast megalithic monuments of Carnac, Avebury and Stonehenge, the extensive 'high places' with *maṣṣebahs*, *asherahs* and groves on hill-tops, or a succession of temples to Yahweh on Mount Zion in Jerusalem; they would not otherwise have erected the hundreds of sublime temples in the Graeco-Roman world, elaborate Hindu edifices in India, or the great basilicas of Rome, Ravenna, Byzantium and Cordoba, and the imposing Islamic mosques. All these sacred places are expressions of deeply ingrained religious beliefs, emotions and spiritual values, just as are modes of worship, ritual and seasonal dramas. The aim of this historical and archaeological investigation of the structure, function and significance of sacred places is to bring together their material and spiritual aspects in as it were a sacramental union, relating the outward and visible manifestations to their inward and spiritual purposes in the religious milieu in which they have emerged. So regarded, sacred places and their equipment become the medium through which basic beliefs, ritual techniques and acts of worship find expression.

Most of the higher living religions arose and developed in the Fertile Crescent and the adjacent and closely connected region in the eastern

Mediterranean and in western Asia, from Iran to north-west India—an area with which I have been familiar for a number of years, together with its Palaeolithic background. Attention has therefore been concentrated in this volume on the data in this vital cradle of civilization. While I have not hesitated to exercise independent judgment in the collection and interpretation of the available evidence in the light of my own observations and inquiries, the most authoritative sources of information have been consulted, as is apparent in the documentation and bibliographies. I am particularly grateful to my friend and colleague Professor I. A. Richmond who has given me the benefit of his unrivalled knowledge of the Roman material and, in the midst of many other commitments, generously undertook to read this section of the typescript, making most valuable criticisms and suggestions. To do full justice to the subject, extensive illustration is essential, and I am indebted to the publishers for the lavish complement of fine plates produced with their customary skill, and for their help and advice in this aspect of the production.

All Souls College,   E. O. JAMES
   Oxford.

CHAPTER I

The Palaeolithic Cavern Sanctuaries

DECORATED CAVES

IT IS NOW CERTAIN THAT EARLY MAN in the Old Stone Age had sacred places to which he resorted, primarily to exercise supernatural control over his food supply by the performance of mimetic rites. This has been confirmed by the discovery in France and Spain of a considerable number of decorated caves which undoubtedly were prehistoric sanctuaries. Their situation, often in the dark, almost inaccessible recesses of damp limestone mountains, sometimes as much as half a mile from the entrance, as at Niaux near Tarascon-en-Ariège in the Pyrenees, and reached only by dangerous, tortuous paths, is indication of the sanctity with which they were regarded. For that which is sacred must be isolated from secular and profane contacts.

CANTABRIA

La Pasiega. The cave of La Pasiega is situated in the Cantabrian limestone hills above the small spa, Peunte Viesgo, south of Santander. To gain access to the cave, a descent has to be made by a narrow passage 6 feet in depth, and then, pursuing a veritable labyrinth of small corridors, one is finally led to a small chamber at the end of which is a stone throne, or altar, hewn out of the rock. On it the explorers found an implement made of limestone which may have been a votive offering. In another gallery on the opposite side, probably reached originally by the ancient entrance to the cave now nearly blocked, a group of tectiforms may have formed an inscription or warnings. Above them are designs of two human feet, and to the left others of uncertain interpretation, belonging to the Aurignacian or the early Magdalenian cultures. Elsewhere are good engravings of horses, and in the main gallery paintings in red or black which include those of the stag, ibex, hind, ox, chamois and wild cattle, numbering in all over 250 and belonging to the Upper Aurignacian, now known as the Gravettian, or the Early Magdalenian cultures.[1] 'Art for art's sake' would hardly have lured the men who executed these paintings along these treacherous passages into the heart of the mountain, with only their flickering lamps. Some more urgent purpose must have impelled them.

Castillo. About half a mile across the valley, a steep scramble up the high carboniferous limestone hill is required to reach a second cave, Castillo, rather nearer to the village. It contains a galaxy of paintings and engravings of bison, horses, hinds, stags, ibexes and an elephant (possibly *Elephas antiquus*), together with a frieze of stencilled human hands, like those at Gargas near Montréjeau in the Pyrenees. On the ceiling of a very obscure alcove are an astonishing number of tectiform (i.e. roof-shaped or club-like) conventional designs representing perhaps tents or traps, shields or weapons, and there is a stalagmite projection forming a kind of altar. At the back is a collection of these signs painted at different periods in the Upper Palaeolithic, the entire setting suggesting that the apse had been a small shrine of the sanctuary for a very long time. The cave, in fact, had been a centre of human activity from Acheulian times, when it may have been a factory site for making flint implements, as is revealed by a stratigraphical succession of industries complete with hearths and of Pleistocene fauna in ascending levels, showing that unlike most decorated caves the mouth of Castillo was inhabited during the greater part of the Palaeolithic period, continuing in use until the Bronze Age.

At first entry was made from the lower end, but by the Magdalenian this entrance had become blocked by successive accumulations of kitchen refuse, flints, bones and blocks of stone, reaching a height of 45 feet. Since then access has been from the side of the hill now facing Puente Viesgo, and the Upper Palaeolithic deposit contains the most complete archaeological section known anywhere in Europe. In its extensive and complex interior every phase of Palaeolithic art is represented, from the Lower Aurignacian to the Upper Magdalenian, and a perpetual succession of initiates must have resorted to it to hold within its sacred precincts the magico-religious rites on which the food supply was believed to depend.[2]

Hornos de la Peña. These complicated neighbouring cavern sanctuaries in the province of Santander are but two examples of many similar grottoes widespread throughout the whole Franco-Cantabrian region. Thus, beyond La Pasiega and Castillo in the direction of San Felice de Puelna, some 6 miles from Torrelavega, lies Hornos de la Peña. It is situated near a farm to the right of the main road at the village of Tariba, and lies half way up a steep approach in a cretaceous limestone range of hills on the right bank of the Besaya river. Beyond a narrow entrance passage are its galleries which contain engravings of horses, primitive oxen, deeply incised bison, ibexes, stags and bulls, many of which have been superimposed on earlier roughly executed Aurignacian designs. Some of the later bison and horses are Perigordian in style but with rather more archaic heads. There is also a deeply engraved human figure in profile, 40 centimetres high, with a tail, and having raised arms like similar figures at Altamira. This, Breuil suggests, may represent the god of the cavern.[3] Wavy parallel lines termed 'macaroni' recur, the meaning and purpose of which, here and elsewhere, is purely conjectural. The horse, bison, and stag are Perigordian in technique, but only one engraving of a horse and four of bisons are Magdalenian.[4] The male figure is unique in Cantabrian Aurignacian art, except for the very lightly scratched examples on the painted ceiling at Altamira, the classic site in the Cantabrian mountains near the town of Santillana del Mar, and west of Santander.

Altamira. It was here in 1879 that the little daughter of Don Marcelino de Sautuola, a pioneer prehistoric archaeologist, wandered into the cave with a lighted candle, while her father was digging at the entrance, and came upon the figures of bison on the ceiling and walls of a chamber leading out of a long gallery. These she mistook for bulls, but Sautola at once recognized the nature and antiquity of the animals depicted in the polychrome frescoes. Little notice, however, was taken of the discovery at the time. Identical engravings of bison were found by four lads in 1895 in the Grotte de la Mouthe near Les Eyzies in the Dordogne, and it was only when these were examined by E. Rivière in 1902, and were eventually accepted as genuine Palaeolithic work, that the significance of the Altamira paintings was realized. In the meantime several other decorated caves had come to light in France—at Pair-non-Pair near Bourg-sur-Gironde in 1897, and at Font-de-Gaume and Les Combarelles near Les Eyzies. This led to a careful re-examination of the contents of Altamira by Emile Cartailhac and the Abbé Breuil, and in 1906 their results were published under the auspices of the Prince of Monaco, and subsequently, by the beneficence of the Duke of Alba, with the assistance of Professor Obermaier.

The Hall of the Paintings, aptly described by the Abbé Breuil as 'the Sistine Chapel of prehistoric art', measuring about 20 yards in length by 9 in width, with a very low roof 6½ feet high at the entrance, 5½ feet in the middle and 3½ feet at the end, is adorned with the fine polychromes which first caught the eye of Maria, groping round with her candle. These are still in an excellent state of preservation, having been protected by becoming slightly fossilized. They are rendered in yellow, red and brown ochre with black shading, and superimposed on older paintings. They were painted on a carefully prepared surface, and some of the figures were partly engraved with flint tools. In the background are club-shaped signs painted in red, while to the right are human hands, made either by stencilling the hand on the wall, or by making a print of the hand on it. The bosses were coloured and skilfully utilized to represent bison lying down with the limbs drawn beneath the body in different postures. The paintings include a wild boar shown running, a bison bellowing in rage, and stretching itself, a horse with a finely shaped head superimposed on an older painting of a hind or colt in lighter red, and a walking bison realistically portrayed.

The elaboration of the technique of the polychromes, often partially engraved, is quite remarkable and unequalled in any Palaeolithic cavern-sanctuary. This reached its height in the ceiling fresco in the 'Hall of the Paintings'; a very fine but a rather more primitive technique is used in the gallery behind. Everywhere, however, there are works of art, whether painted or engraved, which excite admiration through the blending of colour and the portrayal of animal attitudes. Combined with these outstanding artistic achievements are crudely executed, grotesque human figures, geometrical signs and typically Palaeolithic tectiforms, ladder-shaped objects, comb-like red signs, and primitive silhouettes. In all, there are about 150 paintings in Altamira from throughout the Upper Palaeolithic, the great polychromes having been superimposed on earlier paintings and engravings, silhouettes and tectiforms.

Repeated falls of rock from the Solutrean culture phase to the end of the Magdalenian, when a final collapse sealed the grotto, rendered it by no means a secure habitation. It can only have been its inherent sanctity that made it an outstanding centre, frequented by a long succession of votaries. They have left behind at the entrance indications of their presence in stone, bone, ivory, and horn implements (of poor workmanship with geometrical designs in the Lower Magdalenian deposits), and in stag shoulder blades, some of which in the Aurignacian and Solutrean levels were engraved. Even after the fall of the rock which made it uninhabitable, it must still have been visited for purposes of worship since it was then that the polychromes were executed in the great hall, which became the sanctuary *par excellence*.[5] This continued in use until the front half of the roof fell in, closing the cave completely. It was discovered in 1868 by a hunter, who removed some of the boulders when digging out a fox. It then remained for Don Marcelino de Sautuola seven years later to begin excavations which were destined to open a new epoch, not only in the history of the cave but also in our knowledge of the Old Stone Age and its prehistoric sanctuaries.

THE DORDOGNE

It was in France in the department of the Dordogne, mainly around Les Eyzies and, elsewhere, the valley of the Vézère, that the evidence accumulated most rapidly once the existence of decorated caves and their art was recognized and authenticated. Thus, within a radius of 3 miles of this remarkable centre, three outstanding confirmatory discoveries were made in succession, beginning with La Mouthe in 1895 and followed six years later by that of Les Combarelles and Font-de-Gaume, to which now have been added those at Tayat, Cap Blanc, La Grèze, Comarque, Bernifal, and more recently (1940) Lascaux near Montignac on the Vézère, 14 miles from Les Eyzies, with an array of Palaeolithic sites of great archaeological importance (e.g. Crô-Magnon, Laugerie-Basse, Laugerie-Haute, Le Moustier, La Micoque, La Madeleine).

Font-de-Gaume. For our present purpose, Font-de-Gaume, $1\frac{1}{4}$ miles to the south-east of Les Eyzies on the left bank of the Beune, is of particular interest. A rather low long corridor leads to a very narrow fissure, known as the Rubicon, marked off now by an iron ladder and a small gate. This seems to have constituted the beginning of the sacred enclosure, opening as it does into the principal gallery with a smaller low chamber, widening on the left to form the 'Hall of the little Bison'. Along the first part of the tunnel the scaling and weathering of the walls through the action of frost and corrosion by condensation have prevented the survival of any paintings that may have been executed there. Beyond the Rubicon the animal figures are prolific and reach their climax in the series of beautiful polychromes in the principal gallery, finely engraved reindeer and mammoths being superimposed on the polychrome paintings and these, in turn, upon earlier inferior designs. In the large polychrome bison and mammoth all the details of the head and even the pupil in the eye have been rendered. In the very small 'Hall of the little Bison' the walls and roof are covered with engravings and paintings of bison in black and brown, on a surface smeared with red ochre, as in a recess at Altamira. Just before the Rubicon, horses are engraved on a red line-drawing under shaded black, and brown polychromes, which in their turn have been superimposed on tectiforms and vertical lines.

Font-de-Gaume, in fact, contains the most complete record of samples of Upper Palaeolithic art to be found in any decorated cave, ranging from crude Aurignacian designs to the most highly developed polychrome friezes and compositions, including processions of reindeer, bison, mammoths and galloping horses. The prevalence of palimpsests, often polychromes with the finest technique, suggests that certain parts of the sanctuary were regarded as especially sacred and efficacious, and so generation after generation made their contributions displaying their skill at the same spots. However, one figure of a rhinoceros in red ochre had been painted on the vertical wall of a narrow fissure, 10 feet above the surface of the floor, in such a position that the artist must have been forced to climb on to the shoulder of an assistant in order to execute it.[6] As there was plenty of wall-space within much easier reach, it is inconceivable that it was made for aesthetic reasons. A deeper motif of a magico-religious nature must be sought.

Les Combarelles. This applies also to the series of engravings in the form of a frieze along the two walls of the lengthy narrow gallery of Combarelles, about a mile from Font-de-Gaume on the road to Sarlat. When the sanctuary was first entered in 1901 by Capitan, Breuil and Peyrony, the very fine engravings of woolly rhinoceroses, mammoths, horses, reindeer, bison, bears, stags, lions and ibexes, could not be reached without scrambling along the subterranean tunnel, 260 yards in length, which became very narrow before it opened into the little chamber containing the best engravings. Near the entrance hardly any occur, the frieze commencing 175 yards along the gallery and continuing to the end. Besides the Palaeolithic animals there are a few tectiforms, a stencilled hand and thirty-nine human figures, some of which are masked. Superimpositions are numerous, and in addition to the masked anthropoid figures is a human silhouette with a mammoth's head and two arms stretching out in the form of tusks.[7] These in all probability represent hunting devices and disguises, perhaps having a magical significance, either in relation to a mimetic ritual or to mythical beings connected with the sanctuary and its hunting ceremonial. The sanctuary is profusely decorated, mainly in work of the Magdalenian period, notwithstanding the difficulty of access. Here again, only a very compelling reason could have induced the ritual experts so persistently to have performed their rites in the sacred gallery.

Lascaux. In striking contrast is the great cavern discovered on 12 September 1940 by two lads and their dog at Lascaux on the left bank of the Vézère, a mile and a quarter to the north of the little town of Montignac. This most spectacular and spacious sanctuary of cathedral proportions, described by the Abbé Breuil as 'the Versailles of Palaeolithic art', opens with a 'nave', or great hall, impressively decorated with wall paintings in a variety of styles, executed in mauve and purple as well as in the more familiar black and red pigments. It must have been a cult-centre for some thousands of years in view of the succession of techniques and distinguishing features. Almost every form of Perigordian art is represented in it, and within its sacred walls a great variety of rites must have been performed, ranging from magic for hunting and promotion of the food supply to mysterious commemorative symbolism depicting the hazards of the chase. The latter has been rendered in a scene in the seclusion of the 'crypt', which is entered by a drop of some 25 feet at the end of the 'nave'.

On the left wall of a corner in this hole is a stylized anthropoid figure with a bird-shaped head, killed apparently by a bison whose flank has been transfixed by a spear and its entrails exposed. To the left is a woolly rhinoceros apparently walking away, though whether it was he who had ripped up the bison is doubtful as the rhinoceros is painted in a different style. In front of the man is something resembling a bird on a pole, its head similar to that of the anthropoid figure.[8] This is not unlike an Egyptian ceremonial stave, a funeral post, or the effigies made to contain the souls of the deceased in Alaska and among the Eskimoes. The Abbé Breuil, in fact, has suggested that the scene may be a votive painting of a hunter who was buried in the cave,[9] while others have conjectured, with less probability, that it had a malicious intent to encompass his death by black magic.

Although it is not possible to determine the precise purpose of this 'problem picture' there can be little doubt that it was painted in this very inaccessible shaft in a particularly sacred and awe-inspiring spot for some magico-religious reason connected with the supernatural control of the chase and its hazards. Elsewhere in the cave are other enigmatical designs, as, for example, the representation of a mythical animal in the great 'Hall of the Bulls' with a large, sagging body resembling that of a rhinoceros, and a head like that of an antelope, with oval rings on the flanks and two long horns projecting from the forehead and terminating in a tuft. To describe this strange composite creature as a 'unicorn' is a misnomer, but it does not

Fig. 1.   The 'Unicorn' from Lascaux, after Breuil

resemble any known living beast. It could be a sorcerer or shaman clad in a spotted skin of some bovidae, perhaps impersonating an ancestral being believed to be responsible for fertility and success in the chase. It has some resemblance to Chinese paintings of horses with short legs and protruding barrel-like bodies. If the large oval spots represent marks of wounds and not natural dappling, then the purpose in all probability was destruction rather than veneration. No other animal, however, is portrayed in this manner, though at the end of the axil passage a horse is shown falling over a precipice, or into a pit, and the tectiform and other magic signs which frequently appear on the paintings could indicate traps, unless, as Breuil suggests, they were local tribal marks.

Taking the evidence collectively, the setting and equipment are only explicable on the assumption that Lascaux was a sanctuary of supreme importance in the Upper Palaeolithic—from the Gravettian phase of the Aurignacian, not less than 20,000 years ago, until it reached its zenith towards the end of the Magdalenian, dated at about 1300 B.C. by the radio-carbon (Carbon-14) isotopic analysis of the charcoal from a hearth in the shaft of the Dead Man, in association with spears and a number of stone lamps used to light the cave. This raises chronological problems in any attempt to correlate the available data and their place in the last glaciation, and to bring them into relation with the contents of other decorated caves in the region. Nevertheless, even if the Lascaux cultus reached its height about 15,500 years ago and in comparison with most of these sanctuaries was therefore of shorter duration, its equipment shows that it occupied a position of great importance and significance in the second half of Breuil's Aurignacio-Perigordian cycle of development in cave art.[10] It was then that such palimpsests as the frescoes of monumental bulls superimposed on more ancient bovines painted in dark red ochre were produced, covering the walls of this vast cavern with a remarkable display of styles and techniques in a relatively short time.

THE PYRENEES

Niaux. Passing from the Dordogne to Ariège on the French side of the Pyrenees, in the valley of the Vic-de-Sos above the village of Niaux, $2\frac{1}{2}$ miles from Tarascon-en-Ariège, one reaches the great cavern of La Calbière, the channel of an ancient glacial river. The paintings begin about half a mile from the entrance, near the centre of the hill. At about 550 yards inside where the corridor divides, on the floor of the passage to the left, there is an engraving of an ox with wounds marked by three circles on the body and an arrow in the chest. To the right the main artery leads to an apse in the form of an immense 'rotunda', the 'Salon noir', on the walls of which are numerous line-drawings of bison and horses, six ibexes and a red deer in black oxide of manganese, in some cases covered by others larger and better executed (e.g. the fine black horse under a low vault), showing the coats by hatching and occasionally by tinting. Several of the bison have arrows marked in black on their sides. A crevice at the end of the hall has been shaped like the face of a deer to which antlers have been added to complete the resemblance. On the floor in the right-hand corner are engravings of two trout, and near by possibly the print of a naked human foot covered with stalagmite. Near the bifurcation, three small natural hollows on the right-hand wall have been cleverly utilized to represent wounds by drawing round them the outline of a bison and marking the cups with arrows in red ochre. In front of the expiring bison are circles and club-shaped designs depicting missiles.

Montespan. In a region in which decorated caves are so prolific, Niaux may well have been a tribal sanctuary in which esoteric rites were performed in the seclusion and silence of the great 'rotunda' and its 'side chapels' to control the fortunes of the chase. This is even more apparent in the cave of Montespan, near the château of the celebrated Marquise in the Haute Garonne. Here, over twenty clay models of wounded animals were discovered by M. Casteret when he entered it in 1923, after swimming for nearly a mile under the icy water that filled the opening and passing through the neck of a siphon. In a gallery to the left, 110 yards from the siphon, the clay figures of horses were executed on the surface of the floor with numerous closely related engravings on the walls (e.g. in slight relief a horse, deeply incised, and in high relief a finely modelled mare in foal). The statues were attached to the wall and had been broken in pieces, apparently during a magical ceremony, the body, hind-quarters and tail of one of them (probably a lion) lying on the ground, the dust perforated by stabs from javelins. In an adjoining small low chamber, among a number of clay sculptures, was the headless statue of a crouching bear lying on its stomach and showing unmistakable indications of having been pierced by more than thirty javelin thrusts. Near by was the model of a clay lion with similar wounds, and behind it, the incised drawing of a horse with a long flowing mane and adorned with curious symbols.[11] Here then, was a Pyrenean sanctuary in which the magical control of the chase was practised on a grand scale.

Gargas. In the cretaceous limestone spur on the left bank of the Garonne, between Saint Bertrand-de-Comminges and the village of Aventignan in the Hautes-Pyrénées, a few miles from Montréjeau, is Gargas. This cave, formerly the den of the cave bear, is of interest mainly on account of the series of 150 stencilled hands on its walls. On the left wall of the first hall, which was blocked up before the Magdalenian, are sixty-seven left hands, twenty-seven of which are in red and forty in black pigment; on the right side are six right hands in red and five in black. Many are mutilated, having several fingers missing. This distinguishes these Gargas hands from those in other Palaeolithic caves (e.g. Castillo and Altamira). Sometimes the thumb and first two fingers have been removed, or four fingers have been cut off. Groups of isolated fingers also are depicted.

Intermingled with these hand designs are interlacings and arabesques with animal silhouettes, naturalistic in style and technique. As this 'Sanctuary of Hands' was closed by a landslide at the end of the Aurignacian, a *terminus ad quem* is set for its mural ornamentation. In the fourth and principal hall, and in a recess between it and the third hall, the surface of the walls are covered with engravings, in association with stencilled hands and interlacings, which extend to the back of the cave. In the corridor known as the 'Oubliettes' a fine figure of a horse has been drawn on the left-hand wall, together with other drawings on clay, while in a niche in the hall of the 'Crevasses' a small bison is outlined in a rudimentary manner. On the left, only the head, horns and legs are sketched. One such clay figure is covered with stalagmite.[12] The hands, however, are the principal magico-religious objects at Gargas, and their mutilation suggests the practice of removing fingers as offerings in times of sickness, disease, and in mourning rites, or to propitiate malignant powers; this is a frequent practice among primitive people today, such as the Australian aborigines, the Bushmen and the North American Indians. In Morocco representations of hands are used as charms against the evil eye, the hand acting as a screen from the dangerous look. The Moors hang figures of an open hand from the necks of their children, and stretch out the

five fingers of the right hand towards a person who is suspected of having
an evil eye, saying 'Five in your eye', or 'Five on your eye'.[13] Similar
devices were practised by the ancient Egyptians.[14]

It is possible that the arabesques on the walls and roof of the Sanctuary
of Hands in the inner depths of Gargas, uncommonly like the claw-marks
of the cave bear made on the surfaces, had some ritual significance. The bear,
we know, has very often been regarded with awe and veneration because of
its great strength and supposed supernatural powers. Its teeth were worn as
amulets because its mystic qualities were thought to reside in them; its claws
may have been similarly revered, and to reproduce the scratchings would
be a means of assimilating the *mana* analogous to the carrying of a charm
containing it.

Tuc d'Audoubert. These, however, are merely surmises. Eastwards from
Montréjeau to St Girons in Ariège are two more very illuminating cavern-
sanctuaries, situated in the foot-hills of the Pyrenees. Both were hollowed out
by the river Volp when, on its way to rejoin the Garonne at Cazères, it went
underground for 1¼ miles at Enlène and emerged in a small valley near
Montesquieu-Avantes at the Tuc d'Audoubert. It was here, at the Tuc, that
on 12 October 1912 the Count Bégouen and his sons, Max and Louis, with
their friend François Camel, having taken a boat along the Volp for about
90 yards upstream, hacked their way through stalactite pillars and the remains
of a landslide which closed the magnificent stalactite hall at the end of the
Palaeolithic. In the corner of this chamber is a narrow passage containing
Magdalenian engravings of horses, bison, reindeer and a bull, associated with
symbolic magical arrows and club-shaped signs like those at Niaux, Altamira, and at Pindal in Asturias. A high oblique chimney leads to a corridor
containing engravings of mythical animals, one above the other, which may
represent the guardians of the sanctuary. The passage becomes narrower
until it is no larger than a drainpipe. At this point there are a few Aurignacian
engravings and 'macaroni' designs on the roof; beyond lies a large gallery
with beautiful stalagmites, traces of the cave bear and marks in the clay of
bare human feet and fingers. A scraper and a pierced tooth of an ox were
also recovered from this part of the cave, together with the lower jaw of a
bear carefully poised on a piece of rock. Lying against a projecting stone at
the end of the gallery, in the middle of this inner low-roofed sanctuary, were

two bison carefully modelled in clay, a male following a female, measuring respectively 63 and 61 centimetres in length. On the floor in front of them was a third, 13 centimetres long, and several incomplete models of bison and lumps of kneaded clay, still carrying impressions of human fingers on them. Around the hillock there were marks of fifty human heels, which may have been made by dancers engaged in a fertility ritual to promote the multiplication of the species so vividly portrayed in the relief showing the female bison with outstretched neck and raised tail awaiting the male in process of rising upon her. In a recess clay had been kneaded possibly into phallic models.[15]

Les Trois Frères. Two years later, on 21 July 1914, the three sons of the Count Bégouen, Max, Louis and Jacques, followed up their discovery at the Tuc with yet another when they lowered themselves with ropes into a hole at the other end of the subterranean descent of the Volp at Enlène. This proved to be the roof of a narrow gallery leading to an extensive cave. Further investigations, however, were prevented by the outbreak of the first World War, and it was not until June 1918, when the boys were on military leave, that the quest was resumed. This involved crawling for 60 yards through a small vertical shaft at the end of the Enlène cave, not much bigger than a rabbit-hole, to reach the decorated halls and corridors; these were found to contain a vast collection of engravings, paintings, faded red stencilled hands and rows of red and black spots and arabesques. Eventually the narrow passage divided into three, the one on the left leading to the 'Chapel of the Lioness' composed largely of stalagmites. This opened on to a great hall with successive tiers and a stage, resembling a theatre but devoid of decoration. In this chapel the figure of a lioness shaded in black with her cub is painted and engraved on a rock rather like an altar and seems to be guarding the first approach to the sanctuary.

The sanctuary itself, however, is composed of an apse with recesses, a sloping floor and converging walls covered with engravings and paintings in Perigordian and Magdalenian styles belonging to this period. At the end of a steeply sloping and winding passage is an alcove, the vertical walls of which are adorned with engravings of bison, horses, reindeer, mammoths, rhinoceroses and cave bears. On the left, about 12 feet above the ground is an aperture, or window, overlooking the alcove in full view of the frieze of animals. Beside it, to the right, is the masked figure of a man in the attitude of a hunter creeping along with bent knees seeking his prey; the legs are human but the face is enclosed in the mask of a stag with antlers; the eyes are those of an owl, the ears of a wolf, the claws of a lion, and the tail of a horse.[16] The figure, partly painted partly engraved, is outlined in black pigments. If this extraordinary representation was in fact that of a sorcerer or shaman engaged in a ritual dance, as has been suggested by Bégouen,[17] he may have stood at the 'window' or aperture to perform his rites in the presence of the sacred design and of the votaries below, to facilitate hunting and fertility. The Abbé Breuil now thinks, however, that the figure represents the embryonic god of the sanctuary in the form of the living sorcerer.[18] Be this as it may, a cult appears to have been practised in this remarkable sanctuary in which human beings and animals were brought together in some ritual action to establish a mystic communion with the providential source of the food supply and to promote its conservation.

LOT

Pech-Merle. In the department of Lot is the large cave discovered and explored by the Abbé Lémozi on the hill Pech-Merle near the village of Cabreret, 20 miles to the east of Cahors. In addition to representations of mammoths, bison and oxen pierced by spears, and a masked man with arrows, there also occur figures of cattle without eyes or ears. The Abbé Lémozi explains this portrayal as the attempt to deprive the hunted beasts of sight and hearing, thereby rendering them an easy prey for the hunters.[19] However, the paintings in the sanctuary belonging to the end of the Perigordian or very early Magdalenian periods have often been very carelessly executed and have a number of features missing. On the ceiling of the huge gallery there are headless figures of women with an arm or leg omitted, and animal designs in a similarly incomplete condition. This may be merely the result of their having been drawn for magical purposes, since for casting spells on the prey or producing fertility, deficiencies in detail of this nature were of little or no importance. On the other hand, some of the mammoths, bulls, bison and spotted horses have been rendered with great skill, and there is every indication that this very extensive and profusely decorated cavern was a much frequented sanctuary in the Aurignacio-Perigordian culture phase.

On the floor of a low rectangular hall, entered from a narrow passage at the end of the large painted stalagmite gallery, appeared numerous bones and skulls of cave bears, and jaws and ribs of cave bears had been preserved in a pit and their skulls in small earth mounds, suggesting that a bear cult may have been practised here. On the right-hand wall of this so-called 'Ossuary' is a well engraved head of a bear, and on the ceiling and walls are stencilled hands and 'macaroni' interlacings. In addition to the cave bear the mammoth is a prominent cult object, together with oxen and horses, while as usual in these sites the bison also is venerated. For the most part the fauna represented is pre-Magdalenian, and this is also the case in the neighbouring decorated caves investigated by the Abbé Lémozi. Thus, in the adjoining Marcenac cave, horses, bison and stags with twisted antlers (*cervus elephus*) are depicted, while engravings of horned animals and horses, with antlers or heads missing, are prominent in the cavern of Sainte-Eulalie, 16 miles away in the Bajocian limestone cliffs near Figeac.[20]

ROCK-SHELTERS

THE DORDOGNE

La Grèze. In contrast to these very obscure and inaccessible sanctuaries in limestone caves are paintings and reliefs under overhanging rocks in shallow shelters open to the light of day. These tend to be rather later than those in the deep Franco-Cantabrian decorated caves, though most of them were executed before the end of the Palaeolithic, or perhaps early in the transitional Mesolithic period in some cases. In the Dordogne in the picturesque valley of the Beune beyond Combarelles, near the ruins of the Château de Comarque and the smaller Château de Laussel, about 5 miles from Les Eyzies, lie four rock-shelters which are quite definitely Upper Palaeolithic. Where the road rises above the marshy valley on the right bank of the Little Beune, there is a very small chamber, 7 or 8 yards long and 5 or 6 yards wide, called La Grèze, with a few engravings and a very fine deeply engraved Aurignacian bison; the deposit contains Aurignacian and Lower Magdalenian implements.[21]

Cap Blanc. Below, on the other side of the road, is the rock-shelter of Cap Blanc in which a Crô-Magnon skeleton was found and which contains the celebrated frieze of horses and bison sculptured in high relief and covered by a Lower Magdalenian deposit.[22] There are, however, no indications that this magnificent example of Palaeolithic sculpture had any magico-religious significance and, like the Gorge d'Enfer, also near Les Eyzies, it may be one of the very few instances of prehistoric 'art for art's sake'.

Comarque. This hardly applies in the case of a small cave on the opposite bank of the Beune beneath the Château de Comarque, where the bas-relief of the head of a horse occurs in association with traces of other similar figures both in the round and in relief with engravings on the wall facing them.[23]

Laussel. The rock-shelter 126 yards long and 22 yards wide, in the long overhanging cliff in front of Comarque, was occupied successively from Acheulean and Mousterian times to the Aurignacian and Perigordian epochs. It was here, above the marsh to the left of the Château de Laussel, that Dr Lalanne discovered in the Late Aurignacian (Gravettian) deposits the well-known sculptures in relief on blocks of limestone, originally perhaps decorating the walls of the shelter. The most important of these, 46 centimetres long, depicts a nude female with prominent breasts and projecting hips, holding in her right hand an incised bison's horn. Her left hand is placed on the stomach which is thrown forward. The face is featureless and egg-shaped, and the head is turned in profile towards the horn. The modelling had been done carefully and the surface, except the head, polished; the entire figure had been painted red. On the ground were four similar reliefs on small slabs in a fragmentary condition. Two figures held horns and had their heads turned in their direction. One had even more exaggerated hips and breasts; the left arm was raised and bent at the elbow and the right outstretched arm held a curved object. The fourth figure has been interpreted as the representation of a copulation, or as an accouchement. On the fifth slab is a headless male apparently shooting with a bow and arrow, or throwing a javelin.[24] In contrast to the voluptuous female reliefs, this figure is remarkably slender with a belt round the waist and no traces of any sexual features.

While female figurines with pendulent breasts, broad hips, rotund buttocks and excessive corpulency suggestive of pregnancy have been very prevalent in the Middle Aurignacian and Gravettian sites (e.g. at Kostienki Gagarino, Mozine, Malta [Siberia], Brassempouy, Willendorf and Lespugne), having reached Europe from the southern Russian steppes, they would seem to have been primarily symbols of the maternal generative functions. It is true that an esoteric element may have been inherent in the tradition, but as Palaeolithic prototypes of the cult of the Mother-goddess in more advanced stages of civilization, their main purpose was the promotion and conservation of life through the outward signs of female fecundity. Therefore, it was childbirth rather than conception that found expression in these figurines and bas-reliefs, the rock-shelter at Laussel being in the nature of a shrine adorned with sculptural blocks of limestone representing pregnant women holding what may be horns of plenty, and painted with red ochre as a potent life-giving agent. This shrine was situated in the very heart of the cave cultus in the Dordogne.

EASTERN AND SOUTHERN SPAIN

Cogul. It is, however, on the other side of the Pyrenees in a rock-shelter at Cogul, a remote village some 8 miles from Lérida in Catalonia, that an actual scene is portrayed on a very faded fresco: a group of nine women, narrow-waisted, wearing caps and skirts reaching to the knees, but devoid of facial features, are portrayed dancing round a small naked male figure.[25] In its present form a fertility motif is indicated, though hardly of a phallic

Fig. 2. The dancing women fresco from the rock-shelter at Cogul, Spain

nature, as has been suggested, as the penis is not erect. Moreover, the picture seems to have been the work of several generations of late Palaeolithic artists, the little dark-brown male figure having been added to the earlier black group of women. Nevertheless, the insertion of the later figure would appear to have had a fertility significance connected with a rite in which the women were grouped round a male cult object of some kind to promote the production of life. The inclusion of the figure of a bison in the scene indicates its Palaeolithic provenance, though in the present condition of the fresco it is not possible to work out a chronological succession of layers as Breuil managed to establish in the composite painting containing the figure of a rhinoceros in the rock-shelter at Minateda in Murcia, between Chinchilla and Hellín.[26]

Alpera. Not very far from Minateda in the rock-shelter of La Vieja near Alpera in the province of Albacete, a typical eastern-Spanish hunting scene is portrayed in which male and female dancers occur; the women resemble

Fig. 3.   The dancing chieftain scene, detail from the painting in the Alpera rock-shelter

those at Cogul, two of them clad in wide skirts of crinoline type, while the men are unclothed. In the Cueva de la Vieja the figures are depicted in three shades of red, repainted at two successive epochs, comprising some thirty goats or antelopes, twenty-six stags, four bulls, seven wolves, two deer, a horse, an elk, and ten men, most of whom with drawn bows are shooting at animals. Two of them are engaged in a dance with legs apart showing the genital organs and are wearing a head-dress of plumes. The three women have wasp waists and one of them is naked and corpulent. The bodily proportions are well preserved but the hands and faces are oval and featureless. One of the women holds in her left hand an object that might be a statuette, though it is very difficult to determine what it was supposed to be when it is examined *in situ*.[27] In the Cueva del Quesco, close to La Vieja, a human figure is represented lifting another figure by its feet, and among pictures of extinct species are some of the moose, as at Minateda.

It seems, in fact, that these realistic, vivacious paintings in eastern Spain were for the most part executed in the Upper Palaeolithic, but while in all probability they were contemporaneous with their Franco-Cantabrian counterparts, their cultural connexions and origins appear to be Caspian, with possible African affinities, similar designs and techniques occurring as far south as Southern Rhodesia.[28] Although their precise purpose is as obscure as their exact origin and history, it is almost certain that they had a magico-religious significance. The attitudes of the human figures are of those engaged in a sacred dance rather than in hunting, though they hold weapons. They may have been directed primarily to the securing, preservation and increase of the species encountered in the chase, and frequently changed to suit these requirements. This is particularly apparent at La Vieja where oxen were painted over older pictures of stags and then were metamorphosed into stags by the addition of antlers. Finally, they were overlaid by highly conventionalized and geometrical designs of the third and last phase of Spanish art, when influences from the south were being felt in these rock-shelters, as for instance, at Velez Blanco west of Murcia, and at La Pileta Benaojan, near Malaga.[29]

Las Figuras. In the late Neolithic and Chalcolithic Age conventionalized designs and petroglyphs of human and animal forms are distributed sporadically in the limestone or sandstone rock-shelters in southern Spain, especially between Malaga and Cadiz. Las Figuras near Casa Viejas in southern Andalusia, with its five hundred drawings, is the most important example. Although, unlike the great caves of the Dordogne, the Pyrenees and Cantabria, none of the rock-shelters in eastern and southern Spain were concealed from the profane gaze of all and sundry, most of them were never used for human habitation. Thus, the floor of Las Figuras sloping upwards, made it quite impossible to walk about in it, yet the superimposition and alteration of the designs, here and in other similar larger sites, show that they were visited by successive generations of worshippers, probably at seasonal festivals and on other ritual occasions.[30] The smaller shelters may have had some particular sacred significance as domestic or local shrines, at which rites were duly performed as and when occasion required.

THE CULT OF THE CAVES AND ROCK-SHELTERS

One of the reasons for the continued use of the sacred places, often over a great number of years, would seem to have been the practice of a ritual dance in which men and women engaged to control the mysterious processes upon which the food supply and the propagation of the human and animal species were thought to depend. As we have seen, under Palaeolithic conditions the vagaries of the chase and of the seasons were the principal concerns leading the ritual experts to perform their rites in the forbidding recesses of these esoteric sanctuaries in the Dordogne, the Pyrenees, Haute Garonne, Lot, Cantabria and Asturias. If the sanctuaries were inhabited at all, it was only the entrance chamber which was used, as at Altamira and Castillo, and then generally sporadically; the interior was far too damp and dark for permanent human habitation. It is, and apparently always has been, thought necessary to reserve sacred places exclusively for the exercise of their spiritual functions.

THE MIMETIC MASKED DANCE

This dance was devised to meet the requirements of the deep, emotional impulses centred in the perpetual struggle for survival, and to sublimate the tension arising out of it by symbolizing and bringing under control the supramundane forces involved; hence the numerous representations of figures clad in animal masks or skins engaged in mimetic dances portrayed

Fig. 4.   Disguised hunter at Les Trois Frères, after Breuil

at Abri-Mège, Teyjat, Combarelles and the Grotte de la Madeleine in the Dordogne, at Marsoulas in the Hautes-Pyrénées and at Altamira and Hornos de la Peña in Cantabria. The figures in animal disguises suggest that the ritual expert impersonated the spirit of the animals, their qualities, attributes and powers, in a dramatic presentation of a successful hunt preceding the event. Secondarily, because a ritual that involved a more or less realistic reproduction of some practical activity established the *ex post facte* notion of 'sympathetic causation', the rites acquired a magical efficacy. Thus, besides the so-called 'Sorcerer' at Les Trois Frères, a dancer depicted playing a bow-shaped instrument appears disguised as a bison, and two curious beasts are rushing away from him, possibly dancers in the guise of animals.

The situation, however, was complicated by an inherent sense of kinship which Early Man felt existed between himself and the animals, whom he realized had greater strength, virility and dexterity than himself and yet upon whom he depended for his means of subsistence, involving their slaughter. Out of this tension may have arisen the dual aspects of the mimetic masked dances: the one directed to facilitating the fortunes of the chase; the other to establishing a mystical union with the source of providential bounty and beneficence. To these ends the hunter had to become the animal in order to imbibe its essential qualities and to become *en rapport* with it. In the Palaeolithic period hunting was the essential pursuit, as almost all features of everyday life were in some way related to it—skins for clothing, bone and horn for artefacts, needles and tendons for sewing, fat for lamps, and hooks and harpoons for fishing, as well as meat for daily consumption. But the maintenance of the food supply in its several aspects required an organized, collective effort on the part of the community to exercise a ritual control over the chase, to achieve success in hunting expeditions by magico-religious devices and to propagate the species.

Thus, resort was made to the cavern sanctuaries by ritual experts to assist human skill and ingenuity with supernatural power and knowledge, casting spells upon the quarry and employing their superior strength and cunning by identifying themselves with the prey. Therefore, the paintings, engravings and models were marked with spears, darts, javelins and other missiles, the representations and effigies being regarded as the actual creatures portrayed. The same designs or figures were often used repeatedly for this purpose, as in the case of the headless bear in Montespan, and the numerous palimpsests at Lascaux, Marsoulas, Les Trois Frères, and, in fact, in the majority of the more important decorated caves. Sometimes it sufficed to depict only particular parts of the animal, as for example the head or the horns, these being regarded as sufficient to convey the spell to the quarry.

SEASONAL FERTILITY RITES

Securing the prey, however, was only one element in the maintenance of an adequate food supply, the chase depending in the first instance upon the increase of the animals to be hunted. Therefore, it was also to stimulate fecundity among them that fertility dances were held at Tuc d'Audoubert, Cogul and Alpera—very much as the Australian aborigines resorted to such sacred places as Emily Gap near Alice Springs in the Arunta country, where the rocks have been decorated with totemic zoomorphic and phytomorphic designs and conventionalized drawings, to perform their intichiuma ceremonies to make their totems increase and multiply.[31] In the case of the Australian aborigines each clan exercises its functions for the benefit of the community, as the sacred species is tabu to those responsible for its ritual propagation and they may only eat of it very sparingly if at all.

Whether anything in the nature of totemism was practised in the Upper Palaeolithic, as has often been suggested,[32] is very doubtful as the representation of so many different varieties of animals in the same cave, and indeed in the same paintings, is not indicative of a totemic organization. Had the institution been established, each totem presumably would have had its own sanctuary in which its particular rites were performed in relation to its specific designs, as at Emily Gap or Kalurungari on the Calder river in Australia, even though, as Breuil has pointed out, bones of these animals depicted in the Palaeolithic caves are absent in the kitchen-middens.[33] Nevertheless, even if it is improbable that the rites had a totemic sacro-religious setting, there are good reasons to think that seasonal ceremonies were held with similar intentions in the cavern-sanctuaries and at the rock-shelter shrines to facilitate fecundity, especially at breeding seasons and at the annual renewal of nature in the spring, or its equivalent, according to the climatic and local conditions after the maximum glaciation.

THE CULT OF SKULLS

The most mysterious and disturbing phenomenon that arrested the attention of Early Man seems to have been that of death, and one of the earliest features of prehistoric religion was the belief in a continuance of life in the dead, thereby bringing the mystery of the after-life into relation with that of birth, nutrition and fertility. This becomes apparent in the care taken to inter the body in a grave, not infrequently in a cave, and to provide the deceased with implements, ornaments and offerings of food. The skull as the seat of potency was preserved for ritual purposes, the brain sometimes having been extracted and consumed to imbibe its life-giving qualities. The earliest indications of this practice have been found in China in a deep cleft which was once a cave in the Dragon-bone Hill near the village of Chou K'ou Tien, 37 miles from Peking. Remains were found in Middle Pleistocene strata, corresponding probably to the second (Mindel-Riss) interglacial in Europe, estimated at about 300,000 years ago, as far as it is possible to measure even Quaternary geological time in years. It was here that the skull of *Sinanthropus* was recovered in 1929, followed by the discovery of the bones of human skeletons scattered about indiscriminately and split to extract the marrow. This has been thought to suggest a cannibalistic feast, and the absence of the first two cervical vertebrae on the skulls to indicate decapitation after death.[34] This may have been to preserve the crania as trophies, or, as they show signs of injuries, to consume the brain sacramentally as the soul-substance; a custom widely practised in Borneo and Indonesia.[35]

It seems probable from the numerous crania and headless skeletons that have been found in Palaeolithic and Mesolithic sites, especially in Western Europe, that a cult of skulls was prevalent in prehistoric times. Thus, in 1939, a Neanderthal skull was discovered in Goat's Cave in Monte Circeo on the Tyrrhenian coast of the Pontine marshes, showing signs of death from violence and of the extraction of the brain through the foramen magnum after it had been cut away from the spinal column. It was placed in an inner chamber of the cave in a ritual position within a circle of stones, as an object of worship or as a trophy. Beneath it were fractured metacarpal bones of an ox and a deer, and piled up round the walls were the bones of deer, hyena, elephant, leopard and lion.[36]

We see, therefore, that in the last glaciation, from 100,000 to 50,000 years ago, Neanderthal man on occasions deposited the dead ceremonially in a cavern sanctuary used for ritual purposes as a sacred ossuary, and in all probability extracted the brain and partook of it to imbibe its magico-religious qualities and mystic virtue. At Krapina near Zagreb in Croatia in a Mousterian deposit on a terrace belonging to the Riss-Würm interglacial, a quantity of charred human and animal bones had been split to obtain their marrow, suggesting the remains of a cannibalistic mortuary feast, one of the skulls showing cuts suggestive of a violent death.[37] In the Ngandong terraces of the Solo river in eastern Java, in the equivalent in Indonesia of the third (Riss-Würm) interglacial in Europe, skulls appear to have been hacked open, probably at a mortuary feast, and the crania used as bowls.[38] In the Upper Palaeolithic, drinking cups made from the upper part of the dome of human skulls were of not uncommon occurrence, as, for example, in the Solutrean and Magdalenian deposits in a cave, Le Placard, Charente, at Laugerie-Basse near Les Eyzies, and in Castillo, Cantabria.[39]

Rather later, in the Mesolithic deposits in the cave of Ofnet in a spur of the Jura near Nördlingen in Bavaria, a nest of twenty-seven skulls was found in 1907, embedded in ochre and facing westwards. Next to this collection were six skulls in the same position. The cervical vertebrae were attached to them, and from the marks of cutting with flint knives it is apparent that the heads had been severed from the rest of the body after death, and then ceremonially dried. As those at the centre were crushed or distorted by pressure from those nearer the edge, it seems that the heads were added one by one successively. Twenty ornamented with snail shells were of children, nine more elaborately adorned with necklaces of deer teeth and shells were of women, while the four male skulls had no such equipment.[40] It is evident that here again in this ossuary a cult of skulls had been practised, recourse having been made to the sacred cave from time to time to add to the collection and to seek the aid of those whose heads had been preserved.

CEREMONIAL INTERMENTS

Ceremonial interment on a less extensive scale was of frequent occurrence from the Middle Palaeolithic, as is shown by the disposal of a Neanderthal youth in the cave at Le Moustier, the type-station of the flake-tool industry, near Peyzac in the Dordogne. The skeleton had been placed in the extended position, with the forearm under the head which rested on a pillow of flint flakes. A fine Acheulean hand-axe and a scraper were near the left arm, and in the grave were the bones of the wild ox (*urus*), charred and split, suggesting the remains of a funeral feast.[41] In a small, low-roofed cave, near the village of La Chapelle-aux-Saints in the department of Corrèze, there was a similar interment in a pit dug in the floor. It was surrounded with excellent scrapers, quartzite and crystal flakes of various colours together with the foot of an ox, the leg of a bison and the vertebral column of a reindeer. The body had been buried in the contracted position, and the strata above it contained the bones of the woolly rhinoceros, bison, horse and ibex, some of which had been split, presumably by the Mousterian implements found in the deposit.[42] The quantity and variety of the bones suggest that the funerary feasting was not confined to the time of the interment. In the cave at La Ferrassie near Le Bugue in the Dordogne the head and shoulders, the right leg and left forearm of a male skeleton were protected with slabs of stone and covered with bone flakes. With it was that of a woman, and in the adjacent trenches were the remains of two children and those of a baby beneath a tiny mound. A fourth child was buried in a grave in the floor under a stone with artificial cup-markings on it. These seem to have been members of a single family, and they were all orientated from east to west. A number of Mousterian implements were associated with them, and in front of the children's grave was a ditch containing bones and ashes of Pleistocene animals, in what appears to have been a funerary deposit.[43]

The care and equipment bestowed upon these ceremonial interments show that a cult of the dead was definitely established in the Middle Palaeolithic in Western Europe, though of course it was only in districts like the Dordogne where caves and rock-shelters abounded that the burials and grave goods concealed there have survived the ravages of time, weather and wild beasts. With the arrival of the Crô-Magnons and the allied types of *Homo sapiens* at the end of the maximum glaciation, the mortuary cultus became more elaborate. Thus, the bones of the skeleton found at Les Eyzies in the rock-shelter called Crô-Magnon, from which Upper Palaeolithic Man takes his name, had been stained red by pieces of haematite, and with them were found nearly three hundred perforated marine shells, apparently strung together as necklaces.[44] At Brno (Brünn) in Czechoslovakia, above a skeleton of this type, were a mammoth tusk and a shoulder-blade, and around it were more than six hundred conical tubes of a fossil shell (*dentalium badense*)—used apparently as a breastplate—an ivory male figurine without legs, perforated discs in bone, quartzite, stone and three from the tooth of a mammoth. The skeleton was stained with an ochrous powder of iron oxide, this red colouring matter recurring on the statuette.[45] The custom of burying the dead in an ochrous deposit was very widespread, extending from the Grimaldi caves, on the Franco-Italian frontier at Menton, to Paviland on the Gower coast of South Wales, and including interments of this nature at Chancelade near Perigueux, Obercassel near Bonn, and at the Grotte de Hoteaux near Rousillan, Ain,[46] in addition to those already mentioned.

The first of the series of caves at Grimaldi between Menton and Ventimiglia takes its name, La Grotte des Enfants, from the interment of two children clad in a shroud of nearly a thousand perforated *nassa* shells. Below them was the skeleton of a very tall man with a crown of shells round the head and a quantity above the thorax. At the bottom of the grave lay the tightly-flexed bodies of a youth of about sixteen years of age, with his right arm under the pelvis of an old woman, also in the flexed position. Both were adorned with shell ornaments and stained red with iron peroxide. Between their heads, protected by a flat stone, lay two pebbles. The adjoining Grotte du Cavillon contained 7,868 marine shells (*nassa meritea*) of which 875 were pierced. Two hundred of them were placed above the head of a Crô-Magnon man buried in the contracted posture and covered with powdered haematite. On the cranium had been placed a fillet of seashells and near the frontal bones were twenty-two perforated canine deer teeth. Similarly, at Barma Grande, in the fifth cave, a tall man, a very young woman

The Palaeolithic Cavern Sanctuaries

Negative hand impression in the cave of Castillo

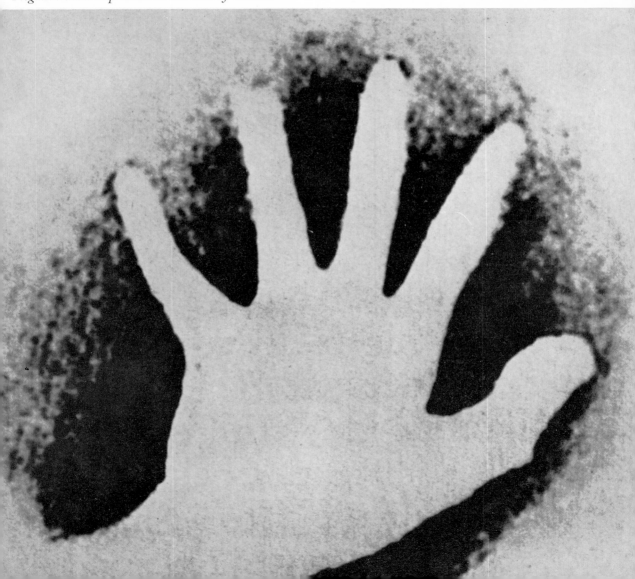

Palaeolithic hunting rituals were performed in deep dark subterranean cave sanctuaries whose walls were richly decorated with paintings of the hunter's prey. At Lascaux (2, 3) succeeding artists covered the gallery with herds of black-maned bistre horses, red deer and outlined bison. The detail of a black bull shows the mastery of form achieved by the anonymous painters whose hands sometimes appear in stencilled friezes, as at Castillo in Spain (1)

4

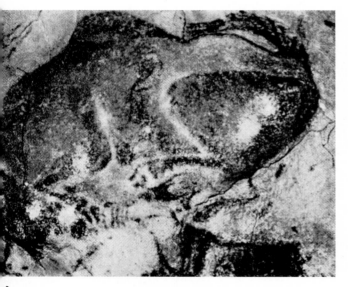

5

Many of these animals are shown wounded and crumpled on their knees, as at Altamira, in the brilliant polychrome frieze of bison and boar (4, 5). The mysterious symbols beside a bison at Niaux (6) were also intended to aid the hunter and had some ritual purpose

6

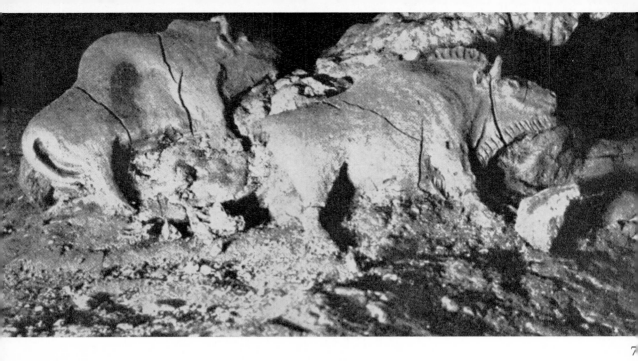

In fertility rites as well
as for hunting rituals,
models of animals were
set apart in the inner
sanctuaries of certain
caves. The mating
bison from Tuc
d'Audoubert formed the
centrepiece around
which the rites were
performed (7) while in
the cave at Montespan,
many models of woun-
ded animals were
pierced by javelins,
including the headless
bear (8)

10

11

The men who performed the hunting rituals are rarely depicted in cave art but the Shaft of the Dead Man at Lascaux shows a hunter apparently lying dead with his broken spear at his side, while a wounded bison stands over him (11). On the wall of the cave at Les Trois Frères, Ariège, is the figure of the 'Sorcerer' (9, 10) a bearded man with a red deer mask on his head and animal skins over his body, performing a ritual dance

The importance of fertility rites at this time is testified by the discovery all over Europe of female statuettes in which the sexual features are grossly exaggerated, as with the Venus of Laussel (12). Opposite are four small figurines modelled in the round from clay or stone. The faces are featureless, except for the delicate ivory head of a girl from Brassempouy

12

The burial of many headless skeletons and actual skulls over the world, particularly in Palaeolithic and Mesolithic sites in Europe, suggest that a cult of skulls was practised as part of a belief in an after-life. At La Chapelle aux Saintes the skull of a Neanderthal man (right) was ceremonially buried in a cave, and during Mesolithic times, at the cave of Ofnet in Bavaria a nest of 27 skulls, 15 of them children, were interred facing west, and covered in red ochre (19)

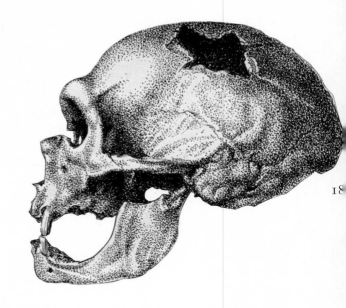

18

19

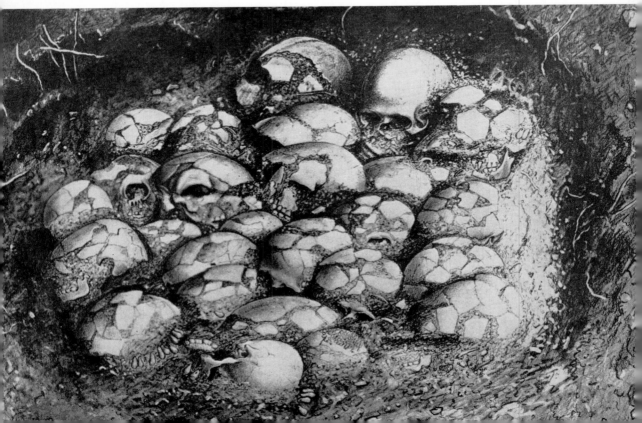

and a boy were deposited in a grave lined with red ochre, and equipped with shells, ivory pendants, necklaces and vertebrae. Above them, at the back of the cave, were two extended skeletons arrayed in the same manner.[47]

These Upper Palaeolithic ceremonial interments in graves containing red colouring matter and an abundance of shells and other ornaments in bone and ivory, bear witness to a developed cult of the dead in which attempts were made to revivify the body with a ruddy surrogate of blood and with life-giving charms and amulets. Thus, at Laugerie-Basse, cowries shaped like the opening through which a child enters the world, were arranged in pairs on the forehead, arms and feet, and four near the thighs and knees.[48] It is most improbable that the flexing of the body symbolized the position of the embryo to secure its rebirth beyond the grave, as it is not very likely that the pre-natal attitude was understood at all clearly in Palaeolithic times, and even if such embryological knowledge was available it is hardly to be expected that it would be interpreted in this mystical manner. Contracted burial with the legs drawn up need not imply more than resort to the normal sleeping posture—when it was not a question of economy of space in the grave. Tightly trussing before *rigor mortis* had set in, like that adopted at Chancelade and at La Grotte des Enfants at Grimaldi, as among primitive people today, may have been a device to prevent the corpse from 'walking' to molest the living. The same may apply in the case of interment under heavy stones with the face towards the ground. Here fear of the deceased would seem to have been the motive, but it is more usual to find indications of respect and regard for the dead. The care bestowed on the disposal of the body and on its funerary equipment, secondary burial, ritual treatment of the skull, and the supply of life-giving agents like red pigments and shells seem attempts to make adequate provision for their survival and well-being in the afterlife, to which the grave seems to have been thought to be the portal, rather than a prison house to be made secure from escape. It was only those who met a violent death, or who for some reason or another had a grudge against their survivors on earth, who had to be prevented from returning to pay off old scores.

Death, like birth, adolescence and marriage, was a sacred, tabu condition and a transitional state requiring *rites de passage* as a protection for the mourners and kinsfolk against a dangerous contagion and malign influences always rampant on such occasions, as well as for the benefit of the deceased.

It was for these purposes that recourse was made to ossuaries and other sacred places hallowed by the presence of the corpse and set apart for the performance of the prescribed mortuary rites. The close association of the cultus that developed around the mystery of death with that of birth and fertility shows how very intimately the quests for life in this world and the next have been related to each other. The belief in rebirth and regeneration for human beings when their allotted span has come to an end under temporal conditions is apparently almost as old as mankind, going back, as we have seen, to the beginning of the Palaeolithic period. At all times the desire for the promotion and conservation of life has been a fundamental urge, arousing the deepest emotions and most heartfelt needs; these have found ritual expression in an analogous cultus practised in sanctuaries and shrines, temples and tombs, selected or constructed either for the disposal of the body, or specifically for funerary rites.

CHAPTER II

Neolithic and Bronze Age Sanctuaries

WHEN THE ICE RETREATED NORTHWARDS at the end of the Pleistocene period some 14,000 years ago, with milder interglacial oscillations the steppes and tundra in Europe became forested, and the prairies of North Africa and Western Asia were transformed into deserts with fertile oases. It was then, after the Magdalenians had evacuated their former haunts following the reindeer towards the Arctic circle, that settlers from an Asiatic cradle-land with Gravettian cultural affinities began to infiltrate into Europe. Their descendants lived under Mesolithic conditions in small groups in the open glades of the forests and on the banks of rivers or on the sides of lakes, hunting, fishing, snaring game and wild fowl. Gradually, at the approach of the Neolithic, animals acquired a domestic status and wild grasses and grains were harvested. Among the houses on the settlements, especially in South-west Asia on the Syrian hills and the Persian highlands somewhere between 8000 and 5000 B.C.,[1] the remains of structures have been found which seem to have been shrines with cult objects.

WESTERN ASIA AND THE EASTERN MEDITERRANEAN

PRE-POTTERY SHRINES AT JERICHO

At Jericho the end walls of a small room in a house had been divided off to form a niche in the base of which was a column of volcanic rock which exactly fitted the pedestal as a sort of *maṣṣebah*, or sacred menhir, comparable to those which were a prominent feature in Semitic sanctuaries. In the centre of a larger rectangular room was a little basin. The floor, walls and basin were covered with burnished plaster scorched by fire. At each end rounded

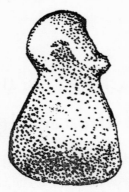

Fig. 5.   Clay female statuette from a Pre-pottery Neolithic shrine at Jericho

annexes were formed with walls curving inwards in the shape of domes. Its unusual plan and the presence of the basin have, in fact, inclined Dr Kenyon to regard it as a temple,[2] and the occurrence of two headless female figurines is certainly suggestive of the worship of the Mother-goddess. One is clad in a long flowing robe gathered at the waist and with the bands placed beneath the breasts. The other is similar, though less well-preserved. It is true they could be children's toys, but the association of animal figurines with them is indicative of a fertility cult.[3] Thus, in the Mosul district of Northern Iraq in the Chalcolithic mound at Arpachiyah, the lowest levels of which go back before 4000 B.C., numerous headless clay female statuettes of this Venus type occur with doves and other animals, constituting an important link between the Palaeolithic and later Chalcolithic and Bronze Age emblems of the cultus in Palestine and Western Asia generally.[4]

OSSUARIES AND THE CULT OF SKULLS

Although prior to the Halaf period, about 3800 B.C., these female figurines were not very prominent or abundant apart from Jericho and Arpachiyah, a cult centred in the processes of birth, generation and fertility seems to have been firmly established in Neolithic times at these two sites. Furthermore, at Jericho in the Pre-pottery levels there are indications of a cult of skulls. The skull of an elderly man was found carefully set in the angle of a room beneath the floor, and in a trench in the west side of the mound was a plastered skull. Deeper in the section lay several other crania, making in all a total of seven, covered with plaster delicately moulded in the form of the features of the deceased, with eyes inset with shells. These realistic portraits were probably of members of a family group.[5] The interior of the head and the eye-sockets were packed with clay, while the crown was left bare; this could have been done only after the soft tissues had decayed. Each head displays individual features and colouring matter had been applied to suggest the living flesh.

These Neolithic portrait-skulls, to which three others now have been added, represent the earliest examples of naturalistic portraiture, dated by Carbon-14 analysis at 6250 B.C. Very likely they may have been preserved beneath the floor of a house as the relics of the deceased members of the particular family for cult purposes, based on the belief that the head was the seat of the spiritual power, as in the cult of skulls elsewhere. Further excavation has now produced about thirty skeletons in a small area, many of which had been decapitated. While house burial was evidently a common practice, this exceptionally large number of skeletal remains seems to suggest that this was an ossuary which may have been the centre of a ritual technique for the benefit and protection of succeeding generations, as well as to render to the dead the respect and service which was their due. Conversely, they may have been removed to this location from some larger central sanctuary.

Be this as it may, the cult of skulls continued in the later Neolithic phases, when the crania were arranged in groups either in a circle facing inwards, or in three sets orientated in the same manner. It was at this stage that child sacrifice, which subsequently became so prevalent in Palestine, began to appear at Jericho. Thus, beside one child interment was a collection of infant skulls with the cervical vertebrae attached, showing that the heads had been systematically cut off.[6] Burial beneath floors of houses continued to be practised throughout the Pre-pottery Neolithic periods, and was normally adopted in the case of the more respected, venerated or feared members of the community. The bodies of the rest may have been disposed of in whatever manner was convenient. Disused passages, for example, have been found filled with skeletons.

In the next occupation of Jericho, about 3200 B.C., the dead were buried in cemeteries in shaft graves sunk in the rock, except in the case of some infant graves in pits. The larger tombs were multiple burials containing over a hundred skulls and skeletons, many of which had been secondary interments inserted after the flesh had decayed. The skulls were detached from

the rest of the bodies, and in due course the bones were collected and burnt
on a funeral pyre in the centre of the tomb, the crania being arranged around
it during the cremation. When this was completed, pots containing offerings
were added, together with beads and other small grave goods. The tomb
was then filled in with the débris until the process was repeated with a new
complement of skeletons. It would seem, therefore, that these large tombs
were in the nature of ossuaries reserved perhaps for the mortal remains of a
family or kinship group, at which no doubt prescribed mortuary rites were
duly performed as occasion required. It is hardly likely that so much care and
labour would have been spent on the excavation of such elaborate and spacious tombs in the rock of the hillsides unless, in contrast to the sparsely
equipped single-burial individual graves in the cemeteries, they had had a
cultic significance over and above the primary interment at the time of
death. Moreover, since there is an absence of temple remains at Jericho, the
tombs are the only indication of a communal cultus at this period apart
from the Pre-pottery Neolithic fertility shrines.

THOLOI AT ARPACHIYAH

Indeed, among the earliest traces of Neolithic culture in Western Asia there
are considerably less signs of the practice of religion and care of the dead
than in Palaeolithic Europe. At Arpachiyah, 4 miles east of the Tigris and
Nineveh, as we have seen, the excavations undertaken by the British School
in Iraq in 1933 brought to light evidence of a fertility cultus centred in
the Mother-goddess. Pendants and paintings of the bull's head and hoof
as symbols of virility, probably the male counterpart of the Goddess, and
amulets representing the dove and the double-axe were also revealed. No
less interesting and significant was the discovery of a large group of circular
tholoi with *pisé* walls and domed roofs, built on stone foundations. Hitherto
structures of this nature were known only in Mycenaean, Maltese, Cretan
and late Cypriot sites, belonging to the middle of the third millennium B.C.
Now it has become apparent that their origin must be sought in Western
Asia in the Neolithic Halaf settlements in northern Iraq. There, in the earliest
levels at Arpachiyah, single chamber tholoi occurred and above them a more
developed type with a long rectangular dromos. In one example of this type
at right angles to the main building was an antechamber, which was partially
sunk in the ground, and roofed, it seems, with a low dome springing from

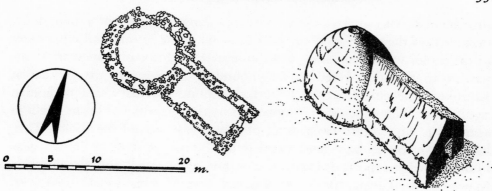

0   5   10   20   *m.*

Fig. 6. Plan and reconstruction of the 'tholos' at Arpachiyah

the floor level. The internal height of the chamber was not more than 5 feet. The care with which they had been preserved free from any disturbance suggests that they were regarded as sacrosanct; two important Halaf burials had been placed against the outer wall of one of them and in another, goddess figurines were found. Although one cannot be certain what rites were performed in them, there can be little doubt, as Professor Mallowan maintains, that they were shrines, perhaps connected with the worship of the Mother-goddess.[7]

KHIROKITIA THOLOI IN CYPRUS

Parallel structures occur at the Neolithic site of Khirokitia in Cyprus (4000–3500 B.C.) where the largest tholos is 33 feet in diameter, and all of them have been built on stone slabs with *pisé* or sun-dried brick superstructures forming a kind of corbelled roof. In the floors graves had been dug containing one or more skeletons. The body of a woman was in a distorted position with the hands bound behind the back,[8] as in some of the Neolithic interments in Jericho. Over the head and chest were heavy stone querns. The body was buried ceremonially beneath a square platform and between two stone piers. Near by, one skeleton lying in a natural position had a necklace of carnelian beads and shells, with fragments of three diabase bowls surrounding it. In a tholos of the upper group the skeletons of twenty-five infants on top of those of adults, or in stone-lined holes, were found in successive floors. On the lower floor was a 'throne' with a seat built of river stones, and three small hearths, on one of which was the skeleton of an adult. A clay human head ornamented with snakes, perhaps representing a male chthonian deity, occurred on the topmost floor. Be this as may, the setting and equipment of the tholoi within enclosing walls indicate that this was a sanctuary comparable to that discovered in the mound at Arpachiyah, except that at Khirokitia the cult seems to have had definite mortuary and chthonian significance. This conclusion is supported by the quantities of burnt bones in association with round tables built of stone slabs around the tholoi. This, however, seems to have been peculiar to Cyprus, as those at Gawra near Nineveh, where the Hassuna culture is not represented, and elsewhere in Mesopotamia, Chagar Bazar, Carchemish and Mersin, do not appear to have been places of burial, though further investigation may reveal interments and remains of a mortuary cult.

The Cypriot tholoi, however, constitute an important link between the Western Asian and the Mediterranean circular sanctuaries, notwithstanding the fact that the stone tholoi at Arpachiyah (with one exception) stood above ground, whereas the beehive tombs at Mycenae were underground.[9] The Cypriot stone vessels are similar to those of the Halaf period at Arpachiyah. The snake design on the back of the clay figure at Khirokitia suggests a connection with the cult of the Cretan Great Mother whose emblem was the snake, but, as we have seen, the chthonian mortuary cultus seems to have been predominant. On the other hand, some of the smaller Khirokitia tholoi were not burial chambers, and some of them may have been habitations or silos for storing grain. In the succeeding culture localized at Erimi (3500–3000 B.C.), which marks the transition from the Chalcolithic to the Bronze Age in Cyprus, and constitutes a connecting link with the latest stages of Khirokitia, the tholoi have a stone substructure of two courses of stones, and a central support. Along the inner face of the stone foundation, post-holes occur, suggesting that there may have been a superstructure of brushwood or reeds covered over with mud and supported by posts. On the floor of rammed earth there were signs of occupation, but burials have been found under the floor and along the outer ridge of the stone foundation. The appearance of terracotta female figurines with prominent sexual features suggests that in addition to the mortuary ritual a fertility cult connected with the Mother-goddess was introduced towards the end of the period. With it came a multiplication of amulets (e.g. beads, pendants, axe-heads) and female figurines in graves.[10]

THE CYPRIOT NECROPOLIS AT VOUNOUS-BELLABAIS

In a later necropolis at Vounous, about a mile to the east of the village of Bellabais in Cyprus (*c.* 2800–2000 B.C.), the tombs, which fall into four groups according to their situation, had been cut in the rock. They varied in size and shape, being either short with roughly parallel sides and rounded back, or, as was more common, long and narrowing towards the end which was either straight or rounded. The long sides of the dromos were straight or sloped inwards and led to the main chamber through a rectangular or rounded doorway. On either side of the dromos were small side chambers blocked by rectangular, rounded or irregular slabs, or rough blocks of limestone. The bodies, clad in their usual clothes, were laid in niches in both the right and left parts of the chamber, with grave goods on the floor; on top of the bodies large vases of red polished ware were laid. Vessels of this nature, in fact, were the customary offerings, usually containing the bones of oxen and other animals, some of the bones also having been scattered about the chamber and on the floor: probably the remains of an animal sacrifice on behalf of the dead, the victim having been placed on the floor of the chamber and subsequently covered with vases. When new burials and their grave goods were introduced the earlier ones were heaped along the sides of the chamber in a disorderly manner.

In one tomb (No. 22) a fragmentary clay model of the sacred enclosure was found, and beside it a bowl with two birds and small cups on the rim,[11] indicating perhaps the connexion of the persons buried in the family tomb with the sanctuary and its ceremonies. But whatever may have been its significance, the model shows that the enclosure was a circular structure surrounded by a low wall, resembling the tholoi at Khirokitia and Erimi, this Neolithic and Chalcolithic tradition having survived in the Early Bronze Age at this site, just as at Mycenae the temenos of the Acropolis is surrounded by a circle of slabs.[12] Moreover, the ritual in all probability was in honour of the chthonian gods as in the Neolithic tholoi at Khirokitia, while the recurrence of figures of the bull in conjunction with the snake on the Vounous enclosure is reminiscent of the chthonian and fertility traditions on the Asiatic mainland. Since the model of the sacred enclosure occurred in a tomb the cultus clearly had a mortuary content, and the sacrifices which formed part of the ritual were offered apparently on behalf of the deceased.

ANATOLIAN SHRINES AT BEYCESULTAN

In western Anatolia shrines have now been revealed belonging to the first half of the Early Bronze Age (2600–2300 B.C.), as a result of excavations at Beycesultan in 1956 by the Institute of Archaeology at Ankara. In a narrow 'barrow-passage' in the side of the hill was discovered a mud-brick structure faced with plaster, surrounded by a mass of broken votive pottery overlaid by charred wood and ashes, and containing the remains of carbonized grain, lentils, grape-stones and pulse. In the centre of the chamber, 16 feet from the south wall facing a doorway, stood a sanctuary outside which was an empty 'bin' which may have been used for the disposal of surplus offerings. Two large side chambers were placed side by side, each equipped with cult objects and a sort of 'altar' at one end in the form of two upright stelae, about 70 centimetres in height, and made of plastered clay. Between them were projections resembling 'horns of consecration', and behind the stelae were large pottery storage-vessels. At the back of the shrine was a screen of wooden posts or columns.[13]

It is possible that the twin sanctuaries were 'male' and 'female' shrines; the former had one concentric curb in front of the 'altar', an upright wooden pillar being set in the periphery of the outer circle facing the shrine; the latter had two concentric curbs enclosing a semicircular area, and a raised sacrificial platform, or 'blood altar', set against the wall, and female figurines of the Goddess type. The charred remains suggest that they were destroyed by fire. Near by in the mound similar shrines of the Late Bronze Age occurred, together with a sanctuary of the Middle Bronze Age in the form of a megaron, and a small altar replacing the hearth. In the later examples the horns of the altar were ornamented with terracotta symbols.[14]

THE MESARA CIRCULAR TOMBS

The squatting Minoan figurines and their associated cult objects have Asian affinities, and Evans suggested that 'the Neolithic culture of Crete (representative of the Aegean islands in general) may be regarded as an insular off-shoot of an extensive Anatolian province'.[15] It would seem that it was from this region that these influences passed to the eastern Mediterranean by way of the Troad, to Cyprus, the Cyclades and Crete, while others made their way to the Aegean islands from Egypt in the third millennium B.C. On the rich plain of Mesara in southern Crete facing Africa the circular tombs containing hundreds of interments represent the oldest architectural remains in Crete except huts and rock-shelters. Those grouped round Koumasa, south-east of Gortyna on the upper slopes of the Kophina mountains, are from 13 feet to 43 feet in diameter. They are composed of dry-stone walling of undressed stones bounded by a quantity of clay, with projections inwards; they had been roofed with a corbelled vault, or with wood and thatch. On the east side was a doorway formed by two large stone uprights supporting a massive lintel. The floor was composed of natural rock, and on the outside of the northern wall a row of five slabs projected from 6 to 8 inches at a height of about 3 feet from the ground, either to serve as scaffolding in the erection of the upper part of the tomb, or, if it was covered with a mound, to make the earth more compact. In front of several of them had been a stone-paved court and before the doorway was a square pit lined with stones.

Inside in the middle of the tholos, beneath the smoke-hole, was a hearth and indications of fires on the floor, but as cremation does not seem to have been practised it must have been used for some other ritual purposes. The bones from the very large number of interments, running into several hundred skeletons, had been dislocated and arranged in heaps in the chamber. The tombs evidently were ossuaries in which burials had been made generation after generation. The grave goods included stone vases and palettes, perhaps copied from Egyptian originals belonging to the Old Kingdom, as well as cylinder seals, Cycladic clay figurines, vases and seals with geometric and spiral motifs, pins, copper awls and daggers. Unfortunately there had been a good deal of looting of the more valuable articles at the various re-openings of the tholoi, but enough have remained to show the nature and cultural connexions of the funerary furniture.[16]

MOCHLOS TOMBS

The prototypes of the Minoan and Mesara vaulted tombs would seem to have been the Assyrian circular corbelled structures going back at Arpachiyah to the fourth millennium B.C. Tholoi also occurred in the Cyclades which connect Crete with the Aegean mainland, and Cycladic figurines and other objects were discovered in the Mesara tombs. In these islands, colonized from Anatolia about 2000 B.C., individual burial in the contracted position was prevalent, as it was also in eastern Crete in the later cists, grouped in small cemeteries. Thus, on the island of Mochlos off the coast of Crete cist graves of the Cycladic type were combined with large ossuaries belonging to the Early Minoan II and III periods, entered through doorways closed by huge upright slabs of stone, while the cists were constructed with walls of similar slabs. Sometimes, however, especially in the Middle Minoan period, they were composed of small stones like those used in building the houses. Occasionally bodies were buried in holes in the rocks with only very few vessels. Later, at the end of the Middle Minoan epoch, large terracotta jars, or *pithoi*, were employed for interment, as, for example, in the cemeteries of Pachyammos and Sphoungaras in eastern Crete where the bodies had been placed in them in the contracted position with the head downwards, the jars standing upside down over the earlier tombs. But complete disregard was shown for previous interments in these cemeteries, groups of jars having been broken and tumbled about in utter confusion.[17]

HAGIA TRIADA SHRINE AND SARCOPHAGUS

Notwithstanding the variety of burial customs and ceramic traditions in Early Minoan times, collective interment was generally practised, as in the rest of the Mediterranean, in communal ossuaries in the form of caves, circular tholoi or rectangular chambers. These may or may not be of megalithic structure and architecture, and while many of them have retained their original sepulchral nature and function, some have become essentially temples, or at any rate sacred sites for the performance of a prescribed ritual which was not exclusively of a mortuary character. Thus, at Hagia Triada near Phaestos on the Libyan Sea a Late Minoan little palace, or royal villa, resembling in its general arrangements the palace of Minos at Knossos on a much smaller scale, contained besides halls and bath-rooms, a shrine of the Minoan Goddess and a remarkable limestone sarcophagus from a neighbouring cemetery in a kind of chamber tomb. On the stucco with which it has been coated are cult scenes depicting an altar with horns of consecration, an olive tree with spreading branches, a pole painted pink with a double-axe sign and a bird, a priestess with a vessel of offerings, a libation jug and a basket of fruit which a man is shown raising in his arms in the act of sacrifice. The blood of a slain bull is apparently being collected in a pail, while a priestess clad in the skin of the victim offers libations at an altar. Behind the bull is a figure playing the double pipes.[18]

While various interpretations have been given to this scene, the emblems suggest that it presents the cult of the Goddess in a funerary setting, with her priestesses as the officiants in a sacrificial oblation on behalf of the deceased interred in the sarcophagus, the life-giving blood of a victim having been poured on the ground through a bottomless pail as an offering to Mother-earth, the ultimate source of rebirth. Professor Pedersen, on the other hand, thinks the episode depicts the sacred marriage of Zeus and Hera and the goddess' bridal bath as a mythical expression of the spring rains renewing nature. The goddess, it is said, is carried away on a chariot drawn by griffins before the end of the year and brought back in a chariot with horses in the spring to be united with the god in the form of a cuckoo, the two leaf-clad pillars symbolizing the union. She then disappears and the pillar is denuded, but the blood of the bull offered in sacrifice effects a renewal, the rebirth of nature being expressed by the offering of the bull and the calves.[19] Similarly, Miss Jane Harrison maintains that 'the picture speaks for itself; it is the passing of winter and the coming of spring, the passing of the Old Year, the incoming of the New, it is the Death and Resurrection of Nature, her New Birth'. In short, it represents the springtime of man and vegetation as recorded in the Hebrew Wisdom literature in the book of Canticles; the bridal song of the new birth in the annual cycle translated into ritual action in the seasonal drama.[20]

As the scenes, however, are on a tomb the natural conclusion is that in the first instance they had a mortuary significance, whatever secondary purposes they may have served. Nevertheless, the symbolism indicates a composite cultus, and if the sarcophagus contained the mortal remains of a Minoan priest-king it may be, as M. P. Nilsson suggests, that they depict the worship of an apotheosized royal hero who had been transported by griffins and accompanied by goddesses to the realms of the gods and there deified.[21] Evans thinks the sacrificial rites were performed temporarily to summon the deceased back to the land of the living, the divinity having been charmed down into its material resting place aided by the music and ritual chants as well as by the sacrifice.[22] Be this as it may, the offerings and sacred symbols, which include the imagery of bulls, trees, pillars, griffins, the double-axe and a votive boat, suggest a composite cult in which the illustrious dead acquired from the goddess divine sanctity and perhaps status beneficial to the living, and were therefore objects of worship at their magnificent tombs.

THE TEMPLE TOMB AT KNOSSOS

When the Mother-goddess made her way from western Asia through the eastern Mediterranean to the Aegean as the 'Lady of the Mountain' she retained her status and life-giving functions which in Mesopotamia extended to the land of the dead. Thus, the royal Temple Tomb in the glen above the palace site at Knossos was her sanctuary. It contained a central pillar, horns of consecration and the double-axe, and led to the sepulchral chamber cut in the rock.[23] In the central shrine in the palace she was arrayed with a high tiara, a necklace, a richly embroidered bodice with a laced corsage and a skirt with a short double apron, made in faience. Her hair is shown falling back behind her neck and on her shoulders, her eyes are black, her breasts spotted with purple-brown. Her body is entwined with snakes: in her right hand she holds out the head of one of them, the rest of its body curling round her arm, behind her shoulders with the tail ascending on her left arm and hand; below the waist two more snakes are interlaced in the form of a girdle round the hips, while a third runs up from the hips, over the bodice to the left ear and round the tiara.[24]

On signet rings from Knossos she appears in her familiar attitude and Minoan-Mycenaean garb, standing on a mountain peak supported by her two guardian lions, holding out a lance or sceptre, with a male god or votary before her in an act of adoration.[25] To the left is a shrine with baetylic pillars and horns of consecration, connecting her with plant and animal life. On a steatite vessel from Knossos a building is represented with horns of consecration surmounting the cornice before which passes a procession of youths

Fig. 7. Seal impression showing the 'Lady of the Mountain'

presenting bowls of offerings. Votaries and priestesses before altars occur frequently on Knossian rings and seals in cult scenes depicting shrines and a sacred tree; sometimes they are shown dancing in a ring in honour of the Goddess. From the sanctuary fresco at Knossos it appears that the pillar cult was brought into conjunction with that of the double-axe and the worship of the great Minoan Goddess whose care embraced all creatures of the land and the sea, and extended to the underworld. It was for her, therefore, that the gifts were placed on a low platform before the altar and to her the images were given.

THE GOURNIA SHRINE

The principal object in the sanctuary of Gournia on the isthmus of Hiera-petra, 4 miles west of Kavousi in eastern Crete, was a primitive unpainted figure of the snake-goddess Eileithyia with raised hands and a serpent twined about her body. She was clad in a bell-shaped skirt in the conventional Minoan manner and reminiscent of the women in the fresco in the rock-shelter at Cogul.[26] In the centre stood a low earthern table with three legs and the base of a vase supporting a bowl, presumably for offerings. Around it were three tubular vessels with a vertical row of three or four handles on either side. Above a large handle was a pair of horns of consecration, and one of the vessels was entwined with two snakes.[27] Here a developed worship of the snake-goddess was established in a sanctuary fully equipped with images, shrines, altars, libation tables and cultic vases, and which, like other Minoan sacred places, was not an integral part of a human habitation, being situated on the summit of a hill some distance from the small palace. In this respect it differed from the shrines in the palace of Knossos and that of Phaestos, though the contents of the public sanctuary at Gournia suggest that it originated in a domestic cult, probably in the Late Minoan I period (*c.* 1500 B.C.). A few traces of the earlier settlements on the rocky ridge remained, however, when the new town sprang up at the end of the Middle Minoan period (*c.* 1700 B.C.), but there can be little doubt that Gournia was inhabited throughout the Bronze Age, the shrine about 12 feet square encircled by walls only about 18 inches in height standing in the centre approached by a narrow paved lane. Within was a sacred tree, and the cult objects were collected together in one corner, except those which were found *in situ*. Crude as many of them were, being made in terracotta with no artistic skill, they nevertheless provide evidence that the shrine was devoted to the worship of the Goddess in association with her characteristic emblems (e.g. snakes, doves, horns of consecration and the double-axe). The small palace on the top of the ridge, unlike its counterparts at Knossos, Phaestos and Tiryns, yielded no indications of having had any religious significance, except possibly a double-axe sign on one of the blocks in the walls.

THE MINOAN-MYCENAEAN SHRINES

In the Aegean mainland Professor Tsountas discovered in tholoi in the lower town at Mycenae two glass plaques with lion-headed demons pouring libations from ewers on to a heap of stones surmounted with a large block, and on to a square pillar.[28] On a gem from the Vaphio tomb the same kind of demons are shown watering a nursling palm-tree from two spouted vases, while on a third plaque from Mycenae the libation is poured into a kind of bowl resting on a column with three supporting legs.[29] Baetylic stones and pillars, in fact, together with horns of consecration and the double-axe, are among the most prominent features of the Minoan-Mycenaean shrines, and are often associated with mythical animals and sacred trees, as embodiments of the indwelling divinity, like the *maṣṣebôth* and *asherôth* in Semitic sanctuaries; hence the pouring of libations on them. The pillar cult was not exclusively centred in a male god, as Evans contended;[30] in the Minoan scenes priestesses and female votaries are represented performing ritual actions in connexion with baetyls in honour of the Goddess.

THE MOUNTAIN CAVE-SANCTUARIES

In Crete it seems that it was under the influence of the palace sanctuaries and their cultus that the earlier aniconic forms assumed an anthropomorphic guise in the Middle Minoan period. For example, in the Neolithic cave sanctuary of Amnisos near Heraklion, the old harbour town of Knossos 4 miles east of Candia, identified with the goddess of birth, Eileithyia,[31] two stalagmites were venerated as her aniconic embodiment as a sacred pillar,[32] though no female figurines have been recorded in the site. In the lower chamber of the double cave of Psychro near Lyttos, often said to be the Diktaean cave, the legendary birthplace of Zeus, there were stalactite columns with double-axe blades and bronze objects placed edgewise on the vertical crevices of the pillars,[33] doubtless as votive offerings.

Neolithic and Bronze Age Sanctuaries

20   *Gold seal ring from Mycenae*

As early as 7800 B.C. the inhabitants of Jericho, one of the oldest-known towns in the world, constructed primitive clay-built shrines for ritual ceremonies (21). By c.6000 B.C. sun-dried bricks were used to build the formal shrines in houses. In one of these (22) a sacred menhir was placed in a plastered niche. The later shrine from Beycesultan in Turkey (23) was dedicated to a male and female diety. Offerings poured from the scattered votive jars were passed over the horned altar

22

24

25

The delicately plastered skull (25) is one of ten from Jericho, each painted and modelled to re-create the individual features of the dead, and buried beneath house floors for cult purposes. Further west, in Crete, the dead were buried in tholoi (26) surrounded by grave gods including Cycladic figurines of the Mother-goddess, modelled with angular simplicity (24)

26

27

The cult of the sacred Double-Axes was one of the most powerful in Crete. Votive axes, such as the golden one shown (28) were placed on the stalagmites of the Amnisos cave sanctuary (27). On the painted limestone sarcophagus from Hagia Triada (29), which portrays religious ceremonies in honour of the Mother-goddess, double-axes are shown mounted on ritual standards

28
29

31

The Mother-goddess was venerated in Crete
as the Snake-goddess. One of the several
faience statuettes shows her in the traditional
tiered skirt, brandishing two snakes (30) and
she also appears on signet-ring intaglios from
Knossos (31) and a gold seal ring from Mycenae
(20) where an attendant holds a double-axe

The Neolithic colonizers of Malta erected vast complex megalithic temples for cult ceremonies, and sacrifices. The walls were made of massive slabs covered with capstones, as at Ta Hagrat (32) the earliest temple. Some stones are decorated with small holes, and occasional motifs, like the plant from the Hagia Qim altar (33). The great rock-cut sanctuary of the Hal Saflieni Hypogeium was later used as an ossuary for 7,000 bodies (34)

33

36

Small statuettes of the Mother-goddess, with heavily modelled thighs and breasts, in which she is portrayed squatting on the ground, are common in Malta. In contrast, the temple figure of the 'Venus of Malta' from Hagia Qim (35) stood some eight feet high

35

37

40

In Sardinia, the dead were buried in rock-cut tombs, known locally now as 'Witch Houses' (38). The three eye idols from Iberia (39–41) all represent stylized forms of the Mother-goddess and were buried with the dead in megalithic tombs

39

41

The cave, like its other Cretan contemporaries, seems to have been a mountain sanctuary of considerable importance since it contains numerous figures of men and animals, clay bulls, engraved gems, a steatite libation table with a Minoan inscription and fragments of similar tables surrounding a kind of altar in a well-defined sacrificial stratum. Although Late Geometric ware and Late Minoan painted pottery occurred in the surface stratum, the bulk of these relics belong to the Middle Minoan period, and in the lower cave the cult flourished at that time before it came to an end in the Geometric age. The imposing Kamares cave on the southern summit of Mount Ida facing Phaestos, while conspicuously devoid of votive objects, or indeed, of any finds other than vessels, can hardly have been other than a mountain sanctuary in Middle Minoan times, as it was seldom free from snow and therefore uninhabitable as a dwelling. The restricted range of pottery did not suggest domestic equipment, whereas for a sanctuary, as Dawkins pointed out, small spouted jars and larger vases, and pithoi with lids would suffice for the making of offerings.[34] Kamares being rather later than Psychro, it may be that only vases and grain were brought to the sanctuary in the Middle Minoan I and II. By the time the Diktaean and Idaean (Psychro) caverns came into use the cultus probably had become more elaborated, thereby requiring a larger assortment of cultic ornaments and techniques.

THE WESTERN MEDITERRANEAN

MEGALITHIC TOMBS AND TEMPLES IN SICILY

In Crete collective burial in caves dates from Early Minoan I to the Middle Minoan, early in the second millennium B.C., with varying degrees of grave furniture. Interment in communal ossuaries in the form of rectangular stone chambers and tholoi, probably of Western Asian origin in the fourth millennium, was established by the first half of the second millennium B.C. (1800–1500), contemporary with those in the Cyclades (e.g. at Melos). It was the end of the period (c. 1500–1350 B.C.) that the great Aegean corbelled chambers, entered through a dromos, were erected on the mainland of Greece, such as the Treasury of Atreus at Mycenae. These appear to represent a development of Crete-Cycladic tholoi, and although they had been rifled when they were first investigated, they contained a number of objects which revealed Cretan influences. Recently, the western origin of these Mycenaean tombs has been urged,[35] but it was in and around the Aegean rather than in the north-west that the megalithic techniques were most firmly established, and it was from this region in all probability that they were diffused by ancient voyagers to Malta, Sicily, Sardinia, the Balearic Isles and Iberia, thence in a north-westerly direction along the Atlantic littoral.

Thus, in the third millennium B.C., the islands of the western Mediterranean became a cultural centre in which collective burial in megalithic tombs was a conspicuous feature. In Sicily, about 2500 B.C., agricultural hilltop settlements of eastern Mediterranean type began to replace the earlier fortified Neolithic villages like Stentinello, which has given its name to this culture. In them the dead were buried in communal pit-graves, whereas the succeeding Siculan I cemeteries (*c.* 2000 B.C.) were composed of rock-cut tombs, usually entered through a dromos which led to circular or oval chambers with a rounded vault, containing a number of interments in association with Cycladic and Middle Helladic pottery and curious Troadic plaques. The narrow portal or window cut out of the slabs at the top, probably a survival of the doorway of the chamber-tomb, was sealed with a megalithic slab which at Castelluccio near Syracuse was decorated with spirals in relief. In the same cemetery another tomb was closed with two carved slabs representing a double-breasted female figure.[36] At Monteracello a vault was later reproduced above ground as a rectangular cist built of squared slabs of limestone set on edge, with a window-entry at one end to represent the door. The chambers, however, were more or less circular in plan, though natural cave-tombs and old flint mines were in use as family graves, and followed the Aegean funerary tradition in its ritual characteristics.[37]

THE MEGALITHIC MONUMENTS AND TEMPLES OF MALTA

Of all the islands in the western Mediterranean, however, the one that was accredited with the greatest sacred significance in the third millennium B.C. was Malta and the little neighbouring island of Gozo. There are no indications of human settlements until Neolithic times when primitive farming people from Sicily began to establish themselves there about 2500 B.C.; this occupation was succeeded by that of the megalithic culture, about 1800 B.C. The dating, however, of the Maltese colonizations is very difficult to determine.

The latest attempt to solve the problem suggests that at the end of the third millennium B.C., a people having Stentinello affiliations settled on these barren shores and transformed the rock-cut tombs into megalithic sanctuaries on the surface of the ground.[38] These vast stone structures became elaborated into labyrinthine apsidal temples like Mnaidra, Hal Tarxien and Hagia Kim in Malta and Gigantija on Gozo, and the hypogeum, or catacomb, of Hal Saflieni to the north-west of the village of Tarxien. Although many cultural influences from Egypt, the eastern Mediterranean and western Asia have contributed to their development, and while they vary in size and complexity, they have certain features in common: they all consist of a central passage or gallery, with two parallel oval chambers in the form of transepts, and ending in an apsidal chamber extending from the centre of the second chamber, in line with the entrance and the middle passage. The walls of the sanctuaries were built of massive stone slabs covered with horizontal capstones.

Notwithstanding the complexity of their structure, the general plan is that of the megaliths of the Siculan and Sardinian type, with corbelled vaulting, a curved forecourt and a passage leading to the several chambers, which sometimes could be entered only by a 'porthole' or 'window' cut in a large slab. The earliest example, the temple of Ta Hagrat (the Stone Heap), near the village of Mgarr, excavated by Zammit between 1922 and 1926, and belonging to the second and third phases of the earliest Maltese culture, consisted of a small oval building entered through a short corridor of three parallel stone slabs, leading to a larger edifice containing several recesses in the form of a horseshoe arranged round a central court. Although no burials have been found in any of these temples except the Hypogeum of Hal Saflieni, this rock-cut monument may represent an early attempt to erect a sanctuary, based on the collective tombs in which the dead were interred. It is possible, in fact, that it was so used at first. There is no evidence, however, of these Maltese temples having been mortuary structures, though the rites performed in them may have been of a chthonian character and the Hypogeum became a vast ossuary extensively employed for burial purposes, estimated at some seven thousand interments with large quantities of grave goods.

As the temples developed as sanctuaries devoted to a highly organized cultus, they conformed to a common architectural plan. Rooms were grouped round a central rectangular court with a massive façade of mega-lithic slabs enclosing a semicircular area in front. In the middle was the entrance with steps leading into a short corridor with recesses or chambers. The façade in the form of a wall of massive upright slabs round the circular platform constituted a temenos. The Gigantija on Gozo, which originally consisted of a single shrine, when a second temple was added became two temples joined together by an outer wall, each having two sets of lateral elliptical areas with niches and 'altars' in the second enclosure.[39] The altars, as the horizontal slabs resting on uprights are called, are in a recess on each side of the entrance to the passage, and like the niches probably were later additions, as the sherds near them belonged to the earlier phase in the pottery sequence. This also applies to the circular stone platform in front of the temples.

In the confused extensive ruins of the Hagia Kim temple-complex near the village of Qrendi on the south coast of Malta, a stone pillar carved in relief with a spiral pattern stood behind an altar, reminiscent of similar Minoan-Mycenaean types. But it was in the final phase of the Maltese temples that these influences became most apparent at Mnaidra and Hal Tarxien. These great megalithic structures undoubtedly owed much to con-tacts with the Aegean, Sicily and Italy, as well as with immigrants practising cremation from the eastern Mediterranean at Hal Tarxian. At Mnaidra, adjacent to Hagia Kim, two elliptical chambers occur, one behind the other, orientated in a south-westerly direction, the southern and earlier building consisting of a paved, vertical and horizontal carefully-dressed masonry. To the left of the entrance stands a trilithon table with a horizontal block above it. A window 16 by 12 inches has been cut in the vertical slab of the wall of the enclosure beyond the aperture, and similar portholes occur in the south-west wall communicating with two other rectangular spaces. The whole of the southern half of the structure is surrounded by a series of rough stones set alternately with the broad faces and their narrow edges outwards. The roofing of the apses was by corbelling, of which a few traces are still visible.[40] The northern half was added later, thereby completing a succession of developments spread over a number of centuries in the Neolithic period.

The most outstanding example of the last phase of Maltese temple architecture, however, is that of the Tarxien complex. This remarkable group, belonging to the end of the megalithic occupation of the island, con-sists of three separate structures erected at different times, with a rather small,

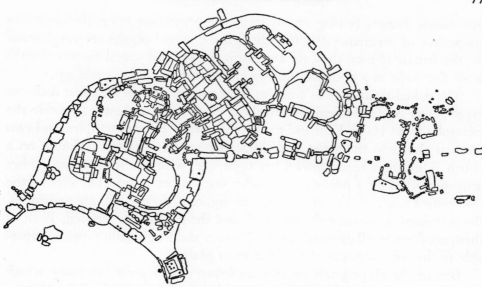

Fig. 8. Plan of the Tarxien complex, Malta

supplementary east building and a few scattered fragments, brought together as a composite whole. The main western temple is now very defective and the large curved façade is in a ruined condition. The entire monument may have been surrounded by an earth mound up to the level of the capstones, while the apses were domed with corbelled cupolas, and the corridors sheltered by long horizontal slabs with the spaces between the apses only open to the sky. The walls were decorated with geometric designs, spirals and friezes of animals, while similar spiral patterns ornamented two altars flanking the entrance to the rear chambers. Charred bones of animals bear witness to the practice of sacrifice in the temple. On a stone were the remains of a huge, headless statue, probably not less than 8 feet in height, though it gives the impression of having been seated like many of the smaller draped figurines found at Hagia Kim and Hal Saflieni.[41] The hands rest on the thighs towards the genital organs; this attitude is repeated in a very small clay female model, the right hand pointing to the vulva.[42] Another small headless female figurine in sitting posture has the knees drawn up against the chest, and pendulous breasts touching the thighs, while on a fragment of a clay female figure among the Neolithic débris a sexual triangle is shown by a deep incision.[43] Again, a female torso in red clay from Mnaidra has very large, protruding breasts resting on an immense projection from the abdomen suggestive of pregnancy.[44] But although the sexual organs are emphasized on the female statues, they are absent on the stylized seated figures clothed from the waist in a flounced skirt so prominent in Cretan paintings.

The naked steatopygous type are most conspicuous in the great rock-cut Hypogeum at Hal Saflieni, where those in clay and alabaster resemble the examples from Hagia Kim and the neighbouring Tarxien temples, and two women naked to the waist with huge breasts are depicted reclining on a couch. The larger figure lies on her right side, with the head resting on her arm supported by a pillow, the smaller one on her face.[45] The hips of the 'Sleeping Lady', as the more complete figure is designated, are enormous, the abdomen is transversely grooved, and the corpulence stressed. Both of them conform in all essentials to the Tarxien and Hagia Kim types, comparable to the colossal torso of the 'Venus of Malta'.

Before the Hypogeum became an ossuary, this great sanctuary which reproduces in three storeys below ground the main features of the Maltese temples on the surface, was undoubtedly the scene of a complex and composite cultus which included a variety of life-bestowing rites, sacrificial, votive and oracular, centred in the worship of the Western Asian Goddess. In the main court at Hal Tarxien she reigned supreme with the representation of her huge body arrayed in a fluted skirt and having pear-shaped legs. She was attended, apparently, by three priests or priestesses in long skirts and short wigs, resembling Chaldaean officials. They were presenting burnt offerings to the statue on the altar near by, and pouring the blood of the victim into a cylindrical stone vessel, decorated on the outside with pit marks, which had a deep cavity at the top to receive the oblation, and a hollow base. In the cup-shaped cylindrical tops of pillars incense was burning.[46]

In addition to sacrificial rites, healing cults, incubation and oracular divination would seem to have been practised in the Hypogeum. This is suggested by the female figures reclining in the attitude of sleep and the cubicles in which votaries may have slept in order to secure oracular dreams interpreted by the priests and priestesses in the sanctuary. It is by no means improbable that devotees resorted for these purposes to the oracular chamber with its remarkable acoustic properties. Next to it is a large circular room with concave walls decorated with spiral designs leading to a small chamber behind a façade, commonly known as the 'Holy of Holies', as it appears to have been set apart for the performance of sacred rites. At the back is an oval chamber with a doorway in the left wall, leading by a staircase to the lower storey. At the bottom step is a recess to this very inaccessible cave beyond the Holy of Holies.[47]

Before it became an ossuary in the middle of the second millennium B.C. the Hypogeum was unquestionably constructed as a sanctuary, served by a priesthood engaged in a variety of ritual functions connected with the cultus of the Mother-goddess, and perhaps with incubation and esoteric mysteries, screened from the uninitiated and performed in subdued light.

If Malta was not actually a 'sacred isle', as Zammit has asserted, it was, nevertheless, an important religious centre in the western Mediterranean where, in the transformation of megalithic tombs into temples, Siculan, Minoan-Mycenaean, Anatolian and western Asian influences were felt. But in spite of Cretan contacts, the island stood apart from the rest of the Aegean world, going its own way to a considerable extent. Long after the use of copper and bronze had become established elsewhere in this region, the Neolithic culture survived among the island colonists whose outstanding achievement was building temples on the grand scale.

SARDINIAN 'GIANTS' TOMBS'

In Sardinia, where collective burial in caves and rock-cut tombs was of common occurrence, the megalithic tradition found expression in cyclopean stone mounds known locally as *tombe di giganti*, which were constructed of rude slabs with flat capstones or corbelling and covered with a cairn enclosed by masonry walls, rounded at the closed end. They were, in fact, a developed form of the gallery grave containing a long burial chamber entered through a huge slab carved and bordered in relief with a small hole at the base and gabled above.[48] The chamber was a family tomb with a semi-circular forecourt from which, in some examples, two wings branched off in the form of an Irish 'horned cairn', though the stones were dressed with metal tools. Contemporary with these giant graves were the *domus di gianas*, or 'homes of the witches and fairies', with an upright slab forming the entrance to both of them from a semicircular space flanked by masonry. In the absence of very much in the way of well-attested furnishings, it is difficult to date these tombs, but the majority seem to fall between 1500 and 800 B.C., contemporary with the truncated circular dry-stone towers of clay mortar and slabs

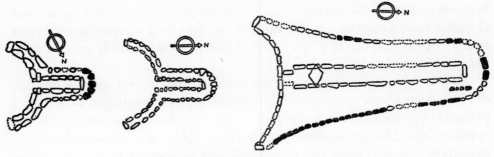

Fig. 9. '*Giants*'' *graves, Sardinia*

called *nuraghi*. The connexion, however, would appear to have been with the Mediterranean tholoi rather than with these fortified refuges, and in association with them the early settlers in Sardinia and their descendants performed their mortuary rites and developed the megalithic and cyclopean techniques in the western Mediterranean.[49]

BALEARIC 'NAVETAS'

In the Balearic Isles the cyclopean tombs in the shape of a ship, known as *navetas*, reproduced above the ground the structure of the rock-cut tombs, with a corridor, antechamber and chamber. A good example is that of Es Tudons ('the wood pigeons') in Minorca 45 feet in length and 15 feet in height standing on slightly rising ground in a sloping valley. The entrance at its western end is nearly square, with three courses of upright masonry inclining towards an angle of 67°; the eastern end is rounded and gathered in at an

Fig. 10. '*Naveta*' *tombs, Minorca*

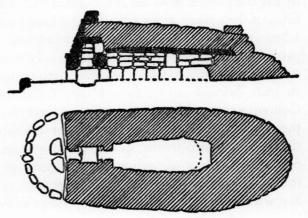

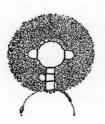
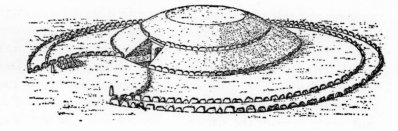

Fig. 11. Tholos at Los Millares, Spain

angle of about 55°, the sides perhaps originally meeting in a ridge before the upper part collapsed; they in fact resemble the square stern and rounded prow of an overturned ship. The monument stands above the level of the rock, on a platform making up the forecourt which is bounded by rough stones. Two slabs stand in front of the entrance and form a second semi-circular area concentric with the forecourt. A groove in the floor suggests that a slab of stone may have been used as the door of the entrance, and through this opening a passage led to an antechamber some 10 feet high. A second narrow passage led to the main chamber, constructed like that in the rock-cut tombs, except that the roof made of great slabs is flat instead of rounded. Like the Sardinian Giants' Graves these navetas were probably reserved for chieftains and their mortuary rites, commoners being buried in the rock-cut tombs.

THE ALMERIAN MEGALITHIC CULTUS

It was, however, on the southern and eastern shores of the Iberian peninsula that the megalithic tradition was strongly represented and developed, notably in Almeria and the surrounding district. Practically every known type of great stone monument, in fact, has been found in the south-east of Spain and Portugal. There settlers of eastern Mediterranean origin may have encountered Neolithic folk with Egyptian affinities, who had established themselves on hill-tops like El Garcel in the third millennium B.C. At Los Millares, very near to the coast and to a region rich in copper, gold, silver and lead, a colony arose in the Almerian hills on the spur of the plateau over-looking the valley of the Anderax river. Behind the town, on a wider ridge, was a cemetery containing circular tholoi in small groups with entrance passages and side chambers, like those at Khirokitia in Cyprus or at Mesara in Crete. The earth mound had a retaining wall composed of a single or double ring of upright slabs, pierced on the side facing the sea (i.e. the east) by a porthole or doorway, frequently divided into a series of antechambers by other doors. The semicircular forecourt outlined by large stones was in the nature of a sanctuary in which the funerary rites and dances were held, and in the interior the slabs forming the walls were plastered and painted. So numerous were the interments that some of the skeletons had been strewn in the passages of the necropolis. Similar cemeteries occur at Almizaraque and Las Canteras, and further to the west at Balmonte, Purcherra, Tabernas and Velez Blancho.[50]

Everywhere the grave furniture was rich and traces of ritual fires occurred, doubtless in conjunction with purificatory rites. The sherds were mainly of Almerian type decorated with incised geometric sacred designs. Highly stylized female figurines with eyes and the facial features incised, made from knucklebones of oxen, were among the cult objects in the graves, together with stone croziers, schist plaques and models of sandals and axes used as amulets. But the emblems of the Goddess become increasingly stylized and degenerate the further they are removed from the great centres of the cult in south-west Spain and the western Mediterranean. While the cult persisted in the hinterland and the north, only a few figurines survived in the process of diffusion from the Mediterranean. Nevertheless, the worship of the Mother-goddess was an integral element in the megalithic tradition and its complicated mortuary ritual, for while it was most prominent in the eastern Mediterranean, the Aegean, Crete and Malta, its symbolism recurred in the menhir-statues in Brittany, the Paris basin, along the Seine, Oise and Marne (S.O.M.) and in the Channel Islands, as well as on the slabs of megalithic monuments in southern Morbihan.

Undaunted by the Atlantic breakers and the storms and hazards of the Bay of Biscay, the megalithic mariners, after colonizing Almeria, the Algave and Estremadura, proceeded northwards to Galicia, Asturias, the Basque provinces and the Pyrenees where small passage-dolmens are mere shadows of the great tombs of the south. The largest concentration, however, lies round the Gulf of Morbihan in Brittany, centred in Carnac; there the cultus of the megalithic builders was most firmly established, and it penetrated to Finistère and the Channel Islands. Small groups of tombs were scattered sporadically along the coast of the Bay of Biscay to Charente, with clusters of galleries and rock-cut tombs in the Loire valley, the Paris basin and in Gard.

NORTH-WEST EUROPE

THE ARMORICAN MEGALITHS

In southern Morbihan the Iberian type of corbelled dry-walled monuments and passage-graves reappear with local variations. To the north-east of Carnac, the great passage circular-tumulus of Kercado, 66 feet in diameter and 11½ feet in height, is surmounted by a menhir over the burial chamber and surrounded by a stone circle like a tholos. Originally an ashlar retaining wall was splayed out to form a forecourt, with a portal composed of massive slabs. A causeway of closely packed stones from 10 to 20 feet wide, flanked by a stone circle, lay at the base of the wall. This seems to have been a development of the ritual enclosure at Los Millares, and in the Aegean tholoi and rock-cut tombs extended to embrace the entire structure.[51] Burnt offerings may have been included in the funerary rites performed within the sanctuary, as traces have been found in the forecourt of two hearths and a slab on which the offerings may have been cooked before they were presented to the dead or to their tutelary spirits.

At the tomb of Mané Rutual, Locmariaquer, behind a smaller rectangular chamber lies a large polygonal chamber covered with a huge slab. Sometimes in Brittany, transepts were added on either side of the gallery at the

Fig. 12. Circular tumulus at Kercado, France

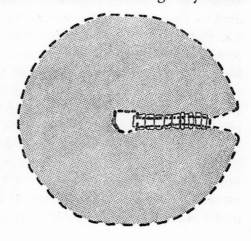

inner end, as in the case of the passage-graves known as Mané-Bras, Goderan, and Clud-er-Yer. We cannot be certain whether these transepted galleries in France evolved from the Iberian tholoi with lateral cells as at Los Millares,[52] or whether, as Dr Daniel now believes, they represent an independent line of diffusion from the gallery-graves related to the Balearic navetas and the Sardinian giganti.[53] As he says, 'there is nothing as yet known from the Breton passage graves to suggest that the Iberian settlers who colonized the Biscay coast from Finistère to the Charente had set out from Iberia before the bell-beaker had become an integral part of the passage-grave culture of Spain and Portugal'.[54] This he suggests occurred not earlier than 1800 to 1700 B.C., and in the Channel Islands from 1500 to 1000 B.C. But until the dating of the Iberian megaliths has been determined with greater certainty, the Breton chronology remains inconclusive.

However, the contents of these Breton tombs show that Brittany became the centre of the megalithic cultus in north-western Europe, attracting devotees from a very wide area. They presumably introduced the gallery-graves and the passage-graves with their forecourt sanctuaries from southern Spain and Portugal and their eastern Mediterranean antecedents, came from the valley of the Loire and southern France and from the Paris basin brought the female figurines and collared flasks characteristic of the S.O.M. region and were responsible for the galleries with portholes. The occurrence of beakers in most of these megaliths, except in the rather rare corbelled tombs in Morbihan and Jersey, indicate that the Beaker folk were a dominant element in the mixed population who had adopted the local cult and practised its rites and burial customs. As well as beakers, undecorated pottery and that of the Chassey style occur in the passage-graves, and although bronze and copper objects are absent, double-axes in stone, imitating their Minoan metal prototypes, form part of the equipment.

Therefore, it would appear that the megalithic sanctuaries in Brittany attracted a variety of worshippers from far and near, sometimes perhaps bringing with them powerful chiefs or heroes to be interred within the sacred precincts, as in ancient Egypt where the tombs of the nobility became clustered round the royal pyramids.[55] The concentration of megalithic graves round Carnac in the south of Morbihan is, in fact, unique in Europe, exceeding even that in the Iberian-Almerian region. There, the alignment of nearly three thousand menhirs reaches a total length of 3,060 yards. They are divided into three distinct groups: the Field of Ménec with a cromlech to the north of the village, the Field of Kermario, and the Field of Kerlescan at the west, which has a stone circle with rounded corners, and like those of St Pierre, Quiberon, is orientated in relation to the solstices. Therefore, they may have been in the nature of vast sanctuaries for seasonal gatherings; those at Ménec and Quiberon for the celebration of the midsummer rites, and those at Kermario for the equinoxial ceremonies in the spring and autumn. But, as alignments often end in tumuli (e.g. at Carnac, Mané-er-Hroeck, Locmariaquer, Clud-er-Yer and Kergo), they appear to have had also a funerary significance in which the cult of the dead played an important part.

The construction, orientation and equipment of the sepulchral monuments in this area, in fact, indicate a highly developed mortuary cultus. This is apparent from great dolmens like the Table des Marchands at Locmaria-quer, or corridor-tombs such as that on the island of Gavr'inis Morbihan, covered with a tumulus nearly 200 feet in diameter and having no less than twenty-two slabs engraved with symbolic cult designs. It is further confirmed by the contents of graves which included necklaces, beads, notably of calläis, and trinkets, including fine greenstone axes pierced at one end for amuletic uses and employed as votive offerings, together with the remains of burnt and unburnt sacrificial victims (horses and oxen). Nevertheless, although megalithic monuments were very frequently employed for collective burial they were by no means confined to this function. They were created over a very considerable period, chiefly in the second millennium B.C., accompanied by a long succession of movements of different peoples in different directions, if, as seems probable, the main stream was from the Mediterranean and the Altantic littoral to the north-west. This protracted process of colonization involved widespread contacts and adaptation to local conditions, but, like the spread of Islam in and after the seventh century A.D., the diffusion was dominated by fundamental religious beliefs and practices.

These found expression in the megalithic tradition and its cultus in which the worship of the Mother-goddess in the setting of the seasonal sequence was a prominent element. The sanctuaries and cult objects were adorned with her image and her symbols, such as the axe and the horns of consecration, going back to the eastern Mediterranean and Western Asia; hence the recurrence of the symbolism on statue-menhirs from southern Spain and Portugal to Brittany, Gard, the Paris Basin, the Marne and the Channel Islands. Female figures with prominent breasts are conspicuous in Aveyron, at the gates of the churchyard of St Martin's, and in that of St Marie-du-Côtel in Guernsey, at Bellehaye near Boury in the department of Oise, at Collorgues in Gard, and on the walls of the artificial caves in the valley of Petit Orin in the chalk country of the Marne.[56]

About 2000 B.C., in the later part of the Neolithic, small groups of colonists from France arrived in southern England and settled on the chalk downs of Wessex. There they mingled with the Windmill Hill farmers, already established there in their causewayed camps. Some two hundred years later they were succeeded by communities of Secondary Neolithic peoples and erected roofed sanctuaries on Overton Hill near the Bath road 4½ miles from Marlborough, and at Woodhenge 2 miles north-east of Stonehenge on the road from Marlborough to Amesbury. Then came an influx of immigrants from the Rhineland about 1700 B.C., bringing with them pottery bell-shaped drinking vessels from which they derive their designation, the Beaker people. They apparently had some knowledge of copper and they were in the habit of burying their dead under round barrows, or in single graves. Moreover, by their contacts with the Battle-axe warriors in central Europe they appear to have become acquainted with the worship of the Indo-European Sky-god.

AVEBURY AND 'THE SANCTUARY' ON OVERTON HILL

In any case, it was they who were mainly responsible for the construction of the vast complex monuments at Avebury on the Marlborough downs enclosing an area of 28½ acres and three-quarters of a mile in circumference, open to the sky. Within the immense surrounding earthwork consisting of a circular, internal ditch with three or perhaps four entrances situated more or less at the cardinal points, lie the remains of two stone circles, about 350 feet in diameter. Originally it contained about a hundred upright blocks of undressed sarsen stone, hauled with great labour for a considerable distance from the downs between Marlborough and Newbury where sarsen nodules occur, weighing up to 40 tons. The largest were placed flanking the entrances; two still remain at the south entrance, and one at the approach to the village from Swindon. The central circle was originally about 320 feet in diameter and had thirty stones, of which only four survive. At its centre stood three

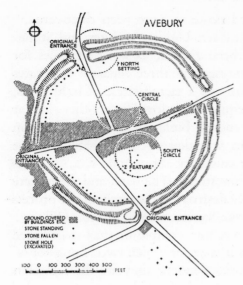

Fig. 13. Plan of the Avebury circles

huge menhirs and in the rather larger southern circle one stood at the centre 20 feet in height, still visible in the eighteenth century, though it had fallen. To the west of the centre was a line of smaller stones (known as the Z stones), and between the circle and the ditch the stump of an isolated 'Ring Stone' has been found. Of a northern circle, if such existed, only three socket holes have survived.

From the south entrance the West Kennet Avenue leads to a second sanctuary on Overton Hill. This is marked by two parallel rows of standing stones, 50 feet apart, those missing having now been indicated by concrete substitutes. The sanctuary consists of two concentric circles with an outer diameter of 135 feet which remained until 1724. Against one of the inner

Fig. 14. Plan of the 'Sanctuary' on Overton Hill

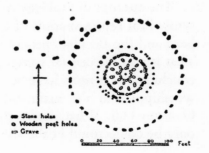

circles, Beaker burials in the contracted position have been discovered,[57] together with Beaker and Peterborough ware. Unlike Avebury and Stonehenge, this sanctuary appears to have been roofed, as series of holes for wooden posts have been excavated representing three separate structures erected one after the other. At the centre was a sacred circle of light posts, open to the sky at the top. This was subsequently enclosed by another circular structure, and then was added a third wooden building, having perhaps an opening for light and ventilation. This was destroyed, probably by the Beaker people when they occupied the sanctuary about 1600 B.C., and was replaced by two concentric circles of sarsen stones. The bank and ditch were produced in the Early Bronze Age, partly destroying the circle in the process of joining the West Kennet Avenue to the Sanctuary on Overton Hill.

When Stukeley first described the Avebury temple in 1723 it included the Beckhampton Avenue from the south-west, of which two 'Longstones' alone survive at the end of the earthwork, if indeed they are the remnants of an avenue that ran towards the Kennet.[58] John Aubrey in 1648 recorded that three stones stood there in his time, and Stukeley mentions the breaking-up of the third stone by Richard Fowler. The other two fell in 1911 and subsequently were re-erected. In 1934, the excavation of the West Kennet Avenue was begun in the hope of ascertaining its exact course and of determining the date of its erection. Although the results have not been very conclusive as regards the development of the temple as a whole and its approaches, nevertheless, it is now reasonably well established that the movement belongs essentially to the Early Bronze Age. The earliest section of it may be the circles at the Sanctuary on Overton Hill and those in the enclosure at Avebury. Later they were surrounded by the outer circle and ditch and finally the West Kennet Avenue was joined to the main circle in the earthwork.

The attempt of Stukeley to interpret the lay of the entire monument as a symbolical representation of a serpent, with the Overton Sanctuary as the head and the Beckhampton Avenue as the tail,[59] cannot be taken seriously. That it was the central sacred place in England, however, is now generally concluded, as it must have been capable of containing a colossal assembly of worshippers in the main enclosure, apart from those who gathered on Overton Hill. What rites were performed within the sacred precincts can only be conjectured in the absence of any conclusive clues.

Brittany became the centre of the megalithic cult during the second millennium. Here chieftains and their subjects were buried in graves formed by walls of monoliths covered with capstones (42). At Carnac were built long avenues of standing stones which stretch for 3,060 yards (43)

The long barrow at West Kennet is one of the most famous of the many which lie scattered over the Wessex chalk downs. Under a mound of chalk some 340 feet long, excavation revealed a gallery made of stones running for 40 feet towards the end chamber (45). On either side of the gallery are four chambers into which human bones and skulls had been placed over a period of time, suggesting that the tomb retained its sanctity for some years

46

47

Large circles of wood or stone, known as 'henges' were erected as places of worship by megalithic cult followers in England. Of these, the sanctuary at Avebury must have been one of the greatest centres. When first built, the site of 28 acres was surrounded by a ditch and bank some 50 feet high, dug by builders who had to rely on primitive antler picks. The eroded earthwork can still be seen clearly from the air (44) but of the complex of three circles only a few monoliths still stand (46). Two hundred stones set in pairs—the West Kennet Avenue—run from the Avebury sanctuary to another sanctuary on Overton Hill (47)

The zenith of monumental building was reached with the enlargement of the sanctuary at Stonehenge. The first henge consisted of a ditch and bank with an inner circle of 56 pits, many containing cremated bones. Over a century later, a great labour force brought blue stones weighing 4 tons each more than 100 miles from Pembrokeshire to form two inner stone circles, but this plan was superceded by the completely new and unique conception of Stonehenge as it stands today (48). Colossal blocks of sarsen weighing up to 50 tons each were dragged to the site from the Marlborough Downs. The stones were dressed and erected to form an outer circle of thirty stones each topped by a lintel, held in place by the tenons on the up-rights (49). Within the outer circle was an inner ring of five trilithons inside which a circle of blue stones was later erected (50)

49   50

The association of Beaker burials with the ritual deposits in the stone-holes, together with flint implements, flakes, sherds and animal bones, indicates the cult of the dead. But in such a complex extensive structure this could only have been incidental to the elaborate rites that must have been performed in the temple and its adjuncts. These, doubtless, were associated with the seasonal cycle in which the sun in all probability played its customary role. The absence of any specific orientations makes it unlikely that it was actually a solar temple, but it appears to have been connected with death and rebirth, as in the case of so many megalithic monuments, in which the Earth-mother probably exercised her customary fertility functions. Superimposed on this basic substratum of the cultus may have been Indo-European beliefs and practices centred in the Sky-god as the most prominent figure, introduced by the Beaker folk through their fusion with the Nordic Battle-axe warriors.

STONEHENGE

This becomes more apparent in the much smaller, if more spectacular, 'henge' monument on Salisbury Plain 2 miles west of Amesbury. As long ago as 1648, Aubrey described the relationship of Avebury to Stonehenge as that of a cathedral to a parish church, but, even so, like many ancient parish churches, one that has undergone a number of reconstructions. In the light of the recent excavations of Professors Atkinson and Piggott, it would seem that about 1800 B.C., the bank ditch, and perhaps the Heel Stone, were constructed by the Secondary Neolithic peoples. The charred remains enclosing a ring of fifty-six ritual pits from 2 to 4 feet in depth, known as the Aubrey Holes after the name of their discoverer in 1666, contained cremated human bones in the chalk rubble which by radioactive analysis (Carbon-14) have been dated at 1848 B.C. ± 275 years. This confirms the archaeological chronology which places the opening phase of the monument between 1900 and 1700 B.C.

On the north-east side of the earthwork is a gap which formed the entrance to an avenue with two parallel banks and a ditch leading across the main road to the river Avon at West Amesbury. Within this avenue lies the Heel Stone, with pointed apex and weighing some 35 tons; there are traces of a circular ditch surrounding its base where Beaker pottery has been found. This ditch appears to belong to the second phase, as the rubble filling it up

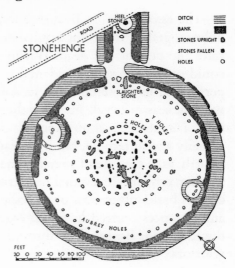

Fig. 15.   Plan of Stonehenge

contained a fragment of unweathered bluestone. It was probably at this time that the ditch was made, perhaps to separate the sacred Heel Stone from profane activities with which the avenue inevitably was associated when the stone circle was in process of construction and development about 1600 B.C. Indeed, Professor Atkinson has suggested that some wooden *sanctum sanctorum* may previously have stood in the centre of the site.[60]

That the Aubrey Holes had a ritual function and were not, as was formerly supposed, sockets for wooden posts is now clear from the cremated burials with them; such remains recur in the rings of pits excavated at Dorchester-on-Thames.[61] In them are no traces of decayed wooden posts or packing as at the Henge monuments at Arminghall and Woodhenge, and they are too shallow for such a purpose, be they wooden or stone structures. Since many of the charred human bones had been inserted after the holes had been dug, they cannot be regarded as primarily sepulchral, and it is possible, as has been conjectured, that they had a chthonian or sacrificial significance. But this has to be considered in relation to the structure and function of the monument as a whole.

The second phase (1700–1600 B.C.) is marked by a double circle of thirty-five or forty bluestones with diameters of 74 and 86 feet respectively. Each pair were set into the two ends of dumb-bell shaped hollows packed with chalk rubble. It was then that the avenue was constructed, probably by the

Beaker people, leading in a north-westerly direction from the causeway of the bank and ditch to the river Avon, the orientation of the entrance of the circle being towards the midsummer sunrise. The eighty odd bluestones of dolorite were brought from the Prescelly mountains in Pembrokeshire 150 miles away; a region colonized by the Beaker folk from which they derived their battle-axes. Dr H. H. Thomas of the Geological Survey has also shown that the so-called 'Altar Stone' is composed of micaceous sandstone from the neighbourhood of Milford Haven.[62] For the greater part of this considerable journey, they may have been water-borne and thence hauled on sledges overland to Stonehenge, probably from the Bristol Avon near to the avenue. But, however the problem of transport was solved, it could only have been undertaken for very compelling reasons connected with the sanctity of the stones and the supreme importance of the sanctuary on Salisbury Plain. It has, in fact, been conjectured that they may have been part of a henge in south Wales. This, however, is not the only place in Wiltshire where bluestones have been found. Since they occur also at Boles Barrow at Heylesbury and in a round barrow near Stonehenge, their sanctity is beyond doubt. It was for this reason that, when the great sanctuary was in process of erection on Salisbury Plain, it had to be adorned with and sanctified by bluestones from another great religious centre of the Beaker people, in spite of all the difficulties involved in their transport.

In the third phase between 1500 and 1400 B.C., the bluestone circle was dismantled and the sarsen outer circle was erected. Five large trilithons, joined by lintels at the top with tenons and mortises, were set up in its place in the area. This enclosure later contained the Altar Stone horseshoe with the 'Slaughter Stone', now recumbent across the axis south-west of the centre but in all probability originally standing erect at the causeway entrance. The fifty-nine sockets surrounding the sarsen circle in two irregular rings, the Y and Z holes with diameters respectively of 130 feet and 180 feet, which were then dug may have been with the intention of re-erecting the bluestones within them. This, however, was never carried out, though in the final phase the sixty bluestones were shaped and erected on the line of the present bluestone horseshoe surrounding the Altar Stone. It would seem, in fact, that a bluestone monument may have existed before the sarsen structure was constructed and demolished and subsequently was used in the completion of Stonehenge about 1500 B.C.[63]

Many of the sarsens bear initials, names or inscriptions on them but it was not until 1953 that, in photographing a name carved on the face of stone 53 of the second horseshoe trilithons, Professor Atkinson detected the forms of a dagger and an axe on the glass of his reflex camera. Closer examination revealed groups of axe-carvings on other stones of the outer circle, and in the previous year a bronze axe had been found within 500 yards of Stonehenge. There is now little doubt that these incised engravings of flanged axes and hilted daggers having Mycenaean affinities are indicative of the penetration to Wessex of the cult of the axe from the eastern Mediterranean in the middle of the second millennium B.C.[64] Moreover, among the symbols on the surface of one of the recumbent trilithons appears an oblong figure resembling similar designs on the Breton megaliths, which suggests that the cult of the Mother-goddess had a place in the complex rites performed at Stonehenge.

It is very probable, as Professor Atkinson says, that between 1500 and 1400 B.C. the sarsens were erected and the bluestones re-arranged by the Wessex chieftains under the inspiration of Mycenaean builders in a co-ordinate effort demanding great skill and ingenuity; Silbury Hill may represent the cenotaph of one of these chieftains.[65] However that may be, it is now becoming apparent that Mycenaean influences penetrated the Wessex culture between 1500 and 1300 B.C.[66] From the Aegean would seem to have come the gold ornaments and gold-mounted amber disks discovered in Wessex graves, and the blue glazed beads worn by Wessex chieftains were of eastern Mediterranean manufacture, while British stone axes were inspired by Minoan *bipennes*.[67] Bronze axes with side-flanges were imported from this region via Spain, and the maritime route as well as the amber route constituted a highway to the Baltic along which the Mycenaean axe cult and the goddess tradition passed. In Wessex they seem to have been an intensive element in the Early Bronze Age, and part of a composite cultus in the great sanctuary of Stonehenge, in which the worship of the Sky-god, with probably a solar element, was combined with that of the Mother-goddess. Both had a vegetation significance associated with the seasonal cycle and the beliefs and customs which, as we have seen, became incorporated in the megalithic tradition as a colonizing movement in western Europe.

What precisely were the rites performed in central sanctuaries like Stonehenge is impossible to say. The supposition (which is by no means established), that at the summer solstice on 21 June the sun rose over the Heel Stone and cast a shadow from it on to the Altar Stone, has led to speculations about a solar cultus, and to romantic theories concerning the site as a Druidical temple. The popular misconception that Stonehenge originated as a Druidical sanctuary is equally unfounded, since this Celtic priesthood was not established in Britain before the La Tène phase of the Iron Age (*c.* 300 B.C.) at the earliest. Therefore, any connexions they may have had with Stonehenge must have been more than a thousand years after its foundation and subsequent developments in the Bronze Age. It is this common fantasy that has given rise to the misnomers 'Slaughter Stone' and 'Altar Stone', based on the unfounded supposition that human sacrifice was practised in the sanctuary.

WOODHENGE

It is true that at the neighbouring circular sanctuary known as Woodhenge, only 2 miles to the north-east on the Amesbury to Marlborough road, the skeleton of a child with its cranium split in half before burial in the contracted position has been found lying across the axis of the central ring of this very complicated structure. It has been assumed that this was a sacrificial offering.[68] But if the conjecture is correct it may well have been only a foundation sacrifice when the sanctuary was first erected. A study of the plan of the dome-shaped sacred site of the Beaker people affords reason to think, as Professor Piggott has shown,[69] that it was a circular gallery with a ridged roof and an open centre. In such a wooden temple designed specifically

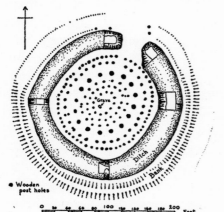

Fig. 16. Plan of Woodhenge

for ritual purposes, like the Sanctuary on Overton Hill, the seasonal drama in spring and autumn, upon which vegetation was believed to depend for its annual renewal, may well have been enacted. The discovery of two ritual axes carved in chalk among the cult-objects at Woodhenge is in accord with such an interpretation of the sanctuary.

CHAPTER III

Egyptian Temples

WHEREAS IN THE CULTUS IN WESTERN ASIA and the eastern Mediterranean and that which found expression in the megalithic tombs and temples, the Mother-goddess was accorded the predominant role, the two most prominent cults in the valley of the Nile at the western extremity of the Fertile Crescent were those of the Sun-god, Re, and of Osiris, the author and giver of life, who himself may have originated in western Asia. Both of them were essentially male deities, and with the rise of the monarchy the Pharaohs were identified with them. Even before the unification of Upper and Lower Egypt and the establishment of the Pharaonic dynasty about 3200 B.C., traditionally attributed to Menes, each clan, or nome, was thought to have been ruled by its local god, and no doubt every town had its 'house of the god' where the deity was believed to dwell, and prayers, lustrations, offerings and gifts were made to him daily, accompanied by dancing, music and processions. At first in prehistoric times each god probably had his own shrine, but in order to secure the favour and beneficence of the various gods responsible for the well-being of the community in its several aspects, others were added. Thus, the temples became increasingly complex structures.

THE HOUSE OF THE GOD

Originally the 'house of the god' appears to have been a hut like that of the goddess Neith, engraved on an ebony tablet of the First Dynasty and portrayed in the hieroglyph for a shrine, with an outer court enclosed by a lattice-work palisade and two high masts with flags at the entrance. In the inner court and vestibule stood the emblem of the goddess in the 'holy place', secluded by reed-mats and hangings. When these simple mud huts reinforced with reeds and, like Woodhenge, covered with a wooden roof gave place to stone structures with additional rooms, they became spacious

Fig. 17.   Ancient reed temple from a
wooden label found at Abydos.
First Dynasty

edifices with three chambers but still retaining the earlier plan consisting of
a portico and an outer and an inner court, a vestibule and the shrine of the
god or goddess. Rectangular in form in accordance with the Egyptian
natural setting and modelled on the hut design, stone temples with five
chambers were attached to pyramids and other royal tombs, those of the
Sun-god Re at Memphis in the Fifth Dynasty being among the earliest.
The first sanctuary mentioned is that dedicated to Horus in the Third
Dynasty (*c.* 2800 B.C.).[1] However, the oldest plan of a temple at Abydos
may be Pre-dynastic in origin; there the sanctuary is enclosed by a wall 16
inches thick entered through a passage between walls 4 feet apart and 3 feet
in length facing south. The more massive structures sometimes had the entrance to the north in the great temenos wall, with store-rooms at the side.
Subsequently in the Fourth Dynasty they were re-modelled to make provision for burnt offerings, and at Abydos, under Pepy I in the Fifth Dynasty,
further expanded to seven chambers.[2]

THE EVERLASTING HABITATION OF THE DEAD

It is evident that the temples at first had a mortuary significance from their
association with tombs in and after the First Dynasty when the simpler Pre-
dynastic pit graves were lined with mud-brick and covered with sand and
stones over a wood roof. A sepulchral chamber was constructed under the
ground, undercut on one side to afford more space at the bottom of the
shaft for the funerary furniture. On the east side of the mound was a doorway to enable the soul to fly out and return. This so-called 'false door'
eventually developed into a chapel of offerings, which in the royal tombs
became a temple. In the Third Dynasty, stone was substituted for brick and
this opened the way for the great mastaba tombs in which a figure in relief
of the *ka*, or guardian *alter ego* of the deceased, was sculptured. In front of it
a small room with a niche was added and there food was laid and drink
poured out into a stone trough on an altar of offerings that was placed

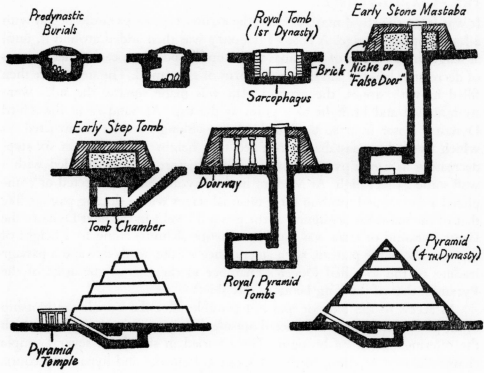

Fig. 18. *Development of the mastaba tomb*

before it. In this life-like statue the ka could take up its abode. When the recess containing the statue was deepened and walled in with masonry across the entrance the jambs of the false door were extended laterally to form a façade. The mastaba was surrounded with brickwork to protect it and a court was added in front for the offerings, but to prevent the façade of the niche being obscured, a cross-passage was left inside the brick enclosure. In order to enable those making offerings for the deceased to enter the chamber, the end of the cross chamber was walled off as a separate closed cell or *serdab*, within the mastaba tomb. In the Sixth Dynasty at Denderah, the passage along the front of the mastaba of Senna contained an increasing number of entrance doors but no serdab. Additional courts and chambers were also added in front of the mastaba, but at Saqqara the serdab was retained within the tombs.

THE PYRAMID-TEMPLES

It was from the royal mastabas that the earliest type of pyramid began with a long sloping passage. A coat of masonry was then added around it, until at length a succession of mastabas were superimposed on each other in steps of decreasing heights and size in the form of a pyramid. The steps were then filled in with stones, the ground plan was made square, the sides were straightened and brought to a point at the top. At Saqqara in the Third Dynasty, Zoser (*c.* 2780 B.C.) had a huge oblong mastaba constructed on which five other mastabas were piled to a height of 200 feet in six steps decreasing in size in pyramid form.[3] This structure was surrounded with a wall some 23 feet high. At Medum in the Fayum, Sneferu erected or completed a flat-topped tomb in three unequal stages with a sloping passage like that of the mastabas beginning at the ground level.[4] In the next Dynasty the Great Pyramid of Giza was built by Cheops (Khufu) rising to a height of 481 feet above the plateau, with an entrance on the north side and a passage leading to the so-called Queen's chamber in the axis of the apex of the Pyramid, that of the king being to one side.[5]

As access to the interior was not possible after the burial, the worship of the pharaoh had to be conducted outside the pyramid in a temple to which the offerings could be brought. These varied in size from several simple chambers, as at Medum, to the elaborate colonnades and hypaethral courts at Abusir on the bank of the Nile with its covered paved passage leading to the pyramids and the mortuary temples. Statues of Chephren (Khafra), the pharaoh, in whose likeness the Sphinx is thought to have been sculptured as an idealized portrait-statue,[6] were placed in the pillared hall of his valley temple at Giza. At a respectful distance around the pyramid were the mastabas of members of the royal family, courtiers and officials, arranged in rows in regular streets. In the centre court of the pyramid-temple at Abusir on a podium stood a great white obelisk, the symbol of the Sun-god, before which was a table of offerings. The lofty walls were elaborately decorated with reliefs depicting the king as a sphinx destroying his enemies. The inner court was open to the sky and opposite the entrance lay the processional hypostyle hall, completely roofed, resting on large columns. The small dark chamber was the shrine of the god; it was narrow, with double doors, and contained the statue of the deity in a richly decorated boat. At the burial of the king the body was washed, probably in the first hall where the purification ceremonies appear to have been held, though they may have been per-formed on the roof of the temple. When the lengthy process of mummifica-tion had been completed the 'Opening of the Mouth' rites followed to re-animate the mummy by restoring the faculties, thereby making it a living soul, or *ba*. This was done in front of the statue in the great hall, or in the mortuary temple east of the pyramid.[7] The entrance was then closed never to be reopened. But the funerary rites were repeated daily, consisting of the presentation of balls of natron, ablutions, libations, censings and offerings of food and drink. These were supplemented on festivals with additional ceremonies, prayers and incantations, and so extensive and complex did the mortuary cultus become that the temples required a large retinue of priests and perpetual endowments continuing for thousands of years.

THE TEMPLE WORSHIP AND ITS PRIESTHOOD

The temples for the worship of the gods differed from those of dead kings in being always structures separate and independent of any other build-ings. As the 'house' of the god to whom it was dedicated, it followed the form of a dwelling with a courtyard in front of the portico with its poles with flags where the festivals were celebrated by large numbers of people. The inner hall and the 'Holy of Holies' were reserved for the more solemn, esoteric rites in conjunction with the shrine and statue of the god which dwelt in it. Within the compound were small chapels or shrines and cham-bers for priests and stores.[8] The pharaoh in his divine capacity as the son of the reigning Horus was in theory the sole officiant in the service of his heavenly father, once the Heliopolitan solar theology was established in the Fifth Dynasty and made the basis of the temple worship in Egypt. He became, in fact, the high-priest of all the local divinities when they were identified with Re, the Sun-god. He was accredited exclusively with having built all the temples, and was depicted on their walls officiating as the media-tor between the gods and mankind. However, it was manifestly impossible for the king to exercise his priestly functions everywhere at the daily temple liturgy and to be at once himself the recipient and bestower of the Toilet ceremonies in the 'House of the Morning', when the coronation ritual was repeated and he underwent the same lustrations at dawn as the cult-image of the Sun-god in the temple at Heliopolis. He was purified with holy water from the sacred pool, identified with the primeval waters of Nun, censed, asperged, vested and arrayed in his royal insignia and anointed with unguents and cosmetics, as was the cult-image.[9] The proceedings concluded with a sacred meal corresponding to the presentation of food and drink offerings in the temple liturgy.[10]

In the temple scenes the pharaoh or his specially appointed deputy is shown as the officiant in all important rites, but since these were a replica of the toilet ceremonial in the palace, his place was taken by one of the retinue of priests attached to the royal household or the local temples. Only very occasionally did he in fact perform his functions in person. Every temple had its high-priest who, in addition to his sacred offices and duties, sacerdotal and administrative, might be a high judicial official, thereby combining spiritual and mundane affairs. The status varied with that of the sanctuary over which he presided, and with the particular nature of the events cele-brated and the actions performed. Thus, the high-priest of Ptah at Memphis had the title of *Sem* because he was the 'chief of the artificers' and of sculp-ture. Consequently he played a prominent part in the 'Opening of the Mouth' of the royal portrait statues and in other mortuary ceremonies.[11] His first duty however was to serve the god of the specific sanctuary for which he was responsible. As the king was the god he embodied, so the priest, being his deputy and representative, was also the son of the god he impersonated for the time being. Even though he only acted as proxy on behalf of the pharaoh, he shared in some measure in his divine personality. But because Re was the ka of the pharaoh, the potency of the sovereign remained unique, his ka alone being depicted on the monuments, and originally the ka was the peculiar possession of the occupant of the throne as an essential aspect of his divine constitution.[12]

The extension of the ka and a future life first to the nobility and then to the rest of mankind, opened the way in the Middle Kingdom for statues of eminent persons to be erected in the courtyards of the temples so that they might participate in the prayers and offerings of the priests on festivals like the New Year or the *Wag* feast on the eighteenth of the first month. To avoid frictions and pluralities, funerary priests were reduced to a single 'servant of the ka', and a 'lector priest' for the recitation of the liturgy at festivals. In the Fifth Dynasty those appointed for the cult of the kings in their mortuary temples were either *web*, meaning 'clean' or 'pure ones', assigned to special sanctuaries of Re, or *sandj*, servants of the god as 'instructors', while between these two classes there was the *yot-neter*, the 'father of the god'. Being attached to specific temples and tombs from which they derived part of their incomes, while their duties were only a subsidiary occupation performed by a succession of alternating priests, they became increasingly influential and well-endowed. Their principal function was to serve the god, bathing, dressing and feeding the image, and to act as the representative and mediator in his service, They might be also high state officials and physicians (*swnw*) and magistrates enjoying many privileges.

Nevertheless, from the number of titles assigned to priestly officials in the Old Kingdom, it appears that one priest must have served simultaneously a multiplicity of small cults in the shrine to which he was attached, and received by way of emoluments only his share of the offerings. Even the office of the greatest of seers in Heliopolis in the Fifth Dynasty is said on the Palermo Stone to have been administered jointly by two persons.[13] In the Middle Kingdom the temple built by Sesostris II to Anubis near his pyramid had a permanent staff restricted to the prince, high-priest, chief scribe, lector (*kherheb*) and eight minor officials. It was not until the New Kingdom that the revenues and status of the temples were very considerably increased so that as a result in the Twenty-second Dynasty (*c.* 1085) the high-priest of Amon-Re and his hierarchy were able to create 'a state within a state' at Thebes under their own rule. And even then the king remained the high-priest *par excellence*, and the entire sacerdotal order acted merely as his deputies or vicars.

The real sovereignty in the Theban sacerdotal state, however, was exercised by the daughter of the ruling priestly house who assumed the role of the 'god's wife' (i.e. wife of Amon). Priestesses were always common in Egypt and those who were members of influential families might become chief-priestesses, often associated with Hathor as wife of the Sun-god Re, and so gain the status of the wife of the god, or 'worshipper of god',[14] the ordinary priestesses being concubines of Amon under the rule and authority of the high-priest's wife from the Ninth or Tenth Dynasty. It was not until the Eighteenth Dynasty when music played a more important part in worship, that they became essentially musicians, their function being to sing and play the sistrum, personifying the goddess Hathor, or as members of the harem of Amon. In the New Kingdom, according to Strabo, the high-priestess at Thebes was the most beautiful virgin of the most illustrious

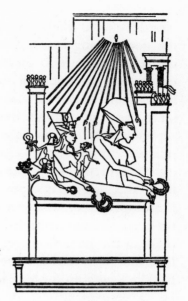

Fig. 19. Ikhnaton and Nefertiti and their family at the 'Window of Appearances' showing the sun disc, 'Aton'. Limestone relief. El-Amarna. Eighteenth Dynasty

family who after cohabiting with anyone of her choice, was then mourned as if dead, and subsequently given in marriage.[15] If he has accurately described the custom, it would appear to have been a survival of the priestess being originally the wife of the god.

By the time of the New Kingdom (c. 1546–1085 B.C.) the local priesthoods had been consolidated in powerful hierarchies and the temples had acquired enormous wealth at the expense of the surrounding lands and were equipped with a large staff and a host of officials engaged in the administration of the estates. It is true that the pharaoh retained his divine priestly status in theory, and even a sickly youth, on ascending the throne in the Eighteenth Dynasty, could set up a new hierarchy and temple organization centred in the Aton as the one and only God manifest in the solar disk, superseding the worship of Amon-Re at Karnak and elsewhere. Indeed, the names of all the gods were erased from the monuments during the reign of Ikhnaton, 'the beautiful child of the Aton', and the capital was removed from Thebes to El-Amarna in Middle Egypt and renamed Akhetaton, 'the Horizon of Aten'; there he was worshipped by his devoted son to whom he alone revealed himself. All anthropomorphic and theriomorphic images were rigidly excluded, the only symbol employed being that of the solar disk with emanating rays.[16]

THE TEMPLE AT EL-AMARNA

Atonism in fact was really a heretical variation of the solar faith instituted by an individualist with fanatical zeal. In his temple at El-Amarna Ikhnaton had rigidly excluded all the ceremonies connected with the royal toilet and the cult-image and although the presentation of food and drink offerings, of flowers and perfumes, censing and libations continued, the temple was devoid of a shrine; the solar disk (Aton) and the pyramidal obelisk, known as *benben*, being the only objects of worship. On the reliefs, the king and queen are depicted as the principal figures, each making an oblation attended at the high altar in the first court by the high-priest and the 'servitor of Aten'. Numerous oxen are also represented as garlanded awaiting sacrifice, while the royal priestesses rattled their sistra and the singers and musicians exercised their functions in the main temple and the smaller 'House of the Benben'.[17]

THE TEMPLE AT LUXOR

At the death of Ikhnaton in 1350 B.C., the return to power of the Theban Amonite priesthood brought Atonism and its sanctuary abruptly to an end. The old régime was restored with a new line of kings, bringing back the worship of Amon-Re in all its traditional splendour. The immense temples that had been created in his honour at Luxor and Karnak by Amenhotep III in the Eighteenth Dynasty (1412–1375) were liberally endowed from the tribute of Western Asia, and subsequently developed with lavish appointment by Rameses II (1299–1232), and his successors. On the banks of the Nile stand the ruins of the palatial temple at Luxor with its great court containing two colossal statues of Rameses II, its colonnades from the pylon

Fig. 20. Plan of the temple of Amon-Mut-Khons, Luxor

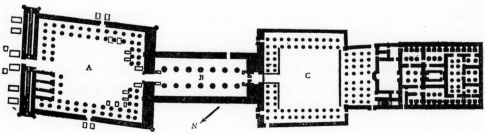

to the chapels behind the shrine, and pillars of the portico on the fourth side; the graceful columns, still bearing the relics of their architraves, have preserved some of its pristine splendour and imposing grandeur. In place of the earlier shrine which stood on the site in the Middle Kingdom, this magnificent sanctuary was constructed in the hey-day of Egyptian prosperity. A second huge hypostyle in front of the great forecourt begun by Amenhotep III was never completed, though fourteen pillars of the central aisle in a double row remain. Formerly they supported a stone roof and are enclosed within side walls on which are scenes depicting the midsummer festival of Amon.

The Festival of Opet. When the floods were at their height and work in the fields was in consequence at a standstill, the feast of Opet was held at Luxor and Karnak in honour of Amon. This New Year Festival usually lasted twenty-four days and was attended by almost the entire population. As depicted in the series of reliefs on the walls on either side of the court in the temple at Luxor, executed in the reign of Tutankhamen (c. 1366–1357), the ceremonies opened with food and drink offerings to the god, his consort Mut and their son Khonsu in their respective sanctuaries in the temple at Karnak, about a mile and a half away from that at Luxor, and connected with an avenue of sphinxes used as a processional way between the two temples. The shrines of each of the three gods at Luxor were in the form of a boat with the small image of the god in the cabin in the centre. On the sacred barque of Amon at the bow and stern were ornaments of rams' horns, that of Mut being adorned with two women's heads and a vulture skin, while two falcon heads were on the image of Khonsu. Poles were attached to the boat-shrines to enable them to be carried in procession by the priests from the temple to the sacred barque on the quayside. In front and behind each boat walked a flabellifer, or ceremonial fan-bearer, and on either side a pair of attendants clad in panther-skin vestments. Preceded by a trumpeter and drummer the three groups were headed by a thurifer, the Pharaoh following the shrine of Amon.

On reaching the edge of the Nile, the boat-shrines were placed on large elaborately decorated vessels, some 60 to 70 feet in length, in the form of a temple with a central shrine, obelisks, sphinxes, statues, and bas-reliefs depicting the king performing the seasonal rites in honour of Amon. On the bow and stern were two huge rams and great crowns, the boats of Mut and Khonsu being similarly decorated with their respective animal symbols. The flotilla of boats then made its way up the river to the main stream of the Nile, towed on the east bank by soldiers headed by a priest chanting the hymn to Amon and accompanied by a negro drummer and dancers. As the priests and priestesses rattled their castanets and sistra the citizens of Thebes clapped their hands and beat tambourines in time with the music. When the procession on the river and the concourse on the banks arrived opposite Luxor the shrines were taken out of the ships and carried into the temple on the shoulders of the priests behind the drummer and trumpeter, the priestesses and concubines dancing and rattling their sistra.[18]

The gods were regaled with food and drink offerings in abundance presented to them by the Pharaoh; from the quantities of food and liquor amassed for the event excessive eating and drinking must have been the characteristic feature, as in most Egyptian feasts. But in addition to these festivities it is probable that the rites included the enactment of episodes in the cult-legend of Amon, borrowed in the first instance perhaps from that of Min, the ancient fertility god of Upper Egypt, of whom Amon may have been a localized form before he was identified with the Heliopolitan Re in the Middle Kingdom. Be this as it may, whatever took place during the twenty-four day sojourn of the gods at Luxor, when the festivities came to an end the procession returned to Karnak by river and the images were re-instated in their shrines in the temple, the same procedure being followed, though with less enthusiasm as prosperity for the forthcoming year had been secured before the rise of the Nile on which it depended.

How firmly established the festival was is shown by its survival in a degraded form in the mosque in the north-east corner of the court at Luxor containing the tomb of the Muslim patron saint, Sheykh Yusef Abu'l Haggag. Here at midsummer a freshly painted boat adorned with flags is placed on a lorry and drawn round the city and the fields by men and boys accompanied by soldiers, musicians, dancers, readers of the Qur'an, men, women and children singing hymns in honour of the saint, and gaily adorned camels led by a muezzin and followed by members of his family and of religious confraternities. Stations are made at the tombs of the other local saints and prayers recited. Finally the boat returns to the mosque and is deposited in it for the rest of the year.[19] Various legends have appeared from time to time to afford an explanation of the observance, but it is clearly an outworn relic of the festival of Opet as depicted on the walls of the colonnaded court at Luxor.

THE GREAT TEMPLE AT KARNAK

The adjoining Great Temple at Karnak, also dedicated to Amon, is connected with that at Luxor by an avenue of ram-headed sphinxes constituting a processional way 1½ miles in length, with a similar avenue leading to the river, and forming the main approach to the western pylon. This imposing edifice was the work of a succession of pharaohs, beginning with the sanctuary of Senusret in the Twelfth Dynasty, built in granite with surrounding chambers. In the Eighteenth Dynasty, after the victory over the Hyksos when Ahmose I made Thebes the capital, ten gateways were added by Thutmose I (*c.* 1525–1509) enclosing a hall with figures of Osiris. A pylon in front was subsequently erected by Seti I (1318–1299) and another on the other side to enclose it. Having enclosed the shrine within three gates Thutmose III carved inscriptions on the walls of the ambulatory which surrounded it, recording his victorious campaigns in Syria and northern Palestine culminating in a detailed description of the defeat of the Syrian princes at Megiddo, the fortress in the plain of Esdraelon, and the tactics employed. The trees, plants and animals which Thutmose III brought back from Palestine were represented on the columns and in one of the rooms at Karnak.

To the north-east and south-west of the great festival hall were other smaller halls, preceded by pyramidal masses of masonry with a cavetto cornice in the form of pythons, and connected by an avenue of sphinxes, like that between the temple of Khonsu built by Rameses III and the temple at Luxor. In the two succeeding dynasties in fact, the achievements of the Thutmoses were completed. Thus, Seti I and Rameses II constructed the gigantic colonnaded hall 170 feet long and 338 feet wide, covering 6,000 square yards. The roof was supported by 134 columns in sixteen rows. Down the centre on either side, forming a kind of nave with five aisles, the columns were 79 feet in height, the roof of the nave being higher than that of the aisles with their clerestory windows. On the walls were highly coloured inscriptions and painted reliefs. Behind the great hall were two lapis-lazuli stelae on either side of the gateway, and in the precincts large gardens with promenades among flowers from many lands, and a sacred lake on which boats containing statues of the gods made ceremonial voyages.

THE TEMPLE OF KHONSU

South of the Great Temple and its lake lie two chapels erected by Thutmose III: the temple of the Middle Kingdom which he extended, and that of Khonsu, the son of Amon and Mut, situated at the end of the sphinx avenue from Luxor to Karnak. The principal structure of this royal temple was built by Rameses III; it is entered from the south through a pylon giving access to the outer court surrounded by a double colonnade of pillars decorated with lotus-bud capitals, and having six other gateways. To the north was a hypostyle hall with eight columns supporting a high central nave flanked by lower aisles on either side. Doors in the north wall led to the ambulatory surrounding the sanctuary containing chapels to minor deities, like those on either side of the axial halls beyond the sanctuary. In one of them occurs the figure of Osiris on a bier lamented over by Isis and Nephthys, and in this 'House of Khonsu' was the magnificent statue of the god designed at the end of the Eighteenth Dynasty, perhaps portraying one of the pharaohs. The inscription on its walls are of considerable interest and importance, recording the confirmation by the high-priest of Amon of the Pharaoh Herihor's appointment to the throne by Khonsu.

THE TEMPLE OF MUT

The temple erected in the Eighteenth Dynasty in Thebes to Mut, the wife of Amon, stood near the sacred lake on the site of an earlier shrine. Before Mut was raised to the dignity of the second member of the Theban triad, she was an ancient deity of the city; she is mentioned on a cylinder inscription of the First Dynasty, in an invocation requesting union with the goddess.[20] As her name suggests, she was represented as a vulture, but when she was given many names and forms, eventually becoming the female counterpart of Amon-Re,[21] she was regarded as the great 'world mother', 'mistress of heaven', and 'queen of the gods', identified with Hathor. She had various cult centres, such as Napata and Diospolis parva, but her principal shrine was her great temple at Thebes built by Amenhotep III in the latter part of the fifteenth century B.C., contemporary with the Great Temple of Amon of which, as we have seen, it was an adjunct connected by a *via sacra*.[22]

It is to him that the original building of the sanctuary has been ascribed, and this is the earliest name that occurs among the ruins that have survived throughout the ages, though it would seem that while he was responsible for its completion the colonnades had already been erected by the enterprising Queen Hatshepsut in a site that had long been sacred to the goddess. After the Ikhnaton reformation, Tutankhamen set up a statue of himself in the temple of Mut, and left records indicating his repudiation of the heresy of his father, and his allegiance to the restored Theban faith in which the goddess occupied an important place. His successors continued the cultus of which the temple remained the centre until the sack of Thebes by Assurbanipal in 663 B.C. when the city and its temples were laid waste. Amon then became again a local deity, never to regain his former supremacy. Nevertheless, although the capital was transferred to Memphis some of the ruined Theban temples were restored and rebuilt by the Ptolemies. Thus, in the temple of Mut the gateway of Seti II was lengthened before the first court (Pylon I), a flight of steps was made leading down to the lake from a small shrine containing three chambers and a niche for a statue erected against the outer wall at the southern end. An enclosing brick wall also was added to complete the circuit meeting the Saite wall round the outer court.

On the west side of the horseshoe lake, a little temple was constructed by Rameses III, consisting of an outer court with a colonnade on the north and south sides entered through a gateway to the north, a hypostyle hall with lateral chambers, and a vestibule leading to three shrines. A second pylon leading to another colonnaded court was flanked by two statues of the Pharaoh. The inner face of the first pylon was decorated with scenes illustrating events in the Libyan wars, such as slaying the captives in the temple before Amon. The outer side of the second pylon contained reliefs and inscriptions relating to the Syrian campaigns.

THE RAMESSEUM

In the mortuary temple of Rameses II, now known as the Ramesseum, on the west bank on the edge of the desert, the great seated colossus of its builder stood in black granite, probably 57 feet high. On the pylon is recorded the battle of Kadesh and the defeat of the Hittites in considerable detail, with briefer references to Rameses' other successful campaigns in Palestine and Ethiopia. Standing not far from the colossi of Memnon, the Ramesseum was

intended primarily to honour the Pharaoh after his death. Thus, four figures
of Rameses in the guise of Osiris stood in the open court in front of it. The
pylon on which these inscriptions occur gave access to an outer court, surrounded apparently by a colonnade with a double row of pillars on one side.
This led to the temple-palace reserved for the royal cultus. On the wall between the outer and inner courts and behind a row of mutilated figures of
Osiris in the form of caryatides, above the accounts of the Hittite war, are
scenes illustrating the festival of Min.

MEDINET HABU

Similar scenes were fully portrayed on the walls at the back of the colonnades in the second court of the main mortuary-temple of Rameses III, built
early in the Twentieth Dynasty (*c.* 1200 B.C.), opposite Thebes at Medinet
Habu, as a replica of that of the Ramesseum. Here the exploits of the King in
his Libyan wars and against the 'Peoples of the Sea' were depicted, and on the
upper part of the walls, behind the colonnades, the great harvest festival of
Min was represented in a series of scenes. Since Pre-dynastic times this god of
fertility and lord of Koptos personified the generative force in nature as the
bestower of procreative power; he was represented as an ithyphallic bearded
man with the thunderbolt as his emblem.[23] In association with Horus and
Amon he acquired a wider cultus in which he was identified with both fertility
and the sky, until by the time of the Middle Kingdom he had become a composite deity, the lord of Koptos and the desert region. Then his principal
festival in the harvest month of Shemon (April) was a universal observance at
which the Pharaoh played the leading role.

The Festival of Min. Thus, in the first scene on the sculpture at Medinet Habu
the King is shown carried on a litter under a canopy from his palace to the
temple, borne on the shoulders of his twelve sons and high dignitaries,
headed by priests and officials bearing the royal insignia, sunshades and fans,
led by a trumpeter and a drummer. On reaching the temple, the Pharaoh
descended and stood facing the shrine containing the image of Min. After
censings and libations the prescribed offerings were made, and the doors of
the shrine were opened. The statue was venerated and placed on a litter to be
carried by the twenty-two priests, and escorted by others waving fans and
bunches of flowers. The Pharaoh, wearing the crown of Lower Egypt, was

accompanied by the Queen and preceded by a white bull sacred to Min. Following were bearers of various emblems of the gods associated with Min and his cultus and the ancestors of Rameses III. But while these included Menes, the traditional founder of the First Dynasty, Nebkheroure who reunited the country, and many of the Eighteenth and Nineteenth Dynasty sovereigns, Queen Hatshepsut and Ikhnaton were excluded, being out of favour in court circles.

Halts were made en route for the performance of dances and the recitation of liturgical hymns and, on reaching the terrace of the temple of Min, birds were released by the priests to announce the enthronement of the Pharaoh to the four quarters of heaven, together with the shooting of arrows north, south, east and west to destroy his enemies symbolically.[24] The god was duly installed in a throne beneath a canopy and offerings were made to him by the King. But exactly what took place at the shrine can only be conjectured from the available illustrations.[25] It is not improbable that a sacred marriage was enacted by the Pharaoh and the Queen during the course of the rites, since at the end of the festival a priest proclaimed, 'Hail to thee Min, who impregnates his mother! How mysterious is that which thou hast done to her in the darkness.' Thus, Min was called 'the Bull of his mother', the marital substitute of Osiris *ka-mutef*, who was thought to have been responsible for the conception of Horus by Isis. Therefore this festival would have been an appropriate occasion for the heir to the throne to have been conceived.

It was then that the union of the god with the King was acclaimed rather than at the actual accession, though the anniversary of the coronation of Rameses III coincided with the annual observance at the beginning of harvest. When Min had been installed, the statues were placed on the ground; in the sculptures the King is then shown with a copper sickle in his hand offering a sheaf of barley (*boti*) 'for his father'. In so doing, as A. H. Gardiner says, he was vindicating his title to the kingship and his patrimony as Horus, the son of Osiris.[26] As the living Horus, Rameses III was equated with Min who personified the fertility of the grain, and he exercised his royal, divine functions at the seasonal ritual to secure a plentiful harvest in the ensuing years. A sacred marriage between the king and the queen at this juncture would be in accordance with the firmly established and widely diffused custom in the Fertile Crescent and throughout the Ancient East.

DEIR EL-BAHRI

The Birth and Accession Scene of Hatshepsut. In the mortuary temple of Hat-shepsut, the daughter of Thutmose I, which she built for herself against the terraces of the adjacent Libyan desert hills at Deir el-Bahri, the Queen's divine birth through the paternity of Amon-Re is recorded in the bas-reliefs on the walls of the middle terrace. An inscription gives an account of the events leading up to her accession to the throne, beginning with the visitation of the Sun-god Amon-Re to the Queen-mother, 'placing in her body' his daughter that she might 'exercise the beneficent kingship in this entire land'.[27] The god Khnum, 'the fashioner of men' and 'maker of the gods', was commanded by Amon to fashion her body and her ka in surpassing beauty, and Khnum's wife Heket was ordered to give her life.[28] To establish her legitimacy to the throne Hatshepsut had a representation of her divine conception engraved, as described in the words attributed to Amon-Re which are inscribed round the scene: 'She who unites herself with Amon, the first of the beloved, behold such shall be the name of a daughter who shall open thy womb, since these are the words that have fallen from thy lips. She shall exercise a beneficial power over all this land, for my soul is hers, my will is hers, my crown is hers, verily, that she may govern the two lands and guide all the living doubles.'[29]

Next the preparations for her birth and the accouchement were portrayed, followed by her presentation to the protecting goddesses who breathed into the child the breath of life. Their leader Meskhent declared, 'I surround thee with protection like Re. Life and good fortune are given to thee more than to all mortals; I have destined thee for life, luck, health, excellence, affluence, joy, sustenance, food, victuals and all other good things. Thou wilt appear as King of Upper and Lower Egypt for many *Sed*-festivals while thou art living, remaining fortunate while thy heart is in joy with thy ka, in these two lands on the throne of Horus for ever.'[30] Then follows the presentation to her heavenly father, Amon, who welcomed her with these words: 'Come, come in peace, daughter of my loins, whom I love, royal image, thou who will make real thy risings on the throne of the Horus of the living for ever.'

Having been duly acknowledged and worshipped by the other gods on her return from a royal progress to her shrines, Hatshepsut, 'beautiful to look upon' and 'like unto a god', was crowned by her actual father,

Thutmose I, at Heliopolis and seated on the throne before Amon-Re in the presence of the nobles and officials who did homage to her. The chief episodes in the coronation ceremony were then portrayed showing the red crown of Lower Egypt and the white crown of Upper Egypt being placed on her head by priests impersonating Horus and Seth, or Horus and Thoth. To symbolize the union of the Two Lands over which she was to reign she was represented seated on a throne between the two gods of the south and north, Horus and Seth, who tie together a lotus flower and bunches of papyrus under her feet. Finally, arrayed in her crown and mantle and holding the scourge and flail of Osiris in her hands, she is shown led in procession round the walls of the sanctuary, to indicate her taking possession of the domains of Horus and Seth; the proceedings conclude with her being embraced by her celestial father in the shrine of Amon.

The reliefs at Deir el-Bahri display the normal procedure for coronation in the Nile valley. It was only Hatshepsut's anomalous position as a woman that demanded particular emphasis on her conception to ensure her validity as the divine heir in spite of her sex. The enthronement ceremonies and proclamation proceeded in the normal manner with the customary purifications and presentation of the new pharaoh as the son of the Sun-god, first to Amon and the goddesses and then to the people.[31]

The Expedition to Punt. Also in this temple, on the southern wall of the middle colonnade, is depicted Hatshepsut's trading expedition to the land of Punt. It was the wish of Amon made known to her, it was maintained, by an oracle vouchsafed to her at this sanctuary. As a result a fleet of five ships was sent down the Nile from Thebes, which on reaching its destination by way of the Red Sea was favourably received by the chief of Punt and his inordinately fat wife. After a pleasant mutual exchange of compliments an agreement was reached and Egyptian necklaces, hatchets and daggers given in exchange for such commodities as gold, ivory, incense, apes, cosmetics, wood, myrrh. The loading of the vessels with this rich cargo is portrayed in the reliefs, and 'never', it is said, 'was the like of this brought for any king that there had been since the beginning'. And it was done 'according to all that the majesty of the god commanded'.[32] Therefore, on its arrival, a lavish thank-offering of the first-fruits of the expedition was made to Amon.

Egyptian Temples

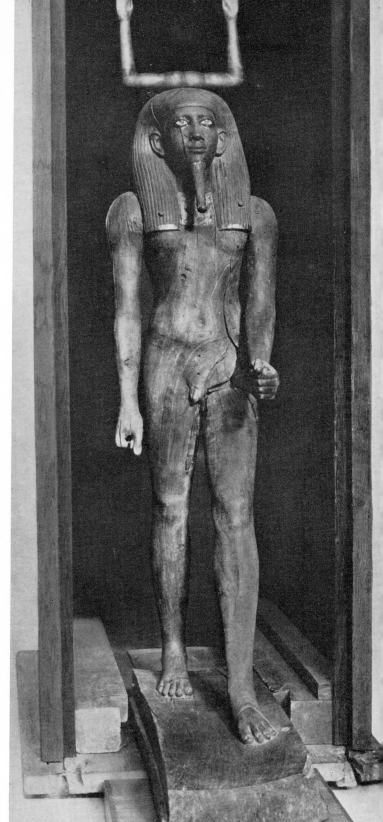

*Wooden 'ka' statue of King Hor, XII
Dynasty, c.2000 B.C.*

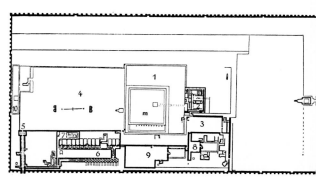

The first example of monumental architecture in Egypt, and the fore-runner of the true pyramid, the tomb of Zoser at Saqqara is at the centre of a vast funerary complex (52–54)

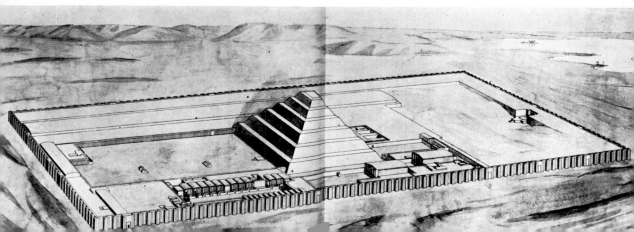

During the next dynasty, three great pyramids rose from the desert at Giza. These belong to Cheops, Chephren and Mycerinus, pharaohs of the Fourth Dynasty. In the mortuary temples which are attached to them, funerary rites and embalming took place

56

Along the banks of the Nile at Luxor lies the Temple of Amon-Mut-Khons (56, 57). Pylons, colonnades and hypostyle halls (57) built by various kings make up the sacred complex. From Luxor a long avenue of ram-headed sphinxes (59) runs to the near-by religious centre at Karnak. Here stands the Great Temple of Amon (60), the Sun-god, and it was here that the divine barque (58) was floated on the sacred lake at the annual festival

57

Rameses II built his mortuary temple on the edge of the western desert (61). The 'Ramesseum' as it is known was intended to honour the pharaoh after his death, and ceremonies were performed daily for the dead king. The façade is adorned by four colossal statues of the king as Osiris (62)

ard against the foot of the Theban
lls, at Deir el Bahri, Hatshepsut
ilt a temple for herself. Carved along
e walls of the porticos are scenes from
r life—her birth and coronation as
e of Egypt's few women pharaohs,
d the expedition which she sent to
e fabulous land of Punt (64).
stream at Medinet Habu lies a
all temple built by Thutmosis I (63)

63

65

On the small island of Philae, sacred to Isis, six temples were erected from Ptolemaic times onward, among which was the pylon (66). Here also the Roman emperor Trajan built the temple known as 'Pharaoh's Bed' (65)

In the temple a garden of Punt was made for Amon with trees planted beside it, as he had instructed in the oracle. The temple became a terraced myrrh-garden for the god, large enough for him to walk in, as recorded in the relief on the wall. However, as in the case of Ikhnaton, the famous queen rapidly fell into disfavour after her death, her successor Thutmose III dismissing her expedition to Punt as a futile operation in comparison with his warlike campaigns in Western Asia. Her temple, therefore, was neglected and after becoming a cemetery in the Christian era, its court was converted into a monastery with cells in the colonnades for the Coptic monks.

DENDERAH

North of Thebes at Denderah, the ancient Tentyra capital of the sixth nome of Upper Egypt, was the Ptolemaic temple of the goddess Hathor, built in the first century B.C. and completed by Augustus. It stood on the site of a much earlier sanctuary, as the Ptolemies erected their temples only on ground long hallowed by shrines. Like Karnak it was the largest of a group of temples and covers an area of about 900 by 850 feet; it is enclosed with a brick girdle wall, and entered by two stone gateways built by the Roman Emperor Domitian. The colonnade that led to the portico with its gigantic pillars no longer exists, but the lofty hypostyle hall, 135 feet in width, remains occupying about a third of the entire magnificent sandstone structure. The roof is supported by two rows of twelve columns, and the façade has six pillars of immense size, about 50 feet in height, adorned with heads of Hathor. A second rectangular hall contains a small hypostyle hall with six columns, and the sanctuary with its little chapels and shrines is surrounded by a corridor into which they open. The first vestibule was devoted to offerings to the goddesses by the king, mainly of a vegetation nature. Near it was a small chamber in which the mysteries were celebrated, while on the west side of the sanctuary is a court and kiosk where the New Year rites were held. On the roof were several chapels dedicated to the cult of Osiris, and within the precincts north-east of the entrance is a 'Birth House', as in all Ptolemaic temples, representing a development of that at Deir el-Bahri, which had been built to emphasize the divine birth of Hatshepsut.

The Death and Resurrection of Osiris. The whole temple including the passages and crypts was decorated with cult scenes, inscriptions and sculptures.

Among the events depicted were the birth of the divine child Hathor, and the funeral rites of Osiris as they were observed at his festival in the month of Khoiak. In the long Ptolemaic inscription inscribed on the walls of the three small chapels set apart for the performance of the Osiris mystery drama, the death and resurrection of the culture hero were portrayed in considerable detail, though the order of the enactment of the rites is by no means clear.[32] According to their description here, they occupied the last eighteen days of the first month of winter (Khoiak), opening with a ploughing and sowing ceremony on the tenth day. The series of scenes show the dead god swathed as a mummy lying on a bier beneath which are four crowns. In front is Horus presenting him with a lotus flower and, in another representation, Nephthys and Isis standing at the head and foot of the bier respectively. Elsewhere he is depicted as an ithyphallic figure wearing a crown, with his soul in the form of a hawk with outstretched wings above him and Isis and Horus standing behind. Sometimes he is portrayed naked and beardless, usually as a mummy, with various gods and goddesses in attendance grouped round the bier. In one example the coffin is enclosed on the branches of a tree, and three small trees also occur beneath the bier.

In the Denderah inscription it is the death and burial of Osiris that constitute the main theme, though resurrection is implied there, and in the basreliefs is clearly indicated. Thus at the conclusion of the festival he is depicted as a mummy raising himself gradually from his bier, sometimes assisted by Nephthys, Isis and Horus, and being presented with the *crux ansata*, the sign of life. Further indications of his revival are the presentation of the lotus flower, the escape of the soul in the form of a hawk, and the references in the inscription to the raising of the *Djed*-column at Busiris on the day of his interment, the thirtieth of Khoiak. This very ancient pillar, resembling a telegraph pole with four or five cross-bars at the top, was unquestionably a symbol of Osiris before it was identified with Ptah at Memphis; it represented perhaps a tree with the branches lopped off,[34] and its ceremonial raising up may have been symbolic of Osiris' restoration from the grave. In the tomb of Kheryaf at Thebes it is shown being raised with ropes by the Pharaoh with the help of the high-priest of Memphis in the presence of the Queen and his sixteen daughters, while a sham fight is in progress between the inhabitants of Buto, the Pre-dynastic capital of Lower Egypt.[35] The Denderah inscription tells that this very ancient rite was held on the day of

Osiris' interment; a coffin containing the hollow effigy of Osiris as a mummy, in which grain was sown, was placed ceremonially in a subterranean tomb on a bed of sand. There it rested until the rite was re-enacted the following year.[36] Inscriptions also occur at Denderah claiming that Osiris made the corn from the liquid that was in him.[37]

From the beginning of the Dynastic period to Roman times, belief in the resurrection and life-giving power of Osiris persisted in the Nile valley. All the gods connected with vegetation and fertilization were identified with him and he with them, as were all those associated with the dead, while his *Djed-*column remained his ancient symbol until eventually it was transferred to Ptah at Memphis. With him, Isis and her son Horus, whom she conceived posthumously from his mummy, impersonated the annual renewal of nature in relation to his restoration, interpreted in terms of the rise and fall of the Nile with which his ritual observances and their symbolism coincided. This was most apparent in the inscription and reliefs in the temple at Denderah which was so intimately connected with the goddess Hathor who eventually had become equated with Isis.

Hathor. Worshipped in the form of a cow, Hathor was regarded as the mother of Horus the Elder but she was never the spouse of Osiris or the mother of his posthumous son Horus, who was always represented as having been born of Isis. It was, in fact, not until all reproductive goddesses became identified with Hathor that her horns were adopted in the symbolism for Isis, and that Hathor as the Mother-goddess *par-excellence* became the nurse of Horus, the son of Isis, in her role as the cow-goddess. Both goddesses however exercised maternal functions and were associated with the kingship. At Denderah seven Hathors were represented as young and beautiful women with cows' horns, solar disks and vulture head-dresses, carrying tambourines in their hands. They comprised the Hathor of Thebes, of Heliopolis, of Aphroditopolis, of the peninsula of Sinai, of Memphis, of Hierakleopolis and of Keset. Such was her popularity that Hathor had shrines not only all over Egypt but also in Sinai, Nubia and at Byblos in Syria.

PHILAE

Isis, however, was the most popular and important of the maternal god-desses, the prototype of motherhood and the embodiment of wifely love and fidelity. The myths and legends and the mystery cult in which she became the central figure gave her a unique position, notwithstanding her not being a Mother-goddess comparable to Hathor, Nut and Neith in Egypt, or of Inanna-Ishtar in Mesopotamia. In the Heliopolitan Ennead she was the daughter of Geb and Nut, and the sister spouse of Osiris, the mother of Horus and the sister of Nephthys the wife of Seth. In the *Contendings of Horus and Seth* she was the daughter of Neith, while Plutarch made her the daughter of Thoth. In fact, there was no deity of any importance in the Nile valley with whom she was not identified, and by the Ptolemaic period as the syncretistic Saviour-goddess of many names she reigned supreme in her great temple on the island of Philae at the head of the First Cataract. There she was worshipped even by the Nubian tribes for whom the Egyptians were the traditional enemies, such was the long-established sanctity of the ancient sanctuary and the reputation of the goddess with whom Isis had become equated. To this shrine came also the Ethiopians to secure fertility for their land by taking her image for an annual visit to her territory in Lower Nubia, extending as it did from the First to the Second Cataract.

The Isis Cult. Like Malta in the Mediterranean, Philae became the sacred island of the Nile from the fourth century B.C. There, within an area 500 by 160 yards six temples were erected, the chief of which was that dedicated to Isis and served by a priesthood who ruled the whole of Lower Nubia, claiming that their authority had been given to them by the Egyptian Pharaoh Zoser in the Third Dynasty. It was not, however, until Ptolemaic times that the cult of Isis was established at Philae after that of Osiris had made its way there from Elephantine; it reached its height in the reign of Ptolemy IV (Philometor), and continued to flourish during the Roman period. Indeed, the worship of Isis spread so rapidly throughout the Hellenistic world that it became a predominant element in the welter of religions in the Empire before and after the Christian era. Philae as its centre was the last stronghold of the mystery, and it was not until the reign of Justinian (A.D. 527–565) that the temple as such came to an end and was converted into a Christian church dedicated to St Stephen by Theodorus about A.D. 577.

The Temple of Nectanebo. The syncretistic character of the worship of 'the goddess of many names' is shown in the temples at Philae in the numerous

shrines to the deities who she comprehended either as counterparts or associates: Osiris, Horus, Hathor, Nephthys, Khnum, Satet and Thoth.[38] In the
reliefs those connected with the Isis, Osiris, Horus myth predominate, the
emphasis being on Isis as the Great Mother. The earliest of the existing
temples, that erected by Nectanebo II at the south end of the island, was
dedicated to Hathor and Isis, though it included the gods of the opposite
island, Bigeh (Senem). The six pillars on the west side have Hathor heads
above the lotus capitals supporting the architrave. The colonnades leading
up to the first pylon are in Ptolemaic style and on the reliefs on the screen
wall, Nectanebo is represented standing before the various figures of Isis
and other gods, most of which have been destroyed by the waters of the
inundation. However, thirty-one pillars supporting part of the roof of the
west colonnade survive, and the outer wall is still intact, decorated with
vultures and with reliefs of Isis, Osiris, Horus and Hathor and various gods
and Ptolemaic Pharaohs. Those on the lofty great pylon were mutilated when
it became a Christian site and a Coptic cross was erected on either side of the
great gateway. The reliefs of Nectanebo before a large figure of Isis and
smaller reliefs of the other deities remain on either side of the walls leading
to the forecourt of the temple of Isis, with the Birth House dedicated to the
goddess and her child, between the great pylon and the second pylon on the
west side.

This was originally distinct from the main structure of the temple,
approached by a processional way to the portico, and decorated with reliefs
of Ptolemy VII and of the Emperor Tiberius in the presence of the usual
gods. On the doorway and the walls of the adytum were reliefs of Hathor
and of the divine birth of the Pharaoh, as at Luxor and Deir el-Bahri. The
two vestibules and the shrine are enclosed by colonnades covered with reliefs
and inscriptions in a similar manner, together with Coptic crosses on the
east side of the doorway. In the forecourt of the temple of Isis was a granite
altar dedicated to Amon-Re, and a number of chambers used probably by
the priests for ritual purposes. A stairway leads to the hypostyle hall, with
a Christian inscription of Bishop Theodorus and a Coptic painting on the
east side, and on the west one of Ptolemy IX making offerings to Isis, Horus
and Unnefer. In the inner court and on the side of the doorway he is shown
being censed on leaving his palace, and above he is making an offering to
Isis. On the east doorway he is represented as crowned and dancing before

Isis, and subsequently worshipping Osiris and Isis and making offerings to Hathor, Sekhmet, Isis and Tefnut. Similar scenes recur in the adytum and vestibule, and the walls of the sanctuary are covered with representations of Ptolemy II before the gods, Isis being the most prominent and persistent figure.

In a chapel at the south-west corner, the death and resurrection of Osiris are depicted, including the restoration and reassembly of the scattered fragments of his dismembered body by Isis and Anubis. He is also portrayed as a mummy lying on a bier and a priest pours water from a pitcher over his body, from which stalks of wheat are growing; this is reminiscent of the watering of the beds of Osiris placed in tombs in the Eighteenth Dynasty to give life to the dead.[39] These associations of Osiris with the sprouting grain taken in conjunction with the autumnal rites with which usually they were connected, show how very intimately the annual renewal in nature was related to his resurrection interpreted in terms of the rise and fall in the Nile with which the festival at the 'Season of Coming Forth' and its symbolism coincided. This deeply laid theme survived in the Ptolemaic period. At Denderah, as we have seen, he was said to have made the corn from the liquid that was in him, and there the interment and rising from the tomb was dramatically enacted in the month of Khoiak and inscribed on the walls of the temple. At Koptos, in the Min Harvest Festival, a sheaf of barley was reaped by the king in his Horus capacity for Osiris. And here again at Philae the same symbolism recurs in a temple in which Isis reigned supreme, and the Pharaoh is constantly depicted in his life-giving aspects and functions in the setting of the Osiris, Isis, Horus myth. Nowhere could these rites have been performed more appropriately than in the temple of Osiris' devoted sister-spouse, Isis, on the island that claimed to be the source of the great river which Osiris personified.

CHAPTER IV
Babylonian and Assyrian Temples

IN MESOPOTAMIA the environmental conditions differed from those in the Nile Valley, resulting in corresponding differences in the two ancient civilizations in these countries. Whereas in Egypt the river, which played such an important part in the development and persistence of the country's cultural achievements, exercised its fructifying functions with a never-failing regularity, the land between the Tigris and Euphrates was subject to the vagaries of an uncertain climate with scorching winds, torrential rainfalls and unpredictable, devastating floods. At the end of the Pleistocene period, the melting snows and glaciers inundated the plain at the head of the Persian Gulf, there being no sea like the Mediterranean to separate the southern diluvial flatlands from the torrents descending from the northern highlands between Samarra and Hit. This, however, brought quantities of silt which gradually produced the alluvial plain of Sumer (Shinar), destined eventually to become Babylonia and Assyria between the two great rivers, the Tigris and Euphrates flowing from the Armenian mountains in the highland zone.

As the Persian Gulf filled up for .125 miles north of Basra and became habitable, the great Mesopotamian civilization was established on its fertile soil. Indeed, while the south was still under water, the northern plain was being cultivated by Sumerian agriculturists, and when the alluvial marshes appeared in the Gulf with their arid climate, scanty rainfall and hot dry summers, the Sumerians reclaimed the area by the excavation of irrigation canals before 3000 B.C. Having rendered the soil prodigiously fertile, barley and wheat were cultivated, and cattle, sheep and goats were reared. It was here in this land of Sumer that the art of writing on clay tablets with the wedge-shaped characters of a cuneiform script was invented and became the medium for many different languages in Western Asia. For a thousand years, in fact, from about 3500 B.C. to 2500 B.C., Sumerian was the only written tongue in Mesopotamia, and it remained for the next two and a half millennia the learned language of the entire region. In addition the script was employed by the Hittites and Hurrians in Anatolia, the Elamites in Susiana, and by the Canaanites at Ugarit, while occasionally it was adopted in Hebrew, Aramaic, Egyptian and Old Persian texts. In Mesopotamia the same system of writing was used for two entirely different languages: that of the original Sumerians and that of the Semitic Babylonians and Assyrians.

THE AL'UBAID TEMPLES

THE EYE TEMPLE, BRAK

From the contemporary records it is clear that, in spite of the climate, the Sumerians in and after the third millennium B.C. established an urban civilization, with well-planned houses built of stone and mud-brick in their villages and temples with a long central hall flanked on either side with small rooms and approached by an entrance porch. In the oblong sanctuary

Fig. 21. Plan of the 'Eye Temple', Tell Brak, Iraq

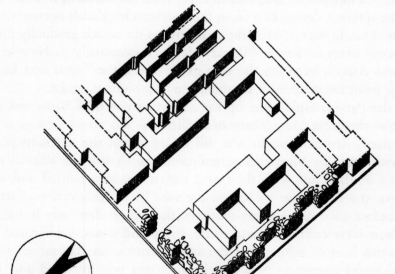

there was a recess in which the cult-image stood, and other indications of the cultus practised there. On the great mound of Brak in the Khabur valley in eastern Syria at the end of the caravan route to the Jabal Sinjar, a series of four temples were excavated by Professor Mallowan in 1937–8, belonging to the Jemdet Nasr period, about 3000 B.C. These he named the 'Eye Temple' because with one of them a quantity of figurines of black and white alabaster were found with staring eyes engraved on them, representing perhaps the Mesopotamian Goddess, as this imagery was later associated with Ninhursag, the goddess of many names (e.g. Inanna-Ishtar).[1]

The Eye Temple was divided into two wings with mud-brick whitewashed walls flanking an oblong sanctuary 60 feet long and 20 feet wide, having two entrances at the north end and a clay altar against the middle of the south wall, the front decorated with a golden frieze, and the walls with stone rosettes and copper panelling.[2] The structure resembles that of the so-called White Temple at Uruk, and is in general conformity with the contemporary sanctuaries in southern Mesopotamia. It was erected on the top of a high mud-brick platform, doubtless approached by a ramp or stairway, and the room on the eastern side may have been the shrine of a subsidiary divinity. The first Eye Temple which was protohistoric in origin, collapsed about 3000 B.C., and four other temples appear to have been erected on the Jemdet Nasr foundations, the last probably belonging to the Uruk period. In the earliest stratification thousands of faience beads were recovered, and amulets and seals were abundant on the site together with eye-figurines similar to those found at Susa, Uruk, and later in Anatolia. The architectural features of the sanctuary and west wing are analogous to those of the earliest Sin Temples at Khafajah, and in general plan resemble the painted temple at Tell Uqair of the Al'Ubaid period,[3] notwithstanding the distinctive characteristics of the eastern wing at Brak.

ERIDU

At Eridu at the head of the Persian Gulf where formerly the Tigris and Euphrates flowed into the sea, the sanctuary of its god Ea, the god of water and wisdom originally called Enki, 'the Lord of the Earth', was superimposed on a succession of sacred edifices. These go back to the small square shrines standing on a platform and built of mud-brick in the late protoliterate Al'Ubaid period (c. 3400–3100 B.C.), corresponding to the Pre-dynastic

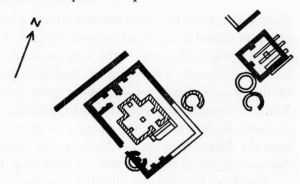

Fig. 22. Plan of the temples,
Levels 15–18, Eridu

in Egypt.[4] These prototypes of the later temples recur at Tepe Gawra
near Nineveh on the caravan route to Iran, and at Uruk on the east bank
of the ancient course of the Euphrates where the remains of three superimposed temples have been excavated on the Anu *ziggurat* mound. The
earliest, known as the White Temple, which belongs to the late protoliterate Jemdet Nasr period, stood on a high terrace on the top of a mound
of débris. On a limestone foundation was a more imposing edifice, while
another, the Red Temple, was so-called because like that at Tepe Gawra
its walls were painted red. The head of the Babylonian pantheon, Anu, the
god of heaven, was worshipped in a temple that covered an area of some
420,000 square feet and which, standing on an artificial mound 40 feet in
height, dominated the surrounding country.

Fig. 23. Plan of the ' White
Temple' and ziggurat, Uruk

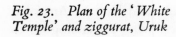

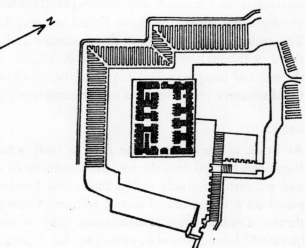

THE ZIGGURAT AND THE 'LOFTY HOUSE'

This represents the earliest example of the *ziggurat*, or temple tower, which became the most conspicuous and characteristic feature of so many Meso-potamian sanctuaries. Standing on a high platform in the west angle of the temenos, or sacred area of the city, it consisted of a series of diminishing and superimposed cubes arranged in storeys, approached by an inclined pathway or a flight of steps. At the summit stood a shrine containing a couch, throne and the image of the god. The huge tower of the temple of Marduk at Babylon, sometimes identified with that immortalized in the Hebrew Babel legend,[5] has been completely destroyed, but that at Ur remains, although lacking the shrine on its summit. Moreover, below the First Dynasty ziggurat terrace lay an older and smaller structure of similar character, as at Al'Ubaid (*c.* 3000 B.C.) with a mud-brick retaining wall and a number of chambers on the north-east side.[6] The protoliterate temple at Tell Uqair on the Euphrates, 50 miles south of Baghdad, has much the same plan and dimensions but it was erected on a mound only 20 feet above the plain.[7] This may have been an incipient mound used as a platform for the later structure, though temples in Mesopotamia were not always equipped with a ziggurat.

When the Sumerians settled on the alluvial plains and marshes of the Euphrates valley they were doubtless compelled to raise their buildings above

Fig. 24. Reconstruction of the Third Dynasty ziggurat. Ur. After Woolley

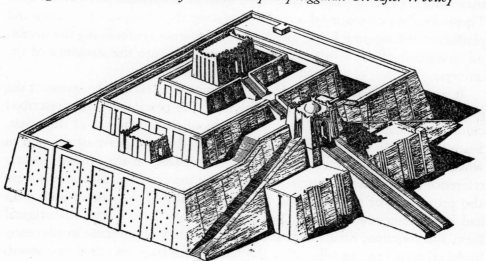

Fig. 25.   Tower of Babel. After Koldewey

the water level on artificial foundations secure against the periodic floods. But apart from this practical necessity, being in origin a mountain people they were accustomed to worship their gods in sanctuaries elevated on hills. Therefore, they continued this tradition placing their temples on mounds and platforms, the ziggurat being given a lofty elevation symbolizing the mythical mountain of the world, representing in miniature the structure of the universe.

It may be that at first an oblong hall with a recess for the statue of the god to whom it was dedicated sufficed for the practice of the prescribed cultus, with the addition of one or two chambers for the use of the priest. Since the temple was not infrequently regarded as the grave of the god in whose honour it was erected, it is not improbable, in the absence of any reference to a primeval pattern established at the creation, that tombs were also prototypes of temples, as in Egypt, especially in the case of gods who had been venerated as heroes. But whatever may have been their original form and function, their erection became a matter of supreme importance. In the creation epic, usually called the *Enuma elish* from its initial two words which mean 'when above', when Marduk defeated and destroyed Tiamat and the forces of chaos the gods showed their gratitude to him by building a shrine.[8] Similarly, it became the first duty of kings to build, endow or embellish a temple in recognition of the services rendered to them by the divine powers. This led to the construction of increasingly elaborate sanctuaries with a costly and complex equipment which frequently revealed their sanctity by their height and designation, 'the lofty house', or 'the house of the shining mountain'. This, of course, was emphasized by the name 'ziggurat', signifying 'high edifice', having the same purpose and significance as the Palestinian 'high places'; it varied from three to seven stages and was dedicated to the patron god.

The monotony of the vast towers was relieved to some extent by the coloured friezes with which they were decorated. The ziggurat at Birs Nimrud (Borsippa), described by Herodotus and excavated by Sir Henry Rawlinson in 1854, which was dedicated to the planets when it was completed by Nebuchadnezzar II in the sixth century B.C., has seven stages, each coloured with the special tint prescribed. At Ur, the first of the four stages was painted black with bitumen, the second white with gypsum, the third red and the fourth sky-blue. The use of coloured bricks became common at Borsippa, Nippur and elsewhere, and as at Ecbatana, according to Herodotus, the seven concentric walls were each distinguished by a particular colour;[9] it has been conjectured that the same practice was used for the stages of the ziggurats.

Fig. 26. The god Marduk, from a piece of lapis lazuli. Babylon

The Etemenanki of Marduk at Babylon. At Babylon, opposite Borsippa, is the temple of Marduk, known as E-sagila, 'the lofty house'; the seven stages of its tower, called Etemenanki ('the house of the foundation of heaven and earth'), were assigned respectively to the principal celestial bodies—the sun, moon and five planets—and the gods with whom they were associated. This gave the ziggurat a cosmic connotation as a reproduction of the abode of the gods. Even though these planetary interpretations were relatively speaking a later introduction under Chaldaean astrological influences during and after the time of Assurbanipal (668–626 B.C.), astrological inscriptions of a much earlier time (e.g. the Enuma Anu-Enlil series) may go back to the Sumerian period, since they contain references to the four-fold division of the world into the lands of Akkad, Elam, Subartu and Amurru, and to such kings as Rimush and Ibin-Sin, who belong to the middle of the third millennium B.C. But although the ziggurats undoubtedly were widely employed for astrological observations, and the Babylonian omen texts were the result of many centuries of the acquisition of astral knowledge going back to Sumerian times, it was not for these purposes that the edifices were constructed in the first instance. Rather were they reproductions of the sacred mountain in a succession of storeys, one superimposed on the other, on an elevated mound and surmounted with a shrine in which the god was reputed to dwell.

That such an erection should be regarded as a means of reaching the heavens[10] is not surprising as on its mystic heights the deity had his abode. While the tower was ascended for religious purposes from time to time, its shrine was too difficult of access to be the centre of worship. Therefore, the sacrifices were offered within the temple area at its base. At Babylon, according to Herodotus, the ornamented altars were made of gold, with a table for offerings and an image of the god in a cell.[11] In front of the altars stood large terracotta jars for ablutions; similar examples have been found at Nippur. There the temple was called 'the Mountain House' and the ziggurat the 'Mountain of Heaven', which facilitated the descent of the god to the earth. The shrine on the apex was a sort of 'Holy of Holies', the mysterious dwelling place of the unseen deity, and possibly the chamber in which the connubium of the goddess and the king was enacted, while the temple and the altar at its base were the sanctuary where the worshippers assembled to engage in the sacrificial cultus.[12]

THE E-SAGILA

In Babylon the temple of Marduk, the E-sagila, regarded as the permanent residence of the head of the Babylonian pantheon, was the predominant feature of the capital. It was approached by a *via sacra* from a triumphal arch, the Ishtar Gate, adorned with zoomorphic emblems of Marduk and Adad, on the north side of the city, through which the processions made their way before proceeding to the E-sagila about a mile away on the east side of the Euphrates. The raised paved road with its walls lined with enamelled tiles was bordered with palaces and temples, which included those of the goddess Ninmah near the Ishtar Gate, and further on the temple of Ishtar of Agade. The E-sagila unfortunately has been so obliterated that its location was in debate until, in 1913, Koldewey excavated the most probable site at Amran and revealed its ground plan and façade.[13] After the capture of Babylon by Xerxes part of it was pulled down, having become a fortress, and although Alexander the Great attempted to rebuild and restore the ancient temples that had been destroyed, he died and Babylon was abandoned before this was accomplished, its E-sagila being left to fall into ruins.

Although little is known directly about its structure and none of its equipment has survived, it was undoubtedly one of the most imposing constructions in the capital in and after the reign of Hammurabi (*c.* 1700 B.C.), occupying a unique position and status as the chief seat of worship in Babylonia until the downfall of the empire. However, an ancient foundation, Ezida, the temple of Nabu at Borsippa on the other side of the Euphrates, going back probably to the time of Sargon and Naram-Sin before Babylon became the capital, was the more important of the two sanctuaries. But once Marduk became the head of the pantheon and the principal deity in Babylonia the E-sagila was supreme. Thus, a cylinder discovered by Koldewey during his excavations contains the declaration by Assurbanipal when he had completed the restoration begun by Esarhaddon after its destruction by Sennacherib: 'under my government the great Lord of Marduk held his entry into Babil with rejoicing and entered upon his dwelling in E-sagila and of the gods of Babylon. I established the protectorship of Babil, I retained.'[14] Nebuchadnezzar called himself 'the fosterer of the E-sagila', contributing to the restoration and embellishment of the sanctuary making it more glorious with silver, gold, bronze, precious stones and cedar wood. The chamber of

Marduk (Ekua) is said to have been made to 'gleam like the sun. Its walls were clothed with solid gold instead of clay and chalk, with lapis and ala-baster the temple area.' The best of his cedars that were brought from Lebanon were used for roofing the Ekua, and they too were covered with gold.[15]

According to the so-called Smith Tablet, first discovered by George Smith in 1876 and after many vicissitudes now in the Louvre (having been re-edited by Koldewey and Thureau Dangin), there were six gates to the E-sagila, the position of which is conjectural. The measurements of the vast sanctuary are also very doubtful as some of them appear to refer to the Etemenanki which is much more fully described on the Tablet and by Hero-dotus. The ground plan of the ziggurat seems to have been about 100 yards square, rising to much the same height, with stairways similar to those at Ur and Uruk, and one frontal flight. There are references to a succession of chambers in the four wings of what is called the 'Nuchar', thought to be identical with the ziggurat; they are located in its temple or chapel at the top and situated at the cardinal points. In the E-sagila section of the Smith Tablet two courts are mentioned, the main building being about 85 by 94 yards, with a large space on the east side enclosed by a wall 98 to 127 yards in length. The outer court was entered from the east from the *via sacra*, the eastern wing of the temple being approached through the outer courtyard to the inner court. A large portal in the western wing apparently led to the lavishly decorated chamber of Marduk, the Holy of Holies, where the most sacred rites were performed. There were, however, several other chapels beside the Ekua in the E-sagila, as for example Ezida, 'the dwelling place of the king of heaven and earth' dedicated to Nabu, the son of Marduk, and Kaduglisug dedicated to the goddess Zarpanitum, in which the respective deities took up their abode during such events as the Annual Festival when they paid their visits to Marduk in his temple.

The chapels may have been detached sanctuaries within the temenos of the E-sagila, set apart for these purposes and for the performance of their own ritual by their priests. Marduk, however, had so distinguished himself at the threshold of creation when he defeated Tiamat and her host of demons that in the *Enuma elish* he was represented as having been exalted above all the gods by Anu and Enlil, the leaders of the pantheon, and given sovereignty both in the heavens and over the universe which he had made. On earth, it was in the E-sagila at Babylon, which the appreciative gods were alleged to have built for his worship, that he reigned supreme when Hammurabi established his unified rule in the new capital as the steward of Marduk, raised up by him to be a 'shepherd who brings peace'. There at the turn of the year in the spring the Akitu festival was held for twelve days in the month of Nisan to awaken the vital forces in the dormant earth and to revivify the processes of vegetation when the crops were reappearing. Akitu, in fact, was the designation both of the festival and of the special sanctuary in which it was held in the E-sagila at the *zagmuku*, or 'beginning of the year'.

The Akitu and the New Year Festival. The Akitu, the annual event in honour of Marduk, began on the second day of the first month, Nisan, with the *urigallu*-priest of Ekua, to whom alone the secrets of the temple were known, performing the preliminary ablutions before vesting and calling upon the god as 'the Lord of Kings, light of mankind, and the fixer of destinies' to bless the city and 'to turn his face to the temple of E-sagila'.[16] After a break in the text, reference is next made to a metal worker and a wood worker being summoned on the third day three hours after the sunrise to make two images for the ceremonies on the sixth day; the one to be constructed of cedar and the other of tamarisk, ornamented with precious stones set in gold. Clad in red garments and holding in their hands emblems of the snake, the images were placed in the temple of Daian, the judge and giver of food from the table of the god. The next day the urigallu continued his prayers to Marduk for his blessing on Babylon and to Zarpanitum his consort to 'fix the destinies of the king, to give life to the children of Babylon', and to plead for them before the king of the gods. He then went into the courtyard and blessed three times the E-sagila, the 'image of heaven and earth'.

Late in the afternoon of the fourth day the *Enuma elish* Creation epic was recited from beginning to end, very much as in the Christian Church the Genesis narratives of creation and the prophecies concerning the Incarnation and the redemption of mankind are read at the transition from the mourning of Good Friday to the triumphant joy of Easter Day. So, in the Akitu the death and revival of Marduk were celebrated with lamentation, mourning, mock battles and commotion in the city during the search for the god imprisoned in a mountain representing the nether regions.[17] Meanwhile the

temple was asperged with holy water from the Tigris and Euphrates, the
sacred drum was beaten by the exorcist (*mashmashu*), the court was censed,
and the incantations and prayers of appeasement were offered.[18] The chapel
of Nabu was purified in the same manner. The doors were smeared with
cedar-oil, and the sanctuary was censed. An executioner was then summoned to cut off the head of a sheep and with the carcass the exorcist wiped
the temple, reciting spells. This accomplished, he threw the body in the
river facing west and the exorcist disposed of the head in the same way.
They then retired to the country until Nabu had left the city on the twelfth
day. Lest he too should be defiled, the urigallu was forbidden to witness or
take any part in the purifying of the temple.

Before sunrise a gold canopy was brought from the treasury of Marduk
to cover the chapel of Nabu. A cathartic invocation was recited, calling
upon Marduk to expel all evil from within the temple, and a table of offerings was prepared on which roast meats, twelve loaves, salt and honey were
placed, and a golden censer set before it. Wine was poured out to 'the most
exalted among the gods'. The offering-table was carried to the banks of the
canal to await the arrival of Nabu in his boat from Borsippa on the sixth day
of Nisan to take up his residence in his chapel, Ezida, in the Esagila. There
the priests had escorted the king to the shrine of Marduk to undergo his
ritual abdication. The urigallu emerged from the Holy of Holies and removed his crown, ring, sceptre and *harpé*, placing them before the statue of
the god. He then returned to the abdicated monarch, struck him on the face
and made him kneel to declare his innocence:

> I have not sinned, O Lord of the land.
> I have not been negligent regarding thy divinity;
> I have not destroyed Babylon; I have not caused its overthrow;
> I have not neglected the temple E-sagila; I have not forgotten its ritual;
> I have not rained blows on the cheek of a subordinate;
> I have not humiliated them;
> I have cared for Babylon; I have not broken its walls.

After a short break in the text of about five lines the reply of the urigallu
is recorded in the name of Marduk as a sort of absolution and renewal
blessing:

Have no fear, for Marduk has spoken.
He will listen to your prayer.
He will increase thy dominion . . .
He will exalt thy kingdom.
On the day of the feast of the new moon thou shalt . . .
Day and night . . .
Thou whose city is Babylon, whose temple is Esagila,
Whose suppliants are the children of Babylon.
Thy god Bel will bless you . . . for ever.
He will destroy thy enemies; he will beat down thy adversaries.[19]

The urigallu then restored the insignia, struck the king on the cheek again, with the intention of making tears to flow as a favourable omen of the good will of Marduk towards him. Forty minutes after sunset, forty reeds of three cubits each were bound together by the urigallu together with a palm branch; a hole was dug in the courtyard of the temple and they were planted in it with honey, cream and oil of the best quality. A white bull was placed before the hole and a fire was kindled in it with a reed. A prayer was addressed to the bull of Anu, as 'the shining light who doth illuminate the darkness', of which only these opening lines have survived.

It is clear that this abdication and re-investiture was an act of renewal of the kingship at this critical juncture in the seasonal sequence. The city was in a state of increasing uproar because the god had disappeared and was held captive in the nether regions, with its reciprocal effects on the decline in the life of nature and the disturbed state of society, given expression in the ritual combats in progress in the streets of Babylon. Comparable are those that occurred during the Persian annual festival Sacraea when the mock king reigned for five days amid general confusion.[20]

It was apparently in the ziggurat called Etemenanki that he was believed to have been incarcerated and,[21] therefore, the commotion was probably centred round this massive temple tower, though the Festival House, or Bit Akitu, on the opposite bank of the Euphrates was also included.[22] But on the arrival of Nabu and the other gods on the sixth of Nisan and the liberation of his father from his tomb, 'the mountain of death', together with the renewal of the king in his throne, order was restored. This was accomplished on the seventh of Nisan and was followed the next day by the determination of destiny in the Ubshukkina, the place of the assembly of the gods in the E-sagila, where the Creation epic had been recited, originally located in the shrine of Enlil at Nippur where at his temple the New Year Festival was an Akitu. To confer upon Marduk their collective strength, the statues of the gods were arranged in order of precedence. The king, acting as the master of ceremonies and holding his sceptre in his hand, summoned the gods in turn and led them to their places in the Great Hall in order to bestow their combined power upon the head of the pantheon who thereby obtained 'destiny beyond compare'.

The Bit Akitu. On the ninth of Nisan the king led a triumphant procession along the sacred way to the Bit Akitu, himself supported by the gods 'taking the hand of Marduk'. On the copper doors the Assyrian kings portrayed the conflict between Marduk and Tiamat in commemoration of their annual visits to the Bit Akitu when they went forth like the victorious army of gods. Thus, Sargon recorded that he 'joyfully entered Babylon in gladness of heart and with a radiant countenance'. He 'grasped the hand of the great Lord Marduk, and made pilgrimage to the House of the New Year's Feast'. In Nineveh, Sennacherib had the scene of the victory over Tiamat engraved on the copper doors of his Bit Akitu of Assur, the Assyrian counterpart of Marduk, with the figure of himself as the 'victorious prince' standing in the chariot of Assur.[23] Whether or not this indicates that the pre-cosmic struggle was enacted in the Bit Akitu with the Assyrian king playing the leading role during the two days from the tenth to the twelfth of Nisan, it was in any case this event that was celebrated in the Festival House before those who had taken part in the great procession returned to the E-sagila for the final episode.

Unfortunately the texts throw little light on what took place in the Bit Akitu. Since, however, the threat of disastrous floods and drought was an ever present anxiety at the turn of the year in the spring and autumn in Mesopotamia, it was to avoid the recurrence of such a catastrophe that the rites were performed at these seasons, interpreted in relation to the primeval defeat of Chaos depicted on the doors of the Bit Akitu. The importance attached to the triumphal procession following the liberation of the captive god, the reinstatement of the king and the determination of destiny, suggested that it constituted the climax of the Akitu, celebrating the victory of

Marduk or Assur and all that this involved in the annual renewal of the processes of nature. It would be appropriate, therefore, for a banquet to be held
in the Festival Hall on the tenth of Nisan in which the king, the priesthood
and their attendants, the effigies of the gods and representatives of the people
took part as an act of thankful rejoicing for what once more had been
accomplished in passing successfully through yet another hazardous transition in the seasonal sequence.[24] Moreover, this very widespread and ancient
feature of the Annual Festival was usually associated with the consummation
of a sacred marriage to the king and queen representing the union of a god
and goddess to promote the fertility of the crops and herds in the ensuing
year.[25]

The Connubium. At Uruk early in the third millennium B.C. the alliance of
Inanna-Ishtar, queen of heaven and 'Lady of the Mountain', with Dumuzi,
the divine shepherd, ruler of Uruk and prototype of Tammuz, was
firmly established in the vegetation cycle, her temple having been
erected near the base of the great sanctuary of Anu on its artificial mound.
Again, at Isin her nuptials were celebrated annually at the spring festival to
awaken the vital forces in the dormant earth, and, as her spouse, the king
who exercised sovereignty over Sumer and Akkad in the third millennium,
controlling Nippur, Erida and Uruk until Ur regained the supremacy. At
the season when the goddess returned from the nether regions their physical
union, as described in a poem addressed to Ishtar as the evening star, was
consummated on a marble bed in the sanctuary, amid universal rejoicing, to
ensure the prosperity of the land.[26] But it was she as queen of heaven and
earth who took the initiative, the king at her invitation sharing her couch.
Indeed, Frankfort has contended that it may well have been only those kings
who were deified who had received such a command.[27]

Be this as it may, the sacred marriage interpreted in these terms was
celebrated during the Annual Festival at Isin and in other cities (e.g. Uruk,
Lagash, Ur) for the purpose of securing a plenteous yield of crops and
cattle.[28] In Babylon the Akitu celebrations were brought to a conclusion in
the evening of the eleventh of Nisan by the king and queen (or a concubine)
repairing to a chamber called *gigunu*, apparently decorated with greenery,
situated it would seem on one of the stages of the ziggurat rather than at the
Bit Akitu. As we have seen, reference was made by Herodotus to the shrine

on top of the Etemenanki equipped with a 'great and well-covered couch' on which the deity was thought to repose when he visited the chamber.[29] This may have some connexion with the connubium at the end of the Akitu though this is more likely to have occurred in the E-sagila than on the ziggurat after the return from the Bit Akitu. There in all probability the newly reinstated king resorted with the queen to engage in a ritual marriage symbolizing the union of the goddess with the king to reinforce the creative powers in nature. It was in such a gigunu, described in the Hymn of Ishtar as 'the seat of joy', that the nuptials of Enlil and Ninlil took place for this purpose.[30] Therefore, it would not be surprising if a similar sacred marriage occurred at the conclusion of the Akitu in Babylon wherever it may have been held.

This affords an adequate reason for the assembly of the gods in the Chamber of Destinies on the eleventh of Nisan to settle the fate of society in the ensuing year before returning to their respective temples on the following day. There the divine decree was ratified confirming the due performance of the rites to secure the renewal of the generative force of nature and the orderly seasonal rhymic sequence. What had been achieved by the victory of Marduk at the threshold of creation had been made operative in the present by all that had been said and done in the temple and its adjuncts in these celebrations at the critical transition in the annual cycle. With confidence, therefore, the gods repaired to their cities and the king to his palace to continue their vital functions, assured of the beneficence of Marduk upon whom had been bestowed the powers of most of the major gods in the Akkadian pantheon. The cultivation of the revitalized soil was resumed in sure and certain hope that, despite the ever-present changes and chances of an unstable environment, with the good hand of their gods upon them all would be well.

It was, however, not only in the great Akitu in the capital that these New Year rites were held. In most of the principal cities in Mesopotamia— Ur, Nippur, Assur, Isin, Larsa, Harran, Dilbat, Uruk, Nineveh and Arbela— they were established events in the local temples, their relative importance depending on the status of the city-god and its ruler. Despite the constantly changing fortunes of the cult-centres and their sanctuaries, the performance of more or less identical Akitu observances either in the spring or in the autumn, for the same purposes everywhere, gave stability to a fluid situation in an insecure milieu. Thus, the temples exercised a very important influence in a unified ritual control of the processes of nature. If this reached its climax in the E-sagila in Babylon, it had behind it a long succession of localized New Year festivals going back to the third millennium B.C., and with the rise of Assyrian domination the Akitu in Babylon was transferred from Marduk to Assur and his temple at Nineveh without any very fundamental change.

In Babylonia it is true no god had a permanently assured status. Anu was a shadowy figure representing the supreme authority in the sky-world over-ruling the universe, but it was Enlil who was the dynamic deity, manifesting his power in devastating storms as well as in the control over the beneficent aspects of nature. Ea or Enki was no less diverse in his powers and operations, and being god of the earth he was in close touch with the world and mankind. These respective attributes and functions found expression in the cultus in their temples. Marduk, though at first an inferior god with solar associations, was, as 'the first-born of Ea', brought into relation with the fructifying waters and the renewal of vegetation in the spring—'the Asaru who restores man to happiness'. Therefore, once Hammurabi ascribed his triumph to him and made him the god *par excellence* of the capital of his empire, he obtained from Enlil the rule over the four quarters of the earth, and was assigned the determination of man and his destinies. Absorbing the powers and attributes of all the great gods, the title of 'Bel', which originally belonged to Enlil of Nippur, was conferred upon him as 'the lord of the land'. It then only remained for the *Enuma elish* to be composed to glorify him, his city and his temple, and made the cult-legend of the E-sagila, for the sanctuary to attain its immense prestige.

THE TEMPLES OF ASSUR

The pre-eminence of Marduk and his worship, however, rested upon the status of Babylon as the political and religious centre in the middle of the second millennium B.C. Therefore, when Assyria succeeded in securing the domination in the next millennium, first in Mesopotamia and then in the greater part of Western Asia, Marduk in his turn was displaced by the national god Assur, and his E-sagila in Babylon overshadowed by that of his successor. The temples of Assyria, however, only played a minor part in the religious life of the nation, despite the imposing structures that were erected in Calah, Arbela, Khorsabad, Nineveh and the new capital Assur, named after its god. Indeed, whereas Marduk was worshipped primarily in Babylon where he had his seat in the E-sagila, temples to Assur were erected all over the Assyrian empire wherever the king had his official residence, symbolized by the erection of his royal standard. There the god had his central sanctuary for the time being, though the cultus continued uninterruptedly in the local temples. In spite of this peripatetic mode of manifestation, Assur was the self-created father and king of the gods, maker of the sky of Anu and of the underworld, author of mankind, living in the bright heavens and ordaining the fate of men. Identified with the might of Enlil, he was essentially a warrior-god leading to victory the king's forces, called the troops of Assur, and was manifest in the king's standard, carried into battle like the Ark of the Covenant by the Hebrews.

As the domination of Assur was extended far and wide by the spread of Assyrian sovereignty, kings ruled as his priests in their several states, and to him in his temples they brought the fruits of their victories as a tribute. It was, however, the course of political events that determined the status and fortunes of the Assyrian supreme deity, as in the case of Marduk in Babylonia. Moreover, the absence of a permanent central sanctuary comparable in status and prestige to the E-sagila in Babylon had a disintegrating effect on the cultus and the temple organization. The attempt of Assurbanipal to establish a religious and intellectual centre in Nineveh failed, and as the empire fell into decay in the reign of Ramman-nirari, both Marduk and the Babylonian Lord of Heaven, Anu, regained the precedence they held prior to the supremacy of Assur, Marduk eventually becoming identified with the planet Jupiter when he acquired astrological zodiacal connotations.

Beside Enlil, Marduk and Assur, to each of whom the establishment of the present cosmic order was attributed in the Creation epic, there had existed Anu and his generation of gods whose struggles and degrees were manifest in mundane events. It was from their conflicts that creation emerged, culminating in the kingship of Marduk and the universal rule of Assur. It was they who deposed Enlil of Nippur and transferred his domain to Marduk of Babylon, and subsequently to Assur in Assyria. From this combination of converging concepts of deity a composite figure under the designation Bel appeared as a proper name for Enlil, Marduk and Assur, as the all-embracing god at particular times and places, with his consort Belit. Thus, when

Marduk regained the supremacy temporarily surrendered to Assur, it was exclusively applied to him as a proper name of the chief god, Bel-Marduk. This was the nearest approach to a genuine monolatry in Assyrio-Babylonian religion inasmuch as he embraced the qualities and attributes of the other members of the triad, Anu, Enlil and Ea, and of the other gods in the pantheon with whom he became blended (e.g. Nabu, Allat, Dagon, Ninib, Sin) in their several capacities. But this did not prevent each and every local god retaining his name and being worshipped in his sanctuary with his own cultus.

In Babylonia every sacred place had a special name to which particular significance was attached, though in Assyria this was not so apparent. There the temple was the house of the god or goddess who occupied it, its designation often being determined by its situation or structure, as in the case of the E-sagila at Babylon, 'the lofty house', or of Ekur, 'the mountain house' of Bel (Enlil) at Nippur. Not only had every city-god his chief sanctuary at his special seat, but the other gods were equally equipped with their temples for their worship. Most of them conform to much the same ground-plan, with a forecourt leading to a large rectangular court at the end of which the image of the god was enshrined in a small sanctuary or recess. Along the sides of the great hall were a number of chambers used as 'sacristies' and apartments for the priests, though some may have been shrines or chapels.

EMAKH, THE TEMPLE OF NINMAH AT BABYLON

Thus, the temple of Ninmah, 'the great goddess of many names', on the north-eastern corner of the Ishtar gate at Babylon, had a large vestibule giving access to a courtyard, apparently open to the sky, with six doorways, presumably opening into rooms which may have been either sanctuaries or storehouses for sacred objects. In the Holy of Holies stood the cult-image, visible from the entrance to the open court, and to the right was a well which was probably used for lustrations and ablutions. Between the court and the holy place was an ante-chapel with a service-room for the shrine; in one corner of its foundations was found an inscribed cylinder, deposited by Sardanapalus referring to his founding of the temple. There are also references to the rebuilding operations undertaken by Nebuchadnezzar inscribed on bricks and tablets recovered from the wall he had erected round the sanctuary.

Behind the shrine and along the north-east wall was a long narrow passage, perhaps the stairways that led up to the flat roof, but its precise purpose is not known. The use of the other buildings in the south behind the temple is also uncertain. Before the entrance stood a brick altar like that in Solomon's temple at Jerusalem erected in the outer court.

Apart from terracotta votive figurines no cult objects have been found in the site, nor have the rites been represented on bas-reliefs. All that is certain is that the temple was built early in the reign of Nebuchadnezzar and that later he strengthened its walls. The plan followed was the same as in the other four temples in Babylon. In all of them the buildings were of sun-dried bricks arranged around an open court with entrances and vestibules flanked by grooved towers. The cult-image was the principal object of veneration by the priests in its ante-chamber and by the worshippers assembled in the court, though the position of the image was not constant.

THE TEMPLE OF NINIB

In the temples of Ishtar and of Ninib, for example, the shrines were on the west side of the great court instead of on the south, and according to Nabupolassar's cylinder, the chamber containing the statue of the god in the temple of Ninib was flanked by two subsidiary shrines, presumably in honour of the deities associated with him. The temple had three entrances and in the front of that on the eastern side stood the altar, opposite the principal shrine. Behind the subsidiary shrines was a narrow passage leading to a chamber at the north corner, and from the grooved gateway towers terracotta cult-figures have been recovered in brick caskets. North-east of the temple clay tablets containing commercial and literary inscriptions have

Fig. 27.   Plan of the Temple of Ninib, Babylon

been found with reliefs of fabulous animals, a bearded head and well-modelled figures belonging to the Assyrian period.

THE TEMPLE OF ISHTAR OF AGADE (AKKAD)

In the temple of Ishtar of Agade (i.e. Akkad) were found caskets; one of them containing the figure of Papsukal, the divine messenger, was discovered where the image of the goddess formerly stood in the niche against the back wall of the shrine. Other brick caskets lay in the doorway of the court. The ground-plan conformed to the general pattern with grooved towers, vestibule, side-chambers opening on the square, shrine, service rooms, priests' apartments, store-rooms, and an entrance chamber to a smaller inner court in which were two circular edifices possibly used as granaries or store-houses. The self-contained block was separated from the wall of the temple by a narrow passage from which southern rooms and a court was reached. Throughout the history of the temple the plan seems to have been very much the same. Little of the earliest structure remains but the later buildings rest upon these foundations without any material alteration in the scheme. The walls for the most part were painted white with a gypsum wash, some of which still survives, the more prominent features (e.g. the main entrance, the doorway leading to the shrine and the niche) having been coloured with a black asphalt solution and adorned at the edges with white vertical lines. A double brick pavement together with an encircling wall or *kisu* was built by Nebuchadnezzar before the overthrow of Babylon by Cyrus in 539 B.C.

THE TEMPLE 'Z'

The unnamed temple, known as 'Z', in the valley between the mound Amran-ibn-Ate and the Ishin Aswad ruins in Babylon, completely rectangular in plan, is divisible into two distinct sections. The eastern portion, constituting the main structure grouped round the central court, was devoted to the performance of the cult; it was therefore equipped with its shrine, ante-chamber, and cult-image on the dais in its niches against the south wall. The smaller western edifice has the appearance of having been the residential quarter of the administrator and his priests. The entire temple was encompassed by a wall with stepped battlements and two gates. In the north-east corner was a room where public business may have been transacted, and the three separate entrances, each with its vestibule and service-chamber, indicate

Fig. 28. *Plan of the Temple 'Z', Babylon*

its several purposes sacred and secular. The altar appears to have stood in front of the northern gate as in the other temples, but in whose honour the temple was erected and to whom it was dedicated are unknown.

PALACE TEMPLES AT KHORSABAD (DUR SHARRUKIN)

At Khorsabad 10 miles north-east of Mosul, Sargon II (721–705 B.C.) built a succession of temples dedicated respectively to Sin, Shamash, Adad, Ea, Ninurta and Ningal (the gods of the moon, the sun, the thunder, the waters and the Mother-goddess) as an adjunct to his immense palace on the banks of the Khanser, a tributary of the Tigris. Nearby stood the temple of Nabu and the ziggurat, approached by a spiral ramp, containing originally either seven or five storeys painted perhaps in various symbolic colours—white, purple, black, blue, red, silver and gold—and surmounted with a shrine of Assur. Sargon's palace was, in fact, the largest royal residence in the Ancient Near East, covering some 25 acres (nearly a million square feet), raised on a huge platform 48 feet above the town level, and dominated by the adjacent ziggurat. The ornamentation, sculpture and decorations were as unparalleled as the gigantic scale of the buildings which were made of sun-dried bricks and arranged round a principal courtyard measuring 300 feet by 240 feet, with smaller courts and rooms representing a religious and administrative complex; this included residences of the priests, state officials and officers of the court, the royal apartments with state rooms in the rear and terraces laid out as gardens.

In view of the proportions and magnificence of the 'peerless palace' Sargon had erected within the city of Dur Sharrukin (Khorsabad), it is hardly surprising that when Paul Emile Botta, the French consul in Mosul, began the excavation of the site in 1842, he thought he had discovered the ruins of Nineveh, some 14 miles away. It soon became apparent however that what had been found was this unique royal residence and its series of sanctuaries in honour of the seven deities for whom Sargon had to cater. Subsequent investigations by Sir Austen Henry Layard, Victor Place, Felix Thomas, and, since 1928, the more intensive work of the Oriental Institute of the University of Chicago,[31] have revealed chambers, shrines, sculptured slabs, figures, bas-reliefs and façades and have determined the ground plan and dimensions. It has now become clear that the area in the south corner of the platform which Victor Place thought constituted the harem was in fact a complex of temples detached from the rest of the palace.[32]

In the most ornate and imposing temples—those of Sin the Moon-god and of Shamash the Sun-god—the centre of activity seems to have been the temple court of the palace with the priests' rooms on the south-east side. From it open five of the six temples, that dedicated to Sin being opposite the approach through the forecourt and its chamber. To the left is the smaller sanctuary of Adad. The central portal of the temple of Shamash lies on the south-west wall to the left, with the much smaller edifice devoted to Ninesta near to it. Towards the north corner of the court is the small temple of Ea, entered through an undecorated doorway. According to Victor Place, walks occurred to and from the entrances near the four corners of the court,[33] though this has not been confirmed by later excavations.[34]

The temple of Sin is entered through a long narrow ante-chamber and thence by way of a corridor-like room to the principal hall. At the end of this lies the sanctuary elevated as a platform approached by a broad flight of stone steps. Here the statue of the Moon-god stood in, or in front of, a niche with half-columns as a background. The cult was probably performed in the central hall, and there doubtless the worshippers assembled, the sanctuary being reserved for the priests and their assistants. Across the width of the temple is an ante-room with plastered walls decorated with glazed bricks, perhaps originally above the arch, serving the purpose of a sort of narthex. In the sanctuary a jar appears to have played some part in the ritual, possibly as a container for holy water or oil, and near by it, before the steps from the central hall, the altar may have stood.

The Shamash temple was similar in structure and design and in it much the same ritual was doubtless performed. In both of them the designs of 'trees' on the façade in the form of tall vertical shafts emerging from behind the portal tableau may indicate an element in the New Year ritual comparable to the 'trees' with bronze bands at Khorsabad. The temple of Adad, adjacent to that of Sin, consisted of a small edifice (19 feet by 36 feet) entered from the north-west corner of the court, with a platform serving the purposes of a sanctuary reached by two flights of steps, and a niche at a higher level. Stone vessels had occupied the customary position on the floors. Though simpler and smaller in structure than the Shamash temple it was designed for the same cult purposes. This also applies to the temples of Ningal, Ninurta and Ea, each with its inscription indicating the nature and attributes of the deity to whom it was dedicated.

THE TEMPLE OF NIMRUD (CALAH)

Botta's discovery of the palace of Sargon at Khorsabad led Austen Henry Layard in 1845 to begin excavations on the site of the second city of the Assyrian empire, Calah, at the extensive ruins at Nimrud on the east bank of the Tigris about 20 miles south of Nineveh. Here was a promising mound which revealed the only complete statue of an Assyrian king (Assurnasirpal II, 883–859 B.C.), recovered in his north-west palace; other discoveries, chiefly from around the ziggurat, were the plan of the royal apartments, throne-room, state halls, with stone bas-reliefs showing his military campaigns and cult-figures. In the palace of Shalmaneser III (859–824 B.C.) was the black obelisk now in the British Museum depicting Jehu kneeling and paying tribute to the king. The Crimean war, however, brought this pioneer work to an end, and apart from brief resumptions at the temple of Nabu by George Smith in 1873, and by Hormuzd Rassam five years later at what seems to have been the temple of Ishtar Kidmurri, it was not until the British School of Archaeology in Iraq inaugurated its first expedition to the site in 1949 under Professor M. E. L. Mallowan that the palace of Assurnasirpal II was fully re-investigated and its contents finally exposed and examined.[35]

THE TEMPLE OF NINURTA

It has now become apparent that the nine temples had been concentrated mainly in the inner city; the most important of these in the ninth century B.C. were the ziggurat and the temple of Ninurta, the patron deity of Calah,

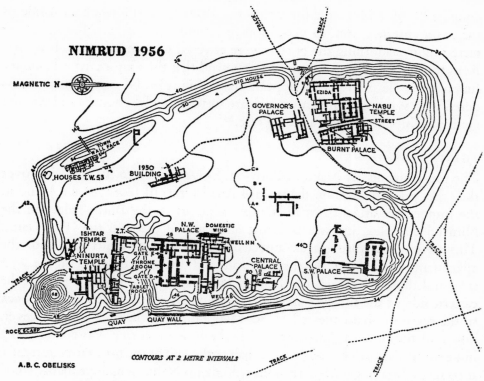

Fig. 29. Plan of the excavations of Nimrud 1956. After Mallowan

at its base, dominating the other sacred edifices. Here also we have an outer court, an entrance leading into a vestibule, a side-chamber with two entrances and a main hall with a niche at the end, but no inner courtyard. The southern side of the sanctuary was flanked with great magazines in which clay jars for storing oil were still standing in position on stone basins. The name of the king, Assurnasirpal, was inscribed on stone oil tanks sunk in the pavement, and on the slabs events in his reign were recorded. The main entrance was ornamented with figures of winged man-lions, and on the doorway leading into the side-room Ninurta was depicted driving out a winged dragon. On a monolith at the side was a portrayal of the king in his divine capacity, and before it stood an altar.[36] Behind the sanctuary beads and cylinder seals of the Kassite and Middle Assyrian periods have been recovered in a deposit under the floor.[37] The smaller temple was similarly equipped with a recess for the statue and altars for libations on each side of the main entrance, but no indication of a vestibule has been found.[38] The sacred figures adorning the portals were covered with inscriptions. It is clear from the bas-reliefs and sculpture at Nimrud that the king exercised priestly functions in the temples; he appears arrayed in splendid vestments embroidered with symbolic emblems which are surrounded by eunuchs and winged genii worshipping before a sacred tree.[39]

THE TEMPLE OF NABU

The pre-eminence of Nabu in Babylon, however, led to his elevation over the other gods in Calah in the time of Adad-nirari III (808–782 B.C.), and to the importance attached to his temple adjacent to the Burnt-Palace in the Nimrud complex, known as Ezida, and entered through the 'Fish Gate'. This gave access through an antechamber to a great courtyard with the apartments of the king, the throne-room and domestic quarters on the west side, and those of officials on the east. Here lay the temple of Nabu on the eastern side of the inner courtyard, the foundations of which may go back to the reign of Shalmaneser I (1280–1260 B.C., or earlier). It was, however, not until the time of Adad-nirari that the new sanctuary was created on a huge stone platform beyond a great hall at the end of the northern courtyard. It contained statues and inscriptions eulogizing Nabu, which probably stood originally in niches at the entrance to the hall and to the sanctuary as at Khorsabad. The temple of Nabu was surrounded by a corridor and approached through an antechamber leading by a flight of steps to a paved holy place; this doubtless contained the cult-image on its pedestal, as portrayed on an inscription of the founder (Adad-nirari) mentioning Nabu and his symbols and depicting the god standing on a pedestal. Under the pavement on an ivory panel an engraving of the bull of Marduk being led in procession by his robed priests was found. Ivories (often burnt) occurred in several chambers on the eastern side of the Ezida, and in those occupied by the scribes cuneiform tablets have been recovered containing incantations, omens, medical texts and hymns, Nabu being the god of wisdom and learning.

Near the temple was a smaller sanctuary, probably dedicated to Tashmelum his wife, as she was mentioned on the doorway in connexion with repairs to her shrine.

Babylonian and Assyrian Temples

7   *Greatly enlarged impression of a cylinder seal showing a worshipper before a ziggurat*

68

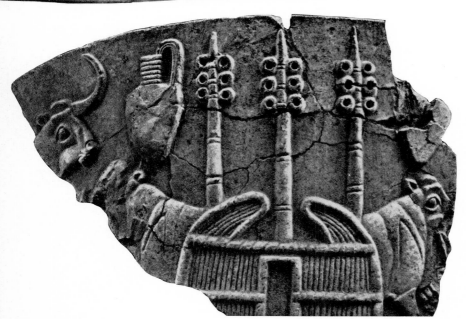

69

Cylinder seal impressions and carved stone fragments (68, 69) are the only records left showing the earliest shrines of southern Mesopotamia. Ritual poles project from the small huts made of reeds, which are shown surrounded by sacred herbs. The alabaster 'eye-idols' (70) come from the temple of Brak in northern Mesopotamia

70

71

72

The ziggurat was the elevated sanctuary of the gods. Today the ziggurat of Ur is eroded by sand and dust (71) but reconstructions show how it may have looked during the Third Dynasty and later under Nabonidus (72, 73). With the rising stages painted in different colours, the ziggurat must have been an imposing sight to the worshippers and is shown on cylinder seal impressions (67)

73

74

The fame of Babylon and its ruins has attracted interest for centuries. Engravings and reconstructions show the city walls and streets with the great temple of Marduk, E-sagila (74, 76 79), and the tower, Etemananki, immortalized as the Tower of Babel (75, 77). The clay stele (78) describes the reconstruction of the temple by Assurbanipal

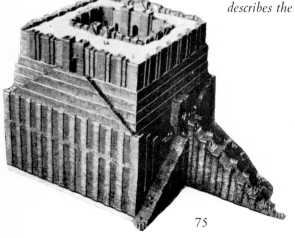

75

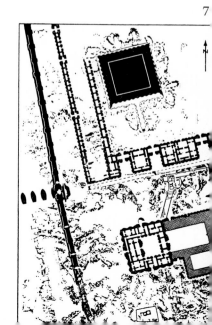

76

77

78

79

80

Even the most sacred buildings in Mesopotamia were made of mud-brick. Temple walls several metres high can still be found preserved beneath the sand in Mesopotamia and the ground plans traced. Above (80, 82) is the Temple of Ninib; below, (81, 84) the Ishtar of Agade Temple and right, (83, 85) the Sin Temple in the Palace at Khorsabad

82

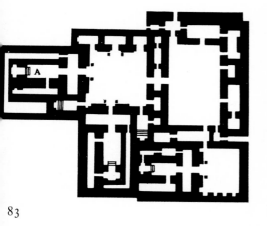

83

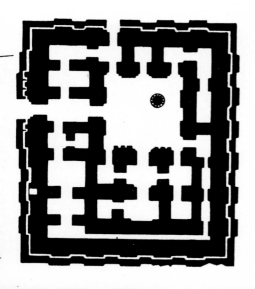

84

85

163

86

87

88

*From the beginning of man's time on earth his artistic
expression has been devoted to his religion. So it was
in Mesopotamia also. Representations, large and
small, of gods and goddesses have been found in their
hundreds, from the earliest cylinder seals to the stone
reliefs lining the walls of Assyrian palaces*

90

Quantities of documents, some of which must have come from the temple of Nabu, were found in the throne-room and its adjacent apartments. Among them appears the account of a treaty between Esarhaddon and the prince of the Medes with the king portrayed between Assur and Ishtar mounted on animals, and Adad with a kneeling figure (perhaps of the king), followed by Marduk on a winged dragon. On the ivory panels processions of foreign tributaries are shown bringing their tributes to the king in a ceremonial procession, indicating that the panels had been engraved and established before the defeat and destruction of the Assyrian Empire in 614–612 B.C., when the Ezida and the temple of Nabu at Calah were sacked, suffering the same fate as Khorsabad, Assur and Nineveh, in the reign of Sinsharishkum. After falling into ruins for the rest of the century the temple was restored in some measure and re-occupied sporadically until in the third century it became a cemetery, the peasants using its stones and bricks in the construction of their tombs.

TEMPLE ORGANIZATION

In all the principal cities in Mesopotamia the temple of the patron deity was the chief edifice, and in very close association with it was usually its ziggurat and smaller sanctuaries dedicated to the gods and goddesses with whom the cultus was connected. Its activities, in addition to its religious and oracular functions, included civil administration, mercantile pursuits of various kinds, commercial transactions, the practice of medicine, astrological observations, mathematical calculations, calendrical intercalations and adjustment to the zodiacal constellations and their relation to the seasonal festivals. To meet these heavy demands involving expert knowledge in a number of fields of sacred learning and social organization, the training in the temple schools became more and more diverse and specialized. This included the study of law, medicine and business, as well as of theology, astrology, divination, ritual techniques and the manifold literary activities in which the priests engaged, producing vast quantities of cuneiform clay tablets dealing with almost every aspect of the life of the community. It was largely in the temples and their schools that this was accomplished. If the first concern was the provision of 'text-books' for candidates for the priesthood, a literary spirit was stimulated and an interest in and appreciation of the learning, wisdom and traditions of former generations were created. The ritual texts, king lists, spells, medical treatises, inscriptions and contracts were not only copied but commented upon and edited, sometimes being transliterated in liturgical versions. In the great collection of texts preserved in the royal library at Nineveh, assembled by Assurbanipal in the last days of the Assyrian Empire (668–626 B.C.), almost every branch of Sumerian and Babylonian learning and knowledge in the possession of the priesthood is to be found, an exhaustive search having been made of the oldest temple archives throughout the country.

These included fragments of the Gilgamesh Epic, one of the finest literary productions of Babylonia going back to about 2000 B.C., covering twelve tablets. It is a composite narrative, containing not less than three thousand lines in the text, relating the story of the legendary founder of Uruk and its temple of Ea, unified into a national epic through the central figure of the hero. Its practical purpose, however, was to stress the importance of proper burial as essential for the peace of the dead in the cheerless nether regions, just as the Creation story recited in the E-sagila at Babylon at the Annual Festival was in the first instance concerned with the building of a shrine in honour of the gods to secure their beneficence towards the city and its people.

The gods owned the land and the temple community acted as the administrators on their behalf; it was a socio-religious institution, the high-priest of the city-god often acting as the governor (*ensi*) of the city. This was the reason for the size, importance and endowments of the Mesopotamian sanctuaries. Their manifold activities spread to almost every field, but above all the New Year Festival, because it was then that the new cycle in nature was symbolized by the divine union between the god and his spouse, with the king acting the part of the divine bridegroom in a sacred marriage as the consummation of the renewal celebrations to secure the restoration of the fertility of the fields, flocks, and men after the blight of winter or summer.

CHAPTER V

Sanctuaries in Palestine and the Temple in Jerusalem

PALESTINE IS A FERTILE LAND, surrounded on the south and east by deserts, on the north by the Taurus mountains and on the west by the Mediterranean Sea. It was on this coast that the discovery of the murex shellfish led to the making of a purple dye which became a valuable export and caused the country west of the Jordan to become known as Canaan, 'the land of the purple'.[1] Having a temperate climate except in the subtropical lower valley of the Jordan, agriculture flourished, and apart from their dyeing industry the people for the most part were peasants with an agricultural economy, dependent largely upon the seasonal sequence as in Mesopotamia.

From the end of October to the middle of April is the wet season when 'the land of hills and valleys drinketh the rain of heaven' and snow appears on Mount Hermon in the north of the central mountain range.[2] Even in spring and summer serious drought is generally prevented by the heavy dew on the western escarpments of Transjordan and through irrigation from the *wadis*; but periods of famine have always been liable to occur from time to time.[3] Normally in April the hillsides in Galilee are decked with a profusion of wild flowers with the green corn waving in the cool breezes on the fields below, the north especially being 'a good land, a land of brooks of water, of fountains and depths that spring out of valleys and hills . . . a land of oil, olive and honey'.[4] Even in the rainless summer famine seldom occurs, but from the end of May there is constant anxiety about the condition of the grain during the dry season, especially when the seasonal rains are pending. This found expression in a Canaanite myth and ritual of the Tammuz type and a seasonal drama, traces of which occur in the texts on the Ras Shamra tablets found in the ancient city of Ugarit since 1929, on the northern coast of Syria, belonging to the middle of the second millennium B.C. In them the Canaanite Baal-Aleyan was the weather-god manifest in the rains of autumn and winter, and in the vegetation they promoted.

THE TEMPLE OF BAAL AT UGARIT AND ITS MYTH AND RITUAL

As in Babylonia these texts were recovered from the archives of a temple prior to the fourteenth century B.C. The alphabetic script in which they were written represents a Canaanite dialect akin to Phoenician and an early form of Hebrew written in a Canaanite-Hurrian adaptation of cuneiform, similar to that which has been discovered at Beth Shemesh and Mount Tabor, but unusual in Palestine. The tablets are in a fragmentary state with numerous lacunae, so that often it is very difficult, if not impossible, to decipher their meaning. The central theme, however, seems to have been a struggle between two opposed forces personified by Baal and Mot, equivalent to those figures playing the leading roles in the seasonal drama elsewhere in Western Asia,[5] Baal being the spring rain, and Mot the summer sun as 'death' and sterility.

As in the Babylonian Creation story and its ritual enacted at the Annual Festival, the threat of chaos was overcome by Prince Baal who subdued the forces of death and destruction and was proclaimed king of the gods. Then follows an involved account of the encounter of Baal with Mot and Prince Sea in which Baal was killed; his body was found in the pastures of Shlmmt and taken by Anat, his sister-spouse, to the heights of Mount Sapan, his former abode, and there buried.[6] Seeking Mot she avenged her brother's death by cleaving his body with a ritual sickle (*harpé*), winnowing him in a sieve, scorching him, grinding him in a mill, scattering his flesh over the fields like the dismembered body of Osiris, and giving it to the birds to eat.[7] In short, she treated him like the reaped grain, thereby rather incongruously making him the slain corn spirit. But because Baal had triumphed by being restored to life, 'the heavens rained oil and the wadis ran with honey'.[8] In the seventh year when the battle was resumed Mot was defeated,[9] the struggle between the two opposed forces being perennial. It was this which was portrayed and re-enacted in the Ugaritic myth and ritual in the agricultural cycle in order to establish the dominion of the beneficent Storm- and Weather-god upon which fertility and prosperity depended.

Thus, a prominent feature in the mythology was the building of a temple for Baal with a lattice, the opening of which produced the autumnal rains:

> Let a window be opened in the house,
> A shutter in the midst of the palace.
> And the clouds shall be opened with rain.[10]

In order that he might exercise his beneficent functions as the rain-producer and 'Rider on the Clouds' it was essential that he should be provided with a house (i.e. a temple) containing a lattice to enable the rain to descend on the earth when he ordered a rift to be made in the clouds and opened the shutter at the appropriate seasons.[11] With the help of various gods the sanctuary in due course was erected, Baal himself taking an active part in the work once the obstacles and opposition to its construction had been overcome. This doubtless represents a mythological reflection of the fact that the temple of Baal at Ugarit was relatively late, subsequent to that of Dagon his father.[12] Being a later introduction in the Canaanite pantheon, Baal was said to be the only god who had no temple, and when his sanctuary was erected at Ugarit it was of exactly the same dimensions, orientation and plan as that of Dagon. But once he became 'the lord of the furrows of the field'[13] responsible for the rain and the kindly fruits of the earth, a series of temples were erected in his honour in Palestine and Syria in and after the fourteenth century B.C.

His temple at Ras Shamra was a considerable structure, approached by a vestibule in front of the hall and a court in which stood a square altar with two steps at the south end. At the east end of the sanctuary was a huge block separated from the inner wall by a narrow passage containing a stone staircase which led to a terrace on the lofty roof surrounded apparently by battlements in the form of a tower (*migdol*), where in the Keret text sacrifices were offered to Baal.[14] If this was composed of two rectangular structures standing back to back on a raised platform, as Schaeffer suggests, with a door in the main axis opening into the first of the towers lower than the one behind,[15] it corresponded to the temple of Baal with its lattice in the middle and an altar in the forecourt. Thus, the text tells how King Keret washes and carries the sacrifice into the house. Then he goes up to the top of the tower (*migdol*), 'rides the shoulders on the wall', lifting up his hands towards heaven and sacrificing to Baal. This completed he descends from the roof.[16]

In the temple of Baal at Ugarit, where it would seem this cult legend was recited and dramatized, it may well have been that at the autumn festival the windows were opened to simulate the clefting of the clouds and the opening of the lattice in a rain-making ceremony. The staircase, which led to the terrace on the roof where in the legend the sacrifices were offered to Baal and El, was placed between the wall and the great block of stone with the face of the god depicted on it. As Schaeffer has conjectured, it may have been ascended in order to make the rain fall through the skylight onto the face of the god on the stele below in the sanctuary, in the presence of the worshippers assembled in the court.[17] As we have seen, temple towers of this nature have invariably been regarded as symbols of a sacred mountain on which shrines have been erected. It is, therefore, not improbable that the migdol at Ugarit may have represented the cultic Sapan where Baal was thought to have dwelt. There he could be encountered in his temple on earth and made to open the windows in heaven and cleave the clouds so that the life-giving rain might descend to fertilize the parched ground, however reluctant he may have been sometimes to exercise this beneficent function.

THE TEMPLE OF DAGON

The neighbouring temple of Dagon is almost identical with that of his son, Baal, except that the walls of the two rooms are much thicker, and while it may have contained a court for public worship like the Baal temple, little is known about either the cult or its legend due to the absence of any equipment in the sanctuary or of mythology comparable to that of the Baal texts. Nevertheless, this Amorite Storm- and Weather-god who was widely worshipped and subsequently adopted by the Philistines, seems to have occupied a prominent position in association with Baal in the cultus at Ugarit where his name occurs on two stelae.[18] As a vegetation deity he was identified with Adad and Enlil, but while in this context he played an important role in Western Asia, where temples were erected everywhere to Adad, or Ramman, as the 'irrigator of heaven and earth', Dagon was singularly devoid of a mythology. But he was firmly established in the second millennium B.C. at Mari on the Upper Euphrates, at Isin, in Phoenicia, in Canaan and Philistia[19] as a god of agriculture and war, described by Philo of Byblos as 'the lord of the grain and tillage' and inventor of the plough.[20] On a seal in the Ashmolean Museum his symbol is represented as an ear of wheat, and the references to him in the Old Testament suggest that he was primarily concerned with the protection of the crops.

It may have been for this reason that the alleged destruction of his image when the Hebrew Ark of the Covenant was brought into his temple at Ashdod was thought to indicate the superiority of Yahweh, who attacked him in his domain and destroyed the crops under his control with a plague of mice.[21] Yet Dagon as one of the oldest Akkadian deities appears to have been regarded originally as a High God, the son of El and the father of Baal, before he acquired vegetation attributes and functions, and then became superseded by the more vigorous young fertility god. Thus, at Ugarit it was the temple of his son that was the active cult-centre and around him its legend was developed, while Dagon receded into the background in spite of his popularity among the Amorites and throughout the Upper Euphrates valley.

THE TEMPLES AT BETH-SHAN

At Beth-Shan situated in a key position at the east end of the Vale of Jezreel which passes through the Carmel mountains from the Jordan to the Plain of Esdraelon, four superimposed temples have been brought to light, ranging apparently from the time of Thutmose III (1501–1447 B.C.), who garrisoned the city about 1450, to that of Rameses III (1168–1137 B.C.), and a final reconstruction of the southern sanctuary in the Graeco-Roman age. Two of the temples stand side by side; that on the south was dedicated in the fifteenth century to Mekal, local god of pestilence, but is conjectured by the excavator, Mr Rowe, to have been the temple of Dagon in which the head of Saul was said to have been nailed after the victory of the Philistines on Mount Gilboa.[22] The temple to the north he associates with the temple of Ashtaroth where the armour of Saul was deposited.[23] Be this as it may, the excavations have proved that the southern sanctuary, which existed under Thutmose III and continued until the Hellenistic period, consisted of a main hall or *cella* with two columns, the bases and capitals of which were of stone while the shafts were of wood. Round the wall was a bench, doubtless for offerings, and on the north, south and south-west of the sanctuary were chambers used possibly as storehouses. The shrine containing the cult-image was on a raised platform approached by steps, in front of which was a stepped altar. In the great courtyard on the west were three tables where the victims may have been dismembered. To the south-west was a chamber which enclosed the baetyl in the form of a conical block of basalt representing the god Mekal with the stele containing his name close by.

Menhirs in the form of a pillar, obelisk or stele, known in the Old Testament as *maṣṣebah*, were prominent adjuncts in Canaanite, Phoenician and Hebrew sanctuaries, and because they were considered to be impregnated with divine life and the abode of the indwelling divinity, were sometimes employed as an altar, or table of offerings.[24] It was, however, for differing reasons and in a variety of forms that *maṣṣebôth* were erected in Palestinian sanctuaries. Thus, they occurred as alignments like those at Carnac in Brittany,[25] or as circles (cromlech), called by the Hebrews *gilgals*, or as mortuary monuments. On occasions they may have had a phallic significance, and their intimate association with sacred posts and trees (*asherah*) gave them a place and function in the vegetation cultus. It was probably on this account that they were regarded with disfavour by the later Hebrew mono-Yahwists who lamented their occurrence 'upon every high hill and under every green tree',[26] and were definitely prohibited in the Deuteronomic code and in the Law of Holiness.[27] Previously, however, they appear to have been generally accepted cult-objects, particularly in the northern kingdom of Israel and its document (E),[28] and by Hosea and Isaiah in the eighth century.[29] Joshua, for instance, is said to have erected a gilgal to commemorate the passage across Jordan,[30] doubtless to give an Israelite interpretation to a cromlech already in existence at a local sanctuary. It was here apparently that Saul incurred the displeasure of Samuel and the judgment of Yahweh for offering a sacrifice there to consecrate the battle against the Philistines.[31] At Shechem, Jacob is alleged to have erected a pillar and named it 'God, the God of Israel', and to have set up another when he made a covenant with Laban.[32]

THE SANCTUARY AT BETHEL

It was chiefly to explain the origin of the Hebrew 'high places' that the patriarchal legends grew up around the ancient sanctuaries at Bethel, Beersheba, Hebron, Mamre, Shechem and Ophrah, where theophanies are said to have been experienced by Abraham, Isaac and Jacob in connexion with sacred trees, wells, springs and stones, as the abodes of an indwelling El, later interpreted as Yahweh in order to transform them into legitimate Israelite places of worship. Thus, the foundation of the sanctuary at Bethel was attributed to an accidental incubation by Jacob, who, when passing the night there on his way to Padan-Aram his ancestral Aramaean home, received a revelation in a dream from its divine occupant.[33] As a result of this incubational experience he is represented as setting up one of the menhirs and pouring oil upon it as an offering to the El, having discovered that it was 'a house of god' (Bethel). Originally the place was called Luz, Bethel apparently being the name of the *maṣṣebah* before it denoted the divinity associated with the shrine, Yahweh being described as the god of Bethel where the stone was anointed.[34]

Recently excavations have revealed levels at this site dating from about 2000 B.C. and continuing to the Later Bronze Age and the Iron Age (*c.* 1500–1000 B.C.), in spite of four destructions by fire in the eleventh and twelfth centuries B.C. There appears to have been a settlement at Bethel at the beginning of the second millennium B.C. (2000–1700), before it became one of the royal Canaanite cities, and it would naturally have its own sanctuary like Shechem and Shiloh in the same region, or Gezer south-east of Jaffa, Megiddo at the entrance to the plain of Esdraelon, and Lachish the modern Tell ed-Duweir. In the Middle and Late Bronze Age it was a well-constructed town before it was reduced to a mass of ruins in the thirteenth century, perhaps by the Hebrew tribes,[35] leaving no traces of its temple. Fresh settlements seem to have been made there after the conquest of Palestine by the invading Israelites before the town was rebuilt in the Iron Age I period, and throughout its checkered history it was essentially a cultic centre.[36] As early as the period of the Judges the Ark apparently was located there[37] before it was removed to Shiloh, and in the period of the monarchy after the revolt of the ten tribes under Jeroboam, calf-worship was practised. It became, in fact, the chief sanctuary in the Northern Kingdom rivalling Jerusalem in the south, and it had behind it an established Yahwistic tradition with its patriarchal cult-legend and its associations with the Ark, Elijah, Elisha and the ecstatic prophets (*nabi*) who had their abode there.[38] To what extent they influenced the worship in a Yahwistic direction it is impossible to say, but in any case while it remained primarily syncretistic it had a Yahwistic element latent in it. Indeed, Kennett has contended that before the

Exile the Aaronite priesthood were in possession and subsequently occupied Jerusalem when the Zadokites were carried away to Babylon.[39] While this raises the problem of the date of Deuteronomy, there seems to be some grounds for thinking that the Aaronites were associated with Bethel and its bull-worship.[40]

The story of the golden calf in the Mosaic narrative, which is doubtless later than the time of Jeroboam, very probably reflects the cultus practised at Bethel and Dan and was legitimate Yahwistic symbolism before the Josiah reformation in 621.[41] It is possible, in fact, that at the accession of David the Ark of the covenant was established at these two sanctuaries (Bethel and Dan) in place of the bull image.[42] In any case, it is clear that bull images representing Yahweh were not innovations introduced by Jeroboam, and that before the seventh century Yahweh was worshipped without hindrance at Bethel and other sanctuaries, quite independently of the Jerusalem cultus in the temple on Mount Zion.

It was in the King's sanctuary at Bethel that Amos, the prophet from Judah, denounced the current sacrificial system and proclaimed the impending judgment of Yahweh when he was driven forth by its priest Amaziah.[43] Bethel had been a royal sanctuary and although it survived after the fall of Samaria in 722[44], its priests seem to have been deported to Assyria, until a plague of lions was attributed to neglect of the worship of Yahweh and an appeal was made for the sanctuary to be reopened. One of the priests was then sent back to teach the people 'the manner of the god of the land'.[45] In addition to its traditional importance and significance, it occupied a key position geographically since it was situated on the road to Jerusalem just over the border of Benjamin in the hill country of Israel. Even while the syncretistic cult continued the Yahwistic tradition was very intimately associated with it, and it is not improbable, in fact, that during the attempt of Manasseh in Judah to suppress the Josiah reform, some of the Judaean reformers may have sought refuge there. Anyway, the Bethelite priesthood contained a Yahwistic contingent, and it was doubtless through its influence and the denunciation of the bull worship by Hosea that worship there became aniconistic.

In the seventh century a determined effort was made to vindicate, formulate and codify the Yahwistic cultus in its ancestral guise handed down, as it was claimed, from the revelation given to Moses in the desert. Thus, in the northern kingdom the Elohistic document was compiled from the traditions that had been current at the great sanctuaries, in the form of a continuous narrative. Bethel and the other high places were assigned a Yahwistic foundation in terms of the patriarchal cult legends before the revelation to Moses of the name of the God of Israel as Yahweh.[46] The collection and reduction of this material probably took place chiefly at Bethel, though it was not confined to this sanctuary. Its priesthood persisted not only during the Josiah reformation in Judah and its aftermath until the fall of Jerusalem in 586 B.C., but throughout the Exile, and it was therefore still exercising its functions when some of the exiles returned to Palestine at the end of the century. The combination of the two pre-exilic documents J and E into a composite narrative after the Exile suggests that the two principal sanctuaries in Palestine during the Hebrew occupation must have been in contact with one another as Yahwistic places of worship, whatever may have been the origin and relationships of their respective priesthoods. The subsequent rivalry of Samaria and Judah and the violent opposition of the Samaritans to the rebuilding of the Temple and the wall of Jerusalem may in some measure be explained by the position which Bethel had occupied in Israel regarded as 'the land of Yahweh'.

LACHISH

Another important cult centre, rebuilt several times, was the temple at Lachish, midway between Jerusalem and Gaza on the site now known as Tell ed-Duweir on the west slopes of the Judaean hills, where settlements and natural caves occurred in the Chalcolithic and Early Bronze Age in the third millennium B.C. These dwellings were subsequently used as tombs, and in the fosse which surrounded the ramparts of the city in the Middle Bronze Age a rectangular shrine about 15 feet wide and 30 feet in depth was erected, probably in the first part of the fifteenth century, with a square antechamber and a small room on one side, the roof supported by wooden columns. Along the back wall of the sanctuary was a bench with three platforms, perhaps used as altars or offerings tables. It was here that the cult seems to have been centred. In front of the middle offering table, two large jars were buried in the floor, and nearby a number of sherds. This earliest fosse temple was later enlarged by a structure double the size of the shrine being superimposed upon it, and the offering table reconstructed in stone instead of in clay to form an elaborate altar with a hearth in front of it, set against the back wall, and a double row of long, narrow 'tables' for offerings along the other three walls, and in an annex behind the sanctuary.

The floor was raised and its columns and roof were rebuilt; a second room was added to the south end of the temple, the two chambers being connected with the sanctuary by a doorway. Later a mud-brick altar was erected against the front of the platform, and to the west a lamp cupboard against the south wall. On the east wall three niches and extra benches were inserted. Around the shrine were quantities of pottery and of bones of birds, sheep and oxen. The only cult image, however, was a bronze statuette of a seated male god, found in the fosse in association with incised pottery containing inscriptions in an early Canaanite script.[47] No Palestinian site, in fact, has produced so much documentary and textual material as Lachish in the Bronze Age, of which the sixth-century ostraca fragments recovered from the floor of a small room in one of the towers of the city gate are the most important, written in pre-exilic Hebrew in the ancient Phoenician script.[48]

GEZER

At Gezer on the lower slope of the Judaean hills above the maritime plain of Philistia some 5 miles from Ramleh, midway between Jerusalem and Joppa, what was claimed to be the largest ancient Palestinian sanctuary was unearthed by Macalister during his exavations of the mound between 1902 and 1908.[49] Several of the essential features of a *bamah* (high place), however, do not occur in it (e.g. a court, altar and *asherah*), and the alignments of eight huge standing stones of unequal size and appearance are not characteristic of such sanctuaries. They may have been merely memorials of the kings of the city,[50] or mortuary monuments.[51] That they had a magico-religious significance of some kind is evident from their occurrence for these purposes in so many similar sites, though not necessarily, or, indeed usually, as part of the equipment of a bamah type of sanctuary. Gezer may have been a mortuary shrine in the first instance, the *maṣṣebôth* having much the same purpose and significance as in the temple of Dagon at Ugarit, or perhaps the funerary stele associated with Absolom.[52] On the east of the northern end of the alignment was the entrance to two natural caverns, connected with each other by a narrow passage and containing a burial. Originally, however, they were inhabited by cave-dwellers although interment and cremation had been practised in them in the Bronze Age (*c.* 1500 B.C.). Until Gezer was captured by Shishak (*c.* 948–924 B.C.) and given to his daughter when she married Solomon, it remained a Canaanite city.

PETRA

At Petra in the mountains of southern Transjordan overlooking the Wadi el-Araba, cave-tombs recur which probably were excavated in the rock by the Nabataeans of Edom. They appear to have evolved from the pylon type about the sixth century B.C. As Petra became an increasingly important centre on the caravan routes to Gaza, Bosra, Damascus, Elath and the Persian Gulf, it came under Syrian, Arabian, Egyptian, Greek and Roman influences, reflected in the tombs and later buildings, when it assumed the character and features of a Hellenistic city in the first century B.C., subsequently becoming more Romanized, until in A.D. 106 it was absorbed into the Roman Empire.[53]

The open-air sanctuaries hewn out of the rock with *maṣṣebôth*, a rock-cut court with a raised platform in the centre had to the west a stepped altar with a depression on its surface perhaps for fire, and 'horns' at three of the corners. Like the tombs of great splendour with elaborate façades copied from Roman temples, they may have been products of the reign of Aretas III Philhellene (*c.* 85–60 B.C.), after the decline of the Ptolemaic and Seleucid kingdoms. A temple excavated by Nelson Glueck in 1937 on the hill called Jebel el-Tannur, south-east of the Dead Sea, erected on a platform facing east, represented a combination of Greek and Nabataean features. Unlike most of the Petra temples which were dedicated to Dusares (Dhu Sharra), Lord of Seir, this high place was in honour of the Syrian Storm- and Weather-god Adad, identified with Zeus, and that of Atargatis (fused with Astarte), the Syrian goddess of Hierapolis where she shared a temple with Zeus. In its later form it belonged to the reign of Aretas IV (9 B.C.–A.D. 40), for whose well-being it was constructed in 7 B.C. Below, however, was an earlier shrine, and while to assign these high places to the days of Moses[54] is an unsubstantiated conjecture, they do conform to the general pattern of ancient Palestinian sanctuaries. Thus, the usual pattern recurs in what appears to have been the royal high place of Edom near the ruins of Petra, first described by Professor G. L. Robinson of Chicago in 1900,[55] near the summit of a high ridge above the Roman amphitheatre. Approached by a rock-cut stairway, it consisted of a large court 47 feet in length and 20 feet in breadth where presumably the worshippers assembled while sacrifices were offered on the altar facing the raised platform. Above, on the brow of the hill, stood two menhirs about 18 feet in height and 100 feet apart, the bamah itself standing on an oval rock dome some 300 feet long and 100 feet broad. Such was its location, construction and prominence that it may well have been the central sanctuary of the Edomites.[56]

SHILOH

So far as Israel was concerned, while Petra possibly may have been the Old Testament Sela, 'the rock', named after the natural fortress, as has been suggested, Shiloh (probably Hirbet Seitun) some 12 miles south of Shechem and 2 miles north of Bethel, was the seat of the Ark and apparently the central sanctuary from the time of the Judges to the establishment of Jerusalem as the capital by David and the erection of the Temple on Mount Zion by his son Solomon. Thus, after the conquest of Palestine was completed, the tabernacle, or 'tent of meeting', was moved from Gilgal near Jericho and set up at Shiloh, which henceforth became the central sanctuary in Israel in the period of the Judges.[57] To it pilgrimages were made on occasions, and at it the Annual Festival was held at the time of vintage.[58] When Samuel took up his abode there with Eli as its priest and guardian of the Ark, it was attended by all within reach of the temple,[59] such was the importance of the shrine and the observance. It was, however, the presence of the Ark there that gave it its prominence and significance, and for its greater safety and reverence a *hekal* (temple) within the sanctuary was erected.

   It may have been of specifically Hebrew origin (*c.* 1200 B.C.) rather than a high place taken over from the Canaanites, and in view of its close association with the Ark Shiloh was probably destroyed when this sacred object was captured by the Philistines (*c.* 1050 B.C.).[60] Thus, when the Ark was recaptured it was taken first to Beth-Shemesh, its former abode being no longer available.[61] Its priesthood then settled at Nob under Ahimelech on the Mount of Olives near Gibeah,[62] where doubtless there was a sanctuary already in existence, to which David as an outlaw repaired.[63] If Shiloh was in fact Tell Seilun, the excavations there by the Danish expedition directed by Hans Kjaer and Glueck in 1926 and in 1929 revealed an extensive settlement from the Middle Bronze Age to Iron Age I (*c.* 1200–1000 B.C.), brought to an end about 1050 B.C. by conflagration.[64] Shut in by lofty limestone hills on the east and north, and standing on a tell some 1800 feet in length, it was only open to attack from the south, but having been destroyed by the Philistines in spite of its seclusion it seems to have been re-occupied only temporarily, and never to have regained its pre-eminence as a sanctuary. Its priesthood, claiming descent from Aaron, soon lost its prestige after the establishment of the monarchy, though Abiathar survived in the priestly organization in Jerusalem until he was deposed by Solomon in favour of Zadok, the line of Eli having never recovered from the defeat and loss of the Ark at Ebenezer.[65]

THE TEMPLE IN JERUSALEM

The transfer of the capital from Hebron to Jerusalem after David succeeded in conquering this Jebusite stronghold about 1000 B.C.[66] was destined to have far-reaching effects on the unification of Israel and its worship in Palestine. As the fortress was neutral territory, strategically situated on the border between Judah and the northern kingdom, it became the natural capital of the country. There David lost no time in strengthening the fortifications and building a palace for himself and his retinue with the aid of foreign workmen and materials supplied by Hiram king of Tyre. He then turned his attention to the reconstruction of the Tabernacle and the installation therein of the Ark so that the recently established 'city of David' might become the religious centre of the nation as well as the capital.

The actual site of the Temple has never been definitely ascertained, but its position can be determined fairly accurately and to some extent its architectural plan can be reconstructed from the literary sources. The threshing floor which David is said to have purchased from Ornan, or Araunah, the Jebusite, (and subsequently identified with Mount Mariah or Mount Zion, 'the mountain of the house'),[67] on which he erected an altar to Yahweh, seems to have been the surface of a rock (*es-sakhra*) which contains cup-markings, on the crest of the eastern hill. It is now enclosed in the mosque, the Dome of the Rock, incorrectly called the Mosque of Omar.[68] This appears to have been an ancient Jebusite place of sacrifice, and a sanctuary stood there, now occupied by the large platform covering some 35 acres, known as the *Haram esh-Sharif*, or 'Noble Sanctuary'. There it may be that David wanted to erect a permanent temple but for reasons which are not clear he never proceeded with the project beyond amassing a considerable amount of money, material, treasure and even artisans for the project.[69] If such was the case, evidently it was not regarded with favour by a section of the mono-Yahwists, who protested through Nathan the prophet that Yahweh declared that he had always dwelt in a tent.[70]

THE TEMPLE OF SOLOMON

It remained for his son Solomon to put the scheme into operation after the death of his father when he enlarged the capital. For his own residence he selected the south side of the eastern hill called Ophel[71] and there he erected a group of buildings which, besides his palace, included the 'house of the forest of Lebanon', so called because of its cedar-wood pillars, a porch of pillars, the throne-room, and in another court a house for Pharaoh's daughter whom he had married.[72] To these he added 'the house of the Lord' as a royal chapel for the worship of Yahweh as an adjunct to the palace, with a private entrance from the king's apartments independent of that on the side provided for the worshippers in general. In fact, it appears to have been primarily for his own use and for the people of the capital that it was constructed originally, certainly with no intention of supplanting the local sanctuaries at Bethel, Shiloh, Hebron, Gilgal, Dan and Beersheba. As we have seen, these continued to exercise their functions long after the temple of Solomon had been established in Jerusalem, and it was not until the seventh century that an attempt was made to make it the sole temple in which the cultus in Israel could be performed legitimately, attributing to Jeroboam I the sin *par excellence* of erecting local high places.

That no such idea was even latent in the mind of Solomon is shown by the brazen altar being so much too small for the burnt offerings required on festivals that he had to hallow the middle of the court in front of 'the house of the Lord' for this purpose;[73] in other words upon the surface of the ancient sacrificial rock. Nevertheless, while the accommodation and equipment may have been under estimated in relation to the requirements of the cult and its worshippers, the actual building, which took skilled Phoenician workmen and craftsmen supplied by Hiram[74] seven years (from about 959 to 952 B.C.) to construct,[75] was an imposing structure designed to impress the neighbouring countries quite as much as for the glory of Yahweh. Its splendour,

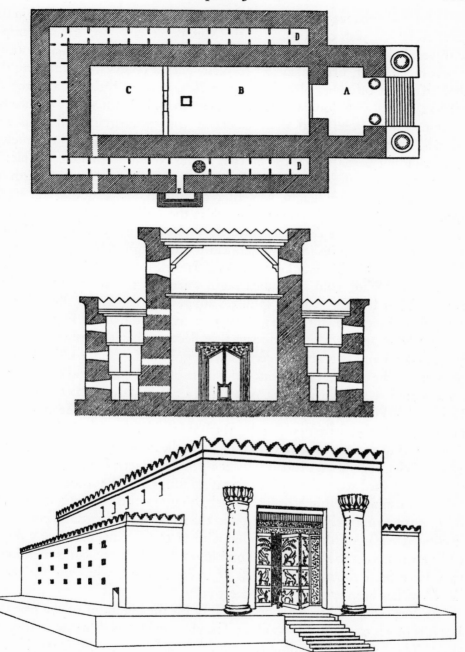

*Fig. 30.   Reconstructed view, plan and section of Solomon's temple at Jerusalem.
After Stevens*

however, did enhance the prestige of the Ark it enshrined. As described in the narratives[76] the plan conformed to the Mesopotamian 'long house' temple with vestibule (broad room), nave (long room) and adytum (square room). It was rectangular, orientated east to west, with a courtyard containing the altar of burnt offerings placed on the *sakhra*, entered through a porch or narthex (*ulam*) with double doors of cypress trees. In front were two bronze columns called Jachin and Boaz, adorned with pomegranate designs and capitals. They are said to have measured 12 cubits in height and 4 in diameter, corresponding perhaps to those erected in the Neolithic Maltese temples.[77]

On the inside of the porch, the holy place (*hekal*), 40 cubits in length by 20 in breadth and 30 in height, was entered through double doors, and dimly lighted by a row of lattice windows high in the wall. Behind the naos was a smaller sanctuary, the *debir*, or 'most holy place' (i.e. the Holy of Holies) on the west, 20 cubits in length, breadth and height, thereby forming a perfect cube.[78] Within was kept the Ark, flanked by two cherubim of olive wood plated with gold, 10 cubits high, guarding it with their spreading wings, rather like the winged sphinxes supporting the king's throne on an ivory from Megiddo and those in Egypt protecting the infant Horus.

The *hekal* and its double doors were decorated with designs of palm-trees, flowers and cherubim, overlaid with gold leaf[79] and within the holy place stood the golden candlesticks, the table of shewbread, and a cedar altar ornamented with gold in front of a flight of steps leading to the Holy of Holies (*debir*) on a raised platform, like the niches containing the cult-image in the Canaanite sanctuaries. On the north side and the south side were small doors, giving access to a stairway connecting the *hekal* with the three storeys of small chambers used probably by the priests as sacristies and storehouses. In the courtyard were the altar of burnt offerings and the so-called 'Bronze Sea', consisting of a huge bronze bowl 10 cubits in diameter and 5 cubits deep, resting on twelve oxen arrayed in threes facing the cardinal points and decorated with gourds.[80] It was filled with water, the quantity being differently estimated in the two biblical narratives, but the 2,000 baths mentioned may have been about 45,000 litres, or 10,000 gallons, while the weight of the bowl has been estimated at some 30 tons.[81]

Its purpose is said to have been merely for the ablutions of the priests,[82] but it is much too high for washing. Josephus attributes its name to its great size.[83] There can be little doubt, however, that it had a cosmic significance of some kind, symbolizing in all probability the Mesopotamian *Aspu*, or subterranean waters from which all fertility was thought to be derived.[84] There were, in fact, tanks of this kind in Babylonian temples and also at Karnak and in Samaria, and the decoration including oxen and bulls is suggestive of a fertility motif so prominent in Canaanite and Israelite religion at this period. The grouping in threes may also have had a seasonal rather than a zodiacal significance. The lavers, or ten bowls on wheels, were likewise decorated with bulls, lions, palm-trees and cherubin, while the altar of burnt offering had similar cosmic symbolism.[85]

The great altar of burnt offering, according to the description in Ezekiel xliii (13–17), was built in the form of a ziggurat with three stages, each with a side 2 cubits shorter than the stage below, and the entire structure, estimated at 11 cubits in height, rested on a base 18 cubits square. The stages were approached by a stairway and on the upper surface were four horns or projections, as in the construction of so many Phoenician and Palestinian

Fig. 31. Reconstruction of the 'Bronze Sea'. Drawing by William Morden. Courtesy, Oriental Institute, University of Chicago

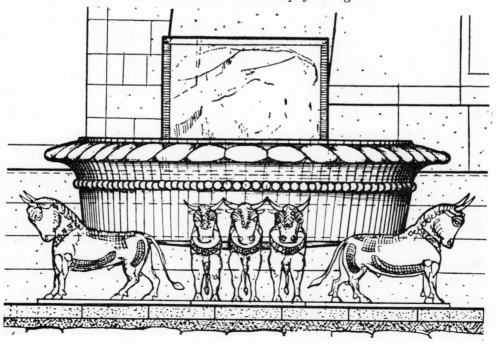

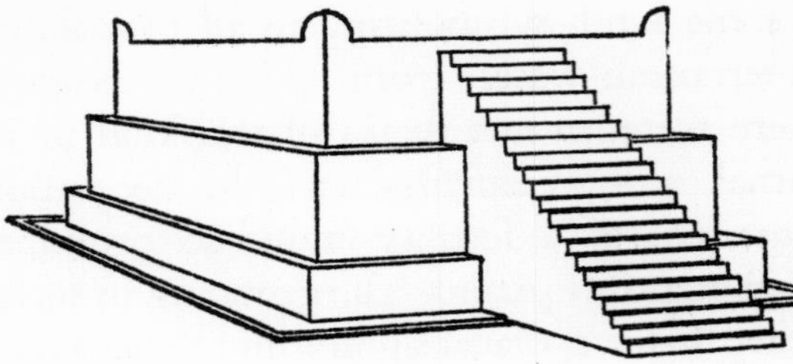

Fig. 32.   Reconstruction of the altar of burnt offerings in Jerusalem, based on Ezekiel xliii, 13–17. After Stevens

altars.[86] On the highest stage burnt offerings were made, the erection being known as *harel*, meaning probably 'the mountain of God', as in the case of many Babylonian ziggurats, it being there that the gods were thought to have their habitation. Similarly, the foundation-platform on which it rested was equated with the 'bosom of the earth' and the underworld. It was removed by Ahaz (736–716 B.C.) from the middle of the court when during a visit to Tiglath-Pileser, the Assyrian king at Damascus, he sent the model and measurements of an altar he had seen in the temple of Hadad to Urijah, the priest in Jerusalem, with instructions to have an identical altar erected in the temple at Jerusalem. It was made of stone with a base 27 feet square and 18 inches high. Above this was a 24 feet square which was 3 feet high surmounted by another square of 21 feet and 6 feet in height. On the top was the hearth of the altar 16 feet square and 6 feet high, approached by steps on the east side. The total height was 17 feet and at its corners were 'horns'.[87] The old bronze altar was to be removed to the northern side of the new Assyrian structure and reserved for the use of the king, probably for omen-sacrifice in the pagan reaction that he instituted.

EZEKIEL'S VISIONARY TEMPLE

Since, as G. E. Wright has reminded us, 'not a single discovery has been made in Jerusalem which can be dated with any certainty to the time of David and Solomon',[88] the accounts of the building, plan and furnishing of the First Temple rest upon the often obscure literary sources which have been handed down from more or less contemporary records and traditions, re-interpreted with the aid of the description of the Temple Ezekiel was said to have seen in a vision, and which of course was never actually built.[89] The exact measurements of the Temple of Solomon, its altars and plan are not known, so complete was its destruction by Nebuchadnezzar between 604 and 562 B.C. Nevertheless, Ezekiel's visionary picture bears a definite relation to the sacred edifice erected after the death of David in the new capital, the dimensions being substantially the same as those given in II Kings vi,[90] and the architecture of the more elaborate ambitious scheme conceived and put into operation by Herod the Great in 20 to 19 B.C., and completed ten years later. Ezekiel's experience may have been based on some recollections of the actual Temple in existence at the time of the Exile, twenty-five years before he had his vision of a sanctuary raised up again and restored along the lines of the former building. Thus, the enclosure was in the form of a square measuring 500 cubits, with three gateways on the east, north and south, each of which gave access to the outer court. To maintain the sacrosanct character of the sanctuary and protect it and its courts from profane secular influences and contacts a second court was introduced with three gateways in the form of fortifications to control the right of entry,[91] the priests alone being permitted to enter the inner court and to officiate at its exalted altar.[92]

Ezekiel's visionary temple, being a separate structure quite independent of a palace or any secular buildings, was set apart wholly for the worship of Yahweh. Only in the outer court could the lay worshippers assemble, and the entire enclosure was encompassed by a wall 6 cubits high and 6 cubits thick, approached at the eastern gateway by a flight of seven steps to the porch. Another eight steps had to be ascended to the inner court and finally ten steps led to the upper terrace to the *hekal* and the *debir*, guarded by sentries for whom rooms were provided. The inner court also was equipped with a number of chambers for the priests as sacristies for the vestments and sacred vessels. In fact, on every side except the east, Ezekiel's temple, like that of Solomon, had some thirty side rooms for sacerdotal purposes arranged in three storeys. The walls of the Holy Place were parallel and decorated with a palm-tree between two cherubim having the face of a man and of a young lion.[93] An altar of cedar wood with horns is the only object mentioned in the *hekal*, corresponding apparently to the table of shewbread in the first temple, but no reference is made to the Ark of the Covenant in the *debir*.

This most sacred object had evidently vanished from the scene by the time of the Exile, having apparently been lost and destroyed during the upheaval in the sacking of the city and the temple by the forces of Nebuchadnezzar. Therefore no place was found for it in the vision of the prophets of the period. Instead the glory of Yahweh was represented as filling the whole of the temple;[94] the whole of the mountain sanctuary in the visionary enclosure was most holy, and everything unclean was excluded from it.[95] Out of it sprang a torrent of living water under the threshold of the house eastward from the south side of the altar, flowing in a south-westerly direction to the Dead Sea, to a lake swarming with fish and surrounded by fruitful trees.[96] Thus, the vision of the prophet closed with a symbolic representation of the restoration of the exiles and the re-creation of the temple from its ruins, when the holy oblation should once more be offered to Yahweh.

THE SECOND TEMPLE

This, however, hardly came up to the prophetic anticipations when after the return of the first batch of the Jews from Mesopotamia in 539 B.C., under the leadership of Zerubbabel and Jeshua, an attempt was made eventually to rebuild the temple. This, according to the Biblical account, was not begun until eighteen years later, in the second year of the reign of the Persian king Darius I (522–485 B.C.) under the inspiration of the prophets Haggai and Zechariah.[97] Cyrus had already returned the silver and gold holy vessels, but beyond re-creating the altar, observing the Feast of Tabernacles and some of the other seasonal festivals, and making a clearance among the ruins,[98] little was done to re-establish the cultus. Even when a start was made it encountered suspicion and opposition from the northern neighbours, and when it was erected eventually and duly equipped five years later (516), it was on a very meagre scale. From the scanty references made in the current literature to what was accomplished, it would seem that it occupied the site of its predecessor, and that it contained a *hekal* with a golden altar of incense, a table for the shewbread, a seven-branched lampstand, and the utensils, but the *debir* was empty, except for a stone (*Eben Shetija*) on which the high-priest placed the censer on the Day of Atonement. Between the two holy places were two veils, in the inner court was an altar of burnt offering of un-hewn stone, and in the outer court cells for the priests and storehouses.

When, before the Maccabaean revolt, this temple was desecrated by Antiochus Epiphanes in 168 B.C. an altar to Jupiter was placed on the altar of burnt offerings and the brazen vessels were seized.[99] Three years later when Judas Maccabaeus restored the worship of Yahweh there a new altar with new furniture was set up in the court and consecrated. The façade was decorated with gold crowns and shields and on 25 December 164 it was purified at the Feast of the Dedication (Hanukkah). The walls and high towers were fortified and subsequently further strengthened by Simon,[100] so that when Pompey first attacked Jerusalem in 63 B.C. it was a very strong fortress taking three months to effect an entry. When at length this was achieved, apart from penetrating into the Holy of Holies, and thereby giving great offence to the conquered Jews, no attempt was made to complete the destruction of the temple or to suppress its worship. It was not until nine years later that it was plundered by Crassus (54 B.C.), and its considerable wealth (more than two million pounds) confiscated.[101]

HEROD'S TEMPLE

In 37 B.C., Herod, the son of the Idumaean Antipater of Maccabaean descent, was made king of Judaea by the Roman Senate at the instigation of Antony. Having laid siege to Jerusalem for two years and being confronted with mistrust and unpopularity everywhere in Palestine, he tried to conciliate his resentful subjects by embarking upon a most ambitious reconstruction of the temple in the eighteenth year of his reign (20–19 B.C.). By sparing no expense or labour in the erection of a most imposing edifice in the Hellenistic-Roman style of architecture, he hoped to enhance his prestige and consolidate his position in the land, and at the same time to mitigate his previous affronts to Jewish piety by taking great care not to offend their religious susceptibilities in the equipment or adornment of their central sanctuary. If his purpose was political and personal, it did in fact result in the erection of a most imposing edifice consecrated exclusively to the honour and for the worship of the God of Israel, ten years being spent on the completion of the elaborate scheme. Indeed, with various interruptions, the work continued almost up to the time of its ultimate destruction by Titus in 70 A.D., so that it was more or less forty-six years in building.[102]

According to Josephus, who was himself a priest, it was nearly twice the size of its predecessor,[103] and was surrounded by a battlemented wall around the edge of the hill with two gates on the south side ('the doors of Huldah'), four on the west, one on the north, and one on the east. The entire perimeter measured just over 1,509 yards, and was trapezoidal in form, surrounded by a paved court bounded by porticos. The two southern gateways opened into a vestibule and led up to the Court of the Gentiles, so-called because non-Jews were allowed to enter this outer courtyard. Within it was a platform

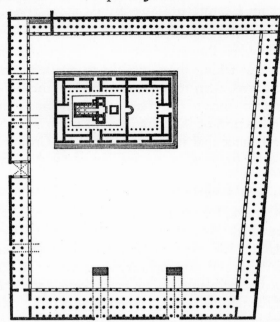

*Fig. 33.   Reconstructed plan
of Herod's temple, Jerusalem*

about 15 cubits high with a terrace surrounding it, reached by a wall
rising to 25 cubits above the ground level. This being the precincts of the
sanctuary, equivalent in sanctity to the *hekal* in the previous temples, it was
forbidden on pain of death for anyone who was not a Jew to enter it,[104] due
warning being given on inscribed tablets in Greek and Latin displayed on a
stone lattice running round it beneath the level of the steps. Jewish women
had access to the first section of the inner court, known as the Court of the
Women, said to have been rather lower than that of the male Israelites,
reached by fifteen steps and shut off by a balcony (*exostra*). This enabled the
women to observe the rites at the Feast of Tabernacles without coming into
contact with the men.[105]

The court of the Israelites (187 by 135 cubits) was entered by six gates
with a seventh sometimes identified with that known as 'Nicanor's Gate' of
the Mishna,[106] opening from the women's court and more ornate than the
rest.[107] That called the 'Gate Beautiful' in the account of the healing of the
cripple in the Acts of the Apostles,[108] would seem to have been at the entrance to the sanctuary, as the apostles are said to have been in process of
entering the temple. This has been regarded as Nicanor's Gate, or that known

as the Corinthian Gate on the east side with its Corinthian bronze doors.[109] It was in these porch-like porticos or cloisters that business was conducted and rites like the presentation of infants were held,[110] the more elaborate ritual observances being performed in the Court of the Priests which was at a still higher level above the Court of the Israelites, and reserved for the priests and their assistants, containing the altar of burnt offering and the laver. Twelve steps higher stood the temple building itself in white marble—the 'house'—60 cubits in height, 60 in length and 20 cubits in breadth.

As in the other temples it was divided into the *hekal* (40 cubits long) and the *debir* (20 cubits long), separated by a veil as in Babylonia. The Holy Place contained the seven-branched candelabra, the table of shewbread, and the altar of incense in the middle, visible to the congregation when on festivals the door was left open. The Holy of Holies screened by a veil was empty and entered annually through the double curtain by the high-priest alone on the Day of Atonement. The porch was 100 cubits in height and breadth in front of the house, with an entrance 40 cubits high and 20 cubits broad, but no door. Along the enclosing wall of the temple were a number of small chambers used as storehouses, sacristies and for the preparation of the offerings, occupying three storeys, as in that erected by Solomon. Above the sanctuary was a flat roof 100 cubits above the level of the lower rooms, comparable with the height of the porch. A golden eagle with outstretched wings on the façade was removed as a Roman emblem distasteful to the Jews shortly before the death of Herod, and the façade was completed by a colonnade supporting the upper storey.[111]

THE CULTUS IN JERUSALEM

PRE-EXILIC YAHWISM

Throughout its long and checkered history the temple of Jerusalem was the central sanctuary dedicated to the worship of Yahweh, the god of Israel. When, however, it was first erected after the death of David it was essentially syncretistic in its appointment, as we have seen, and while the cultus was Yahwistic, Yahweh having become officially the god of the land, the nature and attributes of the Canaanite Baals had been transferred to him. In the local high places the cults were indistinguishable from those of their previous divine occupants, so at Jerusalem David had taken over the priesthood of the god Zedek and placed himself at the head of its hierarchy. The site he selected for the temple was apparently already hallowed ground before it was dedicated to the worship of Yahweh. Yahwism, however, was primarily a Judaean cult, and from the south it dominated all the Hebrew tribes as the cult of the national god under the unifying influence of David and the new capital. Nevertheless, the nature, attributes and worship of Yahweh remained little changed in spite of the mono-Yahwist efforts to rid the official religion of the nation of its Canaanite and other elements alien to the desert tradition.

Once the national sanctuary had been established on Mount Zion and the Ark installed there,[112] Abiathar the high-priest and Nathan the prophet, with the assistance of the Levites, consolidated Yahwism as the State religion, whatever local cults might be practised in the high places outside the capital. There various gods continued to be worshipped in the customary manner at their own sanctuaries, and Ahab did not hesitate to erect a temple to Baal in Samaria when it became the capital of the northern kingdom, and made a grove for him.[113] His son, to the consternation of Elijah, carried on Baalism, appealing to Baal-Zebub when he sustained serious injuries in falling through a lattice in his palace.[114] This continued in Israel until Jehu made an attempt to suppress it.[115] He did succeed in establishing Yahwism officially for a century (842–745 B.C.) but did not in fact eliminate the original worship of the local sanctuaries.[116]

In the south Solomon adopted a much less drastic attitude to the incorporation of other cults in Yahwism than did Jehu, himself worshipping Astarte (Ashtoreth) and Milcom of Ammon, as well as providing a temple for them and the rest of the gods of his many wives.[117] The temple of Yahweh in Jerusalem, as we have seen, was modelled on Phoenician lines with bronze bulls and cherubim and the two colossal obelisks at the entrance, all of which had a syncretistic significance. The adoption of the monarchy in face of the alleged opposition of Samuel[118] could hardly have been entirely independent of the influences of the sacral kingship in the surrounding countries, however much it may have been incorporated in and modified by the Yahwistic conception of the divine covenant (*bērith*), established with the dynasty of David as the anointed servant and son of Yahweh.[119] It was this status that made him and his successors sacred persons and cult leaders exercising sacrificial functions in the temple in Jerusalem like their counter-parts in Egypt, Mesopotamia and elsewhere in Western Asia. Thus, David wore an ephod and danced ecstatically before the Ark when it was taken to its resting place on Mount Zion. When the temple was erected there his son Solomon is said to have offered burnt offerings and peace offerings three times a year on the altar he had erected to Yahweh,[120] and since the principal events in which the king performed his sacred functions in this region was that of presiding over the annual New Year Festival (e.g. in the Akitu in Babylon), it would be surprising if this observance was not celebrated in some form by the Hebrew monarch in the Temple of Solomon.

THE FEAST OF BOOTHS

In Israel the agricultural year commenced in the autumn, and it was then that the Feast of Tabernacles (*Sukkôth*) was held[121] in the month of Ethanim, called the seventh month, Tishri, after the Exile, when the vintage had been completed. The connexion with the ingathering of the grape-harvest shows that it was borrowed from the Canaanite rather than the desert tradition, and that it coincided with the autumnal equinox when the moon was full and the agricultural work of the season had come to an end. In the pre-exilic community it was this observance that was really the New Year Festival, and the time when the Babylonian autumnal rites were celebrated at the 'going out' of the year, although Nisan or Abib became 'the beginning of months' when the Passover was held as the first ripe ears of barley appeared. There were, therefore, virtually two New Year Festivals in Israel, the one in the autumn and the other in the spring, marking respectively the end and the beginning of the growth of the crops, including the vines. Behind this annual sequence and ritual observances lay the most important events in vegetation, symbolized in the sacred drama of the dying and reviving year-god, in which the crucial role was played by the king as the human vicegerent of the god primarily responsible for the control of the weather and the rain. Yahweh, it is true, was never a typical vegetation deity in origin or function, though he was regarded as the giver of fertility, and, as the Carmel incident shows, he could vindicate his supremacy in his land by breaking a drought.[122] He was, in short, the creator standing over and above his creation and its processes as a transcendental deity controlling and ordering natural events and the vicissitudes of history.

This is most apparent in the psalms in which the enthronement of Yahweh was celebrated,[123] and there is reason to think that in all probability they formed an integral part of the New Year liturgy at the autumnal festival, later called the Feast of Booths or Tabernacles.[124] Mowinckel, in fact, has maintained that they were composed for this purpose to commemorate annually the victory of Yahweh over the forces of primeval chaos, reflected in his domination over the kings and nations of the earth. This was symbolized by the carrying of the Ark in procession to the temple where Yahweh was acclaimed as the Lord of the universe,[125] and his blessing was sought on the fortunes of the forthcoming year in the renewal of the covenant (i.e. *bêrith*, the cultus) with the House of David, upon which rain and fertility depended.[126] It is unfortunate, however, that the enthronement psalms are for the most part post-exilic, though Psalm lxxxi, which is paralleled to Psalm xcv, was composed for use at the Feast of the Ingathering at the full moon in Tishri.[127] But if they did originally belong to the New Year liturgy, as is probable, they must have lost a good deal of their significance when they became Sabbath psalms in the later post-exilic worship, the New Year Festival having become associated with the Kingdom of God.

Moreover, although many of those listed by Mowinckel may be subsequent to the Exile, some at least go back to the monarchy (e.g. xlvii, xciii, xcv–c), and may have influenced the Deutero-Isaiah at the end of the Exile. The theme is that of the domination of Yahweh over the physical universe manifest in the seasonal rains, and his beneficent rule over Israel in spite of the recent disasters, along the lines of the cult drama in Mesopotamia and the Ugaritic texts. That the New Year Festival would be the appropriate occasion for the celebration of the victory of Yahweh over the forces of death and destruction in the temple at Jerusalem, as described in several of these psalms (xxiv, xlvii, lxviii), can hardly be denied, notwithstanding the opposition to the vegetation cultus as contrary to the Sinaitic covenant. But the temple with its holy place (*hekal*) remained the 'palace' of the god of the land, in which he resided with his priesthood and servants (i.e. Levites) who engaged in the prescribed daily worship in the presence of a cosmic symbolism over which their God presided enthroned in the darkness of the Holy of Holies with its protecting cherubim.

There is no doubt that the temple was a typical Phoenician structure erected and equipped for the requirements of the established cultus.

Sanctuaries in Palestine and the Temple in Jerusalem

I   *Horned altar from Megiddo*

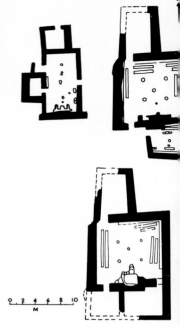

92   93

*The temple at Lachish was an important cult
centre in Canaan and ground plans show how
the building was enlarged during the Bronze
Age (92, 93) so that long altars could be set up
for votive offerings. The horned altar from
Megiddo (91) is one of three, each dedicated to a
Canaanite deity, which stood in shrines in the
temple. The largest cult centre in Palestine is
at Gezer, where an alignment of eight massive
standing stones, possibly mortuary monuments,
were found on the lower slopes of the hills (94)*

94

95

Petra, the capital of the rich trading Nabataean arabs, was founded in the fourth century B.C., high in the mountains of southern Jordan. The ornate façades of tombs and mausolea line the pink cliffs, and there are also two temples hewn from the sandstone (95). Above the city are the 'high places'—open-air sanctuaries of the gods in the ancient Israelite tradition. Two obelisks carved from the solid rock stand in a long ceremonial court (96)

96

97

The second commandment forbade the Jews from making any graven image of their god. We therefore only find figures of pre-Jawhistic cults such as Baal, the Thunder God Teshub and this representation of the Mother-goddess (97–99)

98

99

Furthermore it was apparently at the autumnal festival in the seventh month (Ethanim or Tishri) that Solomon dedicated the temple around the altar he had erected on the ancient holy rock[128] with its Canaanite associations. It was no doubt under the influence of the Deuteronomic movement in the seventh century that the great prayer of the king assumed its present form in which Yahweh was addressed in exclusively monotheistic terms as a celestial Supreme Being whose dwelling was in the heavens rather than in an earthly sanctuary.[129] Nevertheless, the conception of his worship was given a new significance in the light of Ezekiel's visionary experience, the divine presence (*shakan*) being regarded as 'tabernacled' in the less pretentious temple in the post-exilic community.

No information is available about the details of the pre-exilic 'Asith Festival', connected with the full moon at the autumnal equinox, except that it combined both rejoicing and lamentation at the turn of the year.[130] This would be the time for celebrating the triumph of Yahweh and the occasion for the cleansing of the sanctuary, the priesthood and the whole congregation of Israel from the defilements contracted during the year. In its later form as the Feast of Booths or Tabernacles in the Rabbinic literature, a dance is recorded as having been held in the temple on the second night in the Court of the Women, together with a procession round the altar each day in which the branches of palms and a fruit like a lemon (*ethrog*) were held as a fertility charm.[131] These probably were survivals of the earlier harvest observances at the end of the season. That a procession of priests turned to the eastern gate of Jerusalem at sunrise and turned westwards facing the temple was probably a protest against the former custom of facing the rising sun when Yahweh took up his abode on Mount Zion as the King of glory.[132]

The booths made of greenery have been compared with the Babylonian *gigunu* in the Akitu festival, and it is possible that a similar royal sacred marriage may have occurred in the earlier Hebrew ritual.[133] In the Elephantine Papyri Yahweh was associated with Anat, and the worship of the Queen of Heaven was firmly established in Israel before the Exile.[134] Each day of the festival, libations drawn from the pool of Siloam were poured out at the altar by a priest from a golden vessel. This probably was a rain-making ceremony originally, since in the Talmud it is affirmed that on the Feast of Sukkôth waters were offered to Yahweh that 'the rains of the year may be blessed to you'.[135] It was also at this season that, in Ezekiel's vision, women were seen in the temple 'weeping for Tammuz',[136] and 'the lamentation psalms' may have been the Hebrew counterpart of the Tammuz liturgies.[137] If so, behind them lay the fundamental theme in the vegetation cult drama: the fertilization of the earth by the seasonal rains, in which Tammuz played a prominent role.

It was, in fact, because temple appointment and worship was so closely related to the traditional kingship cultus that the prevailing syncretism was regarded with the gravest suspicion by the prophetic movement,[138] and that a determined effort was made in the Second Temple, and subsequently in that of Herod, to prevent its continuance. The fall of the monarch constituted a definite break in the tradition, though to some extent it survived when Zerubbabel on becoming governor of Jerusalem in 520 B.C. was, as a descendant of David, hailed as the deputy of Yahweh, and in conjunction with the high-priest occupied a position in the cultus comparable to that of 'the Prince' in the vision of Ezekiel.[139] When his mission came to an end the hierarchical organization and the temple sacrificial worship was developed around the high-priest, the civic and ecclesiastical functions of the ruler being combined in the same sacred office until the destruction of the temple and the city in A.D. 70.

THE DAY OF ATONEMENT

As the covenant was fundamental in Judaism the sacred community was resolved into a unified theocratic whole, consolidated by the official worship of the temple through which the spiritual bond of the nation and its god was maintained. The transcendence of Yahweh as Lord of the universe and of history prevented the ritual order from gaining supreme control over the cosmic events. He alone could release from sin, and the priesthood was merely his instrument. While it was indispensable for the proper functioning of the covenant, its authority was delegated not absolute. The personal relationship between Yahweh and the individual Israelite, established under the influence of the prophetic movement, found expression in a deepened sense of sin fostered by the post-exilic evaluation of the Law and the ancient symbolism of the Day of Atonement observances, so closely associated with the Feast of Booths in the seventh month. The daily sacrifices in the temple expiated unintentional breaches of the Law. The evening oblation removed those committed during the day, while the morning sacrifice those contracted in the night. The Day of Atonement, however, was an *ex opera operato* piacular to cleanse and carry away the evil of the nation and sins committed with a 'high hand', on the condition that the offering was accompanied by true repentance, thereby moving the action on to a spiritual and ethical plane. Nevertheless, the high-priest entered the Holy of Holies to make expiation by censing and sprinkling the blood of the bullock on the mercy-seat and the altar 'to make atonement for the holy place, and because of the uncleanness of the children of Israel'. Their iniquities were then transferred to the goat selected for the desert demon, Azazel, as the 'sin-receiver'.

According to Ezekiel the sanctuary was to be cleansed twice a year on the first day of the first month, and on the first day of the seventh month.[140] This is the only mention of a twofold purification. In the post-exilic account of the Day of Atonement in the Book of Leviticus, the blood ritual which reached its climax on the tenth day of Tishri, three stages in the development of the rite can be detected. The first belongs to the middle of the fourth century B.C. after the time of Ezra, recorded in Leviticus xvi, 3, 5–10, describing the offering of a bullock for a sin-offering for himself and the rest of the priesthood, and a ram for a burnt offering. Then he had to 'set before Yahweh' two he-goats. Lots were cast upon them to determine which was to be the slain victim and which the 'scapegoat', or sin-receiver and driven forth to the desert to dispose of the uncleanness of the sanctuary and its servants. An elaborate cathartic ritual with detailed regulations about the censings, manipulation of the blood on the mercy-seat in the Holy of Holies and on the altar is described in the second much fuller account of what took place (11–28). First is recorded the offering of the bullock and the censings, together with the sprinkling of the mercy-seat seven times and the cleansing of the holy place and the altar. Then follows the expulsion ritual in connexion with the live goat, and the taking of the carcasses of the bull and the goat to be destroyed by fire outside the city. In conclusion a note was added (29–34a) explaining that the Day of Atonement was to be observed as a 'high Sabbath' during which the congregation of Israel should afflict their souls and do no manner of work.

Although the rite is only described in the post-exilic ritual (i.e. Leviticus xvi), and its spiritual interpretation in the Rabbinical literature, the methods employed for the cleansing of the temple, the priests and the people are so typical of primitive expiation, based on the conception of evil as a substantive pollution or miasma removable by sacrificial blood, censings, and lustrations, and transferable to an animal, that the ceremonial must go back to a very remote period. The fact that it was revived and re-introduced in the cultus at the Second Temple at Jerusalem as the instrument for giving spiritual expression to the conception of sin and atonement shows how deep-rooted it was in Hebrew tradition, and so strong was the association that the observance survived the destruction of the temple and its sacrificial worship in the Jewish liturgy, in which Yahweh who alone can forgive sin and pardon iniquity is besought to 'blot out our transgressions' and 'make our trespasses to pass away year by year, King over all the earth, who sanctified Israel and the Day of Atonement'.

CHAPTER VI

Indian Temples

INDO-IRANIAN CULTURE

THE IRANIAN HIGHLANDS geographically represent the natural position for a common home of the whole range of cultural achievements in the Ancient East in the fourth millennium B.C. In Elam a peasant culture flourished with a concentration of urban life in the third millennium, contemporary with that of Sumer, which seems to have been a reflection of a civilization developed in a more easterly region on the Iranian plateau.[1] This may have been the centre from which similar movements and influences radiated across the Zagros mountains into Mesopotamia, a route doubtless followed later by the Kassites, while groups of Indo-Europeans eventually passed through Iran to establish themselves as the Sanskrit-speaking Aryans in India. Another southward movement finally settled in Iran, and the entire migration was subsequently named Iranians. Traces of an identical ancient agricultural culture have been detected through Baluchistan and the Himalayas to India, and over the Mongolian plain to north and west China. In western Turkestan at Anau, east of the Caspian Sea, further evidence of another outpost of the same civilization has been produced on the alluvial land of Transcaspia, while in Baluchistan Indian pottery has been found in association with wares having Persian affinities.[2]

By 2500 B.C. commercial enterprise between the Euphrates and the valley of the Indus overland through Baluchistan must have been established, Mesopotamia, as we have seen, being the cradle-land of civilization in the latter half of the fourth millennium (the Uruk period), with temple accounts kept on clay tablets. Behind it lay the village society of the Iranian plateau, and while it was to Mesopotamia that the recently discovered Indus civilization looked very largely for its trade relations, the Iranian borderland and Baluchistan provided the source of its colonization and material culture. Thus, the pottery techniques of north and west India were akin to those of the self-contained peasant communities at Quetta, Nal, Kolwa, and the Zhob valley, and at Amru in Sind.[3]

THE INDUS CIVILIZATION

MOHENJO-DARO AND HARAPPA

It is now apparent as a result of the excavations that have been carried out since 1922 at Mohenjo-daro on the Indus river in Sind, and at Harappa on the Ravi, a tributary 400 miles to the north-east in the Punjab, that in north-west India a homogeneous urban civilization was established, unsurpassed by any contemporary urban culture in the Ancient East. Originally it must have occupied a much larger area than either Sumer or Egypt, and included

Fig. 34.   Plan of the excavations at Mohenjo-daro

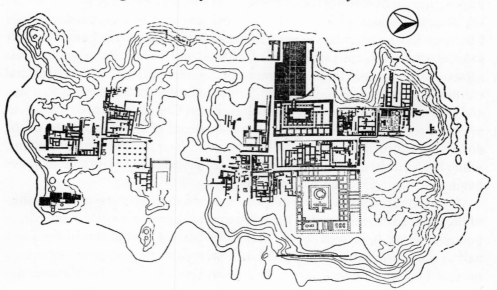

small agricultural towns in the Bahawalpur State, yet to be excavated. The fertile plains of Lärkana, between the Indus and the Kohisthan or Kirthar hills, in the absence of irrigation depended upon the annual inundation for their water supply, when the snow melted in summer or the rainfall was exceptionally heavy. At Mohenjo-daro some of the buildings were raised on platforms and artificial hills in order to place them out of the reach of the flood water, and an elaborate system of drainage had been devised partly probably on this account. Both Mohenjo-daro and Harappa were dominated by a citadel in the form of an artificial mound about 50 feet high upon which the sacred buildings and granaries were erected. It was here that the great bath of Mohenjo-daro stood, described by Sir John Marshall as part of a 'vast hydropathic establishment', with a series of cells and baths for the priests and two pillared halls. Adjacent was a building 230 by 78 feet, which may have been the residence of the high-priest or civic governor, or perhaps a college of priests. The great bath itself was approached by brick steps at the north and south, and a stairway led to an upper storey. On the verge situated on a high brick podium with ventilation passages was the state granary, while a small Buddhist *stupa* and monastery of the second century A.D. surmounted the mound.[4]

THE GREAT BATH OF MOHENJO-DARO

On the acropolis, which appears to have been a sacred hill, the principal structure was a huge bath with an overall measurement of 180 feet by 108 feet, erected in an open quadrangle built of burnt brick, with steps at the north and south leading down to the floor (39 feet by 23 feet) and enclosed with verandahs on its four sides. At the back three of them were rooms and galleries, one of which contained a well. In another room a stairway led to an upper storey, or roof, and at the south-west corner was a covered drain. Drains also descended from the superstructure. Behind the upper storey probably were rooms similar to those on the ground level and, judging from the quantities of ash and charcoal found there, built largely of wood. Subsequently the northern end was filled in solid, and further north were eight small bath rooms measuring 9½ feet by 6 feet, arranged in two rows on each side of a passage, along the middle of which was a drain. Each was paved and had a brick staircase leading apparently to an upper storey now destroyed. As they were so arranged as to make it very difficult for the occupants to see into the rooms from the outside, Mr Mackay, who was responsible for their excavation in 1927–8, suggests that they may have been cells designed for members of a priesthood engaged in a water cult.[5]

Some distance to the south of the stupa mound stood a large hall about 85 feet square, with paved aisles and unpaved strips about $3\frac{1}{2}$ feet wide between them. If Sir John Marshall is correct in thinking that benches originally stood along the strips comparable to those on which the monks sat in Buddhist rock-cut temples,[6] it is conceivable that the building was used for religious gatherings. On the other hand, it may equally well have been a civic hall. That next to it on the west was a similar rather smaller aisled construction suggestive of a place of assembly for some purpose or another. The nearest approach to a central sanctuary was the great bath and its adjuncts on and around the stupa mound some 60 feet above the lower city. It is unfortunate that it has not been possible to excavate beneath the stupa without giving offence to Buddhist religious feelings, as it is highly probable that it was erected there because of the inherent sanctity of the mound, going back perhaps to much earlier times. The practice of constructing places of worship on elevated sites has remained a permanent feature in India. So prevalent, in fact, has it been that it is the exception rather than the rule for a mountain or hill not to have a shrine upon its summit.[7] Beneath the courtyard of the stupa the relics of a building have been revealed by trial trenches, and it is by no means unlikely that they are those of an ancient temple standing on an artificial hill about 20 feet high composed of mud-brick like the other platforms. Thus, Mackay has called attention to the remains of a court with massive walls north of the alleged temple, in a position analogous to that of a similar court at Ur between the quays and the House of Nannar where it is possible that the temple revenues may have been paid.[8]

As Mohenjo-daro had such an excellent water supply from brick-lined wells and many of the largest houses had private bath rooms, the great bath on the citadel would seem to have been a sanctuary rather than a hydro-pathic establishment as Sir John Marshall has suggested. It was certainly the most imposing structure in the city, and the large straggling building closely connected with it may have been either the residence of the governor or the administrative civic centre, unless it was the sacerdotal college for those engaged in the elaborate water cult that was practised on the stupa mound. It is, in fact, not unreasonable to regard it as the prototype of the water worship and ritual bathing that became such a prominent feature in the sacred streams of Vedic India and in modern Hinduism. While it is hardly likely that further excavation will reveal anything at all comparable to the great temples of Mesopotamia and the Fertile Crescent, the proportions of the great bath and its superstructure, its elevation, construction and adjuncts leave little room for doubt about its importance and significance as a cult centre in the Indus civilization.

THE GODDESS CULT

It was not, however, only in association with water worship that sacred edifices were constructed in India and their cultus maintained. Thus, the prevalence of female figurines of the Mother-goddess type, either nudes or with a wide girdle, loincloth and necklace, and a fan-shaped head-dress with pannier-like projections varying in size, suggest that the Great Mother was widely venerated in Sind and the Punjab, notably in the urban centres where terracotta statuettes abounded, some in postures indicative of a ritual dance.[9] To enhance their life-giving properties most of them were painted over with red slip or wash like many Hindu figures today, and as Marshall recognized when he first brought them to light at Mohenjo-daro, there is good reason to think that they represent a goddess with attributes very similar to those of the Great Mother-goddess: 'Lady of Heaven and the special patroness of women'.[10] It is not improbable that, as in India today, they were a prominent feature in the dwellings and streets of the ancient Indus cities, preserved in a niche in the wall of the houses, presiding over childbirth and domestic affairs. Indeed, it may well be that some of the more pretentious structures were shrines erected in the goddess' honour, though in their present ruined condition it is impossible to determine their precise nature, purpose or equipment.

Again, whether or not the goddess or goddesses who controlled the mystery of birth and generation had a male counterpart as her son and/or spouse cannot be ascertained from the available evidence with any degree of certainty. The recurrence on seals of nude male horned figures, associated with the *pipal*-tree and cult animals, side by side with the Mother-goddess, suggests that some such relationship occurred between the two deities as elsewhere in the ancient Near East. On one seal a horned figure is kneeling. Behind is a goat with a human face and a row of seven females, each wearing a sprig on the head and a pigtail behind, but without horns.[11] In another similar scene the male figure has three faces and is flanked with an elephant and a tiger on his right, and a rhinoceros and buffalo on his left. Below are two deer with horns turned towards the dais on which the god is seated with his heels together and arms outstretched in a *yoga* posture. On his chest are triangular necklaces, and on his head a pair of horns with a tall head-dress between them. A projection at the end of the waist-band might be a phallus.[12] Both the form and symbolism indicate that here is portrayed a prototype of the Hindu god Shiva in his aspect of Pasupati, the Lord of the Beasts and Prince of Yoga, who is represented in India in this manner, sometimes with five faces.

While scenes of this nature are of common occurrence on seals and amulets in this region, male gods are not prevalent in the Harappa civilization, and it is relatively seldom that they are brought into conjunction with the Goddess in the iconography. In pottery they are rare and usually are entirely nude and bare-headed, whereas those of the female deity are abundant, though it is uncertain whether she is intended to be represented as a virgin or as a mother-goddess, the consort of the male god. Some of the pottery figures representing gods in animal form are in a very battered condition, and may have come from shrines or temples, whose cultus must have been concentrated upon the processes of birth and generation since the symbolism (e.g. the horned female and male gods, the pipal-tree and supporting animals) has this significance. Moreover, in addition to these figures and scenes a number of limestone conical phallic emblems, *linga*, frequently occur in conjunction with their female *yoni* rings.[13] These iconic fertility representations, so very prominent and deeply laid in the worship of Shiva, are unquestionably phalli and their female counterparts, the yoni or vulva, brought together to indicate the union of the two organs, as, for example, in the yoni bases of linga. Thus, a conventionalized linga in yellow sandstone at Harappa with finely cut coils and necklaces may have had a yoni base, and six occurred in an earthenware jar with small pieces of shell, a unicorn seal, stone pestles and a stone palette. Some miniature conical baetyls have a kind of ring round the body which has been regarded as a possible yoni.[14]

SAKTISM

It would seem, therefore, that the essential elements in what later became known as Saktism in Hindu India as well as in the institution of Yoga, had emerged in the third millennium B.C. in the Harappa civilization. The term *sakti* denoting 'generation', 'power' and 'energy', was always associated with the male deity, Shiva. Nevertheless, he was regarded as an androgynous creator who produced his own consort from the female side of his nature, the one quiescent and the other active, his female energy (*sakti*), usually personified as his wife, inseparable from him and joining with him in the creation, sustaining but sometimes destroying the natural order. Attention, however, was first concentrated on the maternal aspects of generation, with or without the aid and intervention of a male procreator. The primary function was the promotion of fecundity and the guarding of the sacred portal through which life entered the world. In Indo-European tradition this found expression in the conception of the Sky-father (Dyaus Pitar) and the Earth-mother (Prithivi), but the phallic element was foreign to Vedism. This was introduced into Hindusim from pre-Aryan sources, going back to the Harappa civilization where the deeper and more mystical traits in the conception of Shiva appear to have their origin, however crudely these may have been rendered at first in their Dravidian milieu. It is not surprising that they found a prominent place in the household shrines, and it would seem that they also presided over the village and the city as the cult developed, becoming the centre of veneration in the local temples.

In its higher manifestations the duality in unity was the underlying principle in Saktism, and when the worship of the Mother-goddesses received Brahmanical sanction they were personified as manifestations of sakti as the consort of Shiva. Eventually, at a still higher level, sakti was interpreted as the eternal reproductive principle, *prakriti*, united with the eternal male principle, *purusha*, in the generation of the gods and the universe, Shiva being pure spirit and assuming a body to render himself perceptible. The union of the male and female principles, symbolized by the combination of linga and yoni emblems, was a characteristic feature of Saivite shrines. The sacred bull Nandi as the attendant upon Shiva was also depicted in Saivite temples as the guardian of the shrine, and with the linga remained the principal emblem of the cult, the linga being regarded as the symbol of the Ultimate Reality of the evolution and involution of the universe.[15] The original cult objects in becoming mystic symbols, and the ritual actions performed in the shrines and temples in relation to them, have been re-interpreted as allegories embodying spiritual realities, though among the unsophisticated the more sordid aspects of Saktism often have survived and degenerated into unbridled licentiousness.[16]

In Saiva temples the Vedic god worshipped has been Shiva-Rudra, 'the auspicious Rudra', who in the Aryan Rig-veda was invoked as at once benign and destructive, feared for his vengeance upon human beings, their cattle and homesteads, wrought by his storms and forest fires.[17] Identified with the post-Vedic Shiva, Rudra had his abode on mountains, armed with bows and arrows, and wielding the thunderbolt and the lightning shaft. Representing the destructive agency of the thunderstorm he became increasingly feared as malevolent in spite of his beneficence as a healer, because of his association with the mountains whence storms were always liable to wreak havoc. Therefore, the old storm-god Rudra, the father of the Maruts, when he was absorbed by Shiva was worshipped and invoked in his dual capacity as the master of life and death, and at the same time as the first principle of all that exists, sitting enthroned on the fabulous Mount Kailasa, the Indian equivalent of Olympus, surrounded by innumerable gods and spirits.

HINDU TEMPLES

THE KAILASA TEMPLE AT ELLORA

The Kailasa temple, a magnificent rock-cut shrine at Ellora in Aurangabad district north-west of Hyderabad state in the Deccan, was hewn out of the solid rock of the hillside to a length of 164 feet and a height of 96 feet. A rectangular pit was dug from 50 to 100 feet in depth, 160 feet in width and 280 feet in length. In the centre the most impressive of all the Dravidian rock-cut monuments and cave-sanctuaries was constructed and at its completion, between A.D. 757 and 783, it constituted the climax of Indian temple construction. Then it comprised a vast monolithic structure extending over an area comparable to that of the Parthenon in Athens, quarried out of the mountain as a complete whole, purporting to be a replica of the Himalayan sanctuary of Shiva on Mount Kailasa. While it displays the main features characteristic of Hindu temples, and bears considerable resemblance to the much smaller Vurupaksha temple at Pattadakal near Balami, which was also dedicated to Shiva (*c.* A.D. 740) with its terraced roof above the sanctuary, the Kailasa temple is in fact unique.

Approached by an entrance gateway with a porch containing the shrine of the sacred bull Nandi resting on two elephants, and, as in Egyptian temples, flanked by two lofty columns, the courtyard is surrounded with cloisters and preceded by a large square porch supported by sixteen pillars. The three main buildings and the outer gateway are connected by a bridge. Behind the colonnaded terraced roof is the central shrine, or *vimana*, 'the vehicle of the gods', with its stately tower in three tiers surmounted by a cupola rising to a height of 95 feet. Here Shiva dwells as a giant linga in the innermost sanctuary, placed with the rest of the buildings on a podium 25 feet high, giving the appearance of their standing on an upper storey above the courtyard approached by steps. The superstructure is heavily moulded and a frieze of sculptured elephants and lions adorns the sides of the central space. Around the sanctum are five smaller shrines with niches containing statues of gods on the exterior, just as the columns at the entrance bear the ensign of Shiva. All these elements are Dravidian in their decoration and architectural features, representing the final phase of rock-architecture in India as it appeared in the seventh century A.D.[18]

THE DEVELOPMENT OF THE HINDU TEMPLE

From the destruction of the Indus civilization and its cities by the Aryan invaders in the middle of the second millennium B.C., any attempt at temple building which hitherto may have occurred in Sind and the Punjab came to an end abruptly for about a thousand years. The Indo-European-speaking Vedic tribes from east of the Caspian Sea were essentially a pastoral people, who when they penetrated into India from the north-west lived in huts in their villages, often of the beehive pattern with a wooden structure and a circular wall of bamboo, roofed with leaves in the form of a dome, or thatched with grass. These were reproduced in the rock-cut Bihar caves, as, for example, in that called Sudama in the Barabar hills of the Asoka period (*c.* 250 B.C.), consisting of two apartments, one 32 feet 9 inches long and 19 feet 6 inches broad, the other beyond it nearly circular and measuring 19 feet 11 inches by 19 feet. In front the roof hangs down as though covered with thatch.[19] As these huts became oval with a barrel roof they were arranged round a square courtyard, but to what extent these dwellings constituted the prototype of the subsequent temples and shrines cannot be determined since there is no available archaeological and literary data of the Vedic or pre-Buddhist periods. If any temples existed they must have been of wood, the use of stone not having been introduced until the reign of Asoka (273–232 B.C.).

The ravages of time, and of the Hun and Muslim raiders, have left little or nothing to throw light on the problem until the small Hindu shrines at Sanchi, Gran and Tigawa, and the Buddha temples began to make their appearance in the Gupta period (A.D. 320–550), when Hinduism and Buddhism were approximating to each other, and the Vedic gods and their worship were giving place to the Hindu Trimurti, Brahma, Vishnu and Shiva, under the influence of the Bhakti movement and the short-lived triumph of Buddhism in India. It was from then onwards that the magnificent lavishly decorated temples for which India has become world-famous were erected, many of which, mainly in the centre and the south, have survived the wreckage wrought by iconoclasm in the seventeenth and eighteenth centuries. In the north such was the havoc that for the most part Hindu temples tend to be small and undistinguished in spite of the fact that it was along the banks of the Ganges that many of the splendid sacred cities and temples hitherto flourished. Even at Benares the shrines are chiefly in the bazaar and along the river.

In both the Dravidian style in the south and the Indo-Aryan or nagara architecture in the north, there has been a uniformity in the general plan of temple construction. The *vimana*, or central sanctuary, in which in a square cella, or 'womb-house', the cult-image or symbol is enshrined, is surmounted with a pyramidal roof (*sikhara*) containing one or more storeys. In front of the doorway, usually on the eastern side, is a pavilion, or pillared hall (*mandapa*), for the worshippers, and between the wall of the cella and the outer wall is a verandah as a processional passage (*pradaksina*). At first the mandapa was often detached from the rest of the sanctuary and equipped with priests' dwellings or tanks for ablutions, as for instance in the rock-cut temple at Mammallapvram on the coast near Madras, built about A.D. 700. Subsequently, they were brought together as a single building with a vestibule between them, the cella, mandapa and storeyed tower being the three component parts in all Hindu and Jain temples. To these were added a porch (*ardha-mandapa*), and a transept on each side of the central hall (*maha-mandapa*), as in the great Kandariya temple at Khajuraha in central India, erected about A.D. 1000 and elevated on a terrace like the stupas and Mesopotamian citadels. In this way they were resolved into a co-ordinated unit architecturally in a succession of superstructures, entrance porch and separate pyramidal roof and lofty spire over the sanctum.

The wedge-shaped gate-pyramids or *gopuras*, in the stone walls, corresponding to the Egyptian pylons, are a distinguishing feature, and are adorned with mythological scenes. At Srirangam the seventeenth-century temple buildings, decorated in the most florid baroque (*vijayanagar*) style, are seven enclosures leading to the central shrine with a central enclosure full of temples, porches, and halls, and very high gopuras in the walls. In the last phase of Dravidian architecture the temples, numbering nearly thirty, have become virtually a city, that at Madura being a double temple with two separate sanctuaries, dedicated respectively to Shiva and his consort Minakshi, surrounded by nine immense elaborately carved and coloured gopuras at the cardinal points, decorated with crude stucco ornamentation depicting grotesque mythological figures.

The central shrine is enclosed within a series of covered courts and colonnades consisting of a hall, a vestibule and the cella crowned with a small tower (*sikhara*). The second sanctuary to the south is much smaller (225 feet by 150 feet) with only two gopuras, between which is the cupola of the shrine. At the base is the rectangular 'Pool of the Golden Lilies', 165 feet by 120 feet, for ritual ablutions, surrounded by a pillared cloister. On the northeast corner of the outer court a hypostyle hall 240 feet by 250 feet, called the 'Hall of a thousand pillars', was added in A.D. 1560 in the reign of Viswanath, the first ruler of the Nayak dynasty. This had a central aisle with a double row of fantastically carved columns on either side, and a shrine dedicated to Sabhapati. In the first half of the next century (1626–1633) another large reception hall, measuring 330 feet by 105 feet, was erected outside the main enclosure. It had a nave and two aisles with four rows of carved pillars, used perhaps as a temporary abode of the god who presided over a seasonal festival. Thus, as in so many Dravidian temples, the constructions grew up in ever increasing complexity and elaboration around the shrine which originally was the centre of worship.

SHRINE AND TEMPLE CULTUS

It has to be remembered that, for the Hindu, worship is and has always been primarily an individual experience. The twice-born members of the three higher castes perform their religious duties five times daily in their own homes as a private affair without the aid and intervention of a brahmin. Even when temples were erected on a grand scale it was not for purposes of congregational worship according to prescribed liturgical patterns. Each devotee is perfectly free to follow his own devotions addressed to the particular cult and its deity of whom he happens to be a votary (e.g. Saivas, Vaishnavas, Shaktas, Smartas). Indeed, the same individual may practise a variety of forms of worship according to his requirements addressed to the appropriate departmental divinities, sectarianism being completely devoid of exclusive claims upon its adherents. Every village has its shrines and images at which offerings of flowers, perfumes, fruits, leaves, grasses and water are made including, on occasions, animal sacrifices to the dreaded Kali and the local gods. But this does not involve congregational worship or a priesthood to serve the shrines. Nevertheless, in addition to the daily domestic devotions starting before sunrise and continuing until after the evening meal, special collective observances are held on major festivals and at birth, initiation, marriage and death, and in connexion with yogic disciplines. These may be celebrated by household priests in accordance with the sectarian practices prescribed for the occasions in the presence of the cult-image or symbol, often enshrined in a room set apart for the purpose, or at the village shrine.

In the temples dedicated to different deities much the same pattern is followed by the priests, though the personal *rites de passage* are performed in private houses. In fact, in the north and in most of the villages the temples are too small for large-scale public worship. It is mainly in the evening when an elaborate lamp ceremony is held in conjunction with the clothing of the image for the night that the laity attend in person, especially during the week in which the Annual Festival in honour of its principal deity is celebrated. They also assemble in considerable numbers at each of the six seasons into which the year is divided—the summer, rainy, autumnal, winter, dewy and spring seasons—and the festivals set apart for the worship of the different deities in the lunar calendar. Similarly, pilgrimages to holy places have always made a popular appeal, especially to the great ancient shrines honoured and renowned for their sanctity and the sacred persons and events for which they are famous (e.g. Benares on the Ganges, Dwaraka and Mathura, the capital and birthplace of Krishna, Ayodhya in the kingdom of Rama, Hardwar where the Ganges rises, Ujjain, the centre of linga worship, and Conjeaveram in the south sacred to Durga, Vishnu and Shiva). They may be undertaken in fulfilment of vows, in times of stress and misfortune, in acknowledgment of benefits received, or for other personal and private reasons, besides the observance of festivals.

Apart from these special occasions, a daily ceremonial routine is practised in temple worship similar to that in Ancient Egypt, beginning with a lamp rite when the god is awakened at the last eighth of the night with music, prayers and the recitation of sacred texts. After sunrise the cult-image, or in Shiva temples the linga, is bathed and then anointed with sandal paste and venerated. At noon, after a siesta again in the afternoon, food offerings are made to it, sometimes accompanied by an offering of fire. At dusk the lamp ceremonies begin and are repeated intermittently until the god or his symbol is dressed and laid to rest for the night. This daily routine is considerably elaborated in festivals when thousands of pilgrims flock to the temples, as they do also to sit at the feet of a renowned *guru* or pundit. The guru is well versed in the Puranas and epics and is capable of holding the interest and arousing the emotions of his audience, sometimes to the pitch of religious frenzy. Recourse is also made to centres of learning such as Benares by scholars, philosophers and mystics for the study of Vedantic and Yogic theology, metaphysics and law. In recent years this has been done largely in the *ashrams*, 'hermitages', founded by outstanding spiritual teachers and reformers (Rabidranath Tagore, Srii Ramana Maharshi, Ram, Mohun Roy, etc.).

In the later developments of Hindu worship the religion of the Vedas acquired an anthropomorphic guise which found expression in the toilet ceremonies in the temples, the cult-image being treated as a royal personage rather like the Pharaoh in Egypt. The worship of the greater gods, however, has been confined mainly to the higher castes while the Bhakti devotional movement, centred in Shiva and Vishnu and his avatars as personal incarnational deities has made a popular appeal among the less sophisticated classes. In spite of its anti-brahmanical tendencies it has been a powerful influence in the Hindu renaissance, the Bhagavad-gita remaining the most popular and widespread of all the Hindu scriptures throughout the present era.

THE SATRUNJAYA JAIN TEMPLE-CITY

It was, however, largely as a result of the establishment of Buddhism as the official religion of the empire of Asoka in the third century B.C. that structural temples emerged from the cave-temples giving rise to the brahmanical edifices. Thus, those at Ter and Chezarla in the Deccan, and the Lad Khan temple at Aihole in the Bijapur district, were modelled on Buddhist and Hindu cave-chapels, the apse becoming the cella, and the cult-image replaced by the stupa. As Buddhism and Jainism both arose in India as sects within Hinduism they reacted on each other to some extent, though the cultural importance of Buddhism was incomparably greater. Nevertheless, the Jains were prolific as temple-builders, erecting cities with hundreds of shrines of different periods and design, notably in western India. At Satrunjaya, for example, at an elevation of nearly 2,000 feet, more than five hundred Jain temples have been grouped in separate enclosures round a central sanctuary with elaborate sculptured decoration and images of Rishabha, the first of the twenty-four Tirthankara venerated as the first king, ascetic and head of the Jain community. Similarly, at a greater elevation of about 3,664 feet on the hill of Girnar (sacred to Nemi, or Atishtanemi, the twenty-second Tirthankara), another group of temples occurs of which the largest is the Neminatha, standing in a rectangular courtyard 190 feet by 130 feet surrounded by pillared cloisters containing more than seventy cells, each with a cross-legged image of Tirthankara and an enclosure in front of them. The temple consists of a hall 43 feet square with two porches (*mandapas*) and an open space in the centre, constituting the nave, surrounded by a colonnade forming the aisles, while the cella had a central turreted tower and contained a large image of Nemi.[20]

THE TEMPLE OF VIMALA SAHA

In much the same style two Jain temples were erected in white marble on Mount Abu in Rajputana and dedicated to Neminatha. The older of them built by a wealthy banker in A.D. 1031 and named after him as Vimala Saha, was a rather simpler structure with no particular exterior architectural features. Standing within a rectangular walled area surrounded by cells with statues of Tirthankaras and other Jina forming a courtyard measuring 145 feet by 95 feet is the cruciform temple (98 feet by 42 feet) screened by a double arcade of pillars. On the east side is a domed portico facing which is a pavilion, supported by six pillars and ornamented with a design of the Jain holy mountain in the centre, and containing two statues of elephants on which formerly were seated representations of members of the Vimala family in procession to the temple. In the courtyard is an open pillared portico and vestibule with a fine dome, beyond which is a shrine having a pyramidal roof (*sikhara*) and a statue of one of the Tirthankaras.[21] The sculptured decoration of the dome of the nave and its pillars is a remarkable achievement, whatever view may be taken of its aesthetic qualities and architectural deficiencies. The second marble temple with its triple structure built by two brothers who were also bankers, Tejahpala and Vestupala, in A.D. 1230 is similar in design and plan, and together they show the construction and elaborate ornamentation of the Jain temple at its peak, even if Satrunjaya is more famous.

The wealth bestowed upon temple-building and its iconography is an indication of the social position of the Jain community which was out of all proportion to their numerical strength. They never, however, enjoyed imperial patronage like the Buddhists, though in the Deccan they had great influence, Jainism becoming virtually the state religion at Cholan and Pandyan. But being essentially an ascetic movement in origin and purpose they failed to make a popular appeal or to secure the patronage of the court, and with the revival of Hindusim after the disintegration of the Maurya empire in the last century B.C., it was mainly in a few centres where they retained their position, and in the shrines on remote hills in eastern and western India that their temples continued to flourish. Elsewhere the temples either fell into disuse and decay, or were converted into Hindu sanctuaries. Nevertheless, this enabled the Jains to concentrate their resources on those that survived, often in most picturesque places, and to adorn them with excessive ornamentation regardless of cost and labour.[22]

BUDDHIST TEMPLES

While Buddhism enjoyed immense popularity during the reign of Asoka in the third century B.C., like Jainism it was never the predominant religion in India. From time to time it flourished in different parts of the sub-continent but Hinduism remained in possession throughout. Nevertheless, such was the significance of Gautama the Buddha after he had attained enlightenment beneath the pipal-tree at Bodhi Gaya, and had 'set the wheel of the Dharma rolling' that traditional sites connected with his life, death and mortal remains were rapidly established. Thus, the Deer Park at Benares was the scene of his first sermon to the five Jain ascetics in which he enunciated the Three Noble Truths and the Eightfold Path to end the misery of existence and to secure the attainment of the passionless peace of *parinirvana*; there the Mahabodhi temple was erected. The distribution among his disciples of his cremated remains after his death and their enshrinement in stupas, or *dagobas*, in many parts of India, gave rise to shrines which became the centres of prolonged disputes. Everywhere in the states of Kosala and Magadha, where he travelled far and wide for forty-six years, he was claimed to have left footprints in the soil. So numerous in fact, were the places which could boast some association with the Buddha or possession of his relics, that the land became peppered with circular dome-shaped mounds of earth and stone elaborately carved and decorated with symbols (e.g. the Wheel of the Law, the parasol of sovereignty) and allegedly containing his ashes.

THE STUPAS

The stupa was a monumental tumulus built either to enshrine the relics of the Buddha or of a Buddhist sage, or to commemorate a sacred site. In the modern vernacular it is called *tope* or *chaitiya* (funeral pyre, sanctuary, or sacred place).

It seems to have been a particular form of the barrow type of tomb, such as that erected in Kercado in Brittany,[23] built of loose stones with a retaining circular wall round the base and surmounted by a monolith in the centre. Although stupas are essentially a feature characteristic of Buddhist sites, Asoka being said to have erected the fabulous number of eighty-four thousand in three years, they were not confined in India entirely to the movement. The Jains, for instance, employed them, and conical mounds and wooden structures of this nature were erected over the remains of chieftains prior to the rise of Buddhism. Nevertheless, stupas in the strict sense of the term seem to be of Buddhist origin, and it is not improbable that it was Asoka who introduced the practice of building them in stone instead of in wood, and of setting up sacred pillars near ancient funerary monuments to consecrate them by investing them with special sanctity through association with Buddhist relics and events. When they were visited by pilgrims it was to the stupa, as the symbol of the Buddha, that veneration was paid.

The general plan of the structure is relatively simple. Usually it stands on a platform, either square or circular, supporting a hemispherical dome (*garbha*) in the form of a cone. In the centre a square stone pillar is embedded upright in the top over which is a square stone box, or *tee*, covered by a series of thin slabs, each projecting over the one below it. Upon the centre of the tee stands a circular drum, or 'fence', decorated with statues, a parasol towering over the whole edifice, which sometimes has been hung with garlands and gold ornaments. The casket containing the relics has generally been placed in the tee when this has not been a solid block. Its sides usually are covered or moulded in the form of a railing, which doubtless originally was of wood round the parasol. Now sometimes it has been covered by a corbelled roof supported on pillars inside the rail, the tee having become a square house with a railed balcony and windows, and an upper storey, comprising a closed shrine for the cremated remains of the Buddha or of a renowned teacher or sage, just as barrows often have been surmounted by a chapel, for instance, at San Michel or at La Hougue Bie in Jersey.

THE GREAT STUPA AT SANCHI AND THE BHILSA TOPES

The most famous and extensive group of stupas in India is that situated in the Bhopal state near the city of Vidisa or Bhilsa. There are five or six groups comprising nearly thirty examples of 'topes', the chief of which is at Sanchi, erected in the first instance by Asoka in the third century B.C. and subsequently developed during the Indian Middle Ages. In its final form it consists of a massive structure of brick and stone, 120 feet in diameter with a height of 54 feet rising from a stone plinth and surrounded by a stone railing with four highly ornamental gateways. As it now stands there is a lofty terrace (*medhi*), 16 feet from the ground, which formerly was a processional way reached by a double flight of steps (*sopana*) on the southern side. At the ground level was a second ambulatory passage, enclosed by a massive stone balustrade (*vedika*) with entrances at the cardinal points, each with its carved gateway (*torana*). The entire building was then faced with hammer-dressed dry stones, and the crest of the dome was surrounded by a square railing enclosing a pedestal (*harmika*) supporting a triple parasol (*yashti*).

This elaborate structure has clearly undergone very considerable development from the original small brick stupa erected by Asoka with a polished monolithic column of sandstone surmounted by a lion capital on its southern

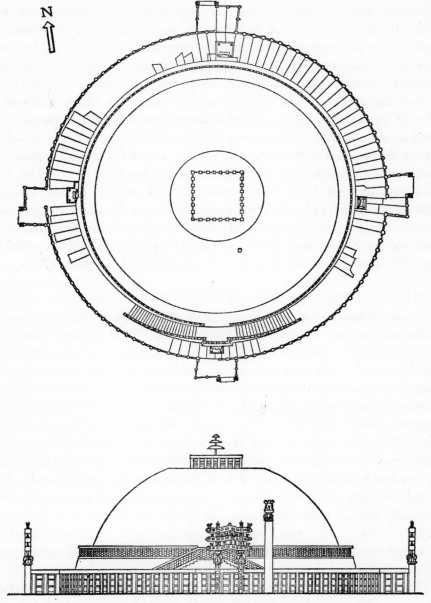

Fig. 35.   Plan and elevation of the Great Stupa, Sanchi

side. It was enlarged to nearly twice its previous size during the next century amid all the confusion of the fall of the Sungas about 70 B.C., and stone railings, gateways and the third balustrade surrounding the sacred parasol added, for it was recognized as a monument of great sanctity and a centre of the religious life of the local Sangha, although it was not connected with incidents in the career of the Buddha or of his disciples. However, the legends and great events in his life and previous births as they are recorded in the Jatakas, are graphically depicted in the reliefs on the pillars and architraves of the gateways, together with the symbol of the Wheel of the Law on elephants or lions. Around the Great Stupa a number of subsidiary sanctuaries were erected from the third century B.C. to the twelfth century A.D. Stupa II, on a ledge on the western side of the hill, is a relic-shrine of much the same dimensions and design, containing the remains of two contemporaries of King Asoka. It may be rather earlier than the Great Stupa, being devoid of a gateway, and the reliefs on the balustrade at the base portraying similar events and scenes and symbols are of primitive and cruder workmanship; these are in an excellent state of preservation, in spite of the destruction caused during the excavations in the last century. Stupa III discovered by General Cunningham, about 50 yards north-east of the Great Stupa at the edge of the plateau, was smaller (49 feet 6 inches in diameter and about 27 feet in height), but almost identical in design, with two caskets in a chamber in the centre of the structure in which the relics of Mahamogalana and Sariputra, two of the disciples of Gautama, were deposited.[24] The stairway and terrace balustrades were similar to those of the Great Stupa in style and decoration, dating probably from the first century B.C., but having only one gateway. An elaborately carved torana on the south was added in the first century A.D. completing the edifice with its dome, railing and umbrella. None of the topes in the considerable Bhilsa group is likely to be earlier than the middle of the third century B.C., or later than the first century A.D.[25]

SARNATH

The best preserved stupa is that marking the spot where Gautama preached his first sermon to the five ascetics in the Deer Park at Sarnath near Benares in Bengal. As the birthplace of the movement Sarnath became the centre of Buddhist activities for a thousand years, and at one stage provided accommodation for some fifteen hundred monks and nuns. Here Asoka erected a number of monuments, most of which as usual have perished through wanton destruction or neglect. The circular Dharmakaya stupa, for example, after having been repaired and enlarged until the twelfth century A.D., was ultimately cleared away by brick-hunters in the eighteenth century. The ruins, which cover an extensive area, are of numerous edifices, ranging from a magnificent temple containing a life-sized brass image of the Buddha turning the Wheel of the Law, a stone pillar about 70 feet high (an object of great veneration) to the Dhamek stupa on a stone platform 93 feet in diameter rising to a height of 150 feet above ground level, situated at the south-east corner of the site in the centre of the monastery area.[26] In the lower part were niches designed apparently for figures of the Buddha, with a beautiful decorated panel of geometric patterns below, encircling the 'tope'. This probably was a later addition, perhaps of the eleventh century A.D., as was the upper part of the tower, neither of which was ever completed.

The buildings, however, continued to flourish until Benares was sacked in 1193 and Sarnath was forsaken. Only the broken stump of the pillar remains, but the lion capital is in the museum near by. To the east lie the ruins of a cylindrical temple called the Main Shrine with chapels on the north, south, and west side, and a portico forming the entrance to the shrine on the east side. This may have been the edifice mentioned by the Chinese pilgrims Fa-hien and Hiuen Tsang in A.D. 640, since it occupied the central position and probably was erected in the Gupta period about A.D. 500, or earlier.[27] Its importance is indicated by the shrines and monasteries which were grouped round it, and by its iconographic sculpture.

MAHABODHI TEMPLE AT BODHI-GAYA

In front of the Bodhi-tree under which Gautama is said to have attained his enlightenment is the much-restored Mahabodhi temple at Bodhi-Gaya which now consists of a plinth 50 feet wide and 20 feet high as the base of a straight-edged pyramidal tower 60 feet in width and rising to a height of 160 feet and surmounted by a stupa with a pedestal (*harmika*) and pointed finial. At each corner of the terrace is a turret, introduced probably under Burmese influence in the fourteenth century, which is a replica in miniature of the main tower. In the surface of the spire are a number of niches for images of the Buddha. According to Hiuen Tsang who visited the temple in the seventh century A.D., it was constructed of blue bricks covered with *chunam*, and the niches contained gold figures. On the eastern front approached by a flight of steps and enclosed by a railing entered through a torana from the east, was a large statue of Gautama preaching his famous sermon. In the courtyard is a lion pillar and a votive stupa erected by votaries to serve the purposes of reliquaries. On each side stand huge figures of *bodhisattvas* as at Sarnath, and along the northern side is a promenade (*chankama*) called the 'jewel shrine of the walk', along which the Buddha was alleged to have walked during his contemplation. To the west is the Bodhi-tree, the spot on which he is supposed to have sat at the time of his illumination being marked on a slab of red sandstone.

KUSINAGARA

The passing of the Buddha into the state of parinirvana in his eightieth year (*c.* 480 B.C.) occurred at Kusinagara, a village in the Gorakhpur district of the Uttar Pradesh, about 120 miles north-east of Benares. There, after having eaten tainted pork, he died in a grove of Sal-trees surrounded by his disciples to whom he gave his last charge. A dispute arose over his remains which were divided among his followers in eight portions and enshrined in stupas in many places. At Kusinagara the stupa bore an inscription in the script of the fifth century A.D. denoting the commemoration of the 'great decease', and around it monasteries and shrines were established as great numbers of pilgrims made their way to the hallowed spot from the fifth to the twelfth centuries A.D. Eventually the main stupa was enlarged by Burmese votaries. No one can be sure which of these, if any, were built on the stupa said to have been erected there by Asoka, or, indeed, whether such a chaiiya ever existed. The earliest now known belong to the Gupta period, though below them may lie sacred edifices of greater antiquity. When Kusinara was visited by Fa-hien and Hiuen Tsang it was in a state of ruin, and subsequent excavations have thrown little light on the problem.

NALANDA

In Bihar a long sequence of sacred buildings, dating from the sixth to the twelfth century A.D. has been excavated at Nalanda, the modern village of Bargaon, extending over a wide area. Here was an important monastic centre, dating perhaps from the time of Asoka, though none of the existing ruins are earlier than the Gupta period. Then it was a flourishing centre of

Mahayana Buddhist learning when it was visited by Hiuen Tsang, having, as he said, no less than ten thousand monks, some of whom obtained a widespread reputation as scholars and teachers. Among the series of temples and parallel rows of monasteries the main temple was rebuilt seven times. In its general structure it consisted of a court with rectangular projections at the four corners, doubtless used as shrines, together with the remains of votive stupas. At the top of the seven successive buildings was a small shrine approached by a long flight of steps. The monasteries were storeyed structures with a central court flanked by a row of cells and a verandah. A huge stupa stands in the middle court in the south-western flank with a number of miniature votive stupas, the four corner towers being decorated with stucco figures, surrounded by rings of stupas. Little, however, remains even of the ruins in this extensive site, though some of the sculpture and epigraphic material have been preserved in the museum, including a number of the seals belonging to the monastery and the contemporary kings of the Gupta and Maukhari dynasties.

On a raised platform at the east end of the courtyard stood the great statue, either of the Buddha or of the goddess Tara, near a beautifully decorated *vihara* (monastery) 200 feet high where Buddha was said to have resided. The chief shrine, however, must have been the Great Stupa at the south-west corner which unquestionably claimed to possess the relics of Gautama. It was at the height of its power and prestige in the seventh century A.D. as the principal centre of Buddhist learning, with innumerable sacred places surrounding the main structure. Indeed, Nalanda was to central India what Cluny and Clairvaux were to France, and its influence in Buddhist lands no less. After its decline at the end of seventh century it continued as a centre of Tantric Buddhism throughout the domination of the Pala dynasty until the Mohammedan conquest in A.D. 1197.

ROCK-CUT CAVE-TEMPLES

The Buddhist monasteries, whether great or small, were arranged on the same general plan with residential cells on four sides of a quadrangle, often reconstructed over and over again, but always retaining their primitive, relatively simple structure. The monks were in the habit of retiring to viharas (monasteries) excavated in remote hillsides, either during the rainy season, or for more permanent sojourn in seclusion. Asoka constructed cave-temples for these purposes in the Barabar hills near Gaya, with polished walls, excellent carvings in relief and paintings, following the usual plan of a central hall with cells and chambers grouped round it and supplied with water from a cistern. It was, however, the Theravada Buddhists who were the chief constructors of this form of settlement from the end of the second century B.C. to the second century A.D.

KARLI

Thus, at Karli on the road from the Deccan to the coast by way of the Bhor Ghaut, in the village of Vehargaon (*Vihara-grama*), one of the finest examples and best preserved chaitiya halls has survived. The apsidal 'nave' is 124 feet long, 45 feet high, and 46 feet wide with a row of thirty-seven columns, octagonal in form in the apse and massive pillars with bell-capitals in the aisles, surmounted by figures on elephants, horses and tigers. These support a vaulted roof with teak ribs and over the apsidal end a rock-cut stupa with a wooden umbrella and a reliquary at the top. In front of the porch is a massive stone column surmounted by a lion capital and an elaborate, decorated façade with an arched window and a gallery, together with two entrances leading to the hall and the aisles respectively. The windows on the side walls of the verandah diminish in size as they rise higher, and later, under Mahayana influence, figures of the Buddha were introduced.

Fig. 36.   Plan of the Karli rock temples

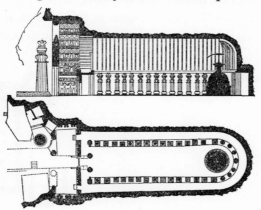

AJANTA

In the volcanic rocks of the Ajanta hills in Khandesh, thirty caves have been excavated in a picturesque lonely glen near Jalgaon dating from the second century B.C. and inhabited until the eighth century A.D. Arranged on the chaitiya pattern with a hall and cells, most of them conformed to the usual plan, five being chaitiya and the rest viharas, lavishly adorned with sculptures of the Buddha and of Bodhisattvas, and magnificent frescoes on the walls, ceilings and columns, representing contemporary scenes and events recorded in the Jatakas and in other sanskrit literature (c. A.D. 550–642). Both architecturally and artistically these rock-cut caves constitute the peak of aesthetic achievement in India and Ceylon, though at Ajanta only relatively few examples of their original glory and magnificence have survived, notably on the walls of the chaitiya halls and on the pillars in caves I, II, IX, X, XI, XVI, XVII and XIX.

Here is displayed a vast drama of scenes in which princes, sages, heroes, men and women, animals, birds and plants are depicted in a great variety of scenes and designs; the earliest examples occur in caves IX and X, and belong to the second century B.C. The façades of these are decorated chiefly with architectural motifs, whereas those of the later seventh century A.D. (XIX and XXVI) are adorned with a vast array of figures of the Buddha, either seated or standing, skilfully sculptured or frescoed, and portraying a great variety of events from his birth to his death as recorded in the Jataka stories.[28]

Here is displayed every aspect of Mahayana Buddhism in a harmonious fusion of the earlier and later conceptions of the 'Great Vehicle', producing a bewildering variety of motifs and forms rendered with a 'baroque' elaboration, marking a considerable advance in this direction on the decoration and design of the façade of the Hinayana sanctuary at Karli.

Fig. 37.   Plan of cave-temple, Ajanta

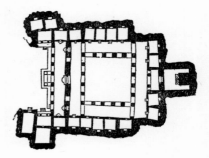

Indian Temples

Female figurine from Mohenjo-daro

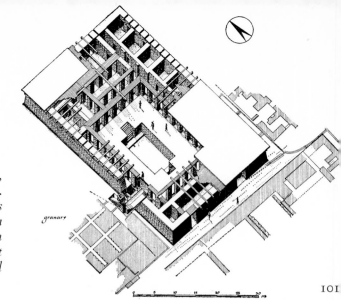

Flights of steps lead down to the Great Bath, high on the acropolis at Mohenjo-daro. The plan shows the arrangement of verandahs and cells surrounding the Bath where a priestly order may have lived. The function of the Bath is not known but it was most probably for ritual bathing, which is still practised in India today (101, 102)

granary

101

102

Terracotta statues of the Mother-goddess from Mohenjo-daro are simply modelled. The one shown left has her arms raised above her head in some kind of ritual dance, and wears a heavy necklace and girdle

103

The proud harsh face portrayed on the steatite figure is that of a Mohenjo-daro 'priest-king', whose robe is decorated with sacred trefoils, a motif which is also found on Sumerian figures

104

The relics of Buddha were believed to have been enshrined in a monumental mound—a stupa. The platforms, dome and umbrellas of a typical stupa are seen in the schist model, which is decorated with the scenes of Buddha's life (105). The most famous stupa in India is that at Sanchi which is over 50 feet high (106). Originally it was covered with stucco, painted black, red and gold. The richly carved gateways were added at a later date

I

I

107

The most sacred of Jain temple cities is that of Satrunjaya in the hills of western India where more than 500 temples are clustered around a central sanctuary. Many of the temples were destroyed during the Muslim invasions and rebuilt in the sixteenth century (107). The Vimala Saha temple on Mount Abu survived and is considered one of the most beautiful and delicate of eleventh century Jain temples. Forty-eight white marble columns support the dome, each heavily carved (108)

108

At Ellora a whole series of temples were hewn from the solid rock (109) and dedicated to the gods of the three Indian religions, Buddhism, Hinduism and Jainism. In the middle of these lies the Kailasa Temple (110) marking the climax of Hindu temple architecture. The sanctuary is cut from the solid rock, with tiered carvings rising to the roof and its four rampant lions

109

110

111

112

Of the 30 caves excavated in the volcanic hillside of Ajanta, chaitiya XIX (111) is perhaps the most magnificent. A profusion of carving on columns, friezes and dagobas, records scenes from Sanskrit literature. The exterior of chaitiya IX (112) shows how architectural styles used in wooden buildings were repeated in stone

The most famous sacred places in China are the later fifteenth century Ming temples, of which the Temple of Heaven in Peking is the most celebrated. Within the temple complex an Altar of Earth stands in a pavilion on a white marble terrace

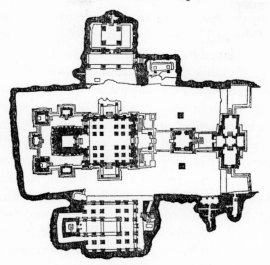

Fig. 38.   Plan of the Kailasa temple, Ellora

Behind it lay a romantic mysticism in which the spiritual and the divine permeated life in all its manifestations, experiences and modes of expression as the ordered pattern of the spiritual values and realities of the universe. So great has been the artistic achievement of Ajanta and so varied, being not merely religious but dramatic, emotional, romantic and lyrical, that artists throughout the Buddhist world in south-eastern and eastern Asia have drawn their inspiration from its successive phases, techniques and traditions.

ELLORA

Among the extensive rock-cut temples of Ellora in the Deccan, twelve of the thirty-four along the southern edge of the ridge were Buddhist creations from about A.D. 550 to 750 These were the prototypes of the later Hindu and Jain temples (from the ninth to the thirteenth centuries), and were simpler in design than the great Kailasa temple dedicated to Shiva, which, as has been noted, was constructed and equipped on the Brahmanic pattern. The Buddhist series are either vihara or chaitya halls arranged in the customary manner, the Visvakarma cave (No. X) being almost identical with the two latest shrines at Ajanta, except that the highly ornamental façade, consisting of a porch and a gallery, has no chaitya window. In front of the stupa a colossal figure of the Buddha in the attitude of teaching has been carved, the apsidal end of the hall behind the image being occupied entirely by the votive chaitiya. The large hall (117 feet by 58 feet) of the fifth cave has twenty-four pillars dividing the nave from the two aisles, as in two other of the Buddhist cave-temples. That known as the Tin Thal (No. XII) has a verandah standing on eight square pillars. Behind the front row are two more lines of eight columns, and six more pillars in the centre behind, making thirty in all. The roof of the lower hall (116 feet by 42 feet and 11 feet high) is supported by twenty-four pillars in three rows, and in the north wall are three cells each containing a stone bench. At the end of the back wall are two more cells, and in the middle is a large antechamber (37 feet wide and 40 feet deep) with two pillars in front and four supporting the roof. To the left of the vestibule to the shrine are figures of the Buddha with attendants carrying flowers, and similar figures appear on each side of the door of the shrine, within which is a huge sculpture of Gautama, 11 feet in height, surrounded with equal figures of Buddhas and of Bodhisattvas holding floral and other symbols (e.g. the lotus, sword, pennon and a book).

The upper storeys are similarly adorned with Buddhas and his attendants, male and female, ornamented with symbolic designs which include the foliage of the Bodhi-tree, the nimbus and umbrellas. The upper floor, measuring 115 feet in length, 64 feet in depth, and over 12 feet in height, is divided into five aisles by rows of eight pillars. At the back is an antechamber $37\frac{1}{2}$ feet wide, divided by two pillars with two in front of the shrine. Large figures of Buddhas seated on thrones with their attendants occur in the recesses at the end of the aisles, while at the south end of the back aisle of the hall is the Buddha on a lion-seat (*sinhasana*) with the Wheel of the Law, perhaps in the attitude of teaching in the Deer Park near Benares. At the other end (north) of this aisle the Buddha is represented in the squatting posture in the act of intense meditation; another shows him ascending to the sky to proclaim his *Dharma* to the gods, while in a third scene he is shown entering the passionless peace of *Nirvana*. To the right are portrayed what seems to be the seven last Buddhas (Vipasyin, Sikhin, Visabhu, Krkucchanda, Kanakamuni, Kasyapa, and Sakyamuni), and each has the foliage of a Bodhi-tree over his head. A similar row occurs on the south side of the wall with umbrellas above them. In the vestibule of the shrine are the figures of two guardians (*dwarpalos*) with lofty head-dresses and arms crossed. On the back wall are three more seated figures holding a symbol; above them are four Buddhas and fire is portrayed on the end walls. In the shrine is a large figure of Buddha in the state of illumination, sitting cross-legged pointing to the earth, and two female figures against the front of the throne. On the sides are Bodhisattvas standing against the wall holding various objects, with a small figure of Amitabha Buddha on the front of their caps, and on the walls above appear five seated cross-legged Buddhas on each side, and two on the front wall.[29]

The rock-cut temples which make their first appearance in India in the reign of Asoka were the result of contacts with the west, originating in all probability, as we have seen,[30] in Egypt and passing to India by way of Persia in the Mauryan era. That they were based on earlier wooden models is indicated by the wooden ribs in the roof and by the umbrella on the stupa. The pillars and their bases, the horseshoe window and arch are reproductions of their prototypes in stone, while beams frequently recur when the more durable material came into general use in the construction of religious edifices. In Ceylon and Burma most of the temples and monasteries have always been made of timber, or when brick or stone has been introduced their general plan has remained little changed.

TEMPLES IN CEYLON AND BURMA

As Buddhism was diffused throughout the Far East in its Theravada and Mahayana aspects, temples arose for its worship outside India. The purpose of these temples in Ceylon and Burma was primarily to house relics rather than images. This has been the determining factor in their structure, with some adaptation according to the materials employed and the local circumstances. Thus, whereas in Nepal where the stupas have not contained relics they have been flattened hemispherical in shape with a square parasol and lofty spire, as in Tibet and China; in Burma they have been bell-shaped erected on a series of platforms with a conical finial, the pagoda being a graceful solid pyramidal relic-shrine. Similarly, in Ceylon the brick pagodas have been solid except for the relic-chamber, rising to a very considerable height (at Anuvadhapura to 300 feet), with a small cella on one side containing several Buddha images, and like the Burmese masonry temples of Pagan centring on huge Buddha statues rather than relics. Therefore, unlike the pagodas they are constructed in gradually diminishing terraces crowned with a spire.

CHINA AND JAPAN

When Buddhism first reached China it found expression in hollowed-out cave-temples with colossal Buddha images, such as that of fifteen storeys which has survived on Sung Shan in Honan (*c.* A.D. 520). The highest recorded pagoda was built in Yung-ning-szu by the Dowager Empress Hu of the North Wei, and is said to have been 900 feet with a finial of 100 feet. Admittedly, the most famous sacred places in China are the comparatively modern imperial temples, dating mainly from the Ming Dynasty in the fifteenth century A.D., and the celebrated Altar of Heaven in a suburb of Peking which is 3 miles in circuit and has a magnificent white marble structure 27 feet high in three circular terraces, approached by four flights of steps and shaded by cypress trees. Nevertheless, Buddhism was the most important influence in Chinese temple architecture. Thus, the Confucian 'halls' and the small Taoist temples with their images in profusion conformed in their general plan to the Buddhist arrangement. This consisted of a series of porches opening from each other and enclosed by a wall with an ornamental gateway. Facing the entrance was an altar and three Buddha images with tables of offerings before them. A second hall contained a pagoda, and often the image of the Bodhisattva was enshrined behind it. The pagoda assumed a variety of forms based on the stupa with reliefs and carvings on the succession of storeys. The earliest now in existence—that of Tzu-en-szu, Si-an—is said to have been modelled on Central Asian prototypes just as the Lama pagoda is of Tibetan origin fashioned on the Indian stupa.

In Japan the Buddhist temples are much more elaborate than the indigenous Shinto shrines; these wayside shrines are placed within sacred enclosures, like the Roman templum, surrounded by branches of trees and derived from primitive huts in wood or stone, tiled or thatched with reeds or straw. The larger shrines like the Grand Imperial Shrine of Ise may originally have contained a hundred smaller shrines of the gods or ancestresses thought to have had their abode there, though it was only under Buddhist influences that the images of deities were introduced. In the second half of the sixth century A.D., after Buddhism had acquired official recognition, pagodas, temples, monasteries and schools were erected, sometimes adorned with ornamentation of Buddhist origin. Eventually, as the sectarian movement developed 'Buddha halls' were constructed in every province, the principal object of veneration in them being the figure of the founder of the sect (e.g. Honen, Nichiren, Shinran, Dengyo), supported by other images. With the rise of popular sects, such as Amida initiated by Honen, which attracted large numbers of adherents, pagodas gave place to large 'golden halls' elaborately decorated, designed for public worship, weddings, funerals and secular entertainment.

In contrast to this was the Zen sect which sought to attain the state of enlightenment by a strict self-discipline and training in quasi-yoga intuitive methods; the monasteries therefore acquired a new importance and significance. In the Hall of Meditation or Zendo, the monks sat in the attitude of contemplation to meditate upon a particular philosophical or religious subject (*koan*) proposed to them by the Superior. As 'Zen only seeks the light which man can find in himself', a carefully prescribed technique has been adopted, practised at fixed times throughout the day and in the evening, with special exercises occupying night and day once a month.[31] Architecture was influenced by its doctrines in the Kamakura period (1185–1335) with a distinctive temple plan in which the altar and shrine were placed in a sanctuary at the end of the temple. Moreover, there was wide aesthetic development in the great Zen monasteries, and Chinese art of the Sung period was introduced into Japan by Zen priests as a result of closer relations with China established by their commercial enterprises.

TIBET

Again from India, Mahayana Buddhism entered Tibet in a syncretistic Tantric form, later than in Japan, arriving there probably in the seventh century A.D., though it made little headway until monasteries were founded in A.D. 749 on the Brahmanputra river about 30 miles south-east of Lhasa. Here a particular form of Tantric mysticism was developed and eventually, in the thirteenth century, an influential hierarchy exercised temporal power. In the fifteenth century priest-kings of Lhasa dominated the whole of Tibet, the Dalai Lama being regarded as the incarnation of the Bodhisattva Avalokita and vice-regent of the Buddha. His Potala palace near Lhasa, and the great monasteries (i.e. Drepung, Sera and Ganden) have been the chief architectural structures in Tibet, occupying large areas, each inhabited by several thousand Lamas.

In their general plan they followed the usual Buddhist model of flat-roofed rectangular temples, with a few Tibetan details such as the pagoda and a number of local images. At one end of the nave stood the three principal statues and their altar, the rest arranged round the side walls. The aisles and pillars have been richly decorated with frescoes, banners, and, in the absence of windows, lighted with lamps. The approach has been by a flight of steps through a gateway guarded by divine beings and leading to a vestibule with side chapels containing the images of lesser gods. Sometimes shrines of the various Buddhas occur on the terraces of the several storeys.

At Lhasa is the three-storied 'cathedral', or *jokung*, with its flat gold roof. In the Holy of Holies, on the west of the pillared hall divided into aisles by a series of colonnades, is a recess containing the image of the Buddha. In the centre is an altar together with other divine images, prayer wheels and relics, and seats for the abbots, officials and for the Dalai Lama as the temporal ruler and the Tashi Lama, the spiritual head and incarnation of Amitabha.[32]

Since the Chinese occupation of Tibet and the exile of the Dalai Lama, many of the monasteries and temples have been destroyed and the monks either killed or expelled, but Lamaism is too deeply ingrained in the country and its inhabitants to be eliminated by communist indoctrination and ruthless methods of suppression. Here, as throughout the Buddhist world, the great temples are likely to remain the most imposing architectural monuments, adapted to the requirements of local conditions.

CHAPTER VII

Greek Temples

JUST AS BUDDHISM was the most important factor in the development of temple architecture in the Far East, there being little variety before in the plan and equipment of the Confucian and Taoist sanctuaries in China or of the Shinto shrines in Japan, so in the west it was largely under Hellenic inspiration and refinement that sacred edifices acquired their most subtle form of architectural and artistic expressions. At first, however, they were apparently patterned on dwellings, the domestic cultus having been practised invariably within the confines of human habitations, be they palaces or houses.

THE DOMESTIC SHRINE AND ITS CULTUS

Thus, there have been no indications that independent buildings set apart exclusively for the veneration of a divinity and the performance of prescribed rites existed in the Minoan civilization. Sometimes they might be little more than shelters, but even so they were associated with dwellings. The only exceptions, as we have seen, seem to be in the case of those in the natural sanctuaries in Crete, in caves, rock-shelters and on mountain peaks, while Gournia was a Minoan shrine equipped for public worship with altars, images, libation tables, double-axes and horns of consecration, situated on a hill independent of the palace.[1] Nevertheless, Nilsson is probably correct in maintaining that it must have originated in the domestic cult,[2] the snake goddess being a house-goddess, connected later in Greece with the house cult and Zeus.

THE TEMENOS

In Crete and the Aegean mainland alike, the *temenos* and its altar and cult-objects, from which the Greek temple in the Hellenic period developed, were normally related in some way to domestic buildings. Small shrines of the megalithic type are represented in intaglio scenes, standing apparently within the temenos, in association with baetyls, sacred trees and ashera, horns of consecration, double-axes, crosses, sacred animals and occasionally dolmens. They are, however, invariably adjuncts of some domestic structure, as in the Knossian frescoes and the gold shrine at Mycenae. At Knossos, the rulers being in fact priest-kings, the palaces (i.e. 'the Place of the Double-Axe' [λάβρυς]), had the character of a temple. Everywhere palaces had their shrine with its *sacra*, and in Mycenae houses as well as the king's palace had their domestic chapels as an integral part of their structure, very much as Solomon's temple was an annexe of the royal residence.[3] Thus, at Palaikastro and Phylakopi in Melos for example, chambers used apparently as shrines were incorporated in the structure of the palace.

While the normal equipment of a sanctuary in Greece at first consisted of an altar with a temenos as at Aegina, Sparta and Ephesus, this no longer sufficed when the gods were represented in large images, though the altar remained the essential requirement wherever it was placed. From the circular hut the temple and its precinct developed into an elliptical, apsidal or horseshoe form, square or oblong, the Mycenaean hall or megaron becoming the most persistent prototype, with its porch, usually supported by two columns, and a large *cella*. Although the temple was the house of the god because in it the cult-statue was enshrined, it was not, however, the place of worship, the cultus being performed in the open air, generally in the temenos in conjunction with the altar, as in the forecourt of the Mycenaean house. There the congregation assembled, the image in the temple not being an object of veneration like that in the toilet ceremonies in Egypt, or the baetyl in Semitic sanctuaries.

As it acquired aesthetic qualities it became at Athens in the time of Phidias (*c.* 490–417 B.C.) and Scopas, in the middle of the fourth century, the expression of abstract divine attributes and values, religious and ethical, and this naturally was reflected in the perfection of the architectural structure and sculpture of the sacred edifice in which it dwelt. But Greek temples always remained relatively small, the surrounding temenos and its altars being the indispensable cult centre, which sometimes included sacred groves, theatres, the tomb of a hero, treasuries, and several temple-shrines, as at Delphi, Olympia, Delos and at the Acropolis at Athens. Altars, in fact, although an essential part of the equipment of a temenos, were not always associated with temples. They could be erected at any place that had acquired particular sanctity, or in the courtyard of a house and at the hearth (*hestia*) in a palace, at which domestic rites were performed by the head of the household, as at the shrines at Mohenjo-daro. Sacred mountains, springs, groves and caves had their own altars, often dedicated to Zeus Καταβάιης, but, nevertheless, though they frequently stood by themselves in market-places and gateways, they were normally set up in sacred precincts in conjunction with a temenos and its temple.

THE EARLIEST GREEK TEMPLES

The temple proper (*naos*) within the temenos consisted of an inner sanctuary (*adyton*), corresponding to the Holy of Holies, behind the cella. A second rectangular chamber was soon added to it, together with columns *distyle in antis*, dividing an open end. At the other end the walls of the porch (*pronaos*) normally terminated in pilasters called *antae*, having various forms. The first stage in this development is to be seen in the rectangular stone building about 40 feet by 24 feet on Mount Ocha near Karystos in the island of Euboea, dedicated to the goddess Hera, the official wife of Zeus. The roof consists of large slabs of stone projecting until they meet at the ridge. A long narrow slit about 19 feet by 18 inches provides an opening for air and light, and in the eastern walls are two other slits flanking a door and serving the purpose of windows.

Next, the walls of the cella were extended beyond the doorway and ended in antae between which two columns were often placed to form a

Fig. 39. Development of Greek temple forms

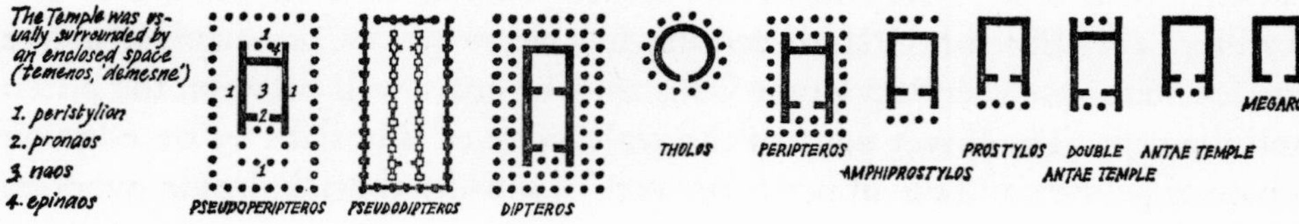

The Temple was usually surrounded by an enclosed space ('temenos, demesne')

1. peristylion
2. pronaos
3. naos
4. epinaos

PSEUDOPERIPTEROS   PSEUDODIPTEROS   DIPTEROS   THOLOS   PERIPTEROS   PROSTYLOS   DOUBLE ANTAE TEMPLE   MEGARON
AMPHIPROSTYLOS   ANTAE TEMPLE

porch with three entrances, or the walls continued in front of the columns when they became the prostyle, forming a portico of not more than four columns in front of the temple. The porch or even the temple can be described as *in antis*, or prostyle, just as the division in the rear may be either an adyton or an open porch, *opisthodomus*, a duplicate of the pronaos, usually with no door, and surrounded by an outer colonnade (*pteron*) covered with the same roof as the rest of the building.

THE SANCTUARY OF THE THERMUM

Except perhaps those in wood in some palaces, there are no Mycenaean precedents for the colonnade. It occurs in a rudimentary form in the Aetolian sanctuary of Thermum in an early type of megaron called 'Megaron B' about 70 feet in length. Nearby are the remains of a rather earlier rectangular and hairpin-shaped building, 'Megaron A', thatched with reeds and containing a porch and two inner chambers. This was a house or palace, whereas Megaron B seems to have been a rectangular archaic temple, dating from the seventh century B.C., divided by cross-walls into three chambers and surrounded with eighteen thin slabs of stone in an elliptical curve. These had wooden posts, the column being based it would appear on Bronze Age models. While they may have been a later addition, they represent the earliest known example of the peripteral architectural plan, on which the temple of Apollo was based.[4]

THE ARTEMIS ORTHIA SANCTUARY AT SPARTA

As early as the tenth century, the cult of the goddess Orthia was practised in the sanctuary at Sparta. The structural remains of this building, as R. M. Dawkins maintained, must date from between the tenth century and 740 B.C. The archaic altar is from the first part of the ninth century, while the remains of the early temple are dated at about 600 B.C.[5] No traces of Mycenaean or Helladic cultures occurred at the site, which undoubtedly was a Dorian foundation dedicated to the Spartan goddess before the cult was equated with that of Artemis, both deities being connected with birth and fertility. Very little of the sixth-century temple, however, has survived above the foundations except the outer walls and the cross-wall between the porch and the cella. The lower parts of the walls were of thin slabs set on edge on a base of pebbles and the upper parts were of sun-dried brick. Inside, wooden posts, on which the cross-beams of the roof rested, had been inserted in stone sockets. As in several Bronze Age Greek temples (e.g. those in Thessaly and at Tiryns and Troy), there was probably a single row of inner columns, and prostyle *in antis*, as in later times. Limestone reliefs of lions seem to have adorned the pediment like those found near the north of the temple, as a gaily painted *poros* fragment of a lion's mane has been discovered in the earth in front of the sixth-century temple. The archaic altar buried in the sand was replaced by a new structure composed of rudely dressed stones, 29½ feet by 5 feet. Its importance and significance is indicated by its increased size.

THE HERAEUM AT OLYMPIA

In the seventh century B.C. when heavy tiles and thatch replaced the clay roofs of the temples, the adoption of rectangular plans with a gable at each end was facilitated, and stronger walls and columns were required to divide the nave from the aisle in the cella. Mud-brick and wood, however, continued until limestone was introduced in the sixth century, and in the next century it was often replaced by marble. Thus, the Heraeum, or temple of Hera at Olympia, belonging to the seventh century B.C., seems to have been superimposed on an earlier peripteral, and a non-peripteral temple, both of which had much the same general plan. This consisted of a peripteral colonnade with six columns at each of the east and west ends and sixteen along the sides at the north and south, in all probability originally in wood.[6] Two rows of columns later divided the cella into a nave and narrow aisles with a flat ceiling under the gabled roof of terracotta tiles; the lower part of the cella wall was of limestone, the rest being of unbaked brick.[7] This was the Doric temple in its earliest construction.

The Greeks, however, were at first by no means convinced of the stability of stone and so they employed monolithic columns of megalithic dimensions with widely projecting capitals, as in the seventh-century temple of Apollo on the island of Ortygia, Syracuse, and in that of Corinth and of Poseidon at Paestum in the next century, where the columns of the cella supporting the ceiling and roof are of these proportions. On the other hand, those thought to belong to a seventh-century sanctuary of Athena Pronaea at Delphi are slender, tapering at the tip, with wide capitals. The Heraeum at Olympia, erected in the sanctuary of Zeus, was probably the earliest large temple in Greece,[8] built to house big images like that of Hermes by Praxiteles. As wood, brick and stone was used in its construction, the heavy columns and thick walls were required to support the superstructure of a different material until they were replaced by stone. At first it would seem that both Zeus and Hera were worshipped in the Heraeum before the classical temple of Zeus was erected in the fifth century as an independent sanctuary, perhaps, as Dr Gardiner suggests, when Pheidon introduced the cult of Hera from Argos after he had seized control of Olympia, probably in the eighth century.[9]

THE ARGIVE HERAEUM

Although it has yet to be established that Hera was a Mycenaean goddess, her Heraeum, 6 miles north of Argos, was one of the most ancient and important sanctuaries in the Peloponnese, if not in the whole of ancient Hellas. It was older by several centuries than that of Zeus, superimposed on a Mycenaean palace site. Nevertheless, outside Argolis her cult was relatively rare. Only in the centres of ancient civilization, Mycenae, Sparta and Argos, and on the island of Samos and Euboea, was it at all prominent, and there it was associated with Argos. Primarily and essentially it was of Peloponnesian origin and provenance, being of no account in Thessaly and the

*Fig. 40. Clay model of the Argive
Heraeum. After G. Oikonomos*

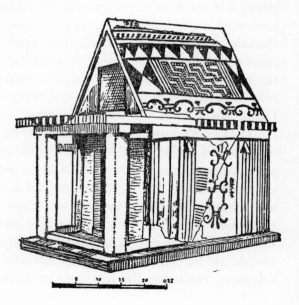

northern littoral, though her union with Zeus may have had an ethnological significance. But it was from the Argive (including Tiryns, Mycenae and the surrounding region) that the worship of Hera was diffused in Boeotia, Euboea, Attica, Olympia, Thrace and Lesbos, as well as in Sicily and Magna Graecia, Rhodes, Cos and Crete, probably in pre-Dorian times.

According to tradition, the Heraeum was founded by Phoroneus at least thirteen generations before Agamemnon and the Achaeans secured ascendancy, and it remained the principal sanctuary during the Tirynthian period, having been perhaps originally a fortified stronghold. Thus, it was from Argos that the Samian temple was said to have been founded by the Argonauts, though the birth of Hera was located on the island,[10] and this derivation is confirmed by all the traditions.[11] In the fifth century Argos conquered the Mycenaeans and from then the city and Heraeum became the political and religious centres in the Argive plain. In 423 B.C. the old Heraeum was burnt down through the negligence of a priestess,[12] whereupon Eupolemus was commissioned to erect a new temple a little below the ancient site. This was built about 420 B.C. while the triangular upper platform upon which the old temple stood, with its apex pointing towards Mount Euboea and its base towards Argos, was still visible. There were three terraces one above the other, the space in front overlooking the plain towards Tiryns and Midea, the entrance being in the south-eastern corner, or from the northeast. The massive Cyclopean supporting walls seen by Pausanias, corresponding to the oldest parts of those of Tiryns with their colossal unhewn blocks, are still in good preservation. On the lowest of the terraces below the old temple the new temple was constructed.

As a result of the extensive excavations of the American School of Classical Studies in Athens from 1892 to 1895, published by Charles Waldstein in 1902, the foundations of both the first and second temples have now been uncovered.[13] The ruins indicate that a Doric structure was erected on the second platform upon which the altar in the old temple appears to have stood on the south and west. Against the southern wall was a magnificent stoa and a flight of steps leading up to the platform of the second temple above, built of stuccoed limestone with gargoyles, carved decoration and sculpture, and the roof covered with white marble tiles. On the northern side of the second terrace was a long stoa, or colonnade, running from east to west and ending in chambers. Below the second terrace stood a large complicated building at the south-west end, with an open courtyard; it was surrounded by a colonnade and had an entrance to the north. It is thought to have been a gymnasium or sanatorium, and two rooms flanking the vestibule were equipped with benches or couches resting on upright blocks of limestone, except in the most easterly of the three rooms. The central court seems to have been paved with irregular blocks covered with limestone, and the fragments of capitals, drums, columns, pediments and metopes give some indication of the decorative art displayed in the temple. This, according to Pausanias, included the portrayal of the birth of Zeus on the eastern pediment, and the capture of Troy on the western one. No trace, however, has been found of the colossal gold seated cult-statue of Hera in ivory and gold described by Pausanias and executed by Polyclitus, though the outlines of the base on which it stood occur. The total height of the image and its base has been estimated at about 26 feet, the seated figure being about 18 feet; in contemporary reproduction she is shown holding her attributes, in her left hand her sceptre surmounted by a cuckoo, and in her right hand a pomegranate.

Many of the numerous marble fragments of sculptures recovered from the temple are of great beauty, such as the life-sized Parian marble head of a woman found in front of the west foundation-wall, with its refined features, grave expression and wavy hair, regarded by Waldstein as quite likely the head of Hera and attributed to a sculptor of the school of Polyclitus in the fifth century B.C.[14] These conjectures, however, are challenged by Professor Furtwängler who relates the sculptures to those at the Erechtheum and the temple of the Wingless Victory on the Acropolis.[15] But other fragments of heads forming adornments of the metropes suggest the work of Polyclitus rather than of the Attic sculptors.

THE THREE ORDERS OF TEMPLE ARCHITECTURE

By the middle of the seventh century B.C. the Doric type of temple had become established in Greece, southern Italy and Sicily, though of course much of the decoration and architectural ornamentation are of a later date. The general structural plan consisted of a cella divided into two chambers and surrounded by a colonnade and walls separated from the columns, often entered through a porch at the rear or by two porches. These features remained typical of Greek temple-architecture, be it Doric, Ionic or

Corinthian, however much architectural refinement and additional equipment might be introduced as skill and requirements increased. The cult-image, for instance, underwent considerable enrichment in form, sculpture, colour and design, as in the case of the gold and ivory statues of Zeus in Olympia and of Athena in the Parthenon at Athens, while the lighter style of Ionic architecture found expression in more slender columns and bases of exquisite beauty, and capitals of lavish sculpture and decoration. Although at first distinct styles, the Doric and Ionic were soon merged. Thus a Doric edifice would be ornamented with an Ionic sculptured frieze, fluted columns resting on bases with a variety of mouldings and graceful capitals, thereby giving lighter and more decorative touches to the more massive constructions. To these were added the Corinthian symmetrical bell-shaped capitals ornamented with acanthus leaves, said to have been invented by Callimachus, a metal-worker who applied his art to the design, perhaps at Bassae where the Corinthian capital first occurred in the temple of Apollo at the beginning of the fifth century B.C.

THE TEMPLE OF APOLLO EPICURIUS AT BASSAE

The Doric temple erected on a mountain in Arcadia near Phigalia was designed according to Pausanias, by Ictinus, the architect of the Parthenon, and dedicated to Apollo Epicurius in fulfilment of a vow for deliverance from plague. Situated on the site of an earlier small temple, it was orientated from north to south. In addition to the first Corinthian capitals, it contained ten tall engaged Ionic columns, and a frieze on the inside of the cella (now in the British Museum) which rested upon the Ionic half-columns. The position, in fact, seems to have been chosen in order to display the whole frieze at once, and was orientated to face Delphi, the seat of Apollo, of which it appears to have been a rather poor imitation. It was, however, closely related to the Parthenon at Athens on a very much simplified and reduced scale and style. The oldest known Corinthian capital gave support to the frieze perhaps with the half-columns on either side similarly decor-ated, as recorded by Pausanias.[16] The temple was completely destroyed by earthquakes, but the capital was described by C. R. Cockerell[17] after it had been re-discovered by a French architect in 1765 and investigated by an international party in 1811–12, who made and preserved drawings of the fragments.

THE PRECINCTS OF APOLLO AT DELPHI

The sanctuary at Delphi on Mount Parnassus was a temenos sacred to Apollo, standing on terraces connected by a winding stairway enclosing the main temple, together with the stadium, monuments, the theatre, treasuries in the form of small Doric and Ionic temples, and the great altar to Athena approached by the *via sacra*. The first shrine was a small primitive structure said to have been constructed of laurel boughs succeeded by one of birds' feathers and wax, indicative doubtless of a primitive sanctuary.[18] The fourth of the alleged series, built of stone, was destroyed by an earthquake or fire in 548, and its successor, a Doric edifice, was completed about 510 with the iberal aid of an Athenian family, Alcmaeonides. Parian marble was substituted for poros on the retaining wall, the east columns and the pediment with its sculptures, and on the flanks of the cornice,[19] the mouldings of which were decorated in red and blue. In front of the supporting wall of the terrace of polygonal masonry stood the colonnade, or stoa, of the Athenians, erected after the Persian wars, with eight very slender Ionic columns much slighter than the older limestone columns at the back. Those in the stoa were so widely spaced that the roof must have been wooden. In Hellenistic times the stoas were added to the precinct, eastward and westward from the temple terrace. The sculptured decoration was archaic in character and included a portrayal of Apollo driving a quadriga accompanied by Artemis and Leto, and animal designs in the corners. It was thrown down by an earthquake about 373 B.C.

After this catastrophe the last (sixth) temple was built in 305 B.C. partly in stuccoed limestone and partly in Pentelic marble by Spintharus, Xenodorus and Agathon. The omphalos stone of the temple was regarded as the navel of the earth, and was kept in the adytum in which the statue of Apollo was enshrined, erected over the sacred spring where the Pythia, seated on her tripod, gave oracles as the prophetess of Apollo. This spring in the crypt was reached by a stairway, and a ramp for processions led up to the entrance of the temple, in front of which was the chief altar of Apollo, called by Herodotus 'the altar of the Chians'[20] because it was they who dedicated it to him. This altar was discovered during the French excavations. It is 28 feet in length and 7 feet in breadth, built of limestone and containing a votive inscription describing its dedication by the Chians, probably in 479 B.C., when they liberated Delphi from the Persians. Near where it stood on the

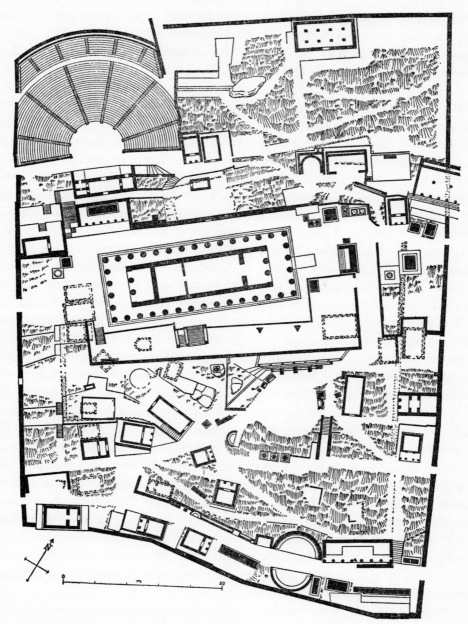

Fig. 41. Plan of the temenos at Delphi. After P. de la Coste-Messeliere

east side of the temenos, fragments of Mycenaean ware have been discovered and there the Earth-goddess Gaea had a sanctuary before it was appropriated by Apollo, who was a relatively late intruder from Delos.[21] The ancient sanctity of the site may account for the dedication of slaves having taken place between the temple and the altar.[22]

THE DELPHIC ORACLE

It was, however, the oracle that for a thousand years of recorded history led Greeks and Romans to the Apolline temple to consult the Pythia on matters great and small, such was the reputation of the shrine where she performed her functions. Although she was the prophetess of Apollo, and Delphi was essentially an Apolline centre during the Homeric period, nevertheless, from the fifth century B.C. the temple became increasingly associated with Dionysus and by the third century the monument in the inner sanctuary was regarded as his grave. By the time of Plutarch two centuries later, he was believed to have taken the place of Apollo at the shrine during the three winter months when Apollo retired to the north,[23] a tradition that may go back to a much earlier period, since the winter absences were established by the sixth century B.C. Who then presided at the temple is not recorded, but the partnership of Dionysus and Apollo at Delphi had a moderating influence on the Dionysian orgies, though it introduced an ecstatic element in the oracular cultus. But the inspiration of the Pythia took a different form from that manifested in the Thraco-Phrygian frenzies. Taking her seat on the tripod in the adytum over the vaporous cleft in the chasm below, or occasionally herself entering the cave, the words she uttered were interpreted by the 'prophet', or chief-priest, and often written down in hexameters as the oracles of Zeus through Apollo with whom she was *en rapport*. If the original home of the oracle was in Anatolia,[24] it doubtless had an ecstatic background, and the Hyperboreans, with whom Apollo is traditionally associated geographically and etymologically, have northern-Asiatic affinities[25] where the shamanistic tradition was very deeply laid. Therefore, as the cults of Dionysus and Apollo coalesced the prophetess and her oracular utterances at Delphi gave expression to a common tradition in a Greek milieu at the temple of Apollo.

When Orpheus, as the hero of the Dionysian cult and the priest of Apollo, found a place in this complex oracle under the influence of the Orphic movement, the Delphians cultivated hero-worship[26] and tendance of the dead.[27] As a result the gulf between mortals and immortals was bridged by metempsychosis and *teletae*, and the soul being purged of its Titanic defilements was brought into union with the chthonian powers, the wilder forms of ecstatic revelation being directed into more refined channels. So great, in fact, became the fame and influence of Delphi that all Greece resorted to it for information on cult procedure, politics, law and personal conduct in everyday affairs, however vague and evasive the responses often might be,[28] especially on critical questions. Nevertheless, it held the allegiance of the entire nation, rulers, statesmen, sages, citizens and athletes assembling periodically at the sacred precincts, its temple, stadium and theatre, to take part in rites and games held in honour of the Pythian Apollo.

Thus, Delphi became a potent consolidating centre in the Greek states, the Pythia and her officials, the *Exegetai Pythochrestoi*, occupying a unique position, Apollo through them saying the last word in answer to oracular inquiries on religious, legal, statutory and personal procedure, especially at time of crisis. By the sixth century B.C. he was the chief standardizing agency in the religious and social structure in Greece, with Delphi as the omphalos. A raid on the sanctuary by the Persians in 480 B.C. was said to have been frustrated by Apollo, who in a storm or earthquake hurled rocks on the invaders. But early in the fourth century the temple seems to have been destroyed by the Phocian defenders of Delphi during the second Persian war (357–346 B.C.), when many of its treasures were melted down. This sacrilege had to be recompensed by annual payments of ten thousand talents, but it ceased to occupy its focal position as the pan-Hellenic sanctuary when they were defeated by Philip of Macedon, though the oracle supported him and his successor, Alexander the Great.[29] After the death of Alexander in 323 B.C. it became little more than a local court of appeal, and no attempt had been made to restore the temple after its destruction by earthquake in 371 B.C. The Hellenistic kings appear to have ignored the Pythia, and on one occasion seduced her.[30] A strenuous effort, however, is alleged to have been made to save the shrine by its prophetesses and the citizens in 279 B.C. when Celtic hordes invaded Macedonia and sacked the temples.[31] But whatever actually happened, although the sanctuary seems to have been plundered, its vitality was renewed in the second century B.C.[32] when, at the end of the Hannibalic war in 207, the oracle was consulted by Roman envoys and at its command the cult of Cybele moved yet further from her original home and was introduced into the capital.[33]

The restored temple again seems to have been seriously injured by northern barbarians in 85 or 84 B.C.,[34] but it was soon repaired, and while Nero removed some of its treasures he is said to have revived the temple on his second visit to Delphi.[35] In the reigns of Trajan and Hadrian it became a sacred city once more, but after a few sporadic utterances the Oracle became silent, and the attempt of Julian to revive it failed.[36] It only remained for the temple to be closed by Theodosius in A.D. 390 and to be demolished by his successor, Arcadius, to bring the great mantic and geographical centre of the Hellenic world to an end. In the Roman Empire it was never the focal point it had hitherto been in Greece, and once the mantic tradition ceased to make a widespread appeal, the oracle lost its *raison d'être* and was reduced to silence for ever.

THE TEMPLE OF APOLLO AT CORINTH

It was not, however, only at Delphi that Apollo was worshipped and consulted. At Corinth a temple of close-grained poros and stucco was built about 540 B.C. in the style of the Old Temple of Athena at Athens, situated to the west of the road leading westwards from the market-place northwards to Lechaeum on the Gulf of Corinth, and north of the road from the market-place to Sicyon. A raised platform of solid rock formed its base, and on the other side of the Sicyon road was the fountain of Glauce, the chambers of which were cut out of the natural rock, with well-preserved stucco on the lower parts of the walls. In front were several water conduits and a large cistern. In a fourth compartment extending beyond the rest in the rear to a back wall were two orifices delivering the water to the fountain house.[37] These reservoirs, similar in shape, were all connected, and the side walls ended in a porch consisting of three columns between two antae. At the back of the porch, approached by a flight of rock-cut steps, was a balustrade with marble lions' heads through which the water overflowed. Lion-headed spouts, two of which have been found, may have been on the façade in the water-tight parapet on the platform.

At the temple, only seven massive Doric columns and a portion of the architrave remain standing, but the plan can be discovered from the cuttings in the rock and the few fragments that have survived, together with four monoliths on the ground. The surface was covered with stucco of marble dust, and each monolith, nearly 21 feet high, had rectilinear tapering and the capital carved in a separate block. At the south-eastern corner of the platform was a broad staircase leading to a porch with two columns *in antis*, and containing two rows of smaller columns. The temple was hexastyle, with fifteen columns on a side, the peristyle being estimated by Dörpfeld at thirty-eight in all, enclosed by a porch, a pronaos and an opisthodomus. The cella was divided into two parts, back to back, each entered by a porch, supposed by Dörpfeld to have been dedicated to two separate deities.[38] But it seems more likely that since the western division has a base for a cult-statue, it was an adytum set apart for the image and its cultus, unless it was the support of a treasury chest as at the temple of Zeus at Olympia. There, however, as we have seen, it was situated between the interior columns. No remains of the frieze have been secured and only small fragments of the pottery and of the cornice (i.e. a number of guttae).

During the Roman re-occupation it was re-roofed, but after Pausanias visited the temple, about A.D. 165, no reference to the site was made until it was described by Cyriacus of Ancona in 1436. Then ten of the columns with their architraves were still standing.[39] The destruction, however, continued intermittently, and in 1745 a British traveller refers to the breaking down of some of the columns to make room for a Turkish villa in the cella. From subsequent sketches by travellers it would seem that twelve of them in fact remained in the eighteenth century though by the time Dörpfeld began his excavations in 1886 they were in their present condition. In 1898 the clearing of the site was begun by the American School of Classical Studies at Athens, and its detailed survey was then undertaken. A museum has now been established in which the contents discovered have been housed and displayed.[40]

THE ACROPOLIS AT ATHENS

It was, however, at Athens that Dr Dörpfeld's excavations were most rewarding. There between the Parthenon and the Erechtheum on the Acropolis in 1885 he identified an early temple, probably originally in the form of a megaron. In fact very little was known of any of the earliest buildings on the Acropolis before their systematic investigation under the direction of the Archaeological Society was begun at the end of the last century. Then it

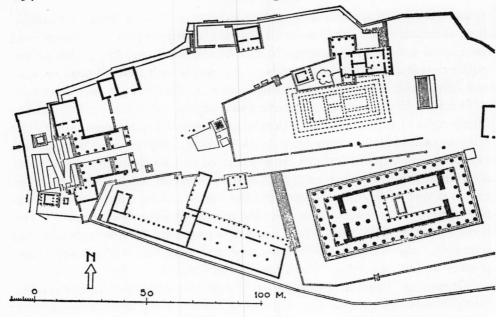

Fig. 42. Plan of the Acropolis, Athens. After A. W. Lawrence

became apparent that below the edifices were deposits containing considerable quantities of sculpture and pottery belonging to the seventh and sixth
centuries B.C., some of the statues and ware revealing great artistic and tech-
nical skill. Over the megaron on ground adjoining the Erechtheum, a small
poros temple about 100 feet long had been erected in the first half of the
sixth century, in which the statue of Athena, the patroness of the city, was
probably enshrined.

THE OLD TEMPLE OF ATHENA

This ancient 'Hecatompedon' appears to have been the only sanctuary on the
Acropolis when it was built, its general plan and foundations suggesting that
it was the precursor of the Erechtheum, though the colonnade may have
been added, perhaps by the tyrant Pisistratus, about 530. Athena originally
was almost certainly a pre-Hellenic goddess, and the house of Erechtheus on
the Acropolis stood on the site of either a Mycenaean sanctuary or palace,[41]
as at other citadels where her cultus may have been established. In the Late

Bronze Age, the settlement around which the sacred site was enclosed with its pre-Greek walls had become one of the most important towns, and when it was dispersed, about 1100 B.C., the Acropolis must have retained its sacred tradition since it became the centre of the worship of Athena and of the deities with whom she was associated.[42]

The exact site of the Old Temple of Athena has not been discovered, and its plan, location and restoration remain in debate. Nevertheless, it seems very probable that it was the predecessor of the Erechtheum, constructed in much the same manner with a cella facing east and having a colonnade and porches of four bays at both ends. An opisthodomus and two chambers, used as treasuries, faced west. The marble metopes on the flanks and rear had red and blue Doric leaves below the fascia; leopards and lions in relief were on the metopes on the east front. The western end with two lions was flanked by serpents, and a marble sima (gutter on the gable). The pediment sculptures of poros limestone portrayed contests between gods (e.g. Heracles wrestling with Triton, Athena and a giant, and fighting animals). About 527 the stuccoed colonnade was added, sometimes attributed to Pisistratus, covered with a marble roof, the foundations being later than those of the Hecatompedon.

During the Persian war the temple apparently was seriously damaged but not completely destroyed. The foundations are in all probability those

Fig. 43.   Possible reconstruction of plan of the Temple of Athena, Athens

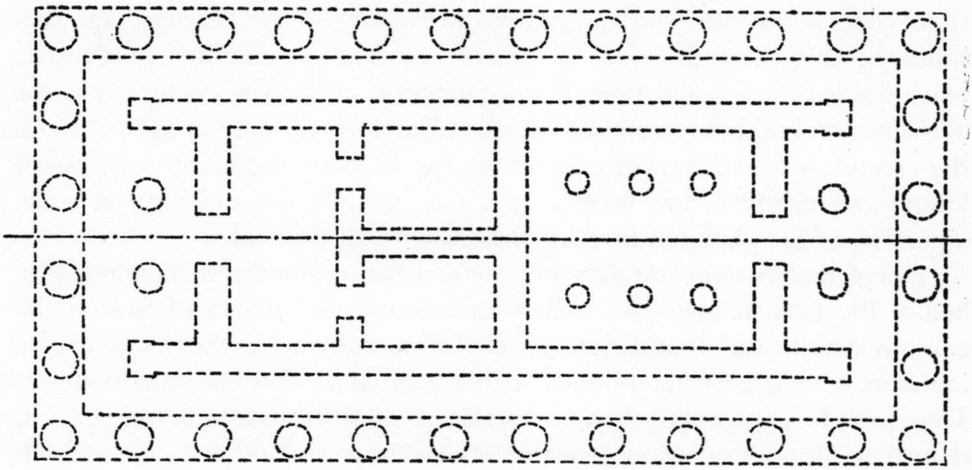

of the previous sanctuary burnt by the Persians, but how the restoration proceeded is very obscure. In 465 the Acropolis was re-fortified by Cimon, and under Pericles the temples were built and reconstructed in all their exquisite beauty by the architect Ictinus and the sculptor Phidias. It was then, between 447 and 438, that the Parthenon became the culmination of Doric refinement, built in Pentelic marble on the stone foundations laid for an earlier Athenian temple, and from the fourth century giving its name to the chief temple of Athena on this ancient sacred site. Slightly later the Ionic Erechtheum was added in 407 with its two cellas and three porches at different levels, and a raised colonnade. Between the Propylaea, or roofed gateway, on the west side and the Parthenon, was built the Chalcotheca, an adjacent hall, in 400, together with the precinct of Artemis Brauronia and the colossal statue of Athena Promachos. What happened to the old temple is not clear but it may have been used for secular purposes. The eastern cella was never rebuilt and the opisthodomus was burnt down.

THE PARTHENON

Whatever may have been the ultimate fate of the original sanctuary on the Acropolis and its various adjuncts, the Parthenon became and has remained the most magnificent Doric temple ever produced. The obvious place for the principal shrine of Athena was that occupied on the natural rock platform by Hecatompedon. This was to be superseded by a building of proportions, design and decoration supremely worthy to give expression to the Marathon victory over the Persians and the prosperity of the Periclean age that followed this triumph, and the newly acquired accessibility of Pentelic marble aided the construction. The conjunction of all these events led to the decision to rebuild the Acropolis on a lavish scale, beginning in 447 B.C. with the erection of a substructure about 40 feet high on the south side, rather longer and narrower than its successor, 256 feet in length and 103 feet wide, a portion of the platform forming a terrace on all four sides.

Dörpfeld, like Ross and Penrose, was convinced that the work was begun before the Persian invasion, calling attention to the marks of fire on the column drums and foundation which he thought were the result of the building having been surrounded with a scaffolding that had caught alight. Therefore, he contended, the Old Parthenon had had two building periods, requiring a longer duration than that between 490 and 480 B.C., going back to about 506 B.C. This would explain the existence of two retaining walls of different techniques for the terraces south of the Parthenon, the one employing polygonal limestone, the other poros ashlar, and the incongruity between the poros and kara limestone crepidoma supporting a marble colonnade.[43] But it has now been shown that there is in fact a unity of design and that potsherds in the bottom of the terrace date up to 490 B.C., making this the earliest date for the commencement of the temple, while the traces of fire show that the building stopped in 480 B.C. This, together with its orientation in relation to the sunrise on the festival of Athena, has led Dinsmoor to suggest 488 B.C. as the most probable year of the beginning of the new construction.[44] It was then burned down when the Persians returned and ravaged the Acropolis, prior to the building of the great outer wall by Cimon and the raising and strengthening of it by Pericles to secure a more extended area for the new Parthenon. In the retaining wall was a stairway descending to the lower level of the Pelasgian wall further south, the carefully worked stylobate of Peiraic limestone being extended about 3 feet 10 inches beyond the line of the late Parthenon to a depth of twenty-two courses at the south-east corner, all of which below the sixteenth having been left unworked because hidden from view.

Erected of Pentelic marble, the interior plan followed that of the old temple of Athena, the cella being 100 feet long divided by a blank wall into two chambers of unequal size and surrounded on three sides by a Doric colonnade. In the larger chamber stood the base of the chryselephantine statue of the goddess designed by Phidias, dedicated in 438 B.C.,[45] the total height of which was, with its base, 40 feet. The goddess was in the erect posture clad in a tunic with a helmet and goatskin, and held a spear in one hand and a figure of victory in the other. At her feet was a shield with a complex design. At the back of the cella was a square chamber supported by four Ionic pillars and used as a treasury for the cult ornaments. This was designated the Parthenon, or Chamber of the Virgin, but since the fourth century B.C., the term generally has been given to the temple as a whole.[46] The rear chamber was entered from the opisthodomus which was enclosed behind a bronze grille between the columns.

In the east cella besides the great statue of Athena were a number of votive offerings and treasures mentioned in the inventories (e.g. golden statuettes, silver censers, ornaments, bowls, candelabra, crowns). Among the abundance of sculptured decoration were forty-four statues in the gables, ninety-two metopes sculptured in high relief over the outer colonnade displaying the battle of the gods and giants, Greeks and Amazons and centaurs, while on the pediments were representations of the birth of Athena, her contest with Poseidon for possession of Attica, and other mythical scenes, and the magnificent heads of Theseus and Olympus.

Round the outer wall of the cella was an Ionic frieze (originally in coloured low relief, with bronze reins and bridles on the horses), probably designed by Phidias about 440 B.C., portraying the procession to the Acropolis at the Panathenaea in the height of summer. This may now be seen in the skilfully rearranged representation of the scene in the Elgin Galleries in the British Museum.[47] When Athens rose to prominence after the Persian war, Pisistratus remodelled the old Athenaea, celebrated on the traditional birthday of Athena, under the name of the Panathenaea. On the first three days contests were held which included boxing, wrestling and chariot races, concluding with a torchlight procession, games and sacrifices on the Acropolis on the seventh night (i.e. 28th of Hekatombaion, July to August).[48] In the frieze on the Parthenon the procession was divided into two streams running parallel to each other, beginning at the south-west corner and moving in either direction towards the east where they converged.[49] On the west frieze the preparations for the procession are indicated, the horseman being shown along the side of the temple as they move northwards with increasing speed in a tumult accompanied by the *thallophori* (elders), musicians, and the animals for sacrifice led by a heifer. Maidens carrying jugs, libation-bowls and incense-burners appear on the east frieze. Above the main eastern doorway of the Parthenon the *peplos*, or new robe woven every four years to drape the statue of Athena, is represented being handed to a priest by a small boy, having been carried through the city to the citadel. The clothing of the goddess in the presence of the twelve Olympian gods with Zeus in the centre was in fact the climax of the festival at the beginning of the Attic year. The rest of the scene is obscure.

The frieze can hardly be regarded as a reproduction of the actual procession as such a cavalcade could not have had access to the Acropolis and its principal temple. Nevertheless, from inscriptions of about 335 B.C., it is clear that there were two separate sacrifices on the Acropolis at the lesser Panathenaea: a smaller one to Athena Hygieia in the old temple (i.e. the

Erechtheum), and the other a great hecatomb of cattle, one of which was offered to Athena Nike and the rest to Athena Polias on the great altar. Deubner suggests that these two offerings are distinguished on the Parthenon frieze by the four cattle and four sheep on the north side depicting those offered at the Erechtheum, and the dozen on the south frieze representing the greater hecatomb, so placed because the sacrifice occurred in the Parthenon.[50] Be this as it may, the central feature and climax of the ritual was unquestionably the clothing of the statue of Athena which it would seem was performed quadrennially at the great Panathenaea in the Parthenon.

To the Pericleans, Athena was the personification of the splendour and achievements of Athens and the highest expression of their Olympian religion exemplified in its perfection in the art of Phidias in form, design and colour. Born from the head of Zeus, according to the Pindarian imagery, Athena partook of his wisdom and power, and to her was attributed the greatness of the city and the prosperity of its citizens, who enjoyed the favours bestowed upon her by her illustrious father. Therefore her victories in battle against the gods, giants, Amazons, Lapiths, Centaurs and the might of Troy, were depicted on the metopes round the Parthenon, which as her most renowned memorial after the triumph over the Persians worthily commemorated all that she had accomplished. It was not until the Greek states and their capital declined, and the Olympian gods were resolved into abstractions under Ionian philosophic influences that Athena Parthenus became a spent force, and at length the Parthenon itself suffered the fate of all pagan temples at the hands of Theodosius II in A.D. 426. After surviving in a mutilated condition as both an Orthodox and a Latin church, and in and after 1458 as a mosque, it fell victim to an explosion in 1687 when Turkish guns were directed upon it. By the end of the eighteenth century, with the rest of the Acropolis, it had fallen into decay and was abandoned as a ruin.

THE ERECHTHEUM

It was not, however, only the Parthenon and the little Ionic temple of Athena Nike that were sacred to the goddess on the Acropolis. The rest of the city and the whole of the land was her domain, and the eastern chamber of the Erechtheum, completed about 407 B.C., was also dedicated to her. Exactly when and by whom it was first constructed is obscure. Dinsmoor suggested that after the ancient image of Athena Polias had been returned from its sojourn in Salamis at the end of the Persian war in 497 B.C. it was sheltered under a baldachin in a temporary shrine in the precinct to the north of the poros temple. In due course the eastern cella and porch of the Erechtheum were built around it and roofed over in 408 B.C.[51] This presupposes that before the destruction wrought on the Acropolis by the Persians there were already two sanctuaries to Athena, the one on the north side and the other on the site of the Parthenon. No traces of an actual temple beneath the Erechtheum, however, have been found or indicated, the fifth-century foundations being of poros ashlar masonry resting on the hard limestone of the Acropolis. Attempts have been made by Holland[52] and Paton[53] to interpret diagonal rock-cutting and two dark brown stones believed to have fallen from the foundation of the Erechtheum as evidence of such a pre-Erechtheum structure erected near the south wall within the classic temenos. But there is nothing to suggest that they were the remains of a sixth-century shrine of Athena. Nevertheless, it is very probable that she was venerated on the Acropolis from very early times as the goddess of fertility *par excellence* under a variety of names and having diverse functions. In the northern sanctuary, where her image of olive wood was duly installed, she may have been the Earth-goddess controlling vegetation before she assumed more militant characteristics in her southern temple as Athena Parthenus.

The Ionic temple on the north side with its superb porches, delicately carved mouldings and frieze and slender columns, all of great beauty, was dedicated jointly to Athena Polias and Poseidon-Erechtheus, a fabulous king of Athens, the son of Gaea, the Earth-goddess, or of Athena by whom he was reared, and brought into conjunction with Poseidon, the god of earthquakes, water and navigation, whose sacred 'token' was the trident. As completed in the fifth century the main rectangular structure, 79 feet in length and 43 feet in width, was divided into four compartments. At the east front was a prostyle-hexastyle Ionic portico, and at the west end the façade consisted of a plain wall surmounted by four half-columns between antae, and a cornice of piers. From it projected the Porch of the Maidens, named after the six draped females statues (κοραι) which supported the roof. These caryatids were erected on a marble podium, and nearly opposite on the north side lay the great north portico with columns arranged in the same manner as the statues of the Maidens: four on the front and two on the east and west. In

the south end of the western compartment was a small door with steps leading up to the higher storey, while under the south-east corner was a crypt
entered through a door in the foundations of the north wall. But the principal entrance to the western part of the temple was in the centre of the south
side of the portico. The two porticos on the north and south, however, were
additions made after the general plan had been devised. Moreover, the
differences of level in the natural conformation of the rock, and the necessity
of enclosing a number of the sacred buildings within a single temenos made
the Erechtheum a unique construction; the ground on the east and south
being 10½ feet higher than that on the west and north at the bottom of the
lowest step of the east and north porticos respectively.

Under the western chamber and its porches dedicated to Erechtheus lay
the pool of Poseidon, alleged to have been created by a blow of his trident,
while outside the temple to the west in the Pandroseum (the sanctuary of
Pandrosus, the daughter of Cecrops, the traditional founder of Athens) was
the olive tree which Athena created in her contest with Poseidon. Among the
sacred 'tokens' in the crypt were the salt sea that poured forth when Poseidon
struck the rock, the tomb of Cecrops under a huge block of marble, and the
altar of Zeus Hypatos, or of Thyechous, the altar to Butes and one to Hephaestus, as well as the ancient image of Athena Polias. Around the walls and
porches were mouldings and a frieze with white marble figures fastened to
black Eleusinian stone by iron dowels and bronze bolts. This, however, is in
too fragmentary a condition to decipher the scenes portrayed. A horse,
doubtless sacred to Poseidon, appears to have featured in the representations,
and a woman holding a child in her lap may be Athena with the boy
Erichthonius (i.e. Erechtheum). The wooden image of Athena Polias, said
to have fallen from heaven, stood in the eastern cella; it bears a crested helmet, and holds a shield in the left hand and thrusts with a spear held in the right
hand, as in the peplos scene. The Ionic doorway in the north porch, though
badly damaged, is of outstanding architectural merit, and the decoration of
the six Ionic columns of the porch and their capitals are of excellent workmanship and great beauty.

THE PROPYLAEA AND THE TEMPLE OF ATHENA NIKE

It was, however, the Propylaea on the west side of the Acropolis that was
the pre-eminent Greek monumental roofed porch, designed by Mnesicles

and begun by Pericles in 437 B.C. It was built of Pentelic marble with Eleusinian black stone steps, dados, copings and thresholds. Although the original plans were never completed owing to the Peloponnesian war, nevertheless it rivalled the Parthenon as one of the priceless treasures of Athens. It was constructed on an older gateway facing south-west antedating the Persian war, and is composed of a large square hall occidentally orientated, 82 feet long and 59½ feet wide, with two wings on either side, and five steps leading up to a walk which has five openings and two porticos, one in front of the other at the rear. The principal entrance in the middle (24 feet high by 14 feet wide) giving access to the road had a lintel composed of two blocks of marble; all entrances had massive bronze doors. On the inner side towards the Acropolis was a portico with six Doric columns, and at the other end of the hall a similar porch facing outwards, with three aisles divided by rows of Ionic columns between the portico and the doors. The outer western front was flanked by two wings projecting at right angles to the main portico with a row of three smaller Doric columns between antae. The doorways were of simple Doric form, the façade being that of a huge prostyle porch. The north wing contained a chamber which doubtless was the room referred to by Pausanias[54] as serving the purpose of a picture gallery, or Pinakothek. On the south side the Nike bastion protruded to the west and here the little temple of Athena Nike was situated, together with the precinct of Artemis Brauronia and the altar of Nike, thereby preventing the creation of a chamber corresponding to that in the north wing. If the original intention of the architect was to complete the central structure with two flanking wings, this was never accomplished owing to the interruption of the Peloponnesian war and the difficulty of the lay-out of the site, the southern front finishing abruptly on the side of the bastion before the shrine of Athena Nike.

The only means of entering the Acropolis is by climbing up to the Propylaea, and it seems the terrace walls supporting the porticos of the west wings were to have been projected much further westwards round the ascent of the hill with gateways leading to the precinct of Athena Nike at the south and to the corresponding terrace at the north. As this could have involved the occupation of a good deal of the sanctuary of Artemis Brauronia on the south and east, it probably encountered the effective opposition of the priesthood both of that sanctuary and of Athena Nike on the south-west. Whether the summit of the bastion in the fifth century B.C. had its present shape is in debate. Apparently it was later than the Propylaea, as it was constructed on the site of an earlier poros temple and altar where perhaps the wooden image of the goddess was housed.[55] There, according to an inscription found in 1897, Callicrates was ordered to erect a marble temple and altar to Athena Nike, but this injunction was not put into operation immediately, as Pericles had decided to reconstruct the whole of the Acropolis, beginning apparently with the Propylaea as an imposing entrance to the sacred citadel. When this had been accomplished by Mnesicles about 450 B.C., or rather later, Callicrates set to work to produce the exquisite little temple of Pentelic marble on the crown of the bastion on the south side of the west approach to the Acropolis. It is probable that the bastion was shaped on its northern side when the Propylaea was built before the work on the temple was commenced to bring it into alignment with the great gateway.

When the temple had been completed with one portico facing the Acropolis and the other towards the sea, no attempt was made to orientate it in relation either to the Propylaea or to the Parthenon. The floor may have been lowered to bring the temple into adjustment with the stylobate of the Propylaea if, as Dörpfeld doubts, there was in fact a difference of level of the pavement and the final step from the Propylaea, as Wolsters has maintained. Otherwise the surface of the bastion may have been lowered after the temple was built to adjust it to the Propylaea, which was in that case a later structure. But the substructure of the Propylaea certainly suggests that it was definitely the earlier foundation.

The temple of Athena Nike was amphiprostyle tetrastyle, with fluted Ionic columns and a frieze of Pentelic marble encircling the entire building, depicting on the front a council of gods, and on the sides a number of deities, battle scenes of Greeks fighting Persians, and Greeks in conflict with Greeks. Before the east front stood the altar of Athena Nike, and around the temple, which was 27 feet in length, 18½ feet in breadth and 23 feet in height from the bottom of the steps, was a balustrade about 3 feet 2 inches in height, decorated with excellent reliefs of winged Victories worshipping Athena. In her wooden cult-statue the Victory was represented as wingless, holding a pomegranate in her right hand and a helmet in her left hand. The parapet round the platform supporting the temple was subsequently (*c.* 410 B.C.) also adorned with a sculptured Victory binding her sandal and another binding that of her sister, and surmounted by a metal grille with holes.[56] Some of

the graceful Victories are shown with their sacrificial victims, others bringing the spoils of war to the Goddess, illustrating no doubt the cultus performed in the temple, which unfortunately was destroyed by the Turks in
1686 to provide material for strengthening the defences of the Acropolis.
The stones, however, were recovered from the bulwarks by Ross, Schaubert
and Hanson in 1835, and skilfully assembled in reconstructing the temple on
its original foundations. This has been further extended as missing fragments
have come to light, and between 1935 and 1940 a complete restoration was
undertaken by the Greek Archaeological Society of one of the most elegant
structures on the Acropolis.

THE TEMPLE OF HEPHAESTUS (THE THESEUM)

Passing from the Acropolis to the Agora, the most conspicuous and externally the best preserved ancient building is the so-called Temple of Theseus.
It is situated to the west of an eminence inside the wall of Themistocles
near the Dipylon Gate. Constructed in Pentelic marble like those on the
Acropolis, it was completed about 421 B.C., soon after the death of Pericles,
about the same time as the Parthenon. As the adventures of Theseus, the
legendary king and unifier of Attica, occur in the sculptures, the temple has
long been known as the Theseum, but it now appears from its position and
the contents of its frieze that it is in fact the building seen by Pausanias[57]
above the market place between the Enneakrounos and the Stoa Poikile, on
the west side of the square, and identified by him with the Temple of
Hephaestus.[58]

It was erected as a Doric peripteral hexastyle *in antis* structure, 104 feet
in length, $45\frac{1}{2}$ feet in breadth, and 33 feet in height, with thirteen rather
slender columns at the sides. The frieze extended across the two ends of the
cella above the porches, though it contained sculptures only in the metopes
of the east front and in the sides adjoining it. Those on the east end represent
the Labours of Heracles, those on the west the struggle of the Lapiths and
the Centaurs, and over the pronaos across the pteron to the colonnade
battle-scenes in the presence of seated gods. On the lateral metopes are the
exploits of Theseus. The zophorus of the cella is of Parian marble, the foundations of limestone, and the background of the metopes and the frieze have
been coloured in red and blue respectively. Among the cult-images may have
been the bronze draped figure of Hephaestus displaying slight lameness,

executed by Alcamenes[59]—as the temple was located in the metal-working region, it was well situated to contain statues by Alcamenes, shops of the metal-workers having been scattered all over the hill. Rows of pots of cuttings excavated in the bedrock running parallel to the temple suggest that the precincts had been planted with a garden, and a water supply introduced by an underground channel from the direction of the Pnyx.[60] This continued in use until late Hellenistic and Roman times, as is shown by the sherds recovered from the site. It suffered slightly when Athens was desolated by Sulla in the first century B.C., and subsequently it was transformed into a Christian church dedicated to St George, the frieze being retained *in situ*. It escaped falling under Turkish rule, and apart from minor injuries it has remained relatively unspoilt externally by the ravages of time and the hazards of events.

THE TEMPLE OF ZEUS OLYMPIOS AT ATHENS

The largest Hellenistic monument, however, was the temple of Zeus Olympios to the south-east of the Acropolis, which was no less than six centuries in process of construction after the foundations were laid by Pisistratus in the sixth century B.C. on an ancient site dating from the time of Deucalion, whose grave was said to be near by this sacred spot where the waters of the flood ran away down a cleft in the enclosure.[61] The sanctuary was reconstructed and considerably enlarged by Cossulius in the time of Antiochus Epiphanes IV between 174 and 164 B.C., and it was the Emperor Hadrian in A.D. 129 who dedicated the temple and the huge cult-image of Zeus in the cella made of ivory and gold and surpassing in size all other statues except the colossi at Rhodes and Rome.[62] The Pisistratian temple on the banks of the Ilissus was a large dipteral, octastyle temple, probably of Doric design, but no bases or capitals have survived to confirm this conjecture. Although, as we have seen, Zeus was worshipped on the Acropolis when he became the guardian of Athens, yet it was upon Athena and her associates that attention was concentrated there after the fall of the Pisistratidæ. When at length it was rebuilt in the first century B.C. by Antiochus and his Roman architect it was as an octastyle Corinthian temple in Pentelic marble, except for the two lower steps of the stylobate, and measured probably about 318 feet in length and 132 feet in breadth, with 104 Corinthian columns, 56 feet 7 inches in height. Of these 48 stood in three rows under pediments, 56 in double rows at the sides.

In the foundations, fragments of the drums of large columns unfluted and of poros stone have been found, probably from the Doric columns of Pisistratus and his sons. A large artificial platform, or *peribolos*, supported by a retaining wall of Peiraic blocks with buttresses has been excavated, but only sixteen columns of the temple have survived, and apart from the drums little is known of the superstructure.[63]

THE TEMPLE OF ZEUS AT OLYMPIA

It was, however, at Olympia that the great temple of Zeus was constructed with the chryselephantine statue by Phidias occupying the place of honour. It was built between 470 and 456 B.C. on a lavish scale, situated in the sacred precinct (Altis) on an elevated substructure reached by three steps, south of the small shrine of the hero Pelops, west of the Altar of Zeus. Here, again, unfortunately nothing remains of the statue, and only a few blocks of the walls of the cella have survived. The plan of the temple, however, and its massive platform surrounded by the great drums of fallen pillars and blocks of the architraves, bases of statues under the rubble of the terrace, altars and votive offerings, ornaments and architectural features, have been preserved. These include marbles thrown down from the pediments and the metopes by earthquakes, and the remains of painted sculptures, waterspouts, marble lionine taenia of the architrave, guttae, mutules and regulae, many of which are now in the museum at Olympia; moreover, busts of Zeus and his image on coins may have been inspired by the statue of Phidias (e.g. on the coins of Elis belonging to the reign of Hadrian, now in Florence, Paris and Berlin; and a head in the Museum of Fine Arts, Boston).

In his description of the temple Pausanias gives the length as 230 feet and the breadth 96 feet, but this included the ramp at the east end of the stylobate, thereby adding some 30 feet to the total measurement. The cella had a prodomos on the east and a piathodomos on the west, and was itself divided from east to west into three aisles by a double row of columns, six at the ends and thirteen at the sides. The throne and its image stood in the western section, a table and statue in the middle division while the easternmost end was the place of public assembly. In height and division it had points of resemblance to the Parthenon, but there is no indication of curvature in the stylobate as in the great temple on the Acropolis. The entasis of the columns at the top was considerable, and they contained the customary twenty flutings and three incised rings round the neck. On the metopes of the prodoms and the episthodoms the Labours of Heracles were depicted, and a stone bench in the episthodomos suggests it was used for orations by orators, philosophers and poets. On the eastern pediment the sacrifice to Zeus before the chariot race between Pelops and Oenomanus was represented in twenty-one colossal figures, and on the west front the contest of Lapiths and Centaurs. In the midst of the first stood Zeus and in the second Apollo as invisible arbiters for the contending heroes. Although perfection is not attained as in the Parthenon sculptures, being in all probability the work of a local school, more is known of this sculpture than of that in any other great Greek temple. In the pronaos a fine Greek mosaic of a Triton with a boy on its tail was found under the Roman marble floor, cut in hexagons, and in the north-east corner another of fishes and sea-birds.

In the spaces between the pillars of the colonnade were bronze statues and votive offerings, while in the cella above the seven Doric columns on either side of the central aisle rose a row of lighter columns with galleries along the side aisles reached by staircases in the corners, perhaps to afford a view of the statue. In the antechamber which extended to the second pillar, the approach to the image was separated by a poros barrier. This unique image of Zeus, invested with attributes borrowed from the Olympian, Platonic and Stoic conceptions of the 'Father of gods and men', and the ideals of the philosopher-king, was one of the chief attractions for the motley crowds who came to Olympia to compete in or watch the games, to sell or to purchase at the booths of the traders, and to venerate the statue. Olympia as a spiritual, athletic and commercial centre became, in fact, a combination of Walsing-ham, Wembley and Widecombe, frequented by all who spoke Greek. Thus, it was to meet the requirements of the statue and its cultus that the gallery had to be inserted in the temple, and its shrine made secure with stone screens and bronze gates, with a priesthood set apart for its tendance. In the fifth century A.D., however, it was gutted by fire and then suffered from earthquakes, and it was only after great efforts by the French Expédition Scientifique de Morée in 1829, followed by the systematic excavation of Ernst Curtiss in 1876, completed by that of Lindau two years later, that the metopes of the opisthodomus, and the eastern parts of the pronaos, were recovered, together with the rest of the sculptured finds, many of which are now preserved in the local museum.[64]

THE TEMPLE OF ZEUS AT AKRAGAS (AGRIGENTO)

In Sicily another colossal temple of Zeus containing the huge figure of Atlas, 25 feet in height, known as Atlantes, appears at Agrigento, the ancient city of Akragas on the south coast, called by the Romans Agrigentum, 2½ miles from the sea. This is the largest of the rows of Doric temples between the Acropolis and the harbour. It is built in red-brown local poros stone with columns about 62½ feet high and a diameter of 14 feet at the bottom. Although not as ancient as the temple called Heracles, or as beautiful as those named Concordia or Juno Lacinia, or as well preserved as either Hera or Concordia, it was nevertheless the greatest of the Akragas group, measuring over 361 feet in length and 173 in breadth. In fact it is, after that of Diana at Ephesus, the largest Greek temple in the world. A succession of disasters since the Carthaginian invasion in 406 B.C., including wars, earthquakes, fires and large-scale pillages in the eighteenth century to procure stone for the making of the harbour of Porto Empedocles, has reduced the gigantic edifice to a ruin.

From the massive foundations now visible, however, it has been possible to reconstruct the ground plan because they were laid beneath the different parts of the building with fillings of rubbish and trodden earth between them. This has left the deeply laid substructures clearly defined, revealing the outlines of the lengthy cella with a very small opisthodomos separated from it by a wall at the western end. Five steps lead up to the stylobate divided into two courses on the north side, a colonnade having been replaced by a wall forming the base for the columns and the shell of the temple. On the outside, colossal figures 25 feet in height, representing perhaps the giants subdued by Zeus, served the purpose of caryatids supporting the architrave until they were thrown down by an earthquake. The discovery of archaic painted terracotta roofing tiles, which invalidates the suggestion of Diodorus that the roof had not been completed when the Carthaginians arrived in 406 B.C., indicates that in all probability the cella, or at any rate the space between it and the peristyle, was covered with a roof, and that the building was finished before the conquest of Akragas by Carthage.[65]

THE TEMPLE OF ASKLEPIUS AT EPIDAURUS

About a mile to the south, two pillars and an anta remain from the temple of Asklepius in which the statue of Apollo attributed to Myron stood before it was carried off to Carthage. It was at Epidaurus that the central sanctuary of the cult of Asklepius was situated. Here on the eastern coast of Argolis, standing on a small rocky peninsula, the god of healing was said to have been born,[66] and to his *hieron*, about 8 miles from Epidaurus, the sick resorted in great numbers to bathe in the sacred stream, sacrifice at the altars, and sleep in the temple in the hope of seeing a vision in the night watches and awakening cured of their infirmity, or, failing immediate relief, to seek from Asklepius advice that would lead to a cure.

The procedure, in the case of a person suffering from blindness, as recorded by Aristophanes in his comedy *Plutus* (*c.* 388 B.C.), was to sleep in the sacred precinct, to be touched on the head by the god, and to have his eyes wiped by him. Two snakes then licked his eyelids to complete the restoration of sight. On one of the Epidaurian inscriptions it is described how a man whose fingers were paralysed saw a vision during his sleep in the temple in which the god jumped on his hand and straightened his fingers one by one.[67] The long list of cures recorded on the inscriptions at the sanctuary leaves little room for doubt that from the end of the fifth century B.C. Epidaurus occupied in Greece a position resembling that of Lourdes in Western Christendom today.

While the cult of Asklepius may have been of Thessalian origin, having arisen probably at Tricca,[68] it was at Epidaurus that it became most firmly established in the fourth century in the sacred precinct, or hieron, with its temples, porticos, priests' houses, baths, gymnasium, hospital, palaestra and tholos. Entered by a propylaeum the chief buildings were grouped together with a stadium and between them and the gymnasium was the theatre outside the hieron. The temple of Asklepius, erected by Theodotus in the fourth century on the site of an earlier shrine, contained the cult-statue of the god in gold and ivory by Thrasymedes of Paros, about half the size of that of Zeus Olympios at Athens. As it was represented on two reliefs, now in the National Museum in Athens, and on contemporary coins, the god was portrayed seated on a throne with a dog near him, a staff in his left hand, and his right hand resting on the head of a serpent. Approached by a ramp at the eastern front, the temple was raised on stages, having six columns at the ends and eleven at the sides. The pronaos was used as a treasury protected by a grille and the doors inlaid with various woods and ivory and gold trimmings. The sculptured pediments were of Pentelic marble, the acroteria

having been executed by Timotheos. On one pediment were two Nereids
on horseback, and on another the scene of a battle between Greeks and
Amazons. To the south of the temple stood a large altar and to the east of it
what may have been an earlier small altar, with the foundations of a little
temple of Artemis. South-west of the temple of Asklepius is the very fine
tholos surrounded by an outer peristyle of twenty-six Doric columns said to
have been erected by Polyclitus the Younger between 360 and 330 B.C.
Inside was a circle of fourteen Corinthian columns standing free from the
wall, one of which was discovered in perfect condition buried three feet
below the ancient floor level. The entablature on the Corinthian columns
had a frieze convex in profile, and below the floor were three circular walls
with doorways in the nature of a subterranean labyrinth or maze, perhaps
used in connection with the snake cult of Asklepius. The beautiful theatre is
divided into three parts; the orchestra circle has an altar of Dionysius in the
centre, and the remarkably preserved semicircular auditorium, 387 feet in
diameter with excellent acoustic properties, has most of its seats and the
steeply radiating stairways intact. Of the stage buildings only the fourth-
century foundations remain.[69] Incubation was practised in the long two-
storeyed portico north of the tholos, called in the inscriptions the Abaton.[70]

THE TELESTERION AT ELEUSIS

Before bringing to a close this survey of the vast collection of Greek temples
that have survived, only a selection of which it has been possible to bring
under review in the space available in this volume, we should consider the
maze of ruins that constitute the remains of the Eleusinian sanctuary. These
occur 14 miles from Athens on the Aegean coast at the end of the Rarian
plain opposite the island of Salamis. According to the legend preserved in
the epic poem known as *The Homeric Hymn to Demeter*, assigned to the end
of the seventh century B.C. (*c.* 600),[71] it was here that the august, fair-haired
goddess Demeter, who had escaped from pirates *en route* from Crete to
Greece, disguised as an old woman, disclosed herself and her mission, and
established her Mysteries. While searching for her daughter Kore, or Persephone, who had been abducted by Pluto while she was gathering flowers in
the rich Rarian meadows and carried off to the nether regions, Demeter
became nurse to Demophon, the infant son of Celeus, the ruler of Eleusis.
Revealing her identity she ordered a temple and an altar to be built on the

hill above the well of Kallichoron, 'the Fountain of Maidenhood', where she first met the king's daughters. In this sanctuary she would teach her initiates the rites which would secure for them regeneration and a happy existence both here and in the after-life.

As Demeter is said to have sown the first seeds of corn on the Rarian plain, behind this complex legend in which a number of myths and traditions have been incorporated may lie an agrarian festival which became centred in the goddess of vegetation in general and in the Corn-mother in particular. As fertility and death are hardly separable, to this in due course was added her bestowal of immortality on her initiates both collectively and individually. In the Eleusinian Telesterion, or Hall of Initiation, the principal episodes in the cult-story were doubtless enacted, prominence being given probably to the abduction of Kore, the grief of Demeter, and perhaps the birth of a holy child called Brimos, or Iacchus, together with the symbolic reaping of an ear of corn in profound silence and in a blaze of light, culminating possibly in a sacred marriage of the hierophant and the chief-priestess in the roles of Zeus and Demeter, or of Pluto and Persephone. Such knowledge, however, as we possess of the esoteric Eleusinian Mysteries is confined to the legend, the fragmentary archaeological data, and references to the rites by Plutarch,[72] Aristotle,[73] and late writers like Hippolytus, who confused the Phrygian Attis cult with that of Demeter.[74] Those who had undergone the carefully prescribed process of initiation, seen the sacred sights revealed to them in the Telesterion and sworn never to divulge the sacred rites in which they had taken part, kept their vow so faithfully that, despite the widespread popularity of the Mysteries as a Pan-hellenic institution, the Eleusinian secrets were preserved for the two thousand years during which the cult held sway in the Graeco-Roman world.

Thus, the way has been opened for endless speculation concerning the nature, purpose and origin of the cult and its sanctuary. From the literary sources we are informed that the *mystae*, or neophytes, were led forth along the Sacred Way from Athens to Eleusis where, after fasting, asperging with water from the well Kallichoron, and undergoing purifications in the sea, they walked about on the shore carrying lighted torches, enacting the search of the Goddess for her abducted daughter. Then came the nocturnal vigil in the Telesterion, on the 22nd of Boedromian, where veiled in darkness and in complete silence they sat on their stools covered with sheepskins to behold the sacred sights which they must never reveal. As the tabu included visible portrayals of the things done the iconography sheds little more light on the problem than do the references found in the ancient authors concerning the real meaning and substance of the Mysteries. Foucart has suggested that the *dromenon* included a journey of the mystae to the grim underworld *en route* for the blissful delights of the Elysian plain,[75] but as Noack has pointed out,[76] such an experience could hardly have taken place in the Telesterion, or on its second storey, with the space and stage-setting available, including the absence of subterranean rooms and passages for the enactment of the lower world scenes.

His attempt, however, to reconstruct the beginnings of the Eleusinian sanctuary requires some revision in the light of the recent excavations at the site undertaken by Dr Kourouniotis and Professor Mylonas. It now appears, as the Homeric Hymn suggests, that the earliest temple attributed to Demeter was probably established in the Late Helladic II, or Middle Mycenaean period, in the second half of the fifteenth century B.C. The absence of Mycenaean remains on the terrace on which the Telesterion was constructed led Noack to the conclusion that the Hall of Initiation was not erected until Eleusis had been annexed by Athens just before the archonship of Solon, about 610 B.C. This seemed to be confirmed by there being no mention of it in the Homeric Hymn. Against this it is now contended that a temple which Demeter in the Hymn ordered to be built was a megaron erected at the end of the Middle Helladic below the acropolis under the fortification wall of the citadel on a rocky projecting spur. The floor is $5\frac{1}{2}$ feet above the level of its court. In front of it stood a platform well placed for the enactment of a sacred drama and the exposition of cult-objects, affording the audience a clear view of a secret ritual protected from the gaze of the uninitiated by the peribolos surrounding the court.[77]

This small unpretentious sanctuary was subsequently destroyed when the sacred area was further developed to accommodate the increasing number of initiates as the Mystery rapidly gained votaries after the union with Athens. In the seventh century the Geometric terrace had been extended to the west and the south, and the retaining wall to the east. The court was enlarged, the terrace became polygonal, and the form of the temple circular or apsidal, as in the case of the other Late Geometric sanctuaries (e.g. the temple of Apollo at Thermos.

Greek Temples

114   *West face of the Parthenon*

115

Sacrifices to Zeus, the father of the gods, were
made in the sacred grove at Olympia, where the
later sixth century temple dedicated to his wife,
the goddess Hera, now stands (115). Cult
images of the two gods were set up here in what
was probably the earliest Doric temple of any
size to be erected in Greece

116

17

The fame and authority of the Pythian oracle brought Greeks and Romans to Delphi for over one thousand years. Here, in the Temple of Apollo (117) high on the slopes of Mt Parnassus, the priestess spoke to delegations from the whole Greek world, many of whom erected treasuries nearby (116) in which to store their gifts for the oracle. Far below in the valley stands the circular temple dedicated to Athena who guarded the Delphic sanctuary (118)

The Parthenon, the most magnificent Doric temple ever built, dominates the Acropolis in Athens (119, 120). Inside the cella stood the statue of Athena by Phidias, and high on the frieze (114) were carved the figures of Athenians in the Panathenaean procession

The graceful Ionic temple
to the west of the Par-
thenon is dedicated to
Anthena Nike, the bringer
of victory. The frieze
shows scenes of battle, the
gods and winged Victories
(121)

121

Within the cella of the Olympian Temple of Zeus stood the fine statue by Phidias. Of this nothing remains, but surrounding the massive platform of the temple lie fallen pillars and columns (123, 124)

3

2

ie Erectheum which lies to the north of the rthenon stands on the most sacred site of the ropolis, where once the Mycenaean palace of e Attic Kings had been, and the first temple of hena. The marble roof of one of the porches is sup- rted by six caryatids, whose draped chitons show mastery of technique achieved by Greek sculptors

Many were the cults of the Greeks. Above, the snake, the symbol of the healing power of Asklepios is seen entwined in a tree; below, is all that remains of the Telesterion, where the secret Eleusinian Mysteries were performed

It may well be that this elliptical building represented the oldest remains of the Telesterion, going back to Late Helladic times, in which the mystae gathered to hear and see the esoteric disclosures. In short, Kourouniotis may be right in regarding the temple of Demeter in the Homeric Hymn and the Telesterion of Eleusis as one and the same building.[78] Outside the sanctuary, in front of the south gate, was a building having three contiguous rooms standing on a terrace, called the Sacred House (Ιερᾶς οἰκίας), and more recently (1952) a similar structure has been found in the north-eastern corner of the foundations of the stoa of Philon,[79] both of which seem to have been used for religious purposes. An ancient well in the rock of this stoa has been interpreted as the Kallichoron of the Homeric Hymn.

After the union with Athens about 600 B.C. the Geometric shrine was entirely rebuilt under Solon on a much larger scale, that probably being the time when the Homeric Hymn was composed. Around the greatly extended sacred area a massive wall was set up, and a large portion of the city was given over to the administrative requirements of the Sanctuary. Gradually the small temple was transformed into the hypostyle structure with its rectangular Telesterion, equipped with seats along the walls, and its roof supported by an array of columns parallel to the four sides. Rebuilt by Pisistratus on the grand scale about the middle of the sixth century B.C., the enclosure was doubled in size and the temple trebled, the interior measuring about 83 feet each way, with five rows of columns, probably Ionic, each row having five columns, a prostyle Doric porch with columns along the east front and the roof-tiles and seats cased with marble. On each side of the hall were two doors, except where it adjoined the rock on the north-west, and in the centre perhaps was a room called 'the palace' (ἀνάκορον) where the rites were performed.

When after the Persian wars the sanctuary was restored and rebuilt, probably by Cimon, the rock in the west had to be cut back and the surface levelled out on the lower slope to allow for expansion. This effort to glorify the temple of Demeter in recognition of her aid in the defeat of the invaders, was hindered by the internecine conflicts and rivalries with which Athens had to contend in the middle of the fifth century B.C. To complete the work begun by Cimon, Pericles solicited the aid of the architect Ictinus, who had just finished the Parthenon, and in consultation with three others new designs were drawn up with new and bolder internal arrangements and the completion of the walls. But perhaps because of the death of Pericles and the architectural difficulties involved in the scheme, it had for the most part to be abandoned. Then came the Macedonian wars in the fourth and the third centuries B.C., and it was not until the Roman period that the building was finally restored. Then the length of the Telesterion was increased to 59 yards from east to west, and the roof was supported by forty-two columns arranged in six rows of seven columns in each row.

Already in 330 B.C. a magnificent marble colonnade had been added to the eastern façade of the Telesterion and early in the Roman domination came a marble propylon at the main entrance to the precinct. Subsequently, in the second century A.D., over the pylon of Cimon, the imposing Greater Propylaea in imitation of that on the Acropolis at Athens was inserted, probably in the days of Marcus Aurelius, together with the paved court and other buildings within it. Nearly opposite the Lesser Propylaea was erected by a Roman nobleman, Appius Claudius Pulcher, a contemporary of Cicero, from which a paved section of the *via sacra* led to the Telesterion. To the right are the meagre remains of another temple constructed in Roman times, though it may have been built on a much earlier sacred site, thought by Noack to have been the temple of Demeter. The temple, however, has been shown by Kourouniotis to have been exclusively a product of the Roman period. Indeed, space would not have allowed such pre-Pisistratian building operations along the east side of the sacred way on the top of the projecting spur of the citadel hill.

Eleusis expanded in the Hellenistic period beyond the circuit of the walls of the sanctuary where public buildings, including a bath, a stadium, and a theatre occurred. But it was the temple and its Mysteries that gave it its unique position in Attica, and eventually throughout the Graeco-Roman world. When the esoteric worship of Demeter ceased in the fourth century with the rise and domination of Christianity, the sanctuary soon fell into ruins and a church was eventually established in the sacred precincts near the Telesterion, while on the Greater Propylaea crosses were incised. For two thousand years the secret rites had met some of the deepest needs of those who found in them assurance and sustenance, hope and joy in this world and, as they believed, beyond the grave.[80] But, like the Delphic Oracle and the powers of the Olympian gods, the Mysteries of Eleusis at length became a spent force, destined to extinction when Christianity was firmly established in the Roman Empire and in the Byzantine world.

CHAPTER VIII

Roman Temples

IN ANCIENT ROME, as in the rest of Italy, temples as architectural edifices were conspicuously absent in the cult of the farm and the field in the earlier phases. The gods and the *numina* were associated with particular places, occasions, and events, such as the annual sequence of the seasons, human occupations, sacred objects and localities, and worshipped or venerated with appropriate rites. To meet these requirements a 'holy acre' was set apart as a *loca sacra* by consecration to cause the divinity to take up his abode therein. Later in the state cult this ritual was formulated in the *jus divinum* which regulated right relations between the human and the divine inhabitants of a locality, and so acquired a special sanctity in the maintenance of the *pax deorum*.

THE TERMINUS

Similarly, boundary stones, or *termini*, marked the division between private and public property in the earlier 'religion of Numa,' protecting all boundary stones and sacred enclosures by virtue of their own numinous qualities before they became personified as a god, Jupiter Terminus. Thus, on the Capitol at Rome a terminus was worshipped either because it marked an ancient sacred precinct there, or as a representative of all boundary stones. In the developed state cult when all other celestial cults had been banished from the Capitol, it survived in the temple of Jupiter Capitolinus, or Terminalis. There was an opening in the roof above so that it could be venerated under the open sky, as in the earlier agricultural cultus of the farm and the field. Here was the centre of the public worship of the State as a whole, though nowhere on the imperial inscriptions is the Terminus described as *deus*. Nevertheless, Ovid addressing the stone exclaimed, 'O Terminus, whether thou art a stone or a stake fixed in the field, thou too has been deified from days of old'.[1] It was to him in a divine capacity that the Terminalia was celebrated on February the 23rd at the end of the year with rural rites in country districts. These included adorning the boundary stones with garlands and erecting an altar on which fire brought from the hearth of the farm was kindled, and fruits of the earth were shaken. A lamb and a sucking pig were then killed and their blood was sprinkled on the boundary stone. The ceremonies ended with a hymn of praise to Terminus and a feast.[2]

The festival no doubt was an annual renewal of the rites performed when the stones were first erected and consecrated.[3] In the state cult they were enacted on the Via Laurentina, doubtless formerly the boundary of the Roman State in the direction of Ostia. How the Terminus became so intimately associated with Jupiter is not very clear unless the temple on the Capitoline Hill was erected on the site of an ancient boundary stone which in view of its sacredness could not be removed. The earliest shrine seems to have been that dedicated to Jupiter Feretrius whose numen was apparently thought to have resided in a sacred oak on the northern summit of the Capitol. There Romulus was said to have hung the *spolia opima* he captured from the King of Caeninensee.[4] Next to it was the still older sanctuary in which the chief cult object was *lapis silex*, probably a stone axe believed to have been a thunderbolt at which solemn oaths were taken and treaties were concluded.

JUPITER

As the Sky-god *par excellence*, the 'ruler and guardian of the universe', the lord of creation, the god of the light and of the heavens, Jupiter became eventually the Roman counterpart of Zeus and his Indo-European prototype, Dyaus Pitar. Originally, however, he was one of the oldest of Italian concepts of deity, and in contrast to Hellenic anthropomorphism, he, like the other gods of ancient Rome, was essentially a cult figure devoid of human form; shadowy, incorporeal and numinous, but, nevertheless, having his abode in natural objects like stones and trees. Thus, whereas in Greece, as we have seen, the temple developed out of the dwelling house as the home of the god or goddess to whom it with its cult statue was dedicated, in Rome before an anthropomorphic element was introduced under Etruscan influence, the sacred precinct was merely an enclosure (*sacellum*) set apart for the divinity or numen indwelling in a terminus, tree or grove, a spring or cave, not in permanent houses (*aedes*).[5]

THE EARLY TRIADS AND THEIR TEMPLES

As the god of the light and the sky Jupiter, as in the case of most sky-gods, established himself mainly on lofty hills,[6] looking down on the Forum and the city from the Capitol and from the Alban Mount where he surveyed the whole of Latium,[7] as the guardian of Rome and the surrounding country. In his Capitoline temple he was the recipient of the sacrifices, vows and the laurel wreath of victory offered to him by the consuls and generals respectively, on their taking office or returning from a victorious campaign.[8] At an early period he was joined in a triad with two other ancient gods, Mars and Quirinus, both of whom had similar functions in an agricultural cultus incorporating warrior and chthonian elements.[9] Next to Jupiter, Mars occupied the highest place in divine honours at Rome, while as an agricultural deity he was worshipped all over Italy from the earliest times; he is invoked in the ancient hymn of the Arval Brothers and in the prayer of Cato's Farmer to protect the crops and herds from all harmful influences, to avert storms, and to give prosperity to the farmer and his household dwelling in woodlands in agricultural clearings.[10] In Rome until the time of Augustus only two temples were dedicated to him, one in the Campus Martius, which until 138 B.C. was merely an altar and, like the other sanctuary outside the Porta Capena, was not within the sacred boundary of the *pomerium*, perhaps because of the warlike character of Mars.

In the heart of the city, however, his spears were kept in a *sacrarium* in the former royal palace (*regia*), where they were brandished by the consul at the outbreak of war, just as the *ancilia*, or sacred shields of his priesthood (the Salii), were carried in the leaping and dancing processions in the March festival as part of the symbolic armoury of the Roman state. The Salii, however, were restricted to twenty-four in Rome, divided into two groups, one belonging to Mars located on the Palatine hill where he was the most prominent deity, the other to Quirinus on the Colline hill. A very ancient sanctuary was, in fact, consecrated to Mars on the Quirinal (from which Quirinus derived his name) near the temple of Dius Fiduis.[11] Having begotten Romulus, Mars also became the father of the people of Rome.

Therefore, Jupiter, Mars and Quirinus were regarded as the three guardian gods of Rome to each of whom King Numa assigned a *flamen*. Together they constituted the chief triad of the ancient Numa religion in which Jupiter continued to reign supreme in his many aspects. If in due course when the Roman gods were hellenized he became the counterpart of Zeus in Latin literature, it was still the old Roman deity who was the principal object of worship, often in conjunction with his two principal associates of the Palatine and the Quirinal settlements and their respective temples and cultus. While each god had his own attributes, functions and distinguishing features, they had a common inheritance deeply rooted in the soil and concerned with the growth of the crops and military campaigns, finding expression in the cult of the farm and the field and of warrior pursuits. It was, therefore, in agriculture and war that the worship of their respective sanctuaries was first centred, and as the gods acquired additional powers with the rise of urbanization and increasing importance, the temples in the capital were multiplied and dedicated to the several aspects and activities of the divinities whom they served. Jupiter as the chief deity may have had a less popular appeal than Mars as the principal agricultural god, to whom numerous temples were dedicated in Rome as well as elsewhere, but he was nevertheless, the guardian of the city and occupied a more exalted position than any other god.

With the rise of Etruscan domination, Juno and Minerva with their western-Asian affinities came into greater prominence in a second triad, but Jupiter bearing the exalted title *Optimus Maximus* still remained supreme in his Capitoline temple. As he was the king of heaven, Juno became queen of the celestial realms by virtue of her nuptial relationship with him. Minerva occupied the third place among these divinities, wielding the thunderbolt of Jupiter as his daughter. As a virgin goddess identified with the Greek Athena, she inherited the latter's attributes and because of her interests in crafts and skill in weaving, medicine, spinning and teaching, she became the patron of the arts and of learning. Her most ancient temple at Rome was probably that on the Capitol built by Tarquin with Etruscan workmen in the Etruscan style, and dedicated to their triad (Jupiter, Juno and Minerva) by the consul Horatius in 509 B.C. Another was erected *extra pomerium* on the Aventine hill, probably dedicated to her on her birthday, 19 March (Quinquatrus), when dramatic poets, actors and skilled craftsmen assembled there.[12] She was also worshipped under the name of Minerva Capta in a shrine on Mons Caelius, when, after the taking of Falerii in 241 B.C., her image was brought to Rome and the temple dedicated on her birthday, as was that on the Aventine.[13]

Thus, the worship of Minerva spread at the expense of that of Mars, and although she had no flamen like the other two members of the earlier triad, nor a place in the calendar, her Aventine temple was nevertheless the religious centre of the most ancient trade-guilds, whose antiquity was so great that they were alleged to have been founded by Numa.[14] That Minerva herself was a pre-Etruscan deity is suggested by these ancient associations of her cult and the fact that she bore an Italian name, Menrva, before she and the arts over which she presided at Falerii in southern Etruria were taken over by the Etruscans, and she assumed the guise and role of Athena Polias.

THE ETRUSCAN CAPITOLIUM

While Etruscan influence in the tranformation of the indigenous customs, cults and beliefs has often been greatly exaggerated, the fact remains that it was at this juncture in the history of Roman religion that temple construction became an established feature, coinciding with the introduction of the anthropomorphic interpretation of the ancient deities, to which reference has already been made. As the conception of *numen* gave place to that of *deus*, the *sacellum* and *locus sacer* as sacred enclosures open to the sky gradually assumed the form and content of architectural temples in conjunction with the Etruscan style and plan. Thus, on the Capitoline hill the sanctuaries of Jupiter Feretrius of Fides and of Fortuna Primigenia, attributed to Romulus, Numa, and Servius Tullius,[15] respectively and other early shrines and altars, were removed to make way for the great triple temples dedicated to Jupiter, Juno and Minerva, who were worshipped in Etruscan cities everywhere as Tinia, Thalna and Minerva.

Relatively few remains of Etruscan temples, however, have been found *in situ*; less in Rome than in the neighbouring cities. Nevertheless, the numerous fragments of friezes in terracotta reliefs, together with cornices, antefixae, and other decorative features of sacred buildings found on the Capitoline, the Palatine, the Esquiline and in the Forum, depicting processions, chariot races, banquets and similar scenes, show in their modelling and colour considerable skill.[16] This must have been very evident when they adorned edifices raised on a podium approached by a flight of steps, and enriched by gilding, with pendant slabs hung round the eaves to protect the walls which were covered with stucco and decorated with paintings. But owing to the perishable nature of the materials employed—unburnt brick, rubble masonry and timber roofs—little has survived apart from these terracotta remains which were introduced into Rome by the Etruscans in and after the end of the seventh century B.C. By the sixth century (525–450 B.C.), the Etruscan culture was firmly established in the capital and reached its architectural climax in the great Capitoline temple of Jupiter Feretrius, Optimus Maximus.

THE CAPITOLINE TEMPLE OF JUPITER FERETRIUS

From the traditions concerning its erection and vicissitudes in the current literature,[17] it appears to have been built as a result of a vow made by Tarquinius Priscus in the Sabine war, and the foundations were laid by Tarquinius Superbus, though it was not finished until the first year of the Republic in 509 B.C.[18] The ambitious scheme proved to be much more costly than was anticipated, and it required the importation of craftsmen from Etruria and much labour from the Roman *plebs*[19] to erect such an edifice where seventy years earlier there had been only a few wattle and daub huts. It now seems that it was from Etruria that the Greek alphabet and much Greek culture was brought to Rome by Etruscans, together with a new reckoning of time which the Greeks had derived from the orient.

According to Dionysius of Halicarnassus and Vitruvius[20] the temple was constructed of the tufa of the hill on a high rectangular platform, measuring about 200 feet on the side facing south, with three parallel cellae side by side, the one in the middle being dedicated to Jupiter and the other two to Juno and Minerva respectively. In the central cella is said to have stood a terracotta cult image of Jupiter with a thunderbolt in his right hand, alleged to have been the work of Vulca of Veii who was called to Rome to execute it.[21] In the chamber on the right may have been a statue of Minerva, and in that on the left of Juno. That of Jupiter was clothed with a tunic decorated with palm branches and victories, and a purple toga embroidered with gold.[22] At festivals the face was painted red.[23] The roof and pediment apparently were similarly decorated with terracotta figures, and the wood of which they were made was protected by a casing of gilded bronze or terracotta. Their style no doubt resembled the Veii sculptures and the portrayal on the coins representing the temple of Catulus, though very few remains of terracotta decoration have been found on the Capitoline hill.

These descriptions of the superstructure of the early Capitoline temple in ancient writings are, however, corroborated substantially by early representations and later excavations, and evidence from other sites of early temples in Etruria and Latium of similar dimensions and construction on stone platforms, with facings of tufa blocks or stucco fashioned to make a decorative stylobate. The dimensions given by Dionysius were doubtless based on those of the temple of Catulus in his own day, but, nevertheless, as these were virtually the same as those of the Etruscan edifice that had been destroyed in 83 B.C.,[24] neither the size nor the form of the two buildings is likely to have been very different, though in detail, such as the introduction of Corinthian columns, and in their respective proportions, they were by no means identical. It was, in fact, the established custom to erect a new sanctuary on the foundations and designs of its predecessor, as, for example, when the *haruspices*, as the Etruscan diviners were called in Rome, in the reign of Tarquinius,[25] ordered Vespasian to build his new temple upon the original foundations and according to the same plan as the previous building, except that it was to be higher, more expensive and splendid.[26] The greater height, however, was not in harmony with that of the stylobate though it proved to be impossible to raise the elevation by lowering the level, as Catulus proposed,[27] to increase the number of steps to the approach, because of the *favissae*, or underground passage beneath the cella, in which the statues from the roof and other gifts were stored.[28] It was this sanctity, combined often with practical considerations, as for instance maintaining the earlier firmly laid foundations intact, that kept the ancient sanctuaries free from change and reconstruction.

Although the temple was rebuilt several times to house a succession of spoils, until it was restored by Augustus about 32 B.C. at considerable public expense[29] it does not seem to have been greatly enlarged or elaborated. The Etruscan temple survived until it was burnt in 83 B.C. and was then reconstructed in marble by Sulla with Corinthian columns from the temple of Zeus in Athens.[30] It was again destroyed by fire in A.D. 70 and then rebuilt by Vespasian in the following year.[31] Finally it was a victim of the great fire in the reign of Titus, and it was restored with Pentelic marble columns by Domitian at heavy cost.[32]

THE TABULARIUM

On the south-east slope of the Capitoline facing the Forum is the well-preserved Tabularium which was erected by the consul Lutatius Catulus in 78 B.C. as the central repository for the state archives.[33] Over a substructure, used later as a jail, grouped round a square court were large vaults, an open colonnaded court with Doric columns belonging probably to the first century A.D., an upper portico, and numerous halls, corridors and staircases. In the rooms were a cornice of the temple of Concordia and another of the temple of Vespasian, with fragments from neighbouring temples, the masonry of *opus quadratum* going back to Republican times. The outer walls were of Gabini stone, the capitals of the half-columns and the imports of the arches were of travertine, the inner walls of Anio tufa, and the vaults of concrete. The entrance from the Clivus Capitolinus is through a well-jointed arch of peperino, now corroded, the Tabularium occupying the entire area between the Clivus Capitolinus on the south-west and a flight of sixty-seven steps leading from the temple of Concordia and the Forum up to the temple of Juno Moneta on the Arx on the north-east. The two portions of the Capitoline were connected by a Doric arcade of peperino columns with eleven arches, but it was blocked up by the erection of the temple of Vespasian and the enlargement of the temple of Concordia.

THE TEMPLES OF VESPASIAN AND OF SATURN

The temple of Vespasian abutting on the Tabularium, begun by Titus in A.D. 80 and completed by Domitian, consisted of an almost square cella with prostyle hexastyle portico with entablature, a sculptured frieze and a beautiful cornice. Three Corinthian columns of white marble at the south-east corner of the pronaos have survived supporting a section of the entablature. The inside wall of the cella was covered with coloured oriental marbles and faced outside with Pentelic marble. On a pedestal, part of which still remains, stood the statues of Vespasian and Titus.[34] As in the temple of Concordia the interior was surrounded by a row of marble columns. On the opposite side of the street near the foot of the Capitoline and on the edge of the Forum, is an Ionic hexastyle portico of massive travertine blocks and marble below, generally thought to belong to the temple of Saturn built against the slope of the Capitoline hill. On this site was traditionally an altar to Saturn, and around it a temple is said to have been erected in 498 or 497 B.C., dedicated at the Saturnalia on 17 December.[35] Although the traditions about its construction vary, it belonged to the beginning of the Republic, and was subsequently rebuilt in 42 B.C. by Munatius Plancus.[36] The blocks belonging to the lofty podium, and remains probably of a drain, are among the few relics that have survived, together with the eight columns of the pronaos and the entablature, but it once stood with a portico approached by a lofty flight of steps. From the earliest times it was the state treasury—the *aerarium populi*.

THE TEMPLE OF JUPITER LATIARIS

Thus, the Capitoline hill and its immediate surroundings were the official centre of the state cult. Here on the south-west peak had stood for more than five hundred years the temple of Jupiter and all that his worship had come to signify under Etruscan and Greek influences as that of Optimus Maximus, the greatest of the gods. Nevertheless, so lofty and civic was the state cult that it made little appeal to the ordinary citizen whose domestic worship remained centred in the genuine ancient Roman religion. It is not surprising, therefore, that the annual festival of the *Feriae Latinae* was held at the ancient seat of Jupiter Latiaris on the Alban hills 13 miles south-east of Rome, where he was the original god of the Latin League, the foundation of his temple being ascribed to the Tarquinii. There in April a Roman pastoral festival of considerable antiquity was held before it was brought under Etruscan influences and overshadowed by the Capitoline temple and its cultus.[37]

THE TEMPLES OF DIANA AT NEMI AND ON THE AVENTINE HILL

Second only to Jupiter Latiaris for the ancient Latins was the goddess Diana whose most famous temple was in the Arician grove in the Alban hills on the north side of Lake Nemi, the worship and legend of which has been immortalized by Macaulay and Frazer. From early times this sanctuary of *Diana Nemorensis*, 'Diana of the Woodland Glade', was a sacred centre of the Latin League, the cult, it is said, having been founded by Egerius Baebius of Tusculum, *dictator Latinus*.[38] The grove was 33 yards in length by 17 yards in breadth, with columns on either side of the pronaos, a retaining wall on the north and east cut into the hillsides, having semicircular niches sunk in them faced with columns forming a series of chapels. The terrace rested on a long wall with buttresses down to the side of the lake.[39]

In this ancient sanctuary of the silvan goddess of Aricia a strange custom was observed: a fugitive slave reigned as *Rex Nemorensis*, 'King of the Wood', having succeeded in slaying his predecessor in a single combat and breaking off a branch of a sacred tree in the grove; he retained this position until he in his turn suffered the same fate. This rule was said to have been still in operation in the time of Strabo[40] and Pausanias,[41] both of whom describe it. This is all we know of the priesthood of Diana,[42] and whether or not Frazer's interpretation of it is correct,[43] Diana certainly was a tree-goddess who had her abode in groves before she was identified with Artemis. Moreover, she was the chief divinity of Aricia worshipped at Nemi by the Latins and the plebeians as their patron deity.

According to Varro her name and cult came from the Sabines,[44] who were essentially Latins and Romans in their worship. When they became plebeians in all probability they erected the temple of Diana on the Aventine as the *commune Latinorum Dianae templum*. It was situated in a numinous grove of holm-oaks outside the pomerium on a separate hill overlooking the Tiber and occupied by plebs in 457 B.C.[45] There the pre-Republic temple of Diana Nemorensis from Aricia was duly installed alongside that of Jupiter Latiaris of the Alban Mount, though by remaining outside the pomerium she retained her independence in the state cult. Nevertheless, without severing her connection with the Latin League, she was inevitably brought into an intimate relationship with the Roman deities and eventually assumed, somewhat artificially, the attributes of Apollo's sister Artemis, though she never had a flamen. Her wooden statue in the Aventine temple, said to be one of the oldest anthropomorphic representations of a deity in Rome, was in fact modelled on an early crude image of Artemis.[46]

While still under the Etruscan kings Rome aspired to become head of the League, and with this end in view the presence of Diana and her temple outside the pomerium on the Aventine hill was welcomed because, though she was not a Roman goddess, yet she was worshipped inside the civic wall. Thereby without losing her status in the Latin League, she was brought into conjunction with Jupiter Latiaris and identified with Artemis whom she resembled in many respects as a forest and fertility goddess; she later acquired human aspects, readily absorbing all the attributes and myths of Artemis.

THE AVENTINE TEMPLE OF MINERVA

Unlike Diana, Minerva who also had a temple on the Aventine, was neither a Latin nor a Roman goddess in origin. Her name is Italic, Menrva, and under this designation she was well known in Etruria and northern Italy, but not in Latium or the south. In Rome her earliest appearance was as a member of the Capitoline triad in association with Jupiter and Juno, though she was not an Etruscan deity. Early in the sixth century B.C. she was established at Falerii, an Italian Etruscan town on the northern bank of the Tiber, strongly under Etruscan influence but essentially Latin in character. There she was intimately connected with handicraft, and when she settled on the Aventine her temple became the religious centre of trade guilds and of skilled craftsmen who assembled there on her chief festival, 19 March (Quinquatrus), which continued for five days, commemorating the dedication of the temple in 484 B.C. Originally a day sacred to Mars, the state was compelled to recognize her status and significance in its pantheon and temples, when the Minerva celebrations became so popular that they completely obscured its Martian associations. She was not, however, assigned a flamen or a place in the calendar.

Because of her interest in crafts, Minerva was identified with Athena when the Greek gods were introduced into Italy and were assigned temples, sanctuaries and shrines in Rome and elsewhere. It is highly improbable that she actually originated from Athena, in view of her name, her provenance and her worship *extra pomerium*. The first mention of the Aventine temple was as the headquarters of the *scribae* and *histriones* in the second Punic war.[47] As restored by Augustus, it was a peripteral hexastyle structure about 49 yards long and 24 yards wide, having thirteen columns on each side, situated between the temples of Luna and Diana. Although exactly when it was founded is not known, its alleged dedication of 19 March connects it with Mars and means it was originally sacred to him. It was after the hellenization of the ancient Roman deities that Minerva was equated with Athena, whose attributes gradually were transferred to her so that she too became regarded as the virgin daughter of Zeus, the patroness of arts and crafts of all kinds including painting, poetry, spinning, weaving, dyeing, medicine and teaching, and the inventor of musical instruments used in religious worship.[48] She also guided men in cunning, courage, and perseverance, especially in warfare and in acquiring skill in their occupations and, like Athena Polias, she was the protectress of cities.

THE GREEK GODS AND THEIR TEMPLES

THE SIBYLLINE TEMPLE AT CUMAE

As the Etruscan domination introduced the building of temples as a constant feature in the religion of ancient Rome, so also from Etruria came the first contacts with Greece, long before the Roman deities were identified with their Greek counterparts as a result of the influences introduced by the Punic wars. It was then that Greek literature became a potent force in Rome, but in the meantime the Sibylline books inspired by Apollo, which eventually were deposited in the Capitoline temple, had played their part in the arrival of the new gods and their cults. In the sixth and fifth centuries floating oracular *dicta* from Asia Minor, emanating from a weird ecstatic woman, made their influence felt in Greece, especially in the Orphic movement and in Apolline circles. Thence the practice spread to Italy and became established at Cumae on the Campanian coast near Naples by Greek colonists who had settled there. On the acropolis was the famous cave of the Cumaean Sibyl which became the scene of intense oracular activity[49] with its 'hundred entrances whence resound many voices'. The principal entrance is on the side of the hill towards the sea. On a terrace above the system of galleries and vaulted passages, most of which are now blocked, leading to a large rectangular covered forecourt, was the temple of Apollo indicating the close association between the two cults.

According to tradition a strange old woman succeeded in selling the Sibylline books at an exorbitant price to Tarquinius Superbus, the last of the Tarquin kings, after she had burned the earlier collection of prophecies which he had refused to purchase. If this legend preserves the memory of the foundation of the Cumaean temple in the fifth century under Sibylline influences, it shows that the movement played an important part in the introduction of the Greek gods and their cultus in Italy, passing from Cumae to Rome in the time of the last Tarquin. The books were deposited in the cellar of the Capitoline temple and their secrets guarded.[50]

It is most probable that it was at Cumae that the oracles were first consulted in Italy since they were established there in charge of *duoviri* before the collections of prophecies were retained on the Capitol in Rome, early in the Republic under the care of *decemviri sacris faciendis*, as the guardians then became.[51] In the disturbances that occurred in the fifth century during the Etruscan struggle for the restoration of the dynasty, application was made to the Sibylline books for consultation and oracular direction. It was at their command that the Greek gods and their cults were introduced and gained a footing in Rome at the beginning of the Republic, and in 499 B.C. for the first time led to the vowing of a temple. Moreover, the oracles were rooted in the cult of Apollo whose centre was at Cumae, and the priestesses of the oracles were drawn from the Greek cities of the Campania and southern Italy. A Greek temple of the fourth or third century B.C., popularly known as '*il tempio dei Giganti*', has survived together with the remains of an amphitheatre, tufa blocks of a brick wall (*Arco felice*), Roman masonry, vases, statues, grave goods and a circular archaic tomb with a conical roof in a necropolis on the north side of the city.[52]

THE AVENTINE TEMPLE OF CERES

Cumae, in fact, became virtually the official seat in Italy of the ancient cult of Apollo and of the closely associated Sibylline oracles, particularly for Rome. From there as early as 496 B.C. by the incantations of the books came the Greek grain-goddess Demeter under the Roman name of Ceres. She was a goddess of fertility whose worship with that of her daughter Kore and of Dionysus, Latinized as Libera and Liber respectively, was ordered to be introduced into Rome, the triad representing the Eleusinian group, Demeter, Kore and Iacchus.[53] The temple near the church of Santa Maria in Cosmedin was erected by Greek architects and under Greek influence in her honour on the slope of the Aventine in 495 B.C., to avert a famine during the war with the Latins,[54] and in obedience to the oracle. The walls were decorated by two Greek artists, Gorgasus and Damophilus, with frescoes and reliefs, the figurative terracotta revetments of the columns in all probability having been previously restored and the roof ornamented with Etruscan statues. Unfortunately, however, after having been twice struck by lightning, the temple was destroyed by fire in 31 B.C. with the result that many of the works of art contained in it perished.[55] It was restored by Augustus and dedicated by Tiberius in A.D. 17.[56]

It had long been the centre of plebeian ritual observances, such as the Cerealia and its games (*ludi*) on 19 April, instituted during the second Punic war about 202 B.C., and placed under a Greek priestess. Ceres, however, was originally *Dea, Dia*, an ancient vegetation deity in the Arval ritual, associated with Tellus,[57] a Roman earth-goddess with a temple on the Esquiline in Carinis whom she closely resembled in nature. Nevertheless, it was in her Greek guise that she was venerated in the Aventine temples which acquired political importance as the headquarters of the plebeian *aediles*, the repository of their archives, the treasury of the fines imposed for assaulting plebeian magistrates,[58] and the centre of distribution of food to the poor. The ludi became increasingly licentious but the temple seems to have played its part in conserving the corn supply brought from Cumae, Etruria and Sicily to relieve the famine.[59] As a result, indirectly at any rate, it brought Greek influences to bear upon the plebs as its ritual was primarily Hellenic superimposed on a Roman substratum.[60]

LIBER PATER AND THE BACCHANALIA

Liber was an ancient corn-spirit who with Libera and Ceres was reintroduced in the Greek cult in Rome by a Sibylline divine injunction to promote the growth of the crops. He appeared in the guise of Dionysus, and later became identified with Bacchus, the god of wine.[61] In the Aventine temple, however, there is no indication of the Dionysiac orgies having been practised during the first three hundred years after its foundation in 493 B.C., Liber Pater being a sober agricultural god. In Greece, as we have seen, the Dionysiac ritual had been shorn of its Thraco-Phrygian excesses by Apolline influences at Delphi[62] before it reached southern Italy, making its way to Rome perhaps from Tarentum when this city was captured by Fabius in 208 B.C. Traces of it occur in an inscription from Cumae belonging to the first half of the fifth century forbidding the burial of any who were not Bacchic initiates in a cemetery reserved for the latter.[63] In the third century licence and debauchery became rife in the Campania. This was attributed to the action of a local priestess, Annia Paculla, who introduced the nocturnal celebration of the rites admitting men into what had been hitherto a female cult.[64] They were then held five times every month instead of three times a year, and so contagious did the Bacchanalian frenzies become that they rapidly spread throughout Italy, and by 185 B.C., after the second Punic war, were firmly established.[65] In the grove beneath the Aventine frenzied women brandishing blazing torches rushed in the darkness to the Tiber to plunge them into the water and draw them out again unquenched amid the strains of wild music, clanging timbrels and cymbals, and sinister howlings. This ecstatic delirium was alien to the state cult and clearly had to be suppressed.

Not only did such unedifying orgiastic practices meet with disapproval but there could be dangerous political and social consequences from a secret foreign cult making a strong appeal to the populace, including slaves and criminals; therefore in 185 B.C. the Senate took rigorous measures to suppress it. Bacchic shrines were closed and their priests and priestesses were forbidden to exercise their functions, and no Roman citizen was allowed to attend a Bacchanalia or any meeting of Bacchae. This would seem to suggest, however, that while Romans were not permitted to become officials or take any part in Bacchic rites, the prohibition was not absolute, it being possible for the Praetor to sanction not more than five persons assembling for the purpose in public,[66] though 'the Halls of the Mysteries' in Bacchic sanctuaries do not appear to have been places where the cult was practised.

Neither Liber nor Dionysus-Bacchus had a temple of his own in Rome. It appears that Liber had a shrine in the imperial gardens,[67] while a shrine to Bacchus stood in *summa sacra via* where the Clivus Palatinus ascended the Palatine.[68] A marble epistyle of a circular structure about 13 feet in diameter, was discovered in front of the basilica of Constantine with an inscription recording the restoration of such a shrine by Antonius Pius, as displayed on a coin of that period found within its colonnade.[69] Moreover, notwithstanding the repression of the Bacchanalia and the break-up of the *thiasoi* by the Senate in the second century B.C., the Bacchic mystery and its rites continued to flourish, especially in southern Italy, as is shown by the Dionysiac designs on sarcophagi and in the great wall paintings in the Villa of the Mysteries of the first century A.D. at Pompeii,[70] and in the series in an underground room of the 'Homeric House' on the Strada dell' Abbondanza.[71] In addition to these scenes representing initiation into the Dionysiac mysteries, figures of Maenads and Satyrs are of frequent occurrence in the houses and villas of Pompeii of the first century B.C. prior to its destruction in A.D. 79, suggesting that the cult was firmly established. Nowhere, however, did it ever secure official recognition or condonation enough to gain a place in the calendar for its observances.

THE MAGNA MATER AND HER PALATINE TEMPLE

The Phrygian Magna Mater, Cybele, on the other hand, though no less foreign and alien to the state cult, found a permanent home in Rome in the third century B.C., some twenty years before the Bacchanalian scandals were suppressed. For twelve years the Punic war had dragged on and its end was still not in sight. Hannibal had succeeded in marching through Italy and remained securely entrenched in the mountains of the south. Moreover, there had been several ominous showers of pebble rain which were thought to portend an approaching calamity. It was decided, therefore, to consult the Sibylline oracles in 204 B.C. in order that a way might be found to drive Hannibal out of the country. The reply was to the effect that this would be achieved if the Idaean Mother, Cybele, were brought to Rome from Pessinus.[72] Following this oracular injunction, an envoy was dispatched to the sacred Phrygian city with the authority of the priestly college of the *decemviri* to open negotiations with Attalus, the king of Pergamos, who had custody of the small black meteorite in which the goddess was believed to be embodied, and to request its conveyance to Rome.

After some demur the request for its removal was granted, and it was placed on a special ship which took it as far as Ostia, where already the Magna Mater had a small temple and high-priest. On its arrival it was welcomed with public rejoicing, and strange things are said to have occurred. The boat was grounded on a sand bank at the mouth of the Tiber and all efforts to release it failed until a matron of questionable virtue, Claudia Quinta, towed it off, thereby clearing herself of a charge of adultery. It was then sailed up the Tiber to Rome by ship[73] or, as Livy describes the event, it was carried to Rome by relays of matrons.[74] However it may have reached the capital, on 4 April 204 B.C., it was installed in the Temple of Victory on the Palatine near the hut which commemorated Romulus, and there it remained until an impressive temple was erected on the hill in Cybele's honour and dedicated to her on 9 April, 191 B.C.[75] In the meantime she had justified her presence in Rome by producing a bumper harvest, and the following year, it was said, that she drove Hannibal out of Italy.

The Palatine temple of Cybele was destroyed by fire in 111 B.C. though the statue of Claudia Quinta in it was preserved and restored the following year. This was repeated in A.D. 3 when it again was burnt and this time restored by Augustus.[76] On the west corner of the Palatine at the top of the Scalae Caci are the ruins of a temple near which inscriptions relating to the Magna Mater have been found, together with fragments of a large statue of a woman seated on a throne, and of paws of lions[77] (animals which are so frequently associated with images of the Mother-goddess everywhere). These remains of the Palatine temple of Cybele suggest that it must have had a massive concrete podium with side walls $12\frac{1}{2}$ feet thick and 18 feet in the rear, faced with stucco, but without strong masonry casing to support the cella walls. This podium was probably added when the temple was rebuilt after the fire in 111 B.C., its total length then measuring 109 feet, and its width 56 feet, built in the prostyle hexastyle Corinthian manner with curved roof and a flight of steps on which stood the statue of the goddess enthroned between lions. In front of the podium are the remains of a fourth-century retaining wall of Grotta Oscura and Fidenae blocks, and from the end of the wall was the base of the pedestal on which doubtless the statue stood. The concrete of the podium, however, belongs to the Augustan reconstruction[78] while the fragments of the peperino columns suggest that material from an earlier edifice (*c.* 110 B.C.) was employed, as peperino was very widely used in the second century B.C.

It would seem, therefore, that the Augustan architect when necessary filled in with new blocks, as well as applying a stucco facing and the current ornamentation to adorn the temple of the Magna Mater, this being the principal Palatine shrine. Recent excavations have revealed in the cella a dump of terracotta ex-votos, statuettes of Attis, figurines, lamps and other objects with traces of fire, suggesting that the dump was made as a result of the fire in 111 B.C. It was probably after this fire that the podium was constructed; and in the subsequent restoration in A.D. 3 some of the material of the super-structure was incorporated in the new Augustan temple.[79]

At first the temple of the Phrygian goddess and her orgiastic cult was regarded as a foreign accretion, although after its dedication on 10 April 191 B.C. it had recognized status among the Roman sanctuaries and its calendrical observances. These observances, however, were confined to the precincts of the Magna Mater on the Palatine which were visited only by the upper

classes when they assembled there on 4 April. But Roman citizens were prohibited from taking any part in the annual celebration of the Megalesia and
its ecstatic procession, *lectisternium* (sacred banquet) and ludi,[80] and although
after the Megalesia and its dramatic performances and games were given a place
in the calendar Romans were allowed to be spectators at the procession and
ludi, the ecstatic ritual itself was performed exclusively by the Phrygian galli.

While every effort was made to keep the procession and its associated
rites within bounds and under Phrygian control, its wild abandon and
frenzied mutilation became contagious to the Roman populace like the
Bacchanalia. This put the Senate in a quandary, as Cybele had demonstrated
her power in the delivery of Rome from the Carthaginians and in giving
fruitful seasons, thereby meriting the erection of her temple on the Palatine
and the introduction of her worship within its precincts and in the streets of
the capital. To suppress the cultus would be an affront to the beneficent
goddess, and to those in her service brought mainly from Anatolia for the
purpose. To ignore them was virtually to condone them and leave the road
open for their adoption as an unedifying foreign intrusion. These regulations,
however, were not relaxed until imperial times when the Megalesia had
become little more than a public holiday in honour of the Magna Mater.
Indeed, by the end of the Republic it had so far declined in public esteem
that when the high-priest from Pessinus appeared in the Forum arrayed in his
vestments and ornaments to demand public expiation for an alleged pro-
fanation of the statue of the goddess he was mobbed by the populace.[81]

With the establishment of the Empire the cult was given a new status by
Augustus in 22 B.C. The ceremonies were extended to six days, beginning
with the procession on 4 April and concluding with the Hilaria of the spring
festival with its games, plays and circuses. The Palatine temple was rebuilt
after the second fire in A.D. 3, and in the Cybele cult legend, having been
brought into relation with the Attis myth, the fertility aspect of the spring
festival was emphasized. The Attis sacred death and resurrection drama was
enacted from 15 to 22 March, reaching its climax on the *Dies Sanguis* on the
24th, when amid loud lamentation, the uttering of piercing cries and the
blowing of pipes, the *archigallus* made an incision in his arm symbolizing the
self-mutilation of the neophytes in the Phrygian rite, the rest of the galli
slashing themselves with knives in a wild dance.[82] After a night of fasting
and vigil at the dawn of 25 March, the empty tomb, in which the image of

Attis had been laid, was opened and the archigallus announced that the god had been saved, and now their toils were over they would find salvation, weeping giving place to rejoicing, sorrow to joy. The resurrection of Attis was then celebrated with feasting, merriment, masquerades and Saturnalian licence, the Hilaria coming to a close on the 27th by the conveyance of the image of Cybele on a wagon to the Almo outside the Porta Capena, preceded by barefooted nobles, to the accompaniment of pipes and tambourines. On the other bank of the river the image, the wagon and the sacred objects were washed by the archigallus who was vested in purple. It was then taken back to its shrine on the Palatine by the wagon adorned with spring flowers, and there it remained until the drama was again enacted at the spring festival in the following March. In addition to this major temple, two other shrines of the Magna Mater occurred in Rome: one in the Circus Maximus; the other in Vaticano on the right bank of the Tiber.

THE TEMPLE OF AESCULAPIUS, INSULA TIBERINA

Thus, through Hellenic influences and their Anatolian contacts a new conception of communion with the divine, centred in Mystery divinities like Dionysus, the Magna Mater and their associates, had become established in Rome largely by the Sibylline books. Along with these orgiastic esoteric cults and their ecstatic rites, so far removed from either the ancient or the state religion of Rome, came a knowledge of the oracle at Delphi and the healing miracles of Asklepius, the son of Apollo, introduced from Epidaurus where, as we have seen,[83] from early in the fourth century B.C. the fame of the cures effected in its sanctuary was such that its cult was transferred notably to Athens and then to Rome. Latinized as Aesculapius, he is said to have taken up his abode on the Insula Tiberina, incarnated in a snake, brought from Epidaurus at the request of an embassy sent from Rome in 293 B.C. asking for the god to heal a pestilence.[84] Having of his own accord swum to the island, a temple was dedicated to him there on 1 January 291 B.C., and the entire island was consecrated in his honour and to his service as its temenos. So sacred was it that, although it is only 324 yards long and 73 yards wide, shrines to Jupiter, Tiberius, Faunus and Semo Sancus were subsequently erected upon it. In commemoration of Aesculapius' swim there from his boat *en route* for Rome, it was shaped by a platform round it to resemble a ship.[85]

A sanatorium for those engaged in divine incubation was built outside the pomerium, and at the end of the Republic the temple was rebuilt without the frescoes displayed in the original edifice.[86] Further extensions may have been made in the Antonine period,[87] but in the absence of any definite remains of the temple it can only be conjectured that some of the columns in the nave of the church of San Bartolomeo, which seems to have been built on the original site of the temple of Aesculapius,[88] did in fact come from this source. The dream oracles of Fannius in Virgil[89] may be merely poetic fancies, but in the Epidaurian cult incubation survived in hellenized Rome as an established practice.[90]

THE TEMPLE OF CASTOR AND POLLUX

Among other gods who obtained a cult centre in Rome whose legend was of Greek origin were the twin brothers Castor and Pollux. Before they assumed their Latin names, they were regarded as the sons of Zeus and Leda and had taken a leading part in the battle of Lake Regillus in 499 B.C. and announced their victory over the Latins to Rome.[91] The Dioscuri were alleged to have been seen in the Forum and consequently a temple was erected on the spot near the *lacus Juturnae* at the south-eastern corner and on its completion it was dedicated to them on 27 January 484 B.C.[92] It became commonly called *aedes Castoris* because the twin-brothers often were known as *Castores*, Pollux always being the obscure partner.

In all probability the cult actually was introduced from Tusculum (Frascati)[93] and as the temple stood within the pomerium near that of Vesta at the end of the Forum under the Palatine, it must have been an early arrival before restrictions were placed on the sanctuaries and shrines of gods of Greek and foreign extraction. In 117 B.C. it was restored by Caecilius Metellus, and completely rebuilt by Tiberius in A.D. 6. The three columns and entablature and most of the existing remains date from the Augustan period.[94] There are traces, however, of earlier structures, including *opus quadratum* belonging to the foundation walls surrounded with *opus caementicium* (concrete) of grey-green tufa (*cappelliccio*) from earlier periods, first introduced into Rome between 121 and 117 B.C., though odd blocks of *opus quadratum* from the temple belonged to the fifth century B.C. This continued in use until in the time of Sulla when it was surpassed and replaced by concrete, except as facing material. The podium of the Concordia temple on the north and west corner of the Forum, restored by Opimius in 121 B.C., is the earliest known monument in *caementicium*, including the mouldings covered over with stucco, and virtually unfaced, while the facing of the temple of Castor has not survived.[95]

The Castor ground-plan does not seem to have changed very considerably through the series of enlargements of the cella and the pronaos. The two rows of four columns and entablature were probably of wood. When it was rebuilt between 484 and 117 B.C., the wall of the cella was apparently made of material of the upper part of the wall and overlaid with concrete, and in the pronaos was only one row of columns. About 127 B.C. when the third reconstruction was undertaken, the ground-plan had not materially altered, if the row of columns round the cella were added in the Augustan restoration in 6 B.C. when the octastyle and peripteral Corinthian temple was erected with eleven columns on each side and a double row on each side of the pronaos. The old core of the podium was left, but heavy walls were constructed and strengthened by travertine and between the spur walls were chambers with metal doors. A flight of eleven steps from the pronaos led down to a wide platform with a railing in front, at the ends of which were two narrow staircases to the ground level. The podium was overlaid with marble and had two cornices and pilasters, one at the top, the other above the doors of the rooms. The three graceful Corinthian columns of the superstructure on the east side are of Pentelic marble, 41 feet in height and 5 feet in diameter. The entablature has a plain frieze and excellent cornice, and with the columns represents some of the finest workmanship among the extant remains in Rome, belonging probably to a restoration under Trajan or Hadrian.

The solidarity of the podium is tremendous, with its massive tufa walls, and columns resting on spurs of walling projecting from that under the cella. Except for a small chamber under the steps the entire podium was filled with a solid mass of concrete to form the platform, from which orations were probably made. Below the later floor of the cella, which seems to have been laid down in the reign of Hadrian, early mosaic, like that in the Regia, suggests that it was fitted as an adornment in the Augustan restoration, probably when it was used as the place of meeting for the Senate and for other civic and popular assemblies, its pronaos serving the purpose of the rostra. In turbulent times, in fact, it seems to have been a rallying point in the Forum, like Trafalgar Square in London or the Place de la Concorde in Paris. In front of its pronaos large political meetings were held and contests between contending parties were fought out on the terrace before the temple, as for instance in 88 B.C. when Sulla and Pompeius Rufus were attacked there by the followers of Martius, or when Cato and Metellus disputed whether or not Pompeius should be recalled from Asia. To bring the cella into direct relation to the palace, Caligula made it the vestibule of his residence.[96]

THE TEMPLE OF VESTA

At the east end of the southern angle of the Forum near the temple of Castor and the fountain of Juturna on the ancient *via sacra* stood the temple of Vesta, founded according to tradition by Numa[97] or by Romulus,[98] because it was the most ancient and the most sacred temple in Rome. Originally it appears to have been a small round hut on the northern foot of the Palatine hill constructed of clay and osiers, having a thatched roof, and similar perishable materials,[99] such as persisted on the eastern side of the Apennines till the fifth century B.C. The oldest representation on a silver *denarius* of the *gens Cassia*, struck by Cassius Longinus in 113 B.C., shows a circular temple with a domed roof, surrounded by a colonnade and surmounted by a conical roof on which a statue was erected. In the centre was an altar or bronze brazier on four legs, on which perhaps the fire offerings were made.[100]

Of the actual remains of the temple all that has survived is the circular concrete platform, 46 feet in diameter, on which it stood, together with the podium consisting of four strata of concrete with facings and fragments of marble columns, entablature, coffered ceiling dating from the time of Augustus, and the foundations of marble steps added later. There are no traces of a restoration by Hadrian.[101] The original building was constantly destroyed by fire, first in 390 B.C. by the Gauls. Before then, according to Ovid, it was roofed with thatch and the walls were wattled with pliant osiers. The shape, however, is said to have been the same.[102] In 241 B.C. it was again burnt, the high priest losing his right arm and his sight (which was miraculously restored) while he was rescuing the Palladium from the flames.[103] In 210 B.C. the temple was saved from burning by thirteen slaves,[104] but in the great fire in the reign of Nero in A.D. 64 it did not escape in the conflagration, though it was soon restored.[105]

Roman Temples

127

Silver denarius of Julia Domna
showing the temple of Vesta

The most exalted god in the Roman pantheon was the omnipotent Jupiter, god of sky and light, and guardian of the city. His temple on the Capitoline Hill (128) looked down on the Forum, and to it came the consuls to make their vows and the generals to offer their laurel wreaths of victory

Jupiter's daughter, Minerva, was the patron goddess of the arts and learning. Her temple on the Aventine was the religious centre for the ancient trade guilds (129). Two Corinthian columns remain of the temple, supporting a frieze in which Minerva is shown teaching the arts. Above is a statue after the original by Scopas

Bacchus, the god of wine, was adopted by
the Romans from the Greeks. By 18_
B.C. the orgiastic rites of the Bacch_
thought to be a political danger and th
cult was officially banned. In spite of thi_
the rites flourished and the room in th_
Villa of the Mysteries at Pompeii date
to the first century A.D. shows scen_
of initiation into the Dionysiac rites (13_

The Phyrgian Magna Mater, Cybel_
was also adopted by the Romans at th_
instigation of the Sibylline oracle. On_
of her sacred relics was brought to Rom_
from Pergamos in 204 B.C. and a temp_
to the goddess was set up at the Palatin_
in 191 B.C. The relief (131) from a wa_
in the Villa Medici shows the entrance t_
the temple

The fame of the healing miracles of Asklepius reached Rome from
Epidaurus. The god is said to have swum to the Insula Tiberina from
a boat bringing him to Rome, and the whole island was then dedicated
to him and a retaining wall, in the shape of a boat, built round it (132)

The Tabularium on the th
Capitoline Hill was erecte
in 78 B.C. by the consul L
Catulus to house the stat
archives (133). The Corin
thian columns which stan
next to it are all that is le
of the Temple of Vespasian
erected in their father'
honour by Titus and Domi
tian in A.D. 79. Opposit
is the façade of the Templ
of Saturn (134), one o
the oldest sanctuaries in th
Forum, dedicated to th
mythical god-king in 49
B.C. The temple, whic
was the state treasury, wa
restored many times. Th
Ionic columns of the pronao
are of grey granite in fron
and of red granite at the side

133

134

Across the Forum, at th
foot of the Palatine Hi
stands the Temple of Casto
and Pollux, (135), the son
of Zeus, dedicated in 48
B.C. A flight of steps le
up to the temple from wher
orators addressed politica
meetings

135

Beyond the Forum was the Atrium Vestae where the Vestals lived and guarded the sacred fire (13?
Colonnades surrounded the courtyard leading to magnificent rooms. Some of the marble statues on th?
plinths describing the virtues of the Vestals still remain on either side. Coins of the time of the Empre?
Julia Domna (127) show the actual Temple of Vesta, the most sacred in Rome

Similarly, in A.D. 191 the fire that swept over the Forum in the reign of Commodus demolished the temple and the Atrium Vestae, the Vestal Virgins fleeing with the Palladium to the Palatine. The reconstruction was undertaken by Julia Domna, the wife of Septimus Severus and mother of Caracalla.[106]

The vignettes, coins and reliefs of the period have preserved representations of the architecture and style of the temple from the end of the Republic to this restoration by the Empress Julia Domna.[107] The magnificent relief in the Uffizi Palace at Florence depicts the temple as a circular edifice with a conical roof, short fluted Corinthian columns and composite capitals with lattice-work between them. A staircase leads to it, and beside it stands an old oak tree to the left of the door. This was the *capillata*, or the tree upon which the hair of the girl cut off at her initiation in the service of Vesta was hung.[108]

THE ATRIUM VESTAE

In the background of the relief the restored Hall of the Vestals was portrayed above and beyond the temple, on either side, indicating that it was the larger of the two buildings. At each end was a fluted pilaster supporting an entablature with plain mouldings forming the architrave, frieze and cornice which rises above the roof of the temple. The name of the convent, Atrium Vestae, doubtless was derived from its spacious courtyard revealed in the excavation of the site since 1883. Adjoining the Regia just east of the Forum at the foot of the Palatine, this luxurious convent as reconstructed by the Empress was certainly befitting the dignity and high esteem of the Vestals, on a scale hardly likely to have been attempted in the time of the Republic. All that remains of the earlier house are a few floors and walls below the level of the later building. In the Empire the precinct of Vesta included the temple, the grove (*locus*) between the Atrium and the Palatine, and the Atrium Vestae where the Vestals resided. So large, in fact, was its colonnaded court that the Senate, it is said, was able to hold its meetings in it,[109] in contrast to the little court surrounded with rooms on the south and west sides of the second-century Republican atrium.[110]

The House of the Vestals, like the temple, was frequently burnt and rebuilt. After the fire of A.D. 64 the structure was restored and enlarged several times by the Flavian emperors and the *tablinum* and rooms at the end added by Hadrian. It was completed by the Antonines and by Septimius

Severus after the fire in 192, on an extended site under the Palatine to the right of the Forum beyond the temple. In its final form it consisted of the spacious cloistered quadrangle with a double colonnade of superimposed columns, one row erected on the top of the other, the lower monoliths being of white cipollino marble, the upper of breccia corallina. As they stood about 13 feet from the wall a cloister gave access to the rooms on the ground floor, and above were three storeys reached by staircases, all similarly adorned with magnificent marbles, porphyries and alabasters, and heated perhaps by hot-air flues, the rooms on the upper storey containing baths.

Besides the private apartments of the six Vestal Virgins, in this luxurious abode were servants' quarters, a bakehouse and offices, and in the centre of the court an octagon that may have enclosed flower beds, unless it served the purposes of a pavilion. Round the court were the marble statues of the *Vestales Maximae*, each with her pedestal inscribed with her virtues.[111] Most of them belonged to the third century and were at the west end in heaps, evidently destined for destruction when long after the Order had been brought to an end in A.D. 394 by Theodosius, the fabric and contents of the famous shrine were ruthlessly burnt into lime by the *fabbrica de S.Pietro* in 1549. Only thirty pieces escaped and were found intact when excavation at the site was commenced in 1877. The most important statues have been preserved in the Museo delle Terme, and much of the upper part of the house and its paved floors has survived. On the ground floor was a large paved hall with fine marbles and a guest room (*tablinum*) reached by four steps at the south-east end of the great court. Running off this were six small chambers, presumably for the private use of each of the Vestals. On the south of the large hall was a smaller one with a sunken circular chamber domed with concentric rings which may have been the *penus*, or storehouse, regarded with great veneration because in it Vesta and the Penates dwelt as divinities of the hearth and the household respectively. On the south-east corner a small room contained a mill used in all probability to grind the corn for the sacred cake of meal, known as *mola*, which the Vestal Virgins mixed with salt and offered to their goddess in her temple at the Vestalia on 9 June. Similar *mola salsa* were prepared and treated in the same way on the Ides of September (13th), and at the Lupercalia on 15 February.[112] Near the Arch of Severus in the Forum a Vestal is shown on a relief on a pedestal holding a box of salt indicating this aspect of her functions.

Rooms cut off from the courtyard at the west end may have been dedicated to the cult of Lares, the spirits probably of the farm and the fields, who as the *Las familiaris* became the guardians of the house. Further to the west were those devoted to the temple requirements of the Vesta cultus. At the east end of the open court, or *atrium*, was a fountain supplying water for domestic purposes, though the water used by the Vestals in sacrifice should strictly have been procured from a sacred grove outside the Porta Capena, where Numa was believed to have met his spouse Egeria to receive divine counsel from her.[113] This ancient practice, however, had ceased long before Ovid referred to it.[114] Near the main entrance to the Atrium from the Forum are the remains of a small shrine (*aedicula*) and of the architrave and frieze, supported formerly by two marble columns; there no doubt a statue of Vesta originally stood. It was erected in the time of Hadrian in the early part of the second century A.D. at the public expense by order of the Senate, as the inscription explains. It was perhaps to give a new impetus to the worship of the great goddess of the hearth who occupied such a conspicuous and significant place in the life of Rome that the image was installed. Through all its vicissitudes the most ancient Roman temple apparently contained no statue of Vesta, from its beginnings as the round hut (said to have been erected by King Numa in 716 B.C. between the Palatine and Capitoline hills forty years after the traditional foundation of the city by Romulus) to its later form as the house in which the sacred fire was kept burning perpetually in the favissa under the dome of the podium, symbolizing the canopic heavens.[115] There the sacred fire reigned supreme, its anthropomorphic representation being confined to the Atrium and the Porticus Deorum Consentium, built in the second or third century B.C. next to the temple of Vespasian under the south-east corner of the Tabularium and the Clivus Capitolinus leading to the highest point of the Capitoline hill. There in a shrine stood the images of the twelve deities of the city among which was the statue of Vesta.[116] This was restored in A.D. 367 by Vettius Praetextatus in an endeavour to resuscitate and maintain the paganism that was then in decline.[117] But all to no avail—Gratian confiscated the house and the endowments of the Vestals in A.D. 382, though the Atrium survived for some centuries inhabited by imperial and papal officials.

For a thousand years the sacredness of the family hearth, later personified in the Vesta and maintained by her Virgins, remained a vital centre of domestic and civic life and the foundation of Roman religion, enjoying even state worship which appropriately took place not in a large temple but in the little circular building at the northern foot of the Palatine hill in the Forum, with its Atrium Vestae adjoining the Regia. In due course, after being overshadowed by the worship of the Emperor as the focus of the state religion, the advent of a more vigorous faith and practice became a new consolidating and regenerative dynamic in an Empire that had run its course. It is upon the Christian basilicas and sacred places, modelled on the Roman structures of the same name and plan, that attention must now be concentrated in bringing this inquiry to its conclusion.

CHAPTER IX

Christian Basilicas and Muslim Mosques

IN GREECE AND ITALY in classical times business was transacted in the open *agorae* or *fora* which in Greece were adorned with spacious double colonnades, the marble or stone columns having entablatures and an upper storey, and in Rome they were surrounded with monumental buildings. In addition to the temples and statues closely associated with the Forum was a rectangular roofed hall sometimes with galleries and surrounded by pillars after the manner of the Greek peripteral temple with the columns within rather than outside, often terminating in an apse or, *exedra*. These basilicas were used for a variety of purposes ranging from commercial undertakings and legal transactions to political disputations, orations and entertainments—in short, to all the activities of the Forum.[1]

THE ROMAN BASILICAS

THE BASILICA PORTIA AND THE BASILICA AT POMPEII

The earliest known example of these structures at Rome was that erected to the west of the Curia by Portius Cato in 184 B.C. for judicial and commercial purposes. It may have been designed on the Athenian model at Athens recently seen by Cato when on a visit to the city, and perhaps for this reason it met with much opposition.[2] In 52 B.C. it was burnt and never restored. At Pompeii an imposing basilica was built at the south-west corner of the Forum, probably about 130 B.C., having an inscription dating from the beginning of the Roman colony there. Architecturally it is the most impressive building in the Forum, though in its original form it was a relatively simple structure, consisting of a long rectangular hall open to the sky with a colonnade surmounted by a loggia in the interior divided into three aisles,

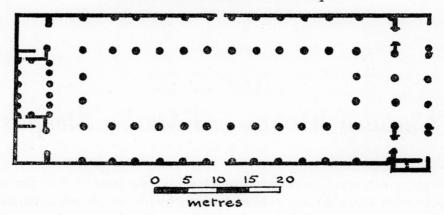

Fig. 44. Plan of the civic basilica, Pompeii

the lateral one being two storeys high. At the end was the tribunal. In fact it was a miniature Forum with the walls and exterior of the edifice decorated with stucco in the Samnite style. Later the middle of the nave was roofed, and in the portico and loggia twenty-eight massive brick columns about 30 feet high supported it, the lower parts of which are still preserved. The five entrances from the colonnade to the Forum were separated by four Ionic columns. On the south was a staircase to the upper storey of the loggia. The plan with its three-roofed nave was based on Greek rather than Roman models and prepared the way for the early Christian basilicas except that in place of the Pompeian corridor on the four sides the churches had only aisles parallel with the nave.

The pagan prototypes being designed primarily for civil, legal and commercial purposes instead of religious worship, no attempt was made to create a numinous milieu by subduing the lighting arrangements. On the contrary, the maximum amount of light was secured by openings in the upper parts of the walls of the main hall where trade was carried on. In the tribunal at the back of the building, with its double colonnade serving the purposes of a court and an exchange, was a raised platform for the judge and counsel or salesmen, the litigants standing in front on the floor. Below was a vaulted chamber, the uses of which are not known, and on the right and left were staircases leading down to it, and up to the second landing. Nothing has remained of the statue at the end of the hall.[3]

THE BASILICA JULIA

Of the six basilicas in Rome the largest and most extensive was that called the Basilica Julia, erected on the southern side of the Forum in 46 B.C., perhaps in honour of Julius Caesar, and restored several times before A.D. 416. It follows the normal plan having a rectangular hall about 110 yards in length and 54 yards in width, and double aisles on the four sides, enclosing a space of about 90 yards by 17 yards, over which were galleries supported by marble pillars of the façade and an inner row of brick faced with white marble. The floor, paved with variegated African and Phrygian marble, was an open arcade divided by marble balustrades joining the pillars. Rooms opened on to the street on the south side. On the north-west side marble pillars adorned with Doric pilasters still survive, as do the high walls of tuffstone and travertine at the back, but many of the brick piers are modern.[4]

Soon after its completion by Augustus it was destroyed by fire. It was rebuilt in an enlarged form and dedicated in A.D. 12 to Gaius and Lucius Caesar, and subsequently, after yet another fire in A.D. 283, in the reconstruction by Diocletian square pillars replaced the earlier colonnade and bricked arches of the former travertine structure.[5] In 377 it was again restored by Probianus, the city prefect, in the time of Valens, Gratian and Valentinian,[6] as recorded on a pedestal on the edge of the steps leading to the Sacra, discovered in 1883. Moreover, he enriched it with works of art and statues procured from the pagan temples that had been closed, which included statues by Praxiteles, Polyclitus and Timarchos, whose names occur on five of the plinths. It continued in use as a law court after the Christian domination, and in the seventh or eighth century the outer aisle was converted into a church, often thought to have been that dedicated to Santa Maria in Cannapara, or to Santa Maria in Foro, but neither of these identifications is convincing.[7] Nevertheless, there are indications of a church having been erected in this part of the basilica between the seventh and ninth centuries.[8]

THE ROMAN CATACOMBS

It was not, however, until Christianity became the religion of the state that these pagan basilicas were found to be adaptable, with slight modifications, to the purposes of corporate worship. The first Christian churches were not derived from these Roman prototypes, but from the fourth century they constituted the typical form of ecclesiastical edifice. Prior to this, in times when public worship was prohibited, Christians on occasions may have resorted to the catacombs in the north-east and south of the capital. It is not improbable, particularly during the Diocletian persecution in the third century, that recourse was made to these subterranean burial places for these purposes, as, for example, to the chapel of St Priscilla, where behind an altar or a stone coffin of the martyr was a platform on which the officiating priest may have stood. The catacomb of Sant'Agnese (over which the basilica of Sant' Agnese Fuori le Mura was built by Constantine, re-erected by Honorius I (625–638) and subsequently restored in 1459 and 1856) was an extensive structure with three rectangular compartments on one side of a corridor and two on the other, connected by a passage intersecting the gallery. The sanctuary may have been at the end containing the altar, as a stone seat, probably reserved for the presiding bishop, occurs in the centre of the rear wall, and a bench for the priests on either side. This could very well have been employed for congregational worship on a small scale, notwithstanding the narrowness of the passage.

It is reasonably certain that the Eucharist was celebrated in the rectangular, circular or polygonal *cubicula*, used as burial places and 'chantry-chapels', at the funeral of the martyrs interred in them, and doubtless on the anniversaries of their death, the tomb serving as an altar. That at St Calixtus on the Appian Way was protected by a marble *transennae*, or lattice screen. But space was too curtailed for large congregations to assemble in these subterranean cubicula. This would not prevent their being used for requiems, and apparently for baptisms, for at San Pontianus in the Vigna di San Michele near the Porta Portese, a basin large enough for immersion, with water from a spring, has been found at the foot of a staircase.

After the final peace of the Church had been granted by Constantine in 313 the cemeteries both below and above ground were embellished with basilicas preserving some of the features of the catacombs, including their mortuary cultus, epitaphs in honour of the martyrs engraved or painted on slabs, marbles or tiles, sealing their tombs. Often they were marked with Christian symbols (e.g. the monogram of Christ, a dove, fish, anchor or olive-branch). Sometimes, however, pagan inscriptions occur on one side of these *opisthographs*, the interment presumably having been made before

313. With the development and embellishment of cemeteries above ground, however, the catacombs ceased to be places of burial, and by the beginning of the fifth century they had become primarily the sanctuaries of the martyrs visited by pilgrims from all parts of the Roman world. Nevertheless, desire to be interred in proximity to these holy acres continued and high prices were paid in the fifth century for sepulchres near the tombs of the martyrs. In their capacity as shrines the catacombs were adorned increasingly with frescoes and ornaments, until in the ninth century the relics of the martyrs were removed and transferred to the churches in the city, after the Lombard invasion of the Campania where in and around Naples frescoed catacombs recurred. Thus, behind the church of San Gennaro, founded in the eighth century on the site of the chapel in which St Januarius was buried, are extensive catacombs containing four main galleries with lateral passages and cubicula. Chambers in the form of niches lie along the walls and below the level of the galleries, decorated in the Pompeian style with figures of the Good Shepherd and other representations of Christ, executed in the fourth and fifth centuries. The bones found in them, however, belonged to victims of a plague in the sixteenth century. But the general plan is that of a basilica, divided into a nave and chancel with a stone altar and episcopal chair behind it. They were doubtless used as such on occasions, though when they ceased to be the burial place of the martyrs and churches were built over them they soon lost their significance, until in the first half of the ninth century they were completely abandoned and worship in conjunction with them came to an end.

THE CHRISTIAN BASILICAS

THE CIVIC AND ECCLESIASTICAL BASILICAS

While the catacombs may have been employed as oratories as well as for the veneration of the martyrs and for mortuary, eucharistic and baptismal rites, it appears to have been the house design that was most influential in the construction of Christian churches after, and perhaps immediately before, the edict of Milan in 312. It was in private houses that Christians first assembled in Jerusalem and the surrounding district for consultation, prayer and worship centred in the Breaking of the Bread (i.e. the Eucharistic offering),[9] and when they were scattered abroad after the martyrdom of St Stephen,[10] this practice was continued and became established in the sub-apostolic period in the Graeco-Roman world. At first it was probably the practice to have one apartment set apart for devotional purposes (where this was practicable) like the *cenaculum* in Jerusalem in which the Eucharist was instituted and to which the disciples repaired after the Crucifixion.[11] Then, as corporate worship developed liturgically the larger Roman houses with their atrium leading to an enclosed hall and smaller chambers, were readily adapted for these requirements. In the third century the *domus ecclesiae* gave way to the *domus Dei*, or *dominicum* (Greek, κυριακόν). This was erected and used exclusively for public worship, but was based on very much the same plan as the 'House of the Church' except that certain parts were omitted while others acquired a sacred character they had not had before.

As the faithful rapidly increased after the Constantine victory in 331, aisles had to be added to the rectangular cella and its apse to accommodate the worshippers. This brought the dominicum more into line with the pagan basilica, as is apparent in the very ancient church of St Saba on the Aventine hill at Rome below the present edifice and devoid of aisles. Santa Croce in Gerusalemme, near the Porta Maggiore, on the other hand, stands on the site of the Sessorian palace and law-court said to have been given by Constantine to the Christians, and subsequently re-created by St Helena after her alleged discovery of the True Cross in Jerusalem and dedicated in its honour. Originally the nave was supported by twelve granite columns, eight of which have survived. The high altar was erected over a sarcophagus containing the relics of SS. Anastasius and Caesarius, and in 501 a synod was held there in the Basilica Sessoriana, as Santa Croce was then called. Similarly, the great patriarchal church of Santa Maria Maggiore on the Esquiline hill was known as the Basilica Liberiana because it originated in the fourth century in the Liberian palaces on a site which is said to have contained a temple of Cybele, while a few hundred yards away was a temple Juno Lucina.[12]

At the end of the fourth century when most of the architects and builders had gone to Constantinople as a result of Constantine's transference of the seat of government to Byzantium, those who remained in Italy in Campania, while starting from the Roman tradition, developed along their own lines the final product of their Italian genius. A notable example of their work occurs in the circular church of Santa Maria Maggiore near Nocera dei

Pagani between Naples and Salerno with its marble pillars, barrel-vaulted ambulatory divided into sections by transverse arches supporting portions of the wall, and an ovoidal dome 49 feet in height at its apex. This type of elevated dome was already familiar in Campania in the third century necropolis of Cumae, in the baths near the Forum in Pompeii, and in the Basilica Severiana, or church of San Giorgio Maggiore at Naples, founded by Severus in the second half of the fourth century, where impost blocks, or pulvins, were introduced in the shape of truncated inverted pyramids similar to those applied to the capitals of the columns of the Basilica Ursiana, the church of the Anastasis, at Ravenna.[13]

In Rome, however, the Latin type of basilica-church, either rectangular or cruciform in plan, predominated when the columns, friezes, capitals and other adjuncts of the pagan basilicas and temples became available for the construction of Christian churches during the Constantine régime. Side by side with the civic basilicas, which continued their customary administrative functions, were ecclesiastical edifices consisting of a narthex in the form of a long narrow vestibule, and an open court or atrium, in both of which the catechumens assembled until they were admitted to the main sanctuary after their baptism, together with penitents before their restoration to communion with the faithful. The long nave had from two to five aisles with a central aisle and clerestory, and an apse at the west end which was provided with seats for the clergy, the bishop's throne being in the middle behind the altar.

Sometimes the altar was raised on a platform approached by steps and separated from the nave by a low screen or railing. When the practice of transferring relics of the martyrs and saints to churches became established these were enclosed in a *confessio* (reliquary) below the steps of the altar. Not later than the fifth century a dome-shaped canopy, or *ciborium*, was built over it resting on four marble pillars, and the underside often covered with mosaics or painted blue with stars in imitation of the sky, where the heavenly action of the Eucharistic offering was consummated. In Eastern Christendom from the fourth century the altar and sanctuary were concealed behind a screen, or *iconostasis*, cutting them off from the congregation, whereas in the west the oblation was made in full view of the worshippers. The apse with the confessio, containing the relics of the patron saint, and its ciborium, was in fact the nucleus around which the basilica was constructed. At first when not much attention was paid to orientation, the altar was usually placed at the west end. The eastward position did not become the rule till later, the earliest example being the basilica of Sant'Agata in Ravenna (425–439). The narthex and the principal entrance were generally at the opposite end to the altar, and there the baptistery, commonly a separate circular or octagonal building, was situated, as at Parenzo in Istria where to the west of the atrium of the cathedral of San Maurus, erected between 535 and 543, stands the now roofless baptistery near the campanile. At Ravenna the octagonal baptistery is adjacent to the duomo and is surmounted with a dome. It was built in the early fifth century by Bishop Ursan round a piscina used for immersion which was originally part of a Roman bath. In 450 the cupola covered by a tiled roof was ornamented with mosaics in a range of colours portraying the baptism of Christ in the Jordan including the bearded nude figure of the river god carrying a pitcher in the background. On a circular band the twelve apostles, holding martyr crowns in their hands, are represented in procession on a blue background with sprays of acanthus leaves between them. Below is another ring of alcoves and niches in mosaic, alternating with four altars and thrones.

ROME

THE LATERAN

The earliest Christian basilica in Rome was that of San Giovanni in Laterano on the Caelian hill, begun in 313 and completed about 324, standing on the site of the ancient palace of the family of the Laterani. It became and remains the chief of the four great 'patriarchal' basilicas of Rome, styled *omnium urbis et orbis ecclesiarum mater et caput*. It was first called 'Basilica Salvatoris' (St Salvator) as it was dedicated to the Redeemer, and since it was given to the Church by Constantine it was also known as the 'Basilica Constantiniana', or 'Aula Dei' as a second Zion. After its destruction by an earthquake in 896, it was reconstructed by Sergius III (904–911) and placed under the patronage of St John the Baptist, and subsequently associated with St John the Apostle. In 1308 it was destroyed by fire and restored by Clement V, and it was again burnt down in 1360, and rebuilt by Urban V (1310–1370). The present edifice was reconstructed under the direction of Fontana and

Borromini in the seventeenth century. The Baptistery to the north-west, traditionally but erroneously said to have been the place of baptism of Constantine, seems to have been erected by Sixtus III (432–440).[14]

Built in the form of a Latin cross (*crux commissa*), orientated towards the west, it had a nave divided by rows of columns into aisles with an atrium in front surrounded by colonnades with a fountain in the middle, and a semi-circular apse. When the ambulatory for which Leo the Great was responsible was enlarged by Sixtus II in 844, the basilica became polygonal. Two mosaic tablets in the ambulatory describe the construction of the church, but although until the fourteenth century the Lateran was the normal residence of the Pope, the basilica has been subject to such extensive and repeated restoration and enlargement that little remains of the original edifice, and its present form with its immense baroque façade hardly does justice to its earlier appearance.

SAN PIETRO IN VATICANO

Like the Lateran, the present church of St Peter's in Rome replaced an earlier basilica, said to have been founded by Constantine on the site of the circus of Gaius and Nero between the Via Aurelia and the Via Triumphalis, where traditionally the tomb of the Prince of the Apostles has been located. The plan was that of the *crux commissa* with a nave, four aisles separated by four

Fig. 45. Plan of San Pietro in Vaticano

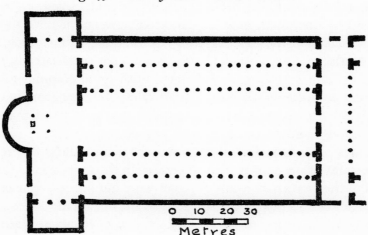

rows of marble columns, transepts, and entered by five doorways. The work, however, was done hurriedly without proper regard for the measurements in relation to the alleged tomb which did not correspond exactly with the axis of the nave. The columns of various styles and ages were collected from a number of ancient quarries, and the obelisk, now standing in the centre of the Piazza di San Pietro, was brought by Gaius Caligula from Heliopolis. This basilica, however, was a relatively simple building until it was transformed into the existing Vatican Basilica, begun in 1506 by Julius II (1503–1513) when Bramante was instructed by Michaelangelo to prepare plans for a new church in Rome dedicated to St Peter.

From the ancient illustrations and plans available it was entered apparently by three gateways through a colonnaded atrium 212 feet by 225 feet. In the centre of the portico, called 'the Paradise', was a magnificent fountain erected in the time of Pope Symmachus (498–511), surrounded by columns of porphyry supporting a dome of gilt bronze. In the middle of a square tabernacle was a pine-cone with two bronze peacocks on either side, and semicircular bronze ornaments in relief on top, crowned by the monogram of Christ. A marble sarcophagus ascribed to Otho II (*c.* 983) stood in the atrium surmounted by a porphyry cover, and above it a mosaic representing Christ between St Peter and St Paul. The nave 80 feet in length, entered by five doors, the chief and most costly of which, the 'Royal Door', was only used on very special occasions, had an open roof supported by ninety-two columns. The four dividing colonnades each had twenty-two Corinthian columns, and the inner ones had arches with a second clerestory, the walls of which were adorned with mosaics. The arch between the nave and the transepts also contained mosaics depicting Constantine being presented by St Peter to Christ offering a model of the basilica. In the relatively small apse under a ciborium was the altar decorated with spiral columns carved with vines which, according to the Liber Pontificales, had been brought over from Greece.[15] The sanctuary was screened by a double row of twelve Parian marble columns, and in the centre was 'the chair of St Peter', as this pontifical throne was described, and beneath it the chapel alleged to contain the mortal remains of the Prince of the Apostles. In the crypt round the foundation wall of the apse a succession of popes were buried, and against the right wall of the nave was placed the fifth-century bronze statue of St Peter procured by Paul V from the monastery of San Martino al Vaticano, and thought by some to have been a figure of Jupiter transformed into that of the Apostle; the right toe of the statue has been worn smooth by the kisses of the faithful.

SAN PAOLO FUORI LE MURA

By comparison with the basilica of St Peter that of St Paul, at the second milestone on the Via Ostiensis, was a very much less inspiring edifice, as the traditional site of the tomb of the Apostle of the Gentiles did not permit extensive rebuilding if, as was always required in these cases, the tomb was to be in the centre of the apse with the front looking towards the east. The space between the façade of the basilica and the road to Ostia running east of the tomb being only 100 feet, the plans had to be circumscribed accordingly,[16] until it was rebuilt by Valentinian II and Theodosius in 386 on the plan of St Peter's. Then by changing the orientation from east to west and extending the site towards the bank of the Tiber, it was possible to construct it as a basilica, with open roof and double aisles, divided by eighty columns of Parian marble supporting arches, the transept and the apse, similar in design and dimensions to St Peter's. Chapels, porticos and fountains, were added in due course, together with churches, hostelries, monasteries, convents, farmhouses, stables, orchards and cemeteries surrounding it. In 846 it was pillaged by the Saracens, and subsequently fortified by John VIII (872–882). Thus it became one of the finest churches in Rome adorned with mosaics and frescoes, until it was almost entirely destroyed by fire on 15 July 1823.

SAN CLEMENTE

Considerably smaller and in its present form later in date, the basilica of San Clemente, between the Colosseum and the Lateran, has preserved intact the original church built in the fourth century on what has been regarded traditionally as the site of the house of St Clement. This apparently was covered over in the ruins after the destruction of this part of the city in 1084 by Robert Guiscard. When a new edifice was erected on the site at a higher level by Paschalis II in 1108 the earlier church formed the crypt, and beneath it lay a chapel of Mithras containing a statue of the Good Shepherd. The upper church is entered through a porch supported on pillars leading to the atrium surrounded by a colonnaded cloister paved with marble and having a fountain in the centre. About a third of the nave is occupied by the choir enclosed by a marble ninth-century screen about 3 feet high, with two ambones installed from the lower church. The slabs are decorated with patterns in low relief and glass mosaic of the thirteenth century. To the west of the octagonal ambone on the Gospel (north) side of the screen stands a large Paschal candlestick ornamented with mosaics. The epistle ambone on the south side is square and has two marble reading-desks facing east and west for the reading respectively of the epistle and the gradual.

Above the choir is the sanctuary reached by two steps and divided from it by a marble screen. In the centre is the altar under a ciborium, supported by two marble columns and a canopy above with its four columns of pavonazzetto. Behind it is an ancient episcopal throne bearing the monogram of Anastasis, the titular cardinal in 1108 when the upper church was built. Mosaics of this century occur on the conch of the apse. On the rood arch is a bust of Christ in the centre with the symbols of the four evangelists, and below figures of St Paul and St Lawrence, Isaiah, St Peter, St Clement and the rood figures on the vaulting. In the lower church, which was a more imposing structure than the later upper church, the walls of the aisles and the narthex were covered with frescoes dating from the seventh to the eleventh century, some being still in excellent preservation.[17] Below the basilica are the remains of earlier buildings of the imperial era and of two massive walls of tufa, probably belonging to the Republican period, together with the Mithraeum.

RAVENNA

SAN VITALE

Outside Rome the most imposing basilica is the octagonal church of San Vitale at Ravenna, the greatest monument of Justinian's time, begun by Archbishop Ecclesius about 526 when Justinian succeeded Theodoric to the imperial Byzantine throne, and consecrated by Archbishop Maximian on 17 May 548 under royal patronage. The interior has an aisle and gallery above encircling it and is crowned by a conical dome supported by eight massive pillars, which in the eighteenth century were adorned with frescoes. The aisle and gallery are covered with cross vaults, transverse arches connecting the piers, and internal buttresses at the angles of the building. On one

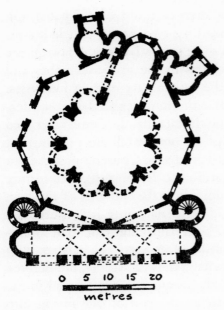

Fig. 46. Plan of San Vitale, Ravenna

O 5 10 15 20
metres

side is the apse flanked by two chambers, each with a niche at the end, and two sacristies with rectangular projections. On the opposite side are the remains of the rectangular narthex with two circular towers.

From the inner octagon the presbytery (or sanctuary) is approached under a triumphal arch frescoed on the under side with the heads of the twelve apostles and of Christ in roundels formed by entwined dolphins. Two triple-arch triforia are finely decorated and the columns adorned with Byzantine capitals. In the large lunette on the left wall scenes from the life of Abraham are depicted. Opposite on the right wall the sacrifice of Abel and Melchizedek are represented, and above to the right of the lunette are the ancestors of the twelve tribes with Aaron, and in another mosaic scene Moses receiving the Law, removing his sandal at the burning bush, and feeding the flocks of Jethro. In the centre of the apse above the altar is a beardless Christ seated on a globe flanked by two angels and handing a martyr's crown to St Vitale, while on the right Archbishop Ecclesius offers him a model of the church. The figures are realistic but rigid, and beneath them are the magnificent portraits in the classic tradition showing the Emperor Justinian holding a dish and wearing a jewelled crown of gold with a nimbus behind his head, preceded by Archbishop Maximian and two priests followed by civic dignitaries and soldiers carrying a huge paten. On the right is the Empress Theodora attended by two priests and ladies-in-waiting bearing a large golden chalice. In these scenes Byzantine portraiture reaches its height in the portrayal of richness in the gorgeous robes and regalia, the stylization of the figures and the authenticity of their likenesses.

San Vitale, indeed, is the greatest Justinian monument and the most interesting building in Ravenna, notwithstanding the fact that the dome was raised too high. In this respect the proportions of its interior fell short of those of SS. Sergius and Bacchus which Justinian had erected in Constantinople about 527, six years before Sancta Sophia. According to Rivoira the architecture of San Vitale was not inspired by Byzantium where the churches of this plan and design are rather later in date. In fact, as he maintains, it constituted a new style resulting from a combination of both pagan and Christian monuments of Rome and Ravenna with those of the Near East. The narthex with a niche at either end, the buttresses and the two tiers of arcades, are derived from the Orthodox Baptistery of Neon. The dome was constructed in the Ravennate conical fashion with tapering tubes, the end of one fitting into the mouth of the other, and without the depression of the cupola as at Sancta Sophia. Finally, the masonry and the method of laying the bricks were according to local custom.[11] The affinities, it is suggested, are to be found not in Byzantium, or in the great rectangular or vaulted Roman basilicas, but in a hall in the Baths of Nero, built in about 228, and in the Basilica Nova in Rome (c. 310–312). The prototype, however, was a Christian baptistery like the Neon at Ravenna or the Lateran at Rome, or such a building as the so-called temple of Minerva Medica at Rome.[19]

With the exception of the baptistery attached to the Lateran and the 'Tomb of Santa Constantia' the circular type of church was not adopted in Rome, though the round church of Santo Stefano on the Caelian hill[20] was erected by Pope Simplicius (468–483) probably on an earlier site, either of a market or as part of the Domus Aurea.[21] Transformed into a church it consisted of a central circular nave 44 feet in diameter, and double aisles. Above the central colonnade with its architrave the elevated drum carried on columns did not support a dome, and in the arcade dividing the aisles it rested on dosserets. As the buildings had not been designed for Christian worship in the first instance, the material employed in the reconstructions was taken from the earlier secular edifices, whereas at Ravenna the basilica of Sant' Apollinare Nuovo, built by Theodoric at the beginning of the sixth century next to his palace, was constructed *de novo* on the basilican plan with Byzantine variations, like Sant' Apollinare in Classe.

SANT' APOLLINARE NUOVO

Sant' Apollinare Nuovo as the principal church of the Arian heresy was designed by Theodoric in 519 to be the most important basilica in the city, and was dedicated to St Martin. Its gilded ceiling gave it the name of San Martino in Coelo Aureo and the walls of the nave and its apse were adorned with fine mosaics and twenty-four cipolline columns with massive Byzantine Corinthian capitals imported from the East, having acanthus leaves and inscribed with Greek masons' letters. Greek workmanship also occurs in the panels of the ancient ambone, and when the basilica was taken over by the Catholics about 561 and re-consecrated in honour of San Martino, a line of female saints led by the Magi, on one side of the walls, and a parallel line of martyrs on the other side were added to the mosaics. In the ninth century the relics of St Apollinaris were transferred there from the church bearing his name in the port of Classe, 3 miles outside the city on the Via Romea. They were placed under the sanctuary and the name of Theodoric's basilica of Ravenna was henceforth known as Sant' Apollinare Nuovo to distinguish it from a neighbouring small church called *in Veclo*, or *in Veteri*. The masonry and decoration of blank arcading are in the Ravennate style, and the cylindrical round campanile, about 125 feet high, resembling towers in the city walls of Rome, was added in the ninth century (850–878).

The mosaics in three parallel bands on the nave walls were executed in the Theodoric period. Those on the left side represented the miracles and parables of Christ, and on the right wall scenes of the Passion. In the apse the original panels contained mosaics of events in the gospel narratives, those on the left side including the marriage of Cana in Galilee (the present design being a copy of the original), the miracle of the loaves and fishes, the calling of St Peter and St Andrew, the healing of Bartimaeus, the woman at the well in Samaria, and the raising of Lazarus; on the right were the events in the Passion story from the Last Supper to the resurrection appearances. The mosaics between the windows portray thirty-two saints and prophets holding a book or a scroll, and the mosaics at the bottom show the Madonna and Child with four angels, the port of Classe and the palace of Theodoric with Christ enthroned on the right. The rest belong to the Justinian period, viz., a procession of saints led by the Magi on the left, and martyrs in white on the right.

THE BASILICA OF SANT' APOLLINARE IN CLASSE

Outside the walls of Classe, about 3 miles from Ravenna on the road to Rimini, Julianus Argentarius erected the imposing basilica in honour of St Apollinaris at the request of Archbishop Ursicinus (533–536). Like San Vitale it was not completed until after the surrender of the city to Belisarius in 540 when it became the capital of the Roman Empire. Then on 9 May 549 it was consecrated by Archbishop Maximian, two years after San Vitale, and has survived as the largest and best preserved of the basilicas in Ravenna. It consists of a spacious nave and two aisles with a narthex at the west end flanked on the left by a high rectangular room, and like Sant' Apollinare Nuovo, with wooden roofs separated by twelve magnificent marble columns on either side surmounted by capitals with acanthus leaves and symbols of the Apostles. At the end of the left aisle a few pieces remain of the original mosaic pavement that formerly had covered the entire floor of the basilica.

The side walls that were once embellished with mosaics and marble were stripped by Leon Battista Alberta in the fifteenth century to adorn the Tempio Malatestiano at Rimini. All that is left of the former decoration is confined to the apse and the triumphal arch at the apex of which is the bust of Christ in a medallion with symbolical figures of the four evangelists on either side, and below the twelve Apostles represented as sheep with fat tails going to Christ from Bethlehem and Jerusalem. This section belongs to the seventh century, and below on the sides of the arch are two palm trees, the figures of the archangels Michael and Gabriel (sixth century) and lower down the busts of St Luke and St Mark (twelfth century). In the centre of the apse St Apollinaris is represented wearing an alb, chasuble and pallium on his shoulder, with upraised arms as an *orante* calling the faithful to prayer. Towards him come the twelve sheep with fat tails and above is a large jewelled cross on a blue ground with gilded stars in the centre of a golden disk. At the sides the Transfiguration is depicted with Moses and Elias; below are the sacrifices of Abel, Melchizedek and Abraham, and on the left restored portrayals of the Emperor Constantine IV, Heraclius and Tiberius bestowing privileges on Archbishop Reparatus (*c.* 671–677). Between the windows are mosaics of the four archbishops, Ursus, Severus, Ursicinus, and Ecclesius.

As a result of the construction of a crypt in the twelfth century, the floor of the sanctuary was raised eleven steps above the ground level, and in a sort of corridor the relics of St Apollinaris were deposited about 1173, before they were removed to the church of Sant' Apollinare Nuovo in the city. Over the crypt is a broad flight of steps leading to the Tribunal and the high altar, while in the aisles are a number of sarcophagi dating from the fifth to the eighth century decorated with symbolic scenes. Originally the western façade was approached by a large atrium closed at either end by a squat tower, the foundations of which have been detected. In the upper part is an ancient triple window, the façade having been strengthened by pilasters at the outer angles. Near the left aisle stands the majestic campanile 123 feet in height, erected as an addition in the late tenth century.

ST MARK'S, VENICE

Great, however, as were the achievements of Ravennate architecture from 404 when Honorius established his imperial palace at Ravenna to its decline as the result of the Lombardic and Frankish invasions in the eighth century, its splendour was short-lived. No sooner were its oriental conquests of the arts complete than they suddenly came to an end as many refugees from the Lombard invasion settled in Venice, which henceforth became the meeting place between Eastern Europe and Western Asia. Here in this impregnable 'city in the sea', erected on piles in the Venetian lagoon at the head of the Adriatic and the Lombard plain known as Veneto, the tradition started in Ravenna was continued and brought to fruition in the successive styles of Byzantine, Gothic, and early Renaissance architecture, reaching its climax in the Doge's Palace and its greatest achievement, the basilica of San Marco.

When it was originally constructed in 829 to receive the relics of St Mark from Alexandria, the chapel was basilican in form, but it was remodelled in the eleventh century in the shape of a Greek cross, like St Front at Perigueux in the Dordogne, with five gilded domes, over five hundred multi-coloured marble columns and mosaics showing Byzantine influences unsurpassed in magnificence. Some of the later additions are somewhat grotesque, though the fifteenth-century Gothic additions to the façade are by no means unpleasing. In 1204 the four bronze horses from the triumphal arch of Trajan in Constantinople were erected over the central entrance, and on the columns supporting the baldachin above the high altar are reliefs of the eleventh century. The Byzantine *Pala d'oro*, originally designed for an ante-pendium in Constantinople in 1105, became the altar-piece. Behind is another altar with alabaster columns and reliefs of the sixteenth century. In an attempt to reproduce the leading features of the church of the Holy Apostles at Constantinople the nave was divided into three square bays like Sancta Sophia. On the outside the walls were decorated with arcades and niches in Lombard style, and the roof vaults covered with lead as in Con-stantinople. The marble casing of the front was executed in the Byzantine manner also on the model of Sancta Sophia, in which all the principal forms of early Christian basilicas are represented.

SANCTA SOPHIA, CONSTANTINOPLE

The church of the Holy Wisdom in the new capital begun by Constantine in 537 marks the highest achievement in Byzantine Christian or Muslim architecture, with its stupendous dome above the spacious nave supported by half-domes over semicircular apses, with arched buttresses and flanked by

Fig. 47. Plan of Sancta Sophia, Istanbul

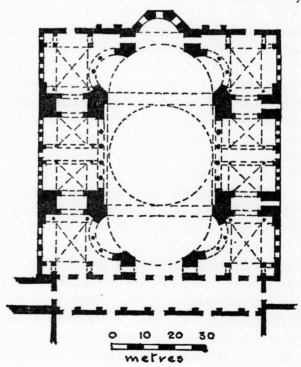

0 10 20 30
metres

galleries rounded off in columned niches. The vast basilica 236 feet in length, 98 feet in width and 175 feet to the apex of the dome, is lighted through numerous windows in the upper and lower storeys and in the domes, showing to advantage the richness of the coloured marbles and the elaborate carving of the capitals. Above the two tiers of columns are two tiers of windows and immense windows in the aisles. The walls of brick encased with their slabs of marble to a considerable height and mosaics on a gold ground above were subsequently coated with stucco when the church became a mosque. The lowest columns are of porphyry and the upper storey of verd-antique. The narthex 204 feet in length with a gallery over it is similarly decorated. In spite of the skill of the original architects, Anthemis of Tralles and Isodorus the Elder of Miletus, the great dome 107 feet in diameter which was supported by four piers collapsed in an earthquake in 558. When it was rebuilt by the younger Isodorus between 558 and 563 the defect in its construction was remedied, its height was increased to 182 feet, and forty circular windows were inserted.[22] The exterior is less impressive with its lack of elevation in relation to its great span and its varied outline and dimensions, to which were added minarets at each of the four exterior angles when, after the Turkish conquest of Constantinople in 1453, it had to be adapted to the requirements of a Muslim mosque.

MUSLIM MOSQUES

THE MOSQUE-CATHEDRAL AT CORDOBA

At Cordoba in Andalusia, Spain, the reverse process occurred. There the Moorish mosque (Mesjid al-Jami) built by Abd-ar-Rahman in 780 on the site of a Roman temple and the Visigothic church of St Vincent, was converted into a Christian cathedral dedicated to the *Virgen de la Asuncia* after the expulsion of the Moors in 1238. In its earlier construction after its original size had been doubled by the caliphs Rahman II and Hisham II between 822 and 976, and made the largest Muslim sanctuary after the Ka'ba in Mecca, it consisted of a rectangle, 570 feet in length and 425 feet in breadth, only slightly smaller than the great basilica of St Peter's in Rome. Up till then the structure erected by Abd-ar-Rahman, the founder of the Omalyade dynasty in Spain in 756, occupied only about a fifth of the present area. It

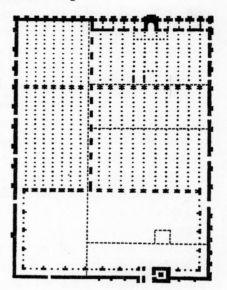

Fig. 48.   Plan of the cathedral-mosque,
Cordoba

consisted of a hall divided longitudinally by ten rows of columns into eleven
sections with twelve aisles, the central aisle ending in the *mihrab*, or semicircular recess facing Mecca which always takes the place of an altar in
mosques. On the north was the court containing the fountain for the obligatory ablutions required before the daily ritual prayers (*salat*) are said with
the prescribed prostrations (*rakah*) at the five appointed times from day-
break to night-fall.[23] In the next reign of Hisham I (788–796) a minaret was
added, from the circular gallery of which the *muezzin* calls the faithful to
prayer, together with an 'open gallery' (*as-sakifa*) for the use of women,
who, although usually excluded from congregational worship in the mosques, did join in the prayers in the theocratic state instituted by Muhammad
at Medina, where they appear to have stood in rows behind the men.

   This adaptation of the Visigothic church to Muslim requirements soon
became inadequate as the Islamic population at Cordoba increased by im-
migration from Arabia, Syria and North Africa. Indeed, it had long been
the ambition of Abd-ar-Rahman that it should become a centre of pilgrimage,
thereby relieving the pressure on Mecca. In 833 he added seven aisles to the
south of the ten rows with eighty new columns and a fresh mihrab. During
the succeeding century the edifice was further enlarged until had it become
the largest sacred place in Islam outside Mecca. In 880 a new minaret was

erected after an earthquake, and the façade of the mosque was restored. Its interior was transformed into one of the most pleasing examples of Moorish architecture, with a veritable labyrinth of some twelve hundred skilfully blended multi-coloured pillars in marble, porphyry and jasper, collected from a great variety of sources—from Constantinople and Carthage to Seville and Nimes—and supporting tiers of Moorish arches 12 feet in height rising to about 35 feet at the ceiling. The climax was reached in the Caliphate of Al-Hakim II (961–976) and that of Abd-ar-Rahman III in the middle of the tenth century. Then with its mosaics it was one of the most magnificent mosques rivalling that of Kairwin at Fez, until a period of decadence set in in the next century when rival claims to the dynasty arose about 1016. This continued until in 1236 the city was captured by Ferdinand III of Castile, and the mosque reverted to its purposes as a Christian church.

During the next two hundred years numerous chapels were inserted, mainly by Moorish masons and workmen, and the high altar (*crucero*) and the cruciform choir with the *Ceco* in the centre of the mosque were additions which marked the transformation from Muslim to Christian worship, thereby introducing anomalous features in the earlier Moorish edifice, as in the case of the substitution of a belfry in place of the minaret. This did not escape the notice of the Emperor Charles V (1500–1558), who on passing through the cathedral in 1526 opined, 'You have built here what you, or anyone, might have built anywhere else; but you have destroyed what was unique in the world'. Nevertheless, if the renovations and additions impaired the harmony of the vaulting and the splendour of the interior, the scenes on the pulpit are excellently carved and those on the stalls are among the finest examples of woodcarving and arabesque ornamentation in Spain, executed by Pedro Cornejo in the first half of the eighteenth century. The court, about 500 feet in length with cypress, palm, and orange trees and five fountains, is entered through a gateway with Christian inscriptions and statues of saints, copper doors with knockers and a Gothic inscription to Allah invoking his aid and protection.

The mihrab, erected by Al Hakim, containing an illuminated manuscript of the Qur'an, was destroyed by the Christians in 1146 and the vestibule made into the chapel of St Peter. Formerly the sacred Ceco was circumambulated seven times by the Muslim pilgrims as was done at the Meccan Ka'ba. The archway was adorned with magnificent mosaics, while the wall below was carved in marble. The marble ceiling is shaped like a shell and below is an arcade; to the right is a Moorish doorway flanked with mosaics and surmounted by a window and on the north is the colonnaded Patio de los Naranjos (the court of the oranges) used for ablutions, with its five fountains erected in 932 opposite the mosque on the south side. Such was the reputation of the sanctity of the Ceco (the House of Purification) at Cordoba that a pilgrimage to it was accepted as a substitute for the *Hajj* to Mecca as one of 'the Five Pillars' incumbent upon every faithful Muslim.

THE KA'BA AND GREAT MOSQUE AT MECCA

Apart from the central sanctuary of the Ka'ba at Mecca, Muslim temples have not been a prominent feature in Islam, and where they have occurred, as at Cordoba and the Ka'ba in Nejran on the Saudi Yemen border in the Arabian highlands, and at San'a, the capital of the Yemen, they have been constructed on sites already hallowed by Christian churches or cathedrals which formerly stood there. Moreover, the cube-shaped building called Ka'ba, which gave its name to the great mosque at Mecca, standing on a base ten inches high in a series of layers of grey-stone from the surrounding hills, had long been a sacred place in Arabia. In Muslim tradition it was alleged to have been founded by Abraham and Ishmael by divine revelation, and the sacred black stone (probably a meteorite) inserted in the building was said to have been received from the angel Gabriel. For this reason it has remained the principal object of veneration, framed in silver in the wall at the south-east corner. But the sanctuary had been rebuilt several times before it was taken over by Muhammad, and in it three goddesses, Al-Uzza identified with the planet Venus, Al-Manat the goddess of fortune, fate and destiny, and Allat a pan-Arabic designation meaning 'goddess',[24] were worshipped, their images and those of their associates being grouped round Hubal, the god of the sanctuary, whom Wellhausen equated with Allah.[25]

This conjecture, however, is based on post-Islamic re-interpretation of the identity of the two gods. Nevertheless, Allat, introduced probably from Syria into Arabia, was regarded as the goddess *par excellence*, the wife of Nabataean Dushara, the head of the pantheon worshipped in a black stone obelisk at Petra. Moreover, her name was a variant of Ilah (Aramaic *Alaha*) in Nabataean inscriptions, as a generic title for Deity. But while it is possible that the Meccans were in the habit of worshipping Allah at the Ka'ba, as the 'lord of the House', for centuries before it was appropriated by Muhammad it was unquestionably primarily a pagan polytheistic shrine. This to some extent was admitted by Muslim legend. It was maintained that it had been originally constructed in heaven two thousand years before the creation of the world, and erected by Adam with stones collected from the sacred mountains Sinai, Olivet, Lebanon, al-Judi and Hira, in the place where Muhammad received his revelation, just below the spot occupied by its celestial prototype. After the Flood it was rebuilt by Abraham and Ishmael and then fell into the possession of Banu Jurhum for a thousand years and became the centre of pilgrimage in Arabia as the chief shrine of the pantheon collected round Hubal. It was from this position that it was rescued by Muhammad when he conquered Mecca and reconstructed the Ka'ba about 608, making it the palladium of Islam.

Up to this time the sanctuary consisted merely of a roofless oblong enclosure with four dry-stone walls, according to Azraqi 32 cubits on the north-east wall, 22 on the north-west, 31 on the south-west and 20 on the south-east, with a height of 9 cubits, or 15 feet. Within it in the centre of a colonnaded quadrangle the Ka'ba stood, built to about the height of a man, as a 'square house', and having been constructed by the Quraysh tribe during the lifetime of Muhammad, partly in wood and covered with a roof.[26] In the Caliphate of Omar (634–644) houses were demolished in 638 to make a sacred enclosure of four walls, covered perhaps with stucco, thereby concealing the fact that they had been a combination of wood and stone before it was burnt down. In the meantime further enlargements had been undertaken by Othman (644–656) which were extended by Abdallah ibn Zobeir (683–684) and his successors, until by the eighth century the great mosque of Mecca had attained its final proportions (c. 783).

Standing on an inclined plane about 2 feet high with a flat roof, the Ka'ba has the appearance of a cube with a door 7 feet above the ground level on the east side. Near it at the south-east corner in three large pieces is the oval black stone about 7 inches from end to end and fragments of smaller stones. In the corner facing the south is the Yemen pillar about $1\frac{1}{2}$ feet in height and 2 inches in breadth, which also is touched with the right hand by the pilgrims as part of the Ka'ba ritual. Between the door and an arch on the north-west wall is a sort of domed pagoda over a hollow in the ground lined with marble, known as al-Mi-jan, venerated as the place where Abraham and

Ishmael were said to have kneaded the clay they used to construct the Ka'ba, and containing the impressions of feet claimed to have been made by them. The roof of the Ka'ba rested on six pillars of Indian wood arranged in two rows of three. The walls were lined with multi-coloured marbles, and the upper half with plates of silver gilt. The floor was paved with a mosaic of marbles and stones, and the exterior was draped with green silk and cotton veils inscribed with legends, invocations, and inscriptions including the ninetieth verse of the third *sura* of the Qur'an, 'Verily, the first house founded for the people was that at Bakka (Mecca), a blessed (house) and a guidance to the worlds'. The sacred precinct (*Haram*) had nineteen entrances and seven minarets, four of which were situated at the corners of the shrine.

THE MOSQUE OF MUHAMMAD AT MEDINA

While the great mosque at Mecca and the Ka'ba have remained the principal holy places for Islam, and the central point to which the mihrab faces everywhere, it was at Medina 300 miles to the north-east of Mecca that Muhammad first established congregational worship in the theocratic state he set up there in 622. According to one tradition it was at his own house in the city, or in that of one of his companions, that he first conducted the *salat*, the daily devotional exercise prescribed in the Qur'an as incumbent upon every Muslim. Another maintains that from the first it was his intention to erect a place of public prayer (*masdjid*, or mosque), and that he was commanded by Gabriel in the name of Allah to do so. But the earliest mosque appears to have been for his own private use rather than a sacred place at which his faithful followers assembled for corporate worship.[27] It may have been sometimes a *magli*, or council-tent, where civic business was transacted and public meetings were held.[28] But in any case it was on the plan of an Arabian dwelling-house with its walls, portico and columns supporting the roof, and chambers opening into a courtyard, that in the first instance most mosques were constructed. At first at Medina the *qibla* was orientated in the direction of Jerusalem, but when all hope of converting the Jews had been abandoned, then, as recorded in the second sura of the Qur'an (145), a revelation was alleged to have been given directing faces to be turned towards Mecca wherever and whenever the prayers were said.

From then onwards Mecca and its sanctuary became, and has remained, the religious centre of Islam, as indeed it had been for all the Arab tribes from time immemorial. Nevertheless, Muhammad's mosque at Medina was regarded as second only in seniority and sanctity to that at Mecca, ranking, in fact, in dignity with the Ka'ba. It was, however, simple in structure, the Prophet having declared that it must not exceed in elevation the temple of Solomon at Jerusalem. When it was rebuilt in 707-9 by Coptic and Greek workmen under the direction of Al-Walid I (705-715), it is said to have measured 200 by 167 cubits, with lofty columns and four minarets one at each of the corners, and to have been decorated with marble panelling and polychrome mosaics. The mihrab was made in the form of a prayer niche, and a block of stone to indicate the direction to be assumed by the congregation. It was first placed against the northern wall, and after the qibla was changed to that of Mecca it was removed to the southern end of the mosque. Further extensions were made on the north side, between 775 and 833, by the addition of ten marble pillars with gilt capitals. After a fire further reconstructions were begun in 1256 and completed in 1589, with embellishments by the sultans of Egypt during the next two hundred years, until it was rebuilt by the nineteenth Egyptian sultan, Qait Bey (1495-1498) in its final form as described by R. F. Burton in 1853.[29]

Prior to the reconstruction of the Ka'ba in 608 and the development of the mosque of Muhammad at Medina after 623, no attempt was made in pre-Islamic Arabia to erect architectural monuments, and when Islam began its long series of conquests after Abu Bakr succeeded to the Caliphate in 632 at the death of the Prophet, it was content for the most part to take over the Christian churches or other public buildings and use them as places of congregational prayer and the delivery of the Friday oration. In the absence of anything in the nature of a sacrificial cultus or of an institutional ritual requiring an elaboration of sacred equipment the adaptation was easily accomplished. It was only at the Ka'ba at Mecca that the pilgrimage ceremonies were retained, based on the traditional rites connected with the sanctuary which included the offering of a sacrifice, circumambulation of the shrine, the asperging and censing of the building, the veneration of the black stone, and libations; a visit to Medina also was highly meritorious.

Nevertheless, although Mecca and Medina for the devout Muslim always have been held in much the same veneration as Jerusalem for the Jew and Rome for those who owe allegiance to the Holy See, Muhammad himself attached little importance to sacred buildings and sites as such. The ritual prayer could be said anywhere, and when Islam moved out of Arabia to Syria, where Christianity was firmly established, churches were converted into mosques either in their entirety or in part, according to local circumstances and requirements. If a town surrendered without opposition it was usually allowed to retain many of its churches. Otherwise they were confiscated completely or divided into two sections, one being used as a mosque, the other as a church or synagogue. Since, as we have seen, many basilicas were themselves built on ancient sacred sites where pagan temples had formerly stood, the mosque not infrequently represented the latest of a long succession of places of worship extending back to remote times.

THE GREAT MOSQUE AT DAMASCUS

Thus, after the capture of Damascus in 636 the Muslim population of the city had increased so rapidly that by the time of Al-Walid (705–715) a mosque of considerable size was required. Already a number of the best churches had been transformed into mosques, partly for devotional and partly for political reasons since the use of such imposing buildings would add to the prestige of the newly established faith. Therefore in 707 Al-Walid took possession of the great ancient temenos in the centre of the town, measuring 1300 feet by 1000 feet, in the middle of which stood a pre-Roman temple on a podium, which had been transformed into the church of St John erected by Theodosius I (378–395) about 379 and enlarged probably by Theodosius II (408–450), covering an area of about 530 feet by 320 feet, enclosed by four walls with square towers at their angles. The actual Umayyad Mosque with its colonnaded halls divided into three aisles with eleven arches, may have been part of the ancient temple buildings, but while the church of St John did occupy a part of the site, it is hardly likely to have extended over the whole of it,[30] as this would have made it second in size only to St Peter's at Rome among early Christian basilicas. However, as a Muslim edifice it ranks next to the mosques at Mecca and Medina and the Dome of the Rock at Jerusalem, and has been described as one of the architectural wonders of the world,[31] but its fame has been achieved largely on account of its decoration.

The great court, measuring 430 feet by 125 feet, surrounded by arcades of columns and piers was arranged in the form of a horseshoe arch surmounted with battlements covered with mosaics. The walls of the mosque were faced with coloured marbles and embellished with mosaics and enamelled

tiles. The capitals and ceilings were gilded and adorned with stucco ornamentation, the dome glittered with gold, and the semicircular mihrab
was inlaid with agate and turquoise. In the centre of the hall was a large
marble tank under a dome supported by marble columns. The pavement of
the court was of mosaic and the windows of the arcade in the northern end
were filled with coloured glass.[32]

Exactly what was the position of the mosque with regard to the church
of St John is uncertain, but there can be no doubt that Al-Walid's aim was to
eclipse the Christian basilicas in Syria and Palestine, regardless of the expense
involved in this excessive elaboration of the Great Umayyad Mosque. It is
said that he spent the revenues of the Empire for seven years on this project,
employing ten thousand men daily for nine years to complete the work,
collecting the gold, precious stones, lead and other materials from all lands,
in spite of protests from the populace who resented this excessive disposal of
public treasure. He maintained, however, that it was for the glory of Allah
that this splendour and magnificence had been bestowed on the mosque,
to which incidentally the city owed its fame. And it cannot be denied that it
has remained the most outstanding achievement of the Caliphate and, indeed,
of Muslim decorative architecture.

THE AQSA MOSQUE AT JERUSALEM

It was, nevertheless, upon Jerusalem that interest was concentrated in the
early days of the expansion of Islam, going back to the time when Muhammad sought the support and allegiance of the Jews and Christians at the
beginning of the movement. It was towards Jerusalem that prayer was said,
as we have seen, and according to Muslim tradition it was to the site of the
temple of Solomon that the Prophet made his noctural journey from the
Ka'ba at Mecca, if this is the correct interpretation of the incident recorded
in the Qur'an.[33] In any case, Jerusalem is known among Muslims as *Al-Kuds*,
or *Muqaddas*, 'the Holy House', a designation derived in the first instance
from the temple on Mount Zion and then applied to the Holy City as a
whole with its several sacred places and associations. When it was sacked by
Chosroes II in 614 and subsequently surrendered to the Caliph Omar in 638,
a mosque known as Al-Aqsa was erected on the temple area. In 691 Abd al-
Malik (685–705) began the construction of the Dome of the Rock over
the sacred stone on which the Jewish altar of burnt-offering had stood, to

prevent, as it was alleged, Muslims being dazzled by the magnificence of the Church of the Holy Sepulchre, which it was made to resemble as closely as possible. Indeed, such was its importance as the sacred spot from which Muhammad was believed to have ascended to heaven that Abd al-Malik endeavoured to make it more beautiful than the Great Mosque at Damascus, as a worthy substitute for the Ka'ba as a place of pilgrimage.

THE DOME OF THE ROCK (QUBBAT AL-SAKHRA)

From the earliest available Arab sources it is very difficult to determine exactly what was the relationship of the Aqsa Mosque to the Dome of the Rock. In the first place it has to be remembered that the Sakhra was a shrine built over the sacred rock not a mosque, as it has been erroneously called 'the mosque of Omar'. That the first Aqsa Mosque may have been built on the site of Justinian's basilica of St Mary the Virgin is by no means improbable,[34] and some of the latter's columns may have been incorporated in the mosque after the church had been destroyed, perhaps in 614 when Chosroes II raided Jerusalem. On the other hand a very primitive place of prayer with upright beams near the east wall on the remains of ruins where once the Jewish temple stood is said by Arculph, a pilgrim from Gaul, who visited the city about 670, to have been frequented by the Saracens.[35] Here it has been suggested the Dome of the Rock was erected, probably of wood, about 691 when Abd al-Malik reconstructed the mosque Al-Aqsa, exploiting the temple site to produce a counter-attraction to Mecca and Medina with the mosque of Al-Aqsa on its southern boundary.

The podium on which the Dome of the Rock was built on Mount Moriah in the centre of Herod's temple was about 56 feet long by 42 feet wide, and 10 feet above the level of the enclosure, approached by a flight of steps with four entrances, each having a marble porch, the largest being on the south side. The sacred rock was surrounded by a lattice screen of ebony and curtains of brocade, the architecture having been attributed to Byzantine workmanship under Constantine to mark the site of the Holy Sepulchre. It is by no means unlikely that Greek architects may have been employed by Abd al-Malik, and many of the columns may have been obtained from the churches destroyed by the Persian raiders, but that it was the work of Abd al-Malik is supported by all the available literary sources and is maintained by the mosaic inscription above the cornice on the base of the dome.

Christian Basilicas and Muslim Mosques

37   *Mosaic showing the Palace of Theodoric, Ravenna*

Until persecution of the Christians was ended by the Edict of Milan, the Catacombs were used as places of worship and as burial chambers. The Catacombs were made in the subterranean tufa quarries of the Appian Way. Galleries in descending tiers led into halls as deep as 70 feet below the surface. The earliest catacomb is that of St Sebastian (138, 139) dating to the end of the first century A.D. where over 250 Christians were buried

The church of San Clemente in Rome is built on the traditional site of the saint's house, which was a meeting place and sanctuary for early Christians. The present building was restored in 1108 after the Norman destruction, using material from the fourth century basilica, the remains of which lie below. The form of the early Christian basilica has been preserved: eight marble columns divide the side aisles from the nave and a four-columned tabernacle stands in the raised chancel

142

Under the patronage of Justinian and his empress Theodora, some of the magnificence of the art and architecture of the eastern Byzantine empire was brought to the imperial court in Italy at Ravenna. The church of San Vitale (141), consecrated in 548 A.D. seems to have followed the plan of Justinian's earlier church of SS. Sergius and Bacchus in Constantinople, but was also influenced by the Ravenna Orthodox Baptistry of Neon (143). In contrast to the external severity of design, the interior of the church is richly decorated with mosaics which glow from the light of three tiers of windows. Some of the detail of the lunettes can be seen (142) as well as the intricate patterns of the arch where the twelve apostles appear in roundels. Carved marble columns line the aisle leading to the open interior under the dome

The basilica of Sant'Apollinare Nuovo was built by the emperor Theodoric in 519 A.D. Above the marble columns which divide the nave from the side aisles, were three bands of mosaics. The palace of Theodoric is shown in one of these with the town buildings beyond (137). Under Justinian, some of the mosaics were replaced: a long procession of saints (144) filled one band, and a similar procession of martyrs was on the other wall. The figures of the saints stand out from a gold background, each in the same pose

143

144

145

146

The height of the First Golden Age and of all Byzantine architecture was reached in December 537 when the great domed basilica of Sancta Sophia was finally completed (145). The Byzantine influence in the Second Golden Age is well shown in Venice where St Mark's was remodelled in the eleventh century in the shape of a Greek cross (147), and the interior made as close a copy of Sancta Sophia as was possible (146, 148)

148

147

149   *As the faith of Islam spread westwards through the Mediterranean, existing places of Christian worship were enlarged and converted to mosques. By the end of the tenth century, the church at Cordoba had become the largest sacred place in Islam outside Mecca (149). In contrast to the open aisles, a labyrinth of some thousand pillars now led to the altar of Mihrab. The mosque of Ibn*
150   *Tulun near Cairo (150) was however, built as a mosque with no Byzantine features*

Jerusalem is a holy city for Muhammadans as well as Christians. Here Muhammad
sought the help of both Jews and Christians during the early years of his movement, and
after his death was believed to have ascended to heaven from the stone beneath the Dome
of the Rock (151) The nearby mosque of Al-Aqsa is also a place of pilgrimage (152)

The huge wooden dome was about 67 feet in diameter on a circular plan surrounded by a double octagonal enclosure with its sixteen windows resting on twelve columns. It has always been the central feature of the structure, but the restorations and redecoration with Christian designs have been so numerous that little remains of the original rotunda, its capitals, columns, arcades and roof.[36] After the fire in 1448 the dome was replaced by a double construction consisting of one dome over the other with a space between them, whereas according to the description given by Ibn al-Fakih in 903, it originally had an inner and an outer cupola. Nevertheless, it was essentially the same in general octagonal plan as that which has persisted throughout the ages, based in the first instance on that of the Church of the Holy Sepulchre except that the decorations of the dome and the walls were arabesques, polychrome mosaics and frescoes in which scenes were rigidly excluded, though some of the columns taken from churches have retained vestiges of the cross on the capitals and mosaics of Persian origin also have survived.

In front of the eastern entrance of the Sakhra is a much smaller rotunda, the Qubbal al-Silsila, the Dome of the Chain, said to have been supported by twenty marble columns with a roof covered with sheets of lead. It is alleged by Arabic chroniclers to have been erected by Abd al-Malik first as a treasury and then as the model for the reconstruction of the Aqsa mosque.[37] This, however, is open to question as the capitals are of various dates taken from other buildings, and the reconstructions have been so numerous that it is impossible to determine with any degree of accuracy its chronological origin and precise sequence; earthquakes and wars having played havoc with the two or three smaller domes on the podium built on different occasions to commemorate events in the noctural journey of Muhammad and subsequently used for other purposes, causing confusion in respect of their origin and significance. Nevertheless, it is beyond doubt that the Dome of the Rock marks the hallowed spot in the temple area at Jerusalem (the Haram ash-Sharif), on which it was alleged the ark of Noah stood after the Flood long before the altar of Yahweh was placed upon it, and the site of the Holy Sepulchre, revered as the omphalos of the world alike by Jews, Christians and Muslims. In the current eschatology it was here too that the last trumpet was destined to be sounded on the Day of Judgment.

As Islam arose essentially as a religious movement based on the revelations and commands which Muhammad claimed to have received from Allah, it was to this extent a new creation that rapidly developed into a widespread civilization, with its own specific beliefs and cultus embodied in the Qur'an imposing on Muslims a distinctive way of life and pattern of culture. In this religious and cultural complex all these elements, spiritual, political, legal and social, many of them being of diverse origin, became fused into a composite theocratic civilization, fundamentally Islamic but embracing, modifying and re-shaping the Christian, Jewish, Persian and Byzantine influences, traditions and structures comprehended within it. This has been most apparent in Muslim architecture and art, notably in the construction, equipment and decoration of mosques. Throughout all their vicissitudes the traditional sanctuary of the Ka'ba retained its original significance and pre-eminence and the mosque established by the Prophet at Medina continued to occupy pride of place as the centre of worship and administration in the Islamic community; these venerated monuments therefore naturally served as models for later mosques. The influence of the Great Mosque of Damascus was also very considerable, and on its general plan those at Aleppo and at Qasr al-Hair, 60 miles north-east of Palmyra in the desert, were erected on a smaller scale. Abd-al-Rahulan I was also influenced by the Mosque at Damascus in his reconstruction of the Spanish cathedral at Cordoba.

Conversely, when existing Christian towns were conquered and the Muslim generals took possession of the churches either in their entirety or in part, as at Jerusalem, Damascus, Kayrawan, Constantinople, and Cordoba, great mosques were created in a new Islamic style of architecture which reflected the merging of Muslim and Christian traditions and their respective modes of prayer and worship. In Turkey several significant changes were made in the process of adaptation to suit the climatic conditions. The open side of the portico facing the court was closed and eventually the courtyard was dispensed with altogether, leaving the pillars and a hall enclosed on all sides, as, for example, in the mosque of Samarra (852) in Mesopotamia.[37]

When in the fourteenth century Konya, the ancient Iconium, became the principal city in the mountain Anatolian province and the meeting point of trade-routes from the three surrounding centres of civilization, it contained a great variety of architectural designs which the Ottomans adopted and utilized in their mosques in the following century. This is revealed in the Syrian skill displayed at Damascus and Aleppo, the Persian and Egyptian craftsmanship, and the Byzantine construction and ornamentation, excluding of course anything of a specifically Christian character. The Aladdin Mosque (1156–1220) had a simple geometric plan and was roofed with clay over wooden rafters resting on arcades supported by columns; a minaret was added, and a conical roof with the circular drum in the central dome super-imposed on the square plan of the main structure. On the whole, however, Turkey kept closest to the Byzantine tradition, with Persian and Muslim details in decoration. This is displayed in the scenes of imperial mosques in Constantinople in the fourteenth and fifteenth centuries in which the dome is the most prominent feature, with an atrium in front of it.

THE MOSQUE OF IBN TULUN

One of the earliest mosques with no Byzantine traits is that of Ibn Tulun at Qattai, a suburb of Cairo (868–879). He was already familiar with the two huge mosques at Samarra erected on piers, though he made no attempt to reproduce either of them at Qattai, except in so far as an open space (*ziyada*) was left between the walls, and an outer enclosing *enceinte* erected on the east, west and north sides. These were new features common to each of the three mosques, the purpose of the circuit walls being doubtless to separate the mosque from the surrounding secular buildings. In the north court were latrines and a fountain for oblations, and near by was the minaret. From the east ziyada six entrance portals led into the arcade. The place of daily prayer was on the southern, or fourth side, with five rows of piers and buttresses, the central open court, or *sahn*, being used to contain the large congregation that assembled on Fridays for the special public prayers, standing in rows side by side facing the qibla showing the direction of Mecca. In the centre was the *fauwara*, or gilt domed pentagon, with latticed windows supported on ten marble columns and sixteen surrounding it, with two columns at each angle. This was destroyed in 986. Under the dome was a large marble basin with a fountain in the middle standing on a marble pavement. On the roof was a sun-dial and a railing of teak-wood,[38] while behind the mosque on the north-west side was a place for ablutions (*mida'a*). On the south side a door in the wall gave access to a chamber (*Dar al-Imara*) used as a sacristy for the Friday prayers.

The outer face of the walls of the internal arcades were ornamented with large niches alternating with windows between smaller niches, and for the first time brick piers carrying pointed horseshoe arches with bell-shaped capitals displaying vine-leaves took the place of the antique columns, probably introduced from the orient.[39] Everywhere the walls and columns were covered with white stucco decorated with ornamental designs in geometrical frameworks and a frieze of rosettes in an octagonal frame above the ornament round the arches. The walls were surmounted with battlements, and like the rest of the mosque built of red brick, but the minaret on the north between the cloister and the outer wall, left of the main axis, was of limestone and divided into four storeys rising to a height of 130 feet. Round it was a stone staircase on the outside leading up to a cylindrical tower with stairs at the top. How it finished is not known, but in the present structure is a small octagonal kiosk above the second circular storey ending in a finial and having an internal staircase. The base consisted of a square block of hard stone 28 feet square and 67 feet high with the octagonal stage above it 20 feet in diameter and 29 feet in height.[40] It has long been suggested that this minaret was copied from the one at Samarra,[41] an assumption going back to the eleventh century and supported by the affinities with the Mesopotamian ziggurats.[42] But it was a much later reconstruction contemporary with the pointed horseshoe arches which made their appearance in Egypt at the end of the thirteenth century (*c.* 1284) coming originally from Iran and Mesopotamia in all probability, and perhaps from India.

The mosque itself taken as a whole, however, was not actually a reproduction of a Samarran prototype, as has been so often alleged in ancient and modern times, even though unquestionably it had points of resemblance to and possible affinities with the two great mosques of Samarra, notably the ziyadas, and other western-Asian features connected especially with the pointed arch, its decoration and the semicircular niches (mihrab). The distinctive claims of Islam to be the final revelation of Allah vouchsafed to mankind through his Prophet, discouraged the imitation of any established characteristic forms of worship, be they of pagan, Christian or Jewish origin and significance. Nevertheless, as we have seen, there was no hesitation in taking over other older sanctuaries and transforming them into mosques, while some of the churches were used as government offices.

As Islam spread in regions devoid of convertible sacred places new buildings had to be erected, especially at spots that could claim historical associations with Muhammad, and where he was said to have performed the salat, or left traces of his footprints. At Mecca and Medina, of course, these connexions with the Prophet and his relatives and companions were almost inexhaustible, and in Palestine were sanctuaries which claimed to have been founded or visited by the Hebrew patriarchs and prophets who had been incorporated in the Muslim tradition and, therefore, required mosques, as did the tombs of the Islamic ancestors. These reproduced for the most part the plan, dimensions and equipment of the prototype in Medina, so far as was possible or reasonably convenient, and occupied a central position in the town. Such associations and design gave sanctity to the edifices, particularly when they became centres of pilgrimage, or acquired a tribal or sectarian status and significance.

The observance of the Friday salat obligatory to all male Muslims who had attained years of discretion demanded the construction of large mosques everywhere as converts increased, though in Egypt and Syria the practice was often restricted to one or two mosques in the towns and villages. Where new mosques were required the original simple plan was retained in principle, but the colonnaded hall was considerably enlarged, the walls, roof and columns were decorated in accordance with local skill and tradition, and a fountain placed in the centre of the court for ablutions. Minarets were added as a permanent feature and tended to become more numerous, whether or not they were borrowed in the beginning from church towers or from ziggurats. Having become an integral part of the mosque they were utilized for the summoning of the faithful to the salat by the muezzin who ascended to the gallery to proclaim the *Kalima*.

With the expansion of Muslim civilization the structure, art and architecture of the mosques underwent repeated modification under Hellenistic, Sassanian, African, Indian and Western influences, with the inevitable result that they differed widely in design. Moreover, so intimately were religion, social organization and politics intermingled in Islam that mosques besides being sacred places were also state institutions in which civic administration, commercial enterprise and secular affairs in general were, and still may be, conducted, the sacred and the secular being two inseparable aspects of the theocratic civilization. In the absence of a priesthood and of a sacramental system mosques have always been devoid of an altar or a sanctuary, their place being taken by the *mihrab* and the *minbar*, or pulpit at its side, and sometimes a *dikka*, or platform raised on columns, in front, from which the sacred words of the Qur'an are read. It has been the numinous quality of these divine utterances by the *imam* that have found outward expression in the prescribed prostrations and formulae at the five daily ritual prayers. As this communal act of worship directed to Allah as the wholly transcendent Creator and sovereign Ruler of all things visible and invisible permits no liturgical drama or iconic representation, the mosque is primarily and essentially a house of prayer.

It is this factor which determined the design of the Ibn Tulun in Cairo, the earliest genuine example of a mosque erected *de novo* without any materials or adjuncts taken from ancient buildings. As we have seen, it consists of a great central court, a prayer chamber four aisles deep on the southeast (Mecca) side, and a double aisle on the other three sides. The brick walls, piers and pointed arches, slightly horseshoe in shape, are covered with stucco decorated with friezes, conventional patterns and geometrical designs. As the 'place of prayer' this was the normal plan adopted even for the elaborate great mosques in India erected by the Mogul emperors at Delhi, Agra and Fathpur Sikri, resembling in design those of Egypt, Syria and Persia, the qibla and mihrab of course being at the west end in India. Throughout all the vicissitudes of its developments and adaptations the mosque as the religious, social, and political centre of the Muslim community has retained its characteristics and occupied a distinctive position in the history of sacred places in antiquity.

NOTES

CHAPTER I

1 cf. Breuil, Obermaier and Alcade del Rio, *La Pasiega a Puente Viesgo* (Monaco, 1913); M. C. Burkitt, *Prehistory* (Cambridge, 1925), pp. 263 *ff.*

2 Obermaier and Breuil, *Congrès Intern. d'Anthrop. et d'Archéol.* (Geneva, 1912); Breuil, *Four Hundred Centuries of Cave Art* (Montignac, 1952), pp. 360 *ff.*

3 Breuil, *op. cit.*, p. 355.

4 Breuil and Obermaier, *L'Anthrop.* xxiii (1912).

5 Cartailhac and Breuil, *La caverne d'Altamira à Santillane près de Santander* (Monaco, 1906); Breuil and Obermaier, *The Cave of Altamira at Santillana del Mar* (Madrid, 1935); Breuil, *Four Hundred Centuries of Cave Art* (Montignac, 1952).

6 Breuil, Capitan and Peyrony, *La caverne de Font-de-Gaume aux Eyzies* (Monaco, 1910); cf. Breuil, *Four Hundred Centuries*, pp. 76 *ff.*

7 Breuil and Capitan, *Rev. de l'École d'Anthrop. de Paris*, xii (1902), pp. 33 *ff.*

8 F. Windels, *The Lascaux Cave Paintings* (1949), pp. 17 *ff.*, 57, 63 *ff.*; A. H. Brodrick, *Lascaux: A Commentary* (1948), pp. 81 *ff.*; Laming, *Lascaux* (1959), pp. 93 *ff.*

9 Breuil, *Four Hundred Centuries of Cave Art*, pp. 131 *ff.*

10 Breuil, *op. cit.*, pp. 38 *ff.*

11 Bégouen and Casteret, *Revue anthropologique* (1923), pp. 533 *ff.*

12 Cartailhac and Breuil, *L'Anthrop.* (1910), p. 129.

13 Westermarck, *Ritual and Belief in Morocco* (1926), vol. i, pp. 445 *ff.*, 471.

14 *E.R.E.*, vol. v, pp. 612 *ff.*

15 Bégouen, *XIIth. Congrès intern. d'anthrop.* (Geneva, 1912), pp. 489 *ff.*; *L'Anthrop.* (1912), pp. 657 *ff.*, cf. *Antiquity*, iii, no. 9 (1929), p. 16.

16 Breuil, *op. cit.*, pp. 166, 176 *ff.*

17 Bégouen, *Antiquity*, iii (1929), p. 17.

18 Breuil, *op. cit.*, p. 176; Breuil and Lantier, *Les hommes de la Pierre Ancienne* (Paris, 1951), p. 315.

19 Lémozi, *La grotte-temple du Pech-Merle* (Paris, 1929), p. 183.

20 Lémozi, *Bull. de la Société préhistorique de France* (1920), pp. 256 *ff.*

21 Breuil, *C.R. Académie des inscriptions* (1905), pp. 105 *ff.*

22 Breuil and Lalanne, *L'Anthropologie*, xxii (1911), pp. 385 *ff.*

23 Capitan, Breuil and Peyrony, *L'Anthropologie* (1915), pp. 505 *ff.*

24 G. Lalanne, *L'Anthrop.* xxii (1911), pp. 257 *ff.*; xxiii (1912), pp. 129 *ff.*; Capitan, *Rev. de l'École d'Anthrop.*, xxii (1912), pp. 316 *ff.*; Passemard, *Les statuettes féminines dites Venus stéatopyges*, Nimes (1938), pp. 121 *ff.*

25 Breuil and Calve Aguilo, *L'Anthrop.*, xx (1909), p. 1.

26 *L'Anthrop.*, xxx (1920), pp. 1–50.

27 Breuil, *L'Anthrop.*, xxiii (1912), p. 529.

28 Obermaier, *Fossil Man in Spain* (1924), p. 257 *ff.*; *L'Anthrop.*, xxxvi (1926), p. 5 *ff.*

29 Breuil, Obermaier, and Verner, *La Pileta à Benaojan* (Monaco, 1915), Pls., xiii, xiv, pp. 41, 43.

30 Breuil and Burkitt, *Rock Paintings of Southern Andalusia* (Oxford, 1929), pp. 11 *ff.*, 86.

31 Spencer and Gillen, *Native Tribes of Central Australia* (1938), pp. 171 *ff.*, 614 *ff.*; *Northern Tribes of Central Australia* (1904), pp. 436 *ff.*

32 Obermaier, *Fossil Man in Spain*, pp. 260 *ff.*; A. B. Cook, *L'Anthrop.*, xiv (1903); Wernert, *Comisión de Investigaciones Paleontologicas y Prehistoricas* (Madrid, 1916), Memoria 12.

33 Cartailhac and Breuil, *La caverne d'Altamira* (Monaco, 1906), p. 139.

34 Black, *Palaeotologia Sinica*, ii (1927), pp. 1 *ff.*; Black, Teilhard de Chardin, *Fossil Man in China* (Peking, 1933), pp. 83 *ff.*; R. Moore, *Man, Time and Fossils* (1954), pp. 237 *ff.*

35 Hutton, *J.R.A.I.*, lviii (1928), pp. 403 *ff.*; Hose and McDougall, *The Pagan Tribes of Borneo*, vol. i (1912), pp. 114 *ff.*; vol. ii, pp. 20 *ff.*; H. I. Marshall, *The Karen People of Borneo*, (1922), p. 222.

36 Blanc, *Accad. Naz. dei Lincei* (1939), p. 205.

37 K. Gorjanovic-Kramberger, *Mitteilungen der Anthropologischen Gesellschaft in Wien*, xxii (1902), p. 189; xxiv (1904), pp. 187 *ff.*

38 Oppenoorth, *Early Man* (Philad., 1957), pp. 349 *ff.*

39 Breuil and Obermaier, *L'Anthrop.*, xx (1909), p. 523; Wernert, *Histoire générale de religion*, vol. i, p. 561; Breuil and Lantier, *Les hommes de la Pierre Ancienne* (Paris, 1951), pp. 280 *ff.*

40 R. R. Schmidt, *Die diluviale Vorzeit Deutschlands* (Stuttgart, 1912).

41 Hauser and Klaasch, *Archiv für Anthropologie*, vol. vii (1909), p. 290

42 A. and J. Bouyssonie and L. Bardon, *L'Anthrop.*, xix (1908), p. 513; xxiv (1913), pp. 616 *ff.*; Boule, *Annales de paléontologie* (1911–13).

43 Breuil, *L'Anthrop.*, xxxi (1921), pp. 343 *ff.*; Capitan and Peyrony, *Revue anthrop.*, xxii (1912), p. 29.

44 Verneau, *Les grottes de Grimaldi* (Monaco, 1906), vol. ii, p. 304; *Reliquiae Aquitanicae*, p. 70.

45 Obermaier, *Der Mensch der Vorzeit*, p. 298, Pl. xxiii, no. 2; Breuil, *L'Anthrop* (1924), pp. 549 *ff*.; Boule, *Les hommes fossiles*, pp. 269 *ff*.

46 Hardy, *La Station quarternaire la Raymonden* (Paris, 1891), pp. 50, 52; Tournier and Guillon, *Les hommes préhistorique dans l'Ain* (Bourg, 1895), p. 61; Boule, *op. cit.*, p. 274.

47 Verneau, *Les grottes de Grimaldi* (1906), vol. i, pp. 64 *ff*.; vol. ii, pp. 23, 33, 260, 277 *ff*., 298 *ff*.

48 *Comptes-Rendus de l'Accad. des Sciences*, lxxiv (1872), pp. 1060 *ff*.; E. Cartailhac, *La France préhistorique* (Paris, 1889), p. 110.

CHAPTER II

1 K. M. Kenyon, *Antiquity*, xxx (1956), pp. 134 *ff*., 184 *ff*.; R. J. Braidwood, *Antiquity*, xxxi (1957), pp. 78 *ff*.

2 K. M. Kenyon, *Digging up Jericho* (1957), pp. 59 *ff*.

3 *op. cit.*, p. 59.

4 M. E. L. Mallowan and Rose J. Cruikshank, *Iraq.*, vol. ii, pt. i (1935), pp. 79 *ff*.

5 In the case of the seventh skull the shells were cowries.

6 Kenyon, *op. cit.*, p. 72.

7 Mallowan and Cruikshank, *Prehistoric Assyria* (Oxford, 1935), p. 34.

8 Dikaios, *Iraq*, vii (1940), pp. 72 *ff*.

9 *op. cit.*, p. 33.

10 Dikaios, *op. cit.*, pp. 77 *ff*.

11 *cf*. Dikaios, *Archaeologia*, lxxxviii (1938), pp. 50 *ff*., 118 *ff*., Pls. vii, viii, xiv (d).

12 M. R. Dussaud, *Syria*, xiii, 26.

13 Seton Lloyd and J. Mellaart, *Anatolian Studies*, vii (1957), pp. 27 *ff*.

14 W. Lamb, *op. cit.*, vi, (1956).

15 Evans, *Palace of Minos*, vol. i, p. 14.

16 S. Xanthoudides, *The Vaulted Tombs of Mesara* (Liverpool, 1924), pp. 4 *ff*.

17 R. B. Seager, *Explorations in the Island of Mochlos* (Boston, 1916), pp. 13 *ff*.; *The Cemetery of Pachyammos, Crete*, University of Penn. Anthrop. Publications (Philad., 1916), pp. 11 *ff*.

18 A. J. Evans, *The Palace of Minos*, vol. i, p. 428; Nilsson, *The Minoan Mycenaean Religion*, pp. 428 *ff*.

19 Paribeni, *Monumenti Antichi*, xix (1909), pp. 11 *ff*.; Picard, *Les réligions préhellénique* (1948) pp. 168 *ff*.; *Der kretische Bildersarg, Arch. Jahrbuch*, xxiv (1909), pp. 162 *ff*.

20 *Themis*, p. 178, p. 168.

21 Nilsson, *op. cit.*, pp. 438 *ff.*

22 *Palace of Minos*, vol. i, pp. 439, 447.

23 *op. cit.*, vol. iv, p. 965.

24 *op. cit.*, vol. i, pp. 500 *ff.*

25 *B.S.A.*, vii (1900), p. 29, ix, Fig. 38.

26 *cf.* Chapter I, p. 31.

27 H. B. Hawes, *Gournia* (Philad., 1906), p. 47, Pl. xi.

28 Tsountas, *Praktika* (1896), pp. 29 *ff.*; Evans, *Tree and Pillar Cult* (1901), pp. 19.

29 Evans, *op. cit.*, pp. 331-9.

30 *op. cit.*, pp. 7, 15.

31 *Odyssey*, xix, 188; Strabo, x, 476.

32 Marinatos, *Praktika* (1929), p. 94; (1900), pp. 91 *ff.*; Nilsson, *op. cit.*, pp. 58, 518.

33 Evans, *J.H.S.* (1897), pp. 350 *ff.*; *Palace of Minos*, vol. i, pp. 625 *ff.*; Nilsson, *op. cit.*, p. 62 *ff.*

34 *B.S.A.*, xix (1913), p. 32.

35 *cf.* Piggott, *The Neolithic Cultures of the British Isles* (1954), pp. 124 *ff.*

36 Bernarbò Brea, in *Annual Report, University of London Institute of Archaeology* (1950), p. 23.

37 F. von Duhn, *Italienische Grabenkunde* (Heidelberg, 1924), pp. 71 *ff.*, 76.

38 J. D. Evans, *Malta* (1959), p. 45, *cf. P.P.S.*, xix (1953), pp. 41 *ff.*

39 Zammit, *Antiquity* (1930), p. 26.

40 Zammit, *The Neolithic Temples at Hagia Kim and Mnaidra* (Valetta, 1927), p. 28; Evans, *op. cit.*, pp. 109 *ff.*

41 Zammit, *Prehistoric Malta* (Oxford, 1930), pp. 7, 80 *ff.*

42 Zammit and Singer, *J.R.A.I.*, liv (1924), Pl. xv, 49

43 *op. cit.*, Pl. xviii, 53, 54.

44 *op. cit.*, Pl. xi, 29, *cf.* Pl. xx, 30

45 Zammit, *The Hal-Saflieni Prehistoric Hypogeum* (Malta, 1910), p. 440; *J.R.A.I.*, *op. cit.*, Pl. ix, 22.

46 Zammit, *Prehistoric Malta*, pp. 15, 84, 96.

47 Zammit, *Hal-Saflieni Hypogeum*, p. 31.

48 D. Mackenzie, *British School of Rome*, vol. v, no. 2 (1910), pp. 101 *ff.*

49 Pallottino, *La Sardegna Nuragica* (1950), pp. 29 *ff.*, 41 *ff.*

50 Siret, *Revue préhistorique* (1908), nos. 7, 81, *Les premiers ages du métal dans le sud-ouest de L'Espagne* (1888); *Revue des questions scientifiques* (Bruxelles, 1893), pp. 522 *ff.*; Leisner, *Arquelogia e Historia*, vol. i (Lisbon, 1945), pp. 13 *ff.*; *Die Megalithgräber der iberischen Halbinsel* i *Der Süden* (Berlin, 1943), pp. 59, 63, 73.

51 Forde, *American Anthropologist*, xxxii (1930), pp. 70 *ff.*; Le Rouzig, *L'Anthrop.*, xliii (1933), pp. 233 *ff.*
52 Forde, *P.P.S.* (1940), pp. 170 *ff.*; Piggott, *Antiquity* (1937), pp. 441 *ff.*
53 *P.P.S.* (1939), pp. 159 *ff.*; *The Antiquaries Journal*, xix (1939), pp. 157 *ff.*; *The Megalithic Builders of Western Europe*, (1958), pp. 99 *ff.*, 122 *ff.*
54 Daniel and Powell, *P.P.S.*, xv (1949), p. 183.
55 *cf.* Chapter III, p. 102.
56 Kendrick, *The Archaeology of the Channel Islands*, vol. i (1928), pp. 21 *ff.*, 32; E. MacCulloch, *Proceedings of the Society of Antiquaries*, viii (1881) p. 32, A. Mortillet, *Bulletin Soc. d'Anthrop.* (Paris, 1893), p. 664; *Assoc. française pour l'advancement des sciences* (Paris, 1890), p. 629; *Bulletin Soc. préhistorique française*, vol. viii (Paris, 1911), p. 669.
57 Cunningham, *Wiltshire Archaeological Magazine*, xlv (1931), p. 313.
58 Keiller and Piggott, *Antiquity*, x (1936), pp. 417 *ff.*
59 Stukeley, *Abury, a Temple of the Druids* (1743), pp. 32 *ff.*
60 Atkinson, *Stonehenge* (1956), pp. 169 *ff.*
61 Atkinson, Piggott and Sandars, *Excavations at Dorchester, Oxon* (Oxford, 1951), p. 88.
62 *The Antiquaries Journal*, iii (1923), p. 239.
63 Piggott, *Antiquity*, xxviii (1954), pp. 221 *ff.*; Atkinson, *op. cit.*, pp. 68 *ff.*; Stone, *Wessex* (1958) pp. 96 *ff.*
64 Crawford, *Antiquity*, xxviii (1954), pp. 25 *ff.*; Atkinson, *op. cit.*, pp. 33 *ff.*, 84 *ff.*, 163 *ff.*; *P.P.S.*, xviii, pt. ii, p. 236; Stone, *op. cit.*, pp. 98 *ff.*
65 Atkinson, *op. cit.*, p. 165.
66 *cf.* Hawkes, *P.P.S.* (1948), pp. 196 *ff.*; Navarro, *The Early Cultures of North-west Europe* (Camb., 1950), pp. 77 *ff.*
67 Childe, *Prehistoric Communities of the British Isles* (1949), p. 122, n. 14.
68 Cunnington, *Woodhenge* (Devizes, 1929), pp. 13, 52.
69 *Archaeological Journal*, xcvi (1939), pp. 20 *ff.*

CHAPTER III

1 Pirenne, *Histoire des institutions et du droit privé de l'ancienne Egypte* (Bruxelles, 1932), p. 313.
2 Petrie, *Egyptian Architecture* (1938), pp. 86 *ff.*; *E.R.E.*, vol. i, p. 723; *Abydos*, vol. ii (1903), pp. 7 *ff.*
3 C. M. Firth and J. E. Quibbell, *The Step Pyramid* (Cairo, 1935–36).
4 Petrie, *Medum* (1882); *Meydum and Memphis* (1910), vol. iii.

5 Petrie, *The Pyramids and Temples of Giza* (1882), *cf.* Ahmed Fakhry, *The Pyramids* (University of Chicago Press, 1962).

6 H. Hassan, *The Great Sphinx and its Secrets* (Cairo, 1953).

7 Lepsius, *Denkmäler*, vol. ii, p. 4; Mercer, *The Pyramid Texts* (1929), vol. iv, pp. 36 *ff.*; Budge, *The Book of the Opening of the Mouth* (1909), vol. i, p. vii.

8 *cf.* S. R. K. Glanville, *J.E.A.*, xvi (1930), pp. 237 *ff.*

9 Blackman, *J.E.A.*, vi (1920), pp. 58 *ff.*; *Journal of Manchester Egyptian and Oriental Society* (1918–19), pp. 51 *ff.*

10 Lepsius, *Denkmäler aus Ägypten und Äthiopien* (Berlin, 1849–59), iii, 48, b. 244, b. 245.

11 Budge, *op. cit.*, vol. i, pp. 155 *ff.*

12 Breasted, *Religion and Thought in Ancient Egypt* (1914), p. 56; Frankfort, *Kingship and the Gods* (Chicago, 1948), pp. 61 *ff.*

13 Palermo Stone, *verso*, 4.2; *Urkunden*, i, 247, 3.

14 Blackman, *J.E.A.*, vii (1912), pp. 8 *ff.*

15 Strabo, xvii, 46.

16 Budge, *Tutankhamon, Amonism, Atonism and Egyptian Monotheism* (1923), p. 79.

17 N. de G. Davies, *Rock-tombs of El-Amarna* (1903–08), vol. i, Pl. x; xxvi *ff.* xxxiii, ii, Pls. xviii, xxvii.

18 W. Wolf, *Das schöne Fest von Opet* (Leipzig, 1931); Blackman, *Luxor and its Temples* (1923), pp. 70 *ff.*

19 G. Legrain, *Louqsor sous les pharaons* (Paris, 1914), pp. 81 *ff.*; J. Hornell, *Man*, xxxviii (1938), pp. 145 *ff.*

20 Petrie, *Ancient Egypt* (1915), pt. ii, p. 80, Fig. 86.

21 Budge, *The Gods of Egypt* (1904), pt. ii, pp. 28 *ff.*

22 *cf.* Benson and Gourlay, *The Temple of Mut in Asher* (1899), pp. 198 *ff.*

23 Wainwright, *J.E.A.*, xvii (1931), pp. 185 *ff.*

24 Moret, *Du caractère réligieux de la royauté pharaonique* (Paris, 1902), pp. 104 *ff.*

25 Gauthier, *Les fêtes du dieu Min* (Cairo, 1931), pp. 230 *ff.*, 239.

26 *J.E.A.*, ii (1915), p. 125.

27 Sethe, *Urkunden des ägyptischen Altertums*, iv (1903), pp. 219 *ff.*

28 Naville, *Deir el-Bahari* (1894), vol. ii, pp. 12 *ff.*

29 Naville, *op. cit.*, ii, Pl. xlvii; Moret, *op. cit.*, pp. 49 *ff.*, 72.

30 Sethe, *op. cit.*, iv, pp. 244 *ff.*; Naville, *op. cit.*, ii, pp. 15 *ff.*

31 For purposes of the succession she was regarded as the *son* of Amon in spite of her sex.

32 Breasted, *History of Egypt* (1906), pp. 275 *ff.*

33 Loret, *Récueil de travaux relatifs à la philologie et à l'archéologie egyptiennes et assyriennes*, iii (1882), pp. 43 *ff.*; (1883), iv, pp. 21 *ff.*; (1884), v., pp. 85 *ff.*; Mariette, *Denderah* (Paris, 1873), vol. iv, Pl. 96.

34 Moret, *The Nile and Egyptian Civilization* (1927), p. 81.

35 Sethe, *Untersuchungen zur Geschichte und Altertumskunde Ägyptens*, iii (1905), p. 134; Brugsh, *Thesaurus*, ii (1891), pp. 1190 *ff.*; Murray, *The Osireion at Abydos* (1904), p. 28.

36 Brugsch, *Zeitschrift für ägyptische Sprache und Altertumskunde*, xix (1881), pp. 94, 99.

37 Blackman, *Analecta Orientalia*, xvii (1938), p. 2.

38 *cf.* Weigall, *A Guide to the Antiquities of Upper Egypt* (1910), pp. 473 *ff.*

39 Gardiner and Davies, *The Tomb of Amenemhet* (1915), p. 115.

CHAPTER IV

1 *Iraq*, ix (1947), pp. 50 *ff.*, 150; Van Buren, *Iraq*, xii (1950), pp. 139 *ff.*; Crawford, *The Eye-Goddess* (1957), pp. 25 *ff.*

2 *Iraq*, ix, Pls. iii–iv.

3 *J.N.E.S.*, ii, no. 2 (1943), pp. 128 *ff.* Pls. iv, v.

4 Fuad Safar, *Sumer* (Baghdad, 1947), vol. iii, pp. 103 *ff.*; vol. iv (1948), pp. 115 *ff.*

5 *Gen.* xi, 1–9.

6 *cf.* Woolley, *Ur Excavations*, vol. v (1939), plans 64, 66.

7 Seton Lloyd and Fuad Safar, *J.N.E.S.*, ii (1943), pp. 135 *ff.*

8 Heidel, *The Babylonian Genesis* (Chicago, 1942), p. 37 (Enuma-elish, VI. 49).

9 Herodotus i, 98.

10 *Gen.* xi, 6 *ff.*

11 Herod, i, 183.

12 *cf.* J. P. Peters, *Nippur* (1897), vol. ii, p. 122.

13 Koldewey, *Excavations of Babylon* (1914), pp. 200 *ff.*

14 Emah, Berlin Museum, 5459, 8–9; British Museum, Budge Collection, 88. 5–12, 75–6, vi, 12 *ff.*

15 *Vorderasiatische Bibliothek*, iv, p. 125.

16 *cf.* Thureau-Dangin, *Rituels accadiens* (Paris, 1921), pp. 129 *ff.*

17 Knut Tallquist, *Sumerisch-akkadische Namen der Totenwelt* (Helsingfors, 1934), pp. 23 *ff.*, 37 *ff.*

18 Thureau-Dangin, *op. cit.*, p. 138.

19 Zimmern, *Der alte Orient*, xxv (Leipzig, 1926), pp. 12 *ff.*

20 Labat, *Caractère religieux de la royauté assyro-babylonienne* (Paris, 1939), pp. 98 *ff.*; Langdon, *J.R.A.S.* (1924), pp. 65 *ff.*

21 Langdon, *The Babylonian Epic of Creation* (1923), p. 35; Pallis, *The Babylonian Akitu Festival* (1926), pp. 241 *ff.*

22 Langdon, *op. cit.*, line 66.

23 D. D. Luckenbill, *Ancient Records of Assyria* (Chicago, 1927), vol. ii, par. 70; Zimmern; 'Zum babylonische Neujahrsfest', *Acta Orientalia*, xxv (1926), p. 18.

24 Pallis, *op. cit.*, pp. 175 *ff.*

25 Frankfort, *Sculpture of the Third Millennium B.C. from Tell Asmar and Khafajah* (Chicago, Oriental Institute Publications, xliv, 1939, pp. 45 *ff.*).

26 Chiera, *Sumerian Religious Texts*, No. 1, col. v, ii, 19 *ff.*; Langdon, *J.R.A.S.* (1926), pp. 15 *ff.*

27 Frankfort, H., *Kingship and the Gods* (Chicago, 1948), p. 297.

28 Luckenbill, *Ancient Records of Assyria* (Chicago, 1927), vol. ii, par. 127, 769.

29 Herod, i, 181 *ff.*; *cf.* S. Smith, *J.R.A.S.* (1928), pp. 849 *ff.*

30 F. Nötscher, *Ellil in Sumer und Akkad* (Hanover, 1927), pp. 19 *ff.*

31 *cf.* G. Loud, *Khorsabad; Excavations in the Palace and at a City Gate* (Chicago Oriental Institute Publications, xxxviii, 1936).

32 Andrea, *Das Gotteshaus und die Urformen im Alten Orient*, 22 *ff.*

33 *Das Gotteshaus und die Urformen des Bauens im Alten Orient*, p. 115.

34 *op. cit.*, p. 88.

35 Mallowan, *Twenty-five Years of Mesopotamian Discovery* (1956).

36 Layard, *Monuments of Nineveh*, Pl. 5; *Nineveh and Babylon.* Pl. 35.

37 *Iraq*, xvii, pp. 93 *ff.*

38 Rawlinson, *Monarchies*, vol. i, p. 387.

39 Rawlinson, *Monarchies*, vol. ii, pp. 232 *ff.*

CHAPTER V

1 *cf. Gen.* xi, 31; J. A. Knudtzon, *Die El-Amarna Tafeln*, no. 8, lines 15, 17, 25; no. 151, line 50.

2 *Deut.* xi, 11.

3 1 *Kings* xviii; *Gen.* xii, 10; *Ruth* lx, 1.

4 *Deut.* viii, 7 *ff.*

5 C. H. Gordon, *Ugaritic Handbook* (Rome, 1947); *Ugaritic Literature* (Rome, 1949); C. F. A. Schaeffer, *Ugaritica* (Paris, 1939), pp. 154 *ff.*; R. de Laughe, *Les Textes de Ras Shamra-Ugarit* (Paris, 1944–45); T. H. Gaster, *Thespis* (New York, 1950); G. R. Driver, *Canaanite Myths and Legends* (Edin., 1956).

6 A.B. 49, ii, 5 *ff*.; iv, A.B. ii, 26; A.B. 67, vi, 8 *ff*.; *cf*. Gordon, *Ugaritic Hand-book*, 62, 2 *ff*.

7 A.B. 49, ii, 20.

8 A.B. 49, iii, 6 *ff*.; *cf*. Joel iii, 18.

9 A.B. 49, vi, 16 *ff*.

10 A.B. 51, vii, 14 *ff*.

11 A.B. 51, 68 *ff*.

12 Schaeffer, *Syria*, xvi (1935), pp. 155, 177.

13 A.B. 49, iv, 27, 29.

14 Keret text, 70–80; 159–72.

15 Schaeffer, *The Cuneiform Texts of Ras Shamra-Ugarit* (1939), p. 68.

16 Keret text, 156 *ff*., 171 *ff*.

17 Schaeffer, *op. cit.*, pp. 67 *ff*.

18 Schmokel, *Revue de l'histoire des religions*, ii, p. 100. *cf. Der Gott Dagon* (Heidelberg, 1925); Obermann, *J.A.O.S.* (1941), pp. 31–45. Dussaud, *Syria*, xvi (1935), p. 177.

19 Langdon, *Mythology of All Races*, vol. iv (1931), pp. 78 *ff*.

20 *Fragmenta Historicorum Graecorum*, vol. iii (Paris, 1928), p. 568.

21 1. *Sam.* v, 1–7.

22 1. *Chron.* x, 10.

23 1. *Sam.* xxxi, 10; A. Rowe, *The Four Canaanite Temples at Bethshan* (1940).

24 E. B. Gray, *Sacrifice in the Old Testament* (1925), pp. 96 *ff*.

25 *cf*. Chap. II, pp. 82 *ff*.

26 2. *Kings* xviii, 10.

27 *Lev.* xxvi, 1.

28 *Exod.* xxiv, 4.

29 *Hos.* iii, 4; x, 1 *ff. Isa.* xix, 19.

30 *Joshua* iv.

31 1 *Sam.* xiii, 9 *ff*.

32 *Gen.* xxxiii, 20; xxxi, 44 *ff*.

33 *Gen.* xxxviii, 10–22.

34 *Gen.* xxxi, 13.

35 *Judges* i, 22–5.

36 *Judges* xx, 18, 26, 31; xx, 18–28.

37 *Judges* xxi, 2.

38 2 *Kings* ii, 3, 5, 23; v, 7.

39 *Journal of Theological Studies*, vi (1905), pp. 161–86.

40 1 *Kings* xii, 28; *Exod.* xxxii, 1–6, 22–5.

41 *cf. Judges* xvii–xviii; 1 *Sam.* xix, 13 *ff*.; xxi, 9 *ff*.

42 *Judges* xviii.

43 *Amos* vii, 12 *ff.*

44 2 *Kings* xxiii, 15, 19.

45 2 *Kings* xvii, 27.

46 *cf. Gen.* xxxv, 2–4; *Exod.* iii, 13–15.

47 Tufnell, Inge and Harding, *Lachish II. The Fosse Temple* (1940), pp. 47 *ff.*

48 H. Torezyner, *Lachish I* (1938); Albright, *B.A.S.O.R.*, lxx (1938), pp. 11 *ff.*; 80 (1940), pp. 11 *ff.*, 82 (1941), p. 24.

49 R. A. S. Macalister, *The Excavation of Gezer*, 3 vols. (1912).

50 C. Watzinger, *Denkmäler Palästinas*, i (1923), pp. 63 *ff.*

51 Graham and May, *Culture and Conscience* (1936), pp. 45 *ff.*

52 2 *Sam.* xviii, 18; Albright, *Archaeology and the Religion of Israel* (1946), p. 106.

53 A. B. W. Kennedy, *Petra: Its History and Monuments* (1925); M. A. Murray, *Petra, the Rock City of Edom* (1939).

54 F. E. Hoskins, *From the Nile to Nebo* (Philad., 1912), p. 366.

55 *cf.* Robinson, *Biblical World* (Jan. 1901), pp. 6 *ff.*; *Palestine Exploration Fund Quarterly Statement* (1908), pp. 8–21; S. R. Driver, *Modern Research as illustrating the Bible* (1909), pp. 61 *ff.*

56 W. H. Morton, *The Biblical Archaeologist*, xix (1956), pp. 25 *ff.*; P. J. Parr, *P.E.F.Q.S.* (1957), pp. 15 *ff.*; N. Glueck, *The Other Side of Jordan* (New Haven, 1945).

57 *Joshua* xviii. 1, 8–10, *cf.* xiv, 6.

58 *Judges* xxi. 19.

59 1 *Sam.* i, 7–21, 29; ii, 19, 22; iii, 3.

60 1 *Sam.* v, 1–22.

61 1 *Sam.* vi, 12; vii, 1 *ff.*; iv, 10 *ff.*; *cf. Jer.* xli, 5; vii, 12.

62 Albright, *Jewish Review*, xxii (1932), p. 413.

63 1 *Sam.* xxi, 2–10; xxii, 6–13.

64 Kyaer, *Journal of Palestine Oriental Society*, x (1930), pp. 87 *ff.*; *I det Hellige Land* (Copenhagen), 1931.

65 1 *Sam.* xxii, 20; 2 *Sam.* viii, 17.

66 2 *Sam.* v.

67 2 *Sam.* xxiv, 18–25; 1 *Chron.* xxi, 18; xxii, 1; 2 *Chron.* iii, 1; *Micah* iii, 12

68 *cf.* Chap. IX *ff.*

69 2 *Sam.* vii, 2, 6; 1 *Chron.* xxii, 8.

70 2 *Sam.* vii, 6.

71 *Micah* iv, 8.

72 1 *Kings* vii, 2–8.

73 1 *Kings* viii, 64.

74 1 *Kings* vi, 38; *cf.* M. B. Rowton, *B.A.S.O.R.*, cxix (1950), pp. 25 *ff.*

75 1 *Kings* v, 1–21.

76 1 *Kings* vi, 1–7, 51; 2 *Chron.* iii, 1–5.

77 1 *Kings* vii, 21 *ff.*; viii, 15–22; 2 *Kings* xxv, 17; 2 *Chron.* iii, 15–17; iv, 12 *ff.*; *Jer.* lii, 17–33. *cf.* Chap. II, pp. 51 *ff.*

78 1 *Kings* vi, 19 *ff.* The cubit was roughly the length from the elbow to the finger tips, approximately half a yard.

79 1 *Kings* vi, 32, 35.

80 1 *Kings* vii, 23 *ff.*; 2 *Chron.* iv, 5.

81 *cf.* Benzinger, *Hebräische Archäologie*, 3rd. ed. (1927), pp. 329 *ff.*; C. C. Wylie, *The Biblical Archaeologist*, xii, no. 4 (1949), pp. 86 *ff.*

82 2 *Chron.* iv, 6.

83 *Ant.*, viii, 3, 5.

84 Jeremias, *Das Alte Testament im lichte des Alten Orient*, 3rd. ed. (1916), p. 488; Albright, *American Journal of Semitic Languages* (1919), p. 185.

85 Albright, *Journal of Biblical Literature*, xxxix (1920), pp. 137 *ff.*

86 2 *Chron.* iv, 1. This altar is not mentioned in 1 *Kings* vi–vii.

87 2 *Kings* xvi, 10 *ff.*

88 Wright, *Biblical Archaeology* (1957), p. 126

89 *Ezek.* xl–xliii.

90 Galling in Bertholot, *Heskiel* (1936), pp. xix *ff.*

91 *Ezek.* xl, 6, 16; *cf.* xliv, 9.

92 *Ezek.* xliii, 13–17.

93 xli, 18.

94 xliii, 1–5.

95 xliii, 13.

96 xlvii, 1–2.

97 *Ezra* v, 1, 2.

98 *Ezra* iii; *Hag.* ii, 14.

99 1 *Macc.* i, 23 *ff.*, 44 *ff.*, 54.

100 1 *Macc.* i, 23 *ff.*; iv, 36–60; vi, 7; xiii, 52.

101 Josephus, *Ant.*, XIV, iv, 4, vii, 1 *ff.*; xiv, xvi, 2 *ff.*

102 *St John* ii, 20.

103 *Ant.*, XV, xi, 3.

104 *Acts* xxi, 28 *ff.*

105 *Ant.*, XV, xi, 6.

106 *Middoth* i, 3.

107 E. Wissenberg, *Journal of Jewish Studies*, iii, no. 7 (1952), pp. 14 *ff.*; *Syria*, vi (1925), p. 99.

108 *Acts* iii, 2 *ff.*

109 Watzinger, *Denkmäler Palästinas*, vol. ii, p. 41.

110 *St. Luke* ii, 22.

111 Josephus, *Jewish War V*, v. 1–7. The measurements and details of the sanctuary differ from those of Josephus in the Mishna tractate *Middoth* written about A.D. 150 nearly a century after the destruction of the Temple of Herod. Therefore, in spite of his exaggerations the account of Josephus, being based on firsthand knowledge of the actual building, is likely to be more reliable than that in the tractate. The literature is immense; one of the best surveys of all the Jerusalem temples is *The Temple of Jerusalem* by A. Parrot (1955).

112 *2 Sam.* vi.

113 *1 Kings* xvi, 32 *ff.*

114 *2 Kings* i, 2.

115 *2 Kings* x.

116 *cf. Hos.* i, 4; xiii, 1; *Amos* iv, 4.

117 *1 Kings* xi, 5 *ff.*

118 *1 Sam.* viii, 5 *ff.*

119 *1 Kings* ix, 25.

120 *Exod.* xxiii, 16; xxxiv, 22; *Lev.* xxiii, 34 *ff.*; *Deut.* xxxi, 10.

121 *Exod.* xxiii, 16.

122 *1 Kings* xviii, 41 *ff. cf.* Ps. lxviii, 9.

123 Ps. xciii, xcv–xcix.

124 Mowinckel, *Psalmenstudien* (Kristiana, 1922), vol. ii, pp. 102 *ff.*; P. Volz, *Das Neujahrsfest Jahwas* (Tübingen, 1912), pp. 15 *ff.*; Johnson, *Sacral Kingship in Ancient Israel* (Cardiff, 1955), pp. 53 *ff.*; Snaith, *The Jewish New Year Festival* (1947), pp. 195 *ff.*; Oesterley, *Myth and Ritual* (1933), pp. 125 *ff.*

125 Ps. xciii; *cf.* xxix.

126 Mowinckel, pp. 301 *ff.*; Schmidt, *Die Thronfahrt Jahves am Fest der Jahreswende im alten Israel* (Tübingen, 1927).

127 Snaith, *op. cit.*, pp. 102 *ff.*; Johnson, *op. cit.*, p. 62, n. 2.

128 *1 Kings* viii, 2, 64.

129 *1 Kings* viii, 27–30.

130 *Lev.* xvi, 20; xxiii, 27, 34, 36, 39–44; *Num.* xix, 7, 12, 18; *Rosh ha-Shanah*, i.

131 *Sukkad*, v, 3, 4; *Tos. Suk.*, iv, 4 *ff.*; *Middoth*, ii, 6.

132 *Ezek.* viii, 16; *Ps.* xxiv, 7 *ff.*; lxxxvi, 1; Thackeray, *The Septuagint and Jewish Worship* (1921), pp. 64 *ff.*

133 S. H. Hooke, *The Origins of Early Semitic Ritual* (1938), p. 54; S. Smith, *J.R.A.S.* (1928), pp. 849 *ff.*

134 *Jer.* ii, 2; *Hos.* ii, 14–20; *Ezek.* xvi, 8.

135 *Sukkah*, iv, 9–10; *Rosh Hashana*, 16, 9.
136 *Ezek.* viii, 14–16.
137 Hvidberg, *Graad og Latter i det Gamle Testamente* (Copenhagen, 1938), pp. 85 *ff.*, 115 *ff.*; Gressman, *The Expositor* (1925), vol. ix, 3, p. 422.
138 *Ezek.* xlv, 13, 20; *Lev.* xvi.
139 *Ezek.* xxxiv, 24; xxxvii, 25; *Zech.* vi, 9 *ff.*; *Haggai* ii, 23.
140 *Ezek.* xlv, 18 *ff.*

CHAPTER VI

1 *cf.* E. E. Herzefeld, *Iran in the Ancient East* (Oxford, 1941), p. 7.
2 Piggott, *Antiquity*, xvii (1943), pp. 162 *ff.*; R. E. M. Wheeler, *Ancient India*, vol. i (1945), pp. 8–26; vol. iv (1948), pp. 162 *ff.*
3 Piggott, *Prehistoric India* (1950), pp. 72 *ff.*; N. C. Majumdar, *Explorations in Sind* (1934); Aurel Stein, *An Archaeological Tour in Gedrasia* (1931).
4 J. Marshall, *Mohenjo-daro and the Indus Civilization* (1931), vol. i, pp. 131 *ff.*
5 Mackay, *Early Indus Civilization* (new edition, 1948), pp. 16, 43 *ff.*
6 Marshall, *op. cit.*, vol. i, pp. 23 *ff.*
7 Dubois, *Hindu Manners, Customs and Ceremonies* (Oxford, 1906), p. 578.
8 Mackay, *Further Excavations at Mohenjo-daro* (Delhi, 1938), vol. i, pp. 16 *ff.*; *Early Indus Civilizations*, p. 40.
9 Mackay, *Further Excavations*, Pls. lxxiii, 8.8; xci, 12; xcii, 1.
10 *op. cit.*, vol. i, p. 339.
11 Mackay, vol. iii, p. 337.
12 Marshall, *op. cit.*, vol. i, pp. 52 *ff.*; Mackay, vol. i, pp. 335 *ff.*
13 Marshall, *op. cit.*, vol. i, p. 56.
14 Vats, *Excavations at Harappa* (Delhi, 1940), vol. ii, p. 370.
15 *cf.* S. Shivapadasundaram, *The Saiva School of Hinduism* (1934), p. 15.
16 G. Grierson, *Imperial Gazeteer of India*, vol. ii (1909), p. 422.
17 Rig-veda, cxiv, 8.
18 J. Fergusson, *History of Indian and Eastern Architecture* (1910), vol. i, pp. 342 *ff.*; B. Rowland, *The Art and Architecture of India* (1953), pp. 174 *ff.*; P. Brown, *Indian Architecture* (Bombay, 1949), pp. 89 *ff.*
19 Fergusson, *op. cit.*, vol. i, pp. 130 *ff.*
20 Fergusson, *op. cit.*, vol. ii, pp. 32 *ff.*
21 Fergusson, *op. cit.*, p. 37.
22 *cf.* K. T. Shah, *The Splendour that was 'Ind* (Bombay, 1930), pp. 155 *ff.*
23 *cf.* Chap. II, pp. 83 *ff.*

24 Cunningham, *The Bhilsa Topes* (1854), pp. 295 *ff.*

25 Cunningham, *op. cit.*; Fergusson, *History of Indian and Eastern Architecture* (1910), vol. i, pp. 66 *ff.*

26 Cunningham, *Archaeological Survey Reports*, vol. i, pp. 107 *ff.*

27 Cunningham, *op. cit.*, vol. i, pp. 16 *ff.*

28 W. Rothenstein, *Ajanta Frescoes* (Oxford, 1915), p. 28; R. Grousset, *The Civilization of the East* (1931), vol. ii, p. 159; *cf.* iv (1934), p. 56; B. Rowland, *The Art and Architecture of India*, pp. 136 *ff.*

29 J. Burgess, 'Report on the Elura Cave Temples', *Archaeological Survey of Western India*, vol. v (1883), pp. 4–22; *Cave Temples of India* (1880), pp. 367 *ff.*

30 Chaps. III and IV.

31 D. T. Suzuki, *Manual of Zen Buddhism* (1950); J. Blofceld, *The Jewel in the Lotus* (1948); B. H. Chamberlain, *Things Japanese* (1898); E. Steinilber-Oberlin, *The Buddhist Sects of Japan* (1938); D. C. Holtom, *The National Faith of Japan* (1938); A. W. Watts, *The Way of Zen* (1957).

32 L. A. Waddell, *Lhasa and its Mysteries* (1905), pp. 361 *ff.*; *The Buddhism of Tibet* (1895), pp. 287 *ff.*; J. E. Ellam, *The Religion of Tibet.*

CHAPTER VII

1 *cf.* Chap. II, pp. 63 *ff.*

2 Nilsson, *The Minoan-Mycenaean Religion* (Lund, 1950), pp. 80, 311.

3 Chap. V, pp. 180 *ff.*

4 D. S. Robertson, *Handbook of Greek and Roman Architecture* (Camb., 1943), pp. 51 *ff.*

5 R. M. Dawkins, *The Sanctuary of Artemis Orthia at Sparta* (1929), pp. 19, 399 *ff.*

6 Pausanias, V, 16, 1.

7 Pausanias, V, 20, 4; W. Dörpfeld, *Alt-Olympia* (Berlin, 1935), vol. i, pp. 35 *ff.*

8 R. Rodenwaldt, in *Mitteilungen des Deutschen Arch. Inst. Athenische Abteilung*, xliv, p. 183.

9 E. N. Gardiner, *Olympia* (Oxford, 1925), pp. 88, 207.

10 Pausanias, VII, 4, 4.

11 *cf.* Clement of Alex. *Protr.* iv, 46; Strabo, vi, 1. 1,; Roscher in *Lexikon der griechischen und römischen Mythologie*, I, pp. 22–75 *ff.*; Waldstein, *The Argive Heraeum* (1902), pp. 5 *ff.*

12 Thucydides, iv, 133.

13 Waldstein, *The Argive Heraeum* (New York, 1902).

14 *The Argive Heraeum*, p. 23.

15 *Meisterwerke d. griech. Plastik*, pp. 557, 576 *ff.*; *Archäologische Studien von H. Brunn dargebracht* (Berlin, 1893), p. 90.

16 Pausanias, VIII, 41–8.

17 Cockerell, *The Temple of Apollo at Aegina and Bassae* (1860).

18 *cf.* Frazer, *Pausanias*, vol. V, pp. 239 *ff.*

19 Herodotus, v, 62.

20 Herodotus ii, 135.

21 Aeschylus, *Eumenides*, 1 *ff.*; Pausanias, II, 33, 2; Strabo, viii; Courby, *Fouilles de Delphes*, vol. v, pp. 1 *ff.*; Poulsen, *Delphi* (1920), pp. 4 *ff.*, 60 *ff.*; Nilsson, *The Minoan-Mycenaean Religion*, pp. 466, 576.

22 H. Pantow, *Beiträge zur Topographie von Delphi*, pp. 38 *ff.*

23 Plutarch, 389 c.

24 Latte, *Harvard Theological Review*, xxxiii (1940), pp. 9 *ff.*

25 Guthrie, *The Greeks and their Gods* (1950), pp. 78 *ff.*

26 Pausanias, X, 6, 24.

27 Dem. Macart. 1072.

28 Plutarch, III. 404 d., 511 b.

29 Plutarch, *Demosthenes*, 20; Cicero, *de Div.* ii, 57, 118.

30 Siculus, XVI, xxvi, 6.

31 Cicero, *op. cit.*, I, xxxvii, 81; Diodorus Siculus, XXII. *Frags.*, ix, 4, 5; Pausanias, X, xxii, 12–xxiv.

32 Diodorus, *op. cit.*; Strabo iv, 188; Livy, xxxviii, 2, 9, 48; *Homeric to Apollo*, 23 *ff.*

33 Diodorus, xxxv, xiii; Livy, xxix.

34 Jerome, *ol.*174.1; Eusebius, *Chronic.*, xxxv, vol. ii, p. 133 (Schone).

35 Aeschines, *contra Ctesiph.*, 116, p. 335 (Schultz).

36 Julian, *Contra Galilaeos*, 198 c.; Prudentius, *Apotheosis*, 438 *ff.*; *Bulletin de correspondence hellenique*, xx, pp. 719, 128; Paule Wissowa, *Real-Encyclopadie*, 'Delphoi', 2583.

37 R. B. Richardson, *Journal of American Archaeology*, iv, (1900), pp. 458 *ff.*

38 *cf.* *Mitteilungen des Deutschen Archäologischen Instituts, Athenische Abteilung*, xi (1886), pp. 297 *ff.*

39 Cyriacus, *Epigrammata per Illyriam*, p. xvii.

40 B. Powell, *A.J.A.*, ix (1905), pp. 44 *ff.*; H. N. Fowler and R. Stillwell, *Corinth: Excavations by the American School of Classical Studies at Athens*, vol. i (1932), pp. 114 *ff.*; S. Weinberg, *Hesperia*, viii (1930), pp. 191 *ff.*

41 *Odyssey*, vii, 81; *Iliad*, ii, 549.

42 Dörpfeld, *Ath. Mitt.* xi (1886), pp. 337; xii (1887), pp. 25 *ff.*, 190; xxii (1897), pp. 159 *ff.*

43 *Ath. Mitt.* (1897), pp. 167 *ff.*; (1902), p. 399.

44 *A.J.A.*, xxxvii (1934), p. 447.

45 Plutarch, *Pericles*, xxxi, 214.

46 Demosthenes, c. *Androt*, 13, 76.

47 A. S. Murray, *The Sculptures of the Parthenon* (1903); B. Ashmole, *Short Guide to the Sculptures of the Parthenon* (1950); Gardener, *J.H.S.*, xxxii (1912), pp. 179 *ff.*; Collignon, *Le Parthénon* (Paris, 1914), pp. 173 *ff.*; Dinsmoor, *The Architecture of Ancient Greece* (1950), pp. 159 *ff.*

48 Deubner, *Attische Feste* (1932), pp. 22 *ff.*; Ziehen, *Revue des Études*, xviii, 3, col. 457 *ff.*

49 G. P. Stevens, *Hesperia* Supplement iii (1940), v (1936), pp. 443 *ff.*

50 *op. cit.*, pp. 26 *ff.*

51 *A.J.A.*, xxxv (1932), pp. 318 *ff.*; li (1947), pp. 109 *ff.*

52 *A.J.A.*, xxviii (1924), pp. 2 *ff.*; Heberdey, *Poros-Skulptur*, pp. 174 *ff.*

53 Stevens, *Erechtheum* (1927), pp. 10 *ff.*, 431, n. 2.

54 Pausanias, I, 22, 6.

55 Pausanias, V. 26, 6.

56 Dinsmoor, *A.J.A.*, xxxiv (1926), pp. 1 *ff.*

57 Pausanias, I, 3, 1–14.

58 H. A. Thompson, *Hesperia*, vi (1937), pp. 65 *ff.*

59 Cicero, *De natura deorum*, i, 30.

60 D. B. Thompson, *Hesperia* vi (1937), pp. 396 *ff.*

61 Pausanias, I, 18, 7 *ff.*

62 Pausanias, I, 18, 6.

63 *cf.* Penrose, *J.H.S.*, viii (1887), p. 273; Welter, *Ath. Mitt.* xlvii (1922), pp. 61 *ff.*; xlviii (1923), pp. 182 *ff.*

64 E. N. Gardiner, *Olympia: Its History and Remains* (Oxford, 1925), pp. 234 *ff.*; E. Curtiss, and F. Adler *Olympia: Die Ergebnisse der von dem deutschen Reich veranstalteten Ausgrabungen*, vol. ii (Berlin, 1892).

65 D. Randall-MacIver, *Greek Cities in Italy and Sicily* (Oxford, 1931), pp. 199 *ff.*; P. Marconi, *Agrigento* (Florence, 1929).

66 Pausanias, II, 26, 8.

67 Dittenberger, *Syllage Inscriptionum Graecarum*, 1168.

68 Strabo, 437; *cf. Iliad*, 4, 202.

69 Pausanias, I, 29; II, 275.

70 R. Caton, *The Temples and Ritual of Asklepios at Epidauros and Athens* (1900); A. Fossum, *A.J.A.* xxx (1926), pp. 70 *ff.*; P. Cavvadias, *Fouilles d'Epidaure* (Athens, 1891); A. Defrasse and H. Lechat, *Epidaure, restauration et description des principaux monuments du sanctuaire d'Asclépios* (Paris, 1895).

71 Allen, Halliday and Sykes, *The Homeric Hymn* (1936), pp. 111 *ff*.

72 *de profect. virt.* 81 e.

73 *Synesius, Dion.* p. 48a.

74 Hippolytus, *Refutatio Omnium Haeresium*, v. 8; Farnell, *Cult of the Greek States*, iii. pp. 177, 183.

75 Foucart, *Les Mystères d'Eleusis* (1914), pp. 392 *ff*.

76 Eleusis, *Die baugeschichtliche Entwicklung des Heiligtumes* (1927), pp. 236 *ff*.

77 K. Kourouniotis, *Archiv für Religions wissenschaft*, 32 (1915), pp. 52 *ff*.; G. E. Mylonas, *The Hymns to Demeter and her Sanctuary at Eleusis* (Washington, 1942); *Eleusis and the Eleusinian Mysteries* (1961), pp. 38 *ff*.; Kourouniotis and Travlos, *Telesterion* (Deltion, 1933–5), pp. 54 *ff*.

78 *Archiv.*, xxxii, pp. 53 *ff*.; *A.J.A.*, xxxvii (1933), pp. 274 *ff*.

79 Mylonas, *Praktika* (1952), pp. 56 *ff*.; Kourouniotis, *Praktika* (1937), pp. 42 *ff*.

80 Sophocles, *Frag.* 719 (Dindorf); Pindar, *Frag.* 102; Cicero, *De Legibus*, 2, 14, 36.

CHAPTER VIII

1 *Fasti.* ii, 641.

2 *Fasti*, ii, 643 *ff*.

3 Siculus Flaccus, *Gromatici veteres*, i, 141.

4 Livy, i, 10; Aust, 'Jupiter' in Roscher, *Lexikon der griechischen und römischen Mythologie*, ii, p. 673; *Die Religion der Römer* (Munster, 1899).

5 Festus, 318 (ed. Lindsay), p. 422.

6 Livy, i, 10, 33; xliii, 55.

7 Festus, s.v. *Sacer Mons*.

8 Ovid, *Ex Ponto*, iv, 9, 5. Livy, xxi, 63, xli, 32, xlii, 49; *Fasti*, iv, 621.

9 Festus, 238 (Lindsay); Ovid, *Fasti*, ii, 476 *ff*.; iv, viii. 9, 6.

10 Henzon, *Acta Fratr. Arv.* (1874), p. 26; Cato, *De Re Rustico*, 141.

11 Varro, *De ling. Lat.* v, 52.

12 Ovid, *Fasti*, iii, 809; vi, 728; Platner and Ashby, *Topog. Dict*, p. 342; *C.I.L.*, i, pp. 234, 312.

13 *Fasti*, iii, 836; Livy, *Per.* xx; Varro, *De Lingua Latina*, v, 47.

14 Plutarch, xvii; Carter, *Religion of Numa* (1906), pp. 47 *ff*.; Waltzing, *Étude sur les corporations romaines.*

15 Plutarch, *de fort. Rom.*, 10; Livy, i, 21, 4; Dionysius Hal., ii, 75.

16 Van Buren, E. Douglas, *Figurative Terra-Cotta Revetments in Etruria and Latium in the VI and V Centuries* (1921).

17 Livy, i, 38, 55; Dionysius iii, 69, iv, 59–61; Cicero, *Rep*, ii, 20; Tacitus, *Historiae*, iii, 72.

18 Livy, i, 38, 7; 53, 5; ii, 8, 6–8; vii, 3, 8.

19 Livy, i, 56; Cicero, *Veer.*, v, 19, 48.

20 Dionysius Hal., iv, 61; Vitruv., iii, 3, 5, iv, 7.

21 Ovid, *Fasti.*, i, 201 *f.*; Pliny, *Naturalis Historia*, xxxiii, 112 *ff.*; xxxv, 157.

22 Livy, x, 7, 10; xxx, 15, 11–12.

23 Pliny, *op. cit.*

24 Tacitus, *Hist.*, iii, 72; iv, 53.

25 Livy, i, 56, 415.

26 Tacitus, *op. cit.*; Dionysius, iv, 61; *cf.* Gjerstad, *Early Rome* (Lund, 1960), vol. iii, pp. 168 *ff.*

27 Gallius, ii, 10.

28 Gallius, ii, 10.

29 Livy, iv, 20, 7. *Monumentum Ancyranum*, iv, 5, 9.

30 Pliny, xxxvi, 4, 5.

31 Suetonius *Vitellius*, 15; Vespasian, 8; Tacitus, *Hist.* iv, 53.

32 Suetonius, *Domitianus* 5; Dio Cassius, lxvi, 24; Plutarch, *Publ.*, 15.

33 Tacitus, *Hist.*, iii, 72; Dio Cassius, xliii, 14.

34 Jordan, i, 2, 192 *ff.*, *Topog. der Stadt Rom in Alterthum* (1878).

35 Dionysius, i, 4, 34; Macrob. *Sat.*, i, 8, 2.

36 Suet, *Aug.*, 29.

37 *C.I.L.*, vi, 2021; Macrobius, i, 16. 16; *cf.* W. Warde Fowler, *Roman Festivals* (1899), p. 96.

38 Cato, *Origines*, 2, fr., 21 (Jordan).

39 *Notizie degli Scavi* (1885), pp. 159 *ff.*, 192 *ff.*, 254 *ff.*, 317 *ff.*, 478 *ff.*; Vitruvius *de Architectura*, iv, 7, 4.

40 Strabo, iv, 180; v, 3, 12.

41 Pausanias, II, 27, 4.

42 *cf.* Servius on Virgil, *Aenead*, vi, 136; Ovid, *Ars Amatoria*, i, 259 *ff.*; Suetonius, *Caligula*, 35, 3.

43 *The Golden Bough*, i, pp. 8 *ff.*; *Early History of Kingship* (1905), Lect., vii.

44 *de Lingua Latina*, v, 74.

45 Varro, *op. cit.*, 5, 43.

46 Strabo, iv, 180.

47 *Festus*, ed. Muller (1839), p. 333.

48 Ovid, *Fasti.*, iii, 809.

49 J. Geffcken, *Timaios Geogr. d. Westens*, 145; *Aeneid*, vi, 2, 14 (Norden, pp. 133 *ff.*).

50 Warde Fowler, *Religious Experience of the Roman People*, pp. 257 *ff.*

51 Livy, xxii, 27.

52 Blakeway, *J.R.S.*, xxv (1935), pp. 135 *ff.*; A. Maiuri, *Compania Romana* (Naples, 1938), i, pp. 99 *ff.*

53 Chap. VII, pp. 270 *ff.*

54 Dionysius, vi, 17, *cf.*, i, 33.

55 Van Buren, *Figurative Terra-cotta Revetments* (1921), pp. 31 *ff.*

56 Tacitus, *Annales*, ii, 49.

57 Dionysius, viii, 79; Servius, *Aeneid*, viii, 361; Livy, viii, 6, 10.

58 Mommsen, *Staatsrecht*, ii, 467 *ff.*, 490.

59 Livy, i, 56; ii, 9; Dionys. Hal., vii, 1.

60 Ovid, *Fasti*, iv, 681 *ff.*

61 Wissowa, *Religion und Kultus der Römer*, p. 138.

62 *cf.* Chap. VII, pp. 250 *ff.*

63 Cumont, *Les Religions orientales dans le paganisme romain* (Paris, 1929), p. 197.

64 Livy, xxxix, 9.

65 Livy, xxxix, 8–19; Wordsworth, *Fragments and Specimens of Early Latin* (Oxford, 1874), pp. 172 *ff.*

66 *C.I.L.*, i, 196, 581.

67 Pausanias, VIII, 46, 5.

68 Martial, i, 70, 9–10.

69 *cf.* Platner and Ashby, *op. cit.*, p. 321.

70 Servius, *ad Ecl.*, v, 29; M. I. Rostortzeff, *Mystic Italy* (New York, 1927), pp. 40 *ff.*

71 V. Macchioro, *Zagreus* (Bari, 1920), pp. 82 *ff.*; E. G. Rizzo, *Memorie d. Acc. di Napoli* (1918); E. Pottier, *Rev. Arch.* (1915), vol. ii, pp. 321 *ff.*

72 Livy, xxix, 10–14.

73 Ovid, *Fasti*, iv, 326 *ff.*, 331 *ff.*

74 Livy, xxix, 14, 12 *ff.*

75 Livy, xxxvi, 13, 4, *cf.* Graillot, *Le Culte de Cybèle* (Paris, 1912), pp. 25 *ff.*

76 *Fasti*, iv, 347 *ff.*; Valerius Maximus, i, 8, 11.

77 *C.I.L.*, vi, 496, 1040, 3702, 30967, *cf.*, xii, 405.

78 E. B. Van Deman, *A.J.A.*, xvi (1912), p. 393.

79 G. Carettoni, *Journal of Roman Studies*, vol. l (1960), pp. 200 *ff.*; C. Hülsen, *Mitteilungen des Deutschen Archäologischen Instituts, Römische Abteilung* (Rome, 1895), 1–28; (1906), 227; Jordan, *Topographie der Stadt im Altertum. I.* pt. 3 (1906), pp. 51 *ff.*; Platner and Ashby, *op. cit.*, pp. 324 *ff.*; T. Frank, *Roman Buildings of the Republic* (1924), pp. 96 *ff.*

80 Livy, xxix, 14; xxxiv, 54; xxxvi, 36; Cicero, *De Haruspicum Respondis*, 12, 34; Ovid, *Fasti*, iv, 181; 221 *ff.*

81 Diodorus Siculus, xxxvi, 6; Plutarch, *Marius*, 17.

82 Apuleius, *Metamorphosis*, viii, 28; Tertullian, *Apol*, 25; Lucian, *Deorom Dialogi*, xii, i; Hepding, *Attis, seine Mythen und sein Kult* (Giessen, 1903), pp. 158 *ff.*

83 *cf.* Chap. VII, pp. 269 *ff.*

84 Livy, x, 47; *Epitomae*, xi; Ovid, *Fasti*, i, 289 *ff.*; *Metamorphoses*, xv, 622–745.

85 *Annali dell'Instituto di Correspondenza Archaologica* (Rome, 1867), pp. 389 *ff.*

86 Varro, *de Lingua Latina*, vii, 57; Livy, xliii, 4.

87 Jordan, *Topographie der Stadt Rom im Altertum* (Berlin, 1906), vol. i, pt. 3, p. 144.

88 *Bibliothèque des écoles francaises d'Athènes et de Rome.* Fasc., 87 (1902), pp. 152 *ff.*, 235.

89 *Aeneid*, vii, 81 *ff.*, *cf.* Ovid, *Fasti*, iv, 649 *ff.*

90 Flavian *C.I.L.*, vi. 8, 14; R. Heinzey, *Vergil's Epische Technik* (1908), p. 174, n. 2.

91 Diony. Hal. *Ant. Rom.*, vi, 13, 1–2.

92 Livy, ii, 20, 12; 42, 5; Diony. Hal. *op. cit.*; Ovid, *Fasti*, i, 705 *ff.*

93 Wissowa, *Rel. und Kultur der Römer*, pp. 269 *ff.*

94 Cicero, *In Verram*, i, 129–54; Cassius Dio, lv, 27, 4; Ovid, *Fasti*, i, 707 *ff.*; Van Deman, *A.J.A.*, xvi, (1912), p. 393, n. 6.

95 A. W. Van Buren, *The Classical Review*, xx (1906), pp. 77 *ff.*; E. B. Van Deman, *A.J.A.* (1912), p. 249; *Proc. Brit. School at Rome*, xxx, 1962, pp. 18 *ff.*

96 Cicero, *In Verrem*, i, 129; *C.I.L.*, 586; Cicero. *De Haruspicum Responsu*, 27; Plutarch, *Sulla*, 33; Jordan, *op. cit.*, vol. i, Pt. 2, pp. 369 *ff.*; Lanciani, *The Ruins of Ancient Rome*, pp. 272 *ff.*; C. Hülsen, *The Roman Forum* (Rome, 1909), pp. 161 *ff.*; *The Forum and the Palatine* (New York, 1928), pp. 3 *ff.*, 37 *ff.*; Platner and Ashby, *op. cit.*, pp. 102 *ff.*

97 Dionysius Hal. *Ant. Rom.*, ii, 66, 3; Cicero, *de divinatione*, i, 45, 101; Livy, v, 32, 6; Horace, *Satirae*, i, 9; Ovid, *Tristia*, iii, 1, 28.

98 Plutarch, *Romulus*, 2.

99 Varro, *Aulus Gellius*, 147, 7; Ovid, *Fasti*, vi, 261 *ff.*

100 Asconius, *Pro Mione*, 40; E. Babelon, *Monnais de la republique romaines*, i, pp. 329 *ff.*

101 *A.J.A.* (1912), p. 393.

102 *Fasti*, vi, 265; 281; *cf.* Livy, v, 42; Plutarch, *Camilus*, 21.

103 Pliny, vii, 43; Valerius, Maximus, i, 4, 4.

104 Livy, xxvi, 27.

105 Tacitus, *Annales*, xv, 41; *Historiae*, i, 43.

106 Herodotus, i, 14, 4; Cassius Dio, lxxii, 24.

107 E. Babelon, *op. cit.*, i, pp. 329 *ff.* Dressel, *Zeitschr. für Numismatok* (1900), pp. 20 *ff.*; Lanciani. *L'Atrio di Vesta* (1884), Pl. xix; Hülsen, *Roman Forum*, p. 198. Excavations between 1930 and 1931 disclosed an archaic wall (*c.* 7th century B.C.), and a later Republican wall (*c.* 3rd century) containing votive material. *cf.* Carettoni, *J.R.S.* (1960), pp. 193 *ff.*

108 Pliny, xvi, 85.

109 Servius, *Aeneid*, vii, 151.

110 E. Van Deman, *Atrium Vestae* (1909); Jordan, *op. cit.*, vol. i, pt. 2, pp. 299, 423, 427 *ff.*; Hülsen, *The Roman Forum*, pp. 204 *ff.*; Platner and Ashby, *op. cit.*, pp. 58 *ff.*

111 *A.J.A.* (1908), pp. 324, 342; *C.I.L.*, vi, 32409, 32428.

112 Servius, *ad ecl.*, viii, 82; Festus, s.v. 'Mola', pp. 124 *ff.* (ed. Lindsay); Ovid, *Fasti*, vi, 311 *ff.*

113 Plutarch, *Numa*, 13; Livy, i, 21, 3.

114 *Fasti*, vi, 249.

115 *Fasti*, vi, 295 *ff.*; Dionysius Hal. ii, 64, 66; Plutarch, 11, 1.

116 Varro, *Rerum rusticarum*, i, 1, 4; Apuleius, *De deo Socratis*, 2.

117 H. Dessau, *Inscriptiones Latinae Selectae*, no. 4003.

CHAPTER IX

1 Vitruvius, v, 1; Pauly-Wissowa, *Realencyclopaedie der Klassischen Altertums*, iii, 83 *ff.*

2 Livy, xxxix, 44; Plutarch, *Cato Minor*, 5. *Maior*, 19.

3 R. C. Carrington, *Pompeii* (Oxford, 1936), pp. 104 *ff.*; A Mau, *Pompeii, its Life and Art* (1899), pp. 72 *ff.* Vitruvius, p. 134.

4 Jordan, *Topographie der Stadt Rom im Altertum* (Berlin, 1912), i, pp. 385–94; Pliny, *Ep.* vi, 33; G. T. Rivoira, *Roman Architecture* (Oxford, 1925), pp. 202 *ff.*

5 R. Lanciani, *The Ruins of Ancient Rome*, pp. 275 *ff.*

6 *C.I.L.*, vi, 1156b., 1658 (Dessau, 5537).

7 *cf.* Hülsen, *The Roman Forum* (1909), pp. 321, 335.

8 *Archivo Storico dell'Arte* (1896), p. 164; Frotheringham, *Monuments of Christian Rome* (1908), p. 83.

9 *Acts* ii, 46; *Rom.* xvi, 5; 1 *Cor.* xvi, 15; *Col.* iv, 15; *Philemon* 2.

10 *Acts* viii, 4.

11 *Acts* i, 13. *cf.* St. *John* xx, 19, 26.

12 C. Cecchelli, *Mater Christi* (Rome, 1946), vol. i, pp. 89, 198 *ff.*

13 Rivoira, *Roman Architecture* (Oxford, 1925), pp. 253 *ff.*

14 A. Valentini, *La Patriarcale Basilica Lateranense* (1836); J. Sauer, *Lexikon für Theologie und Kirche*, vi (1934), cols. 401–4.

15 Duchesne, *op. cit.*, Silvester, xvi, p. 176.

16 P. Belloni, *Sulla grandezza e disposizione della primitiva basilica Ostiense* (Rome, 1835).

17 J. Mullooly, *St. Clement Pope and Martyr and his Basilica in Rome* (1873).

18 G. T. Rivoira, *Lombardic Architecture* (Oxford, 1933), vol. i, pp. 73 *ff.*

19 Rivoira, *Roman Architecture*, pp. 182 *ff.*; Lanciani, *The Ruins and Excavations of Ancient Rome*, p. 401.

20 Jordan, *Topographie*, i, p. 237.

21 Lanciani, *op. cit.*, pp. 355 *ff.*

22 *Corpus Scrip. Hist. Byz.* Theophanes, *Chronographia*, vol, i, pp. 395 *ff.*; Agathias, v, 9.

23 Qur'an v, 9.

24 Qur'an liii, 19–20.

25 *Reste arabischen Heidentums* (Berlin, 1897), pp. 117 *ff.*

26 Azraqi, *Chroniken der Stadt Mekka* (Würstenfeld, ed.), I. 110, p. 112. 12.

27 *cf.* Caetani, *Annali dell'Islam*, vol. i, pp. 432 *ff.*

28 Lammens, *Rivista degli Studi orientali*, vol. iv, pp. 240 *ff.*

29 Burton, *Personal Narrative of a Pilgrimage to El Medinah and Meccah* (1855), vol. i, pp. 345 *ff.*

30 *cf.* Rivoira, *Moslem Architecture* (Oxford, 1918), pp. 103 *ff.*

31 Maqrizi, *Histoire des Sultans Mamalouks de l'Egypte*, vol. ii, p. 276.

32 *Ibn Jubayr Diary*, ed. W. Wright (Leiden, 1836), pp. 252 *ff.*, 286 *ff.*; Le Strange, *Palestine under the Moslems* (1890), pp. 233 *ff.*

33 Qur'an, xvii, 1.

34 *cf.* Vogue, *Le Temple de Jérusalem*, pp. 69 *ff.*, 99 *ff.*

35 C. R. Conder, *The City of Jerusalem* (1909), p. 287.

36 E. T. Richmond, *The Dome of the Rock* (Oxford, 1924), pp. 11 *ff.*; K. A. C. Creswell, *The Origin of the Plan of the Dome of the Rock* (1924).

37 Le Strange, *op. cit.*, p. 153; De Vogue, *op. cit.*, p. 104.

38 Chassinat, *Memoires publiées par les membres de l'Institut Français d'archéologie orientales du Caire*, vol. vii, p. 13.

39 Ibn Duqmaq, iv, p. 123.

40 Briggs, *Muhammadan Architecture* (1924), pp. 56 *ff.*

41 R. Williams, *Egyptian Gazette* (Alexandria, 1918); Creswell, Burlington Magazine (1919), pp. 42 *ff.*; Corbet, *J.R.A.S.* (1891), pp. 552 *ff.*

42 Chassinat, *op. cit.*, vol. xix, pp. 473 *ff.*; Rivoira, *op. cit.*, p. 147.

BIBLIOGRAPHY

ABBREVIATIONS

A.B. Aleyan-Baal Texts
A.J.A. American Journal of Archaeology
B.A.S.O.R. Bulletin of the American Schools of Oriental Research
B.S.A. Bulletin of the British School at Athens
C.I.L. Corpus Inscriptionum Latinorum
E.R.E. Encyclopaedia of Religion and Ethics (Hastings)
L'Anthrop. L'Anthropologie, Paris
J.A.O.S. Journal of the American Oriental Society, New Haven
J.E.A. Journal of Egyptian Archaeology
J.H.S. Journal of Hellenic Studies
J.N.E.S. Journal of Near Eastern Studies
J.R.A.I. Journal of the Royal Anthropological Institute
J.R.A.S. Journal of the Royal Asiatic Society
J.R.S. Journal of Roman Studies
P.P.S. Proceedings of the Prehistoric Society
P.T. Pyramid Texts

CHAPTER I

BOULE, H., *Les Hommes Fossiles*, 3rd. ed., Paris, 1946

BREUIL, H., *Four Hundred Centuries of Cave Art*, Montignac, 1952. E. T. by M. E. Boyle

BREUIL, H. and BURKITT, M. C., *Rock Paintings of Southern Andalusia*, Oxford, 1929

BREUIL, H., CAPITAN, L. and PEYRONY, D., *La Caverne de Font-de-Gaume aux Eyzies*, Monaco, 1910

BREUIL, H. and OBERMAIER, H., *The Cave of Altamira at Santillana del Mar*, Madrid, 1935

BREUIL, H., OBERMAIER, H. and VERNER, W., *La Pileta à Benaojan*, Monaco, 1915

BRODRICK, A. H., *Lascaux: a Commentary*, 1948

BROWN, G. BALDWIN, *The Art of the Cave Dweller*, 1928

BURKITT, M. C., *Prehistory*, Cambridge, 1925

JAMES, E. O., *Prehistoric Religion*, 1957

LAMING, A., *Lascaux*, 1959, E.T. by E. F. Armstrong

LEMOZI, A., *La Grotte-Temple du Pech-Merle*, Paris, 1929

LUQUET, G. H., *The Art and Religion of Fossil Man*, E.T. by J. T. Russell, Oxford, 1930

MOORE, R., *Man, Time and Fossils*, 1954

OBERMAIER, H., *Fossil Man in Spain*, New Haven, 1924

PARKYNE, E. A., *Prehistoric Art*, 1915

SPENCER, B. and GILLEN, F. J., *Native Tribes of Central Australia*, 1938; *Northern Tribes of Central Australia*, 1904

VERNEAU, R., *Les Grottes de Grimaldi*, Monaco, 2 vols. 1906

WINDELS, F., *The Lascaux Cave Paintings*, 1949

CHAPTER II

ATKINSON, R. J. C., *Stonehenge*, 1956

CHILDE, V. G., *The Dawn of European Civilization*, 5th ed., 1950

CUNNINGTON, M. E., *Woodhenge*, Devizes, 1929

DANIEL, G. E., *The Megalithic Builders of Western Europe*, 1958

EVANS, SIR A. J., *The Palace of Minos at Knossos*, vol. i, 1922; *Mycenaean Tree and Pillar Cult*, 1901

EVANS, J. D., *Malta*, 1959

FORDE, C. DARYLL, Early Culture of Atlantic Europe, *American Anthropologist*, 32, 1930

GRAY, H. ST. G., Avebury Excavations, *Archaeologia*, 84, 1935, pp. 99–162

HARDING, G. LANKESTER, *The Antiquities of Jordan*, 1959

HARRISON, J. E., *Themis*, Cambridge, 1912

HAWES, H. B., *Gournia*, Philadelphia, 1908.

KENDRICK, T. D., *Archaeology of the Channel Islands*, vol. i, 1928 (vol ii J. Hawkes, 1940)

KENYON, K. M., *Digging up Jericho*, 1957

MALLOWAN, M. E. L. and CRUIKSHANK, ROSE J., *Prehistoric Assyria*, 1935

NEWELL, R. S., *Stonehenge*, 1959

NILSSON, M. P., *The Minoan-Mycenaean Religion*, 2nd ed., Lund, 1950

PIGGOTT, S., *The Neolithic Cultures of the British Isles*, Cambridge, 1954

STONE, E. H., *Wessex*, 1958; *The Stones of Stonehenge*, 1924

STUKELEY, W., *Abury, a Temple of the British Druids*, 1743

XANTHOUDIDES, S., *The Vaulted Tombs of Mesara*, Liverpool, 1924

ZAMMIT, T., *The Neolithic Temples at Hajar Kim and Mnaidra*, Valetta, 1927; *Prehistoric Malta, The Tarxien Temple*, Oxford, 1930; *The Hal-Saflieni Prehistoric Hypogeum*, Malta, 1910

CHAPTER III

BLACKMAN, A. M., *Luxor and its Temples*, 1923

BREASTED, J. H., *Development of Religion and Thought in Ancient Egypt*, 1914; *The History of Egypt*, 1906

BUDGE, E. A. W., *The Book of the Opening of the Mouth*, 1909; *The Gods of Egypt*, 1904

EDWARDS, I. E. S., *The Pyramids of Egypt*, 1960

FAKHRY, AHMED, *The Pyramids*, 1962

FIRTH, C. M. and QUIBBELL, J. E., *The Step Pyramid*, Cairo, 1935–36

FRANKFORT, H., *Kingship and the Gods*, Chicago, 1948

GAUTHIER, H., *Les fêtes du dieu Min*, Cairo, 1931

HASSAN, H., *The Great Sphinx and its Secrets*, Cairo, 1953

MARIETTE-BEY, A., *Denderah*, 1873

MAYASSIS, S., *Mystères et initiations de l'Égypte ancienne*, Athènes, 1957

MERCER, S. A. B., *The Pyramid Texts*, 1929

MORET, A., *Du caractère religieux de la royauté pharaonique*, Paris, 1902; *The Nile and Egyptian Civilization*, 1927

MURRAY, M. A., *Egyptian Temples*, [1931]

NAVILLE, E., *Deir el-Bahari*, 1894

PETRIE, W. M. F., *Egyptian Architecture*, 1938; *The Pyramids and Temples of Giza*, 1882

SMITH, W. S., *Art and Architecture in Ancient Egypt*, 1958

WEIGALL, A., *A Guide to the Antiquities of Upper Egypt*, 1910

WOLF, W., *Das schöne Fest von Opet*, Leipzig, 1931

CHAPTER IV

ANDREA, M., *Das Gotteshaus und die Urformen im Alten Orient*

CHIERA, E., *Sumerian Religious Texts*, Upland, 1924

CRAWFORD, O. G. S., *The Eye Goddess*, 1957

DHORME, E., *Les Religions de Babylonie et d'Assyrie*, Paris, 1949

FRANKFORT, H., *Sculpture of the Third Millennium B.C. from Tell Asmar and Khafajah*, Chicago, 1939; *The Art and Architecture of the Ancient Orient*, 1954

HEIDEL, A., *The Babylonian Genesis*, Chicago, 1942

KOLDEWEY, R., *Excavations at Babylon*, 1914; *Die Tempel von Babylon und Borsippa*, Leipzig, 1911

KRAMER, S. N., *Sumerian Mythology*, Philadelphia, 1944

LABAT, R., *Caractère religieux de la royauté assyro-babylonienne*, 1939

LANGDON, S., *The Babylonian Epic of Creation*, 1923

LAYARD, A. H., *Monuments of Nineveh*, 2 vols., 1849–52

LOUD, G., *Khorsabad: Excavations in the Palace and at a City Gate*, Chicago, 1936

LUCKENBILL, D. D., *Ancient Records of Assyria*, Chicago, 1927

MALLOWAN, M. E. L., *Twenty-five Years of Mesopotamian Discovery*, 1956

NÖTSCHER, F., *Ellil in Sumer und Akkad*, Hanover, 1927

PALLIS, S. A., *The Babylonian Akitu Festival*, 1926

TALLQUIST, KNUT, *Sumerisch-akkadische Namen der Totenwelt*, Helsingfors, 1934

THUREAU-DANGIN, G., *Rituels Accadiens*, Paris, 1921

WETZEL, F. and WEISSBAD, F., *Das Hauptheiligtum des Marduk in Babylon*, Leipzig, 1938 (Esagila und Etemenanki)

WOOLLEY, C. L., *Ur Excavations*, vol. v, 1939

CHAPTER V

ALBRIGHT, W. F., *Archaeology and the Religion of Israel*, 1946

DRIVER, G. R., *Canaanite Myths and Legends*, Edinburgh, 1956

GASTER, T. H., *Thespis*, New York, 1950

GLUECK, N., *The Other Side of the Jordan*, New Haven, 1945

GORDON, C. H., *Ugaritic Literature*, Rome 1949; *Ugaritic Handbook*, Rome, 1947

GRAHAM, W. C. and MAY, H. G., *Culture and Conscience*, 1936

HOOKE, S. H., *The Origins of Early Semitic Ritual*, 1938

HOSKINS, F. E., *From the Nile to Nebo*, Philadelphia, 1912

JOHNSON, A. R., *Sacral Kingship in Ancient Israel*, Cardiff, 1955

KENNEDY, A. B. W., *Petra: Its History and Monuments*, 1925

LANGDON, S., *Mythology of All Races*, vol. iv, 1931

LAUGHE, R. DE, *Les Textes de Ras Shamra-Ugarit*, Paris, 1944–45

MOWINCKEL, S., *Psalmenstudien*, Kristiana, 1922–24, vols. i–vi

MURRAY, M. A., *Petra, the Rock City of Edom*, 1939

PARROT, A., *The Temple of Jerusalem*, 1955

ROWE, A., *The Four Canaanite Temples at Bethshan*, 1940

SCHAEFFER, C. F. A., *Ugaritica*, Paris, 1939; *The Cuneiform Texts of Ras Shamra-Ugarit*, 1939

SCHMIDT, H., *Die Thronfahrt Jahves am Fest der Jahreswende im alten Israel*, Tübingen, 1927

SNAITH, N. H., *The Jewish New Year Festival*, 1947

TOREZYNER, H., *Lachish I*, 1938

TUFNELL, O., INGE, C. H. and HARDING, L., *Lachish II, The Fosse Temple*, 1940

WATZINGER, C., *Denkmäler Palästinas*, 1933

WRIGHT, G. E., *Biblical Archaeology*, 1957 (with bibliography of articles on the Temple at Jerusalem)

CHAPTER VI

AYYERM, P. V. JAGADISA, *South Indian Shrines*, Madras, 1922

BROWN, P., *Indian Architecture*, Bombay, 1949

BURGESS, J., *Cave Temples of India*, 1880; *Archaeological Survey of Western India*, vol. v, 1883; *Ancient Monuments, Temples and Sculpture of India*, 1897

COOMARANSWAMY, A. K., *History of Indian and Indonesian Art*, 1927

CUNNINGHAM, A., *Archaeological Survey Reports I; The Bhilsa Topes*, 1854

FERGUSSON, J., *History of Indian and Eastern Architecture*, 1910, 2 vols.

FRÉDÉRIC, LOUIS, *Indian Temples and Sculpture*, 1959

HAVELL, E. B., *Indian Architecture*, 1927; *Ancient and Medieval Architecture of India*, 1915; *Handbook of Indian Art*, 1920

HERZEFELD, E. E., *Iran in the Ancient East*, Oxford, 1941

HOLTOM, D. C., *The National Faith of Japan*, 1938

KRAMRISCH, S., *The Hindu Temple*, Calcutta, 1940

MACKAY, E. J., *Early Indus Civilization*, New ed., 1948. *Further Excavations at Mohenjo-daro*, Delhi, 1938

MAJUMDAR, N. C., *Explorations in Sind*, 1934

MALLAYAM, N. V., *Studies in Sanskrit Texts on Temple Architecture*, 1954

MARSHALL, SIR J., *Mohenjo-daro and the Indus Civilization*, 2 vols., 1931; *Guide to Sanchi*, 1918

PARANAVITANA, S., *The Stupa in Ceylon*, 1947

PIGGOTT, S., *Prehistoric India*, 1950; *Art and Architecture of Ceylon*, 1954

ROWLAND, B., *The Art and Architecture of India*, 1953

SAHNI, D. R., *Guide to the Buddhist Ruins of Sarnath*, 2nd. ed., 1926

SHAH, K. T., *The Splendour that was 'Ind*, Bombay, 1930

SHIVAPADASUNDARAM, S., *The Saiva School of Hinduism*, 1934

STEINILBER-OBERLIN, E., *The Buddhist Sects of Japan*, 1938

SUZUKI, D. T., *Manual of Zen Buddhism*, 1950

VATS, M. S., *Excavations at Harappa*, Delhi, 1940

VERNEUIL, M. P., *L'Art á Java*, Paris, 1927

WATTS, A. W., *The Way of Zen*, 1957

YAZDANI, G., *Ajunta*, 3 vols., Oxford, 1931–46

CHAPTER VII

ANDERSON, W. J. and SPIERS, R. P., *The Architecture of Ancient Greece*, revised by W. B. Dinsmoor, New York, 1927

CATON, R., *The Temples and Ritual of Asklepios at Epidauros and Athens*, 1900

COCKERELL, C. R., *The Temple of Apollo at Aegina and Bassae*, 1860

COURBY, M. F., *Fouilles de Delphes*, vols., ii and v., Paris, 1927

DAWKINS, R. M., *The Sanctuary of Artemis at Sparta*, 1929

DEFRASSE, A. and LECHAT, H., *Épidaure*, Paris, 1895

DEUBNER, L., *Attische Feste*, Berlin, 1932

DINSMOOR, W. B., *The Architecture of Ancient Greece*, 1950; *The Temple of Apollo at Bassae*, New York, Metropolitan Museum, IV, 1933

DÖRPFELD, W., *Alt-Olympia*, Berlin, 1935

FARNELL, L. R., *Cult of the Greek States*, vol. iii, Oxford, 1907

FOUCART, P., *Les Mystères d'Eleusis*, Paris, 1914

FOWLER, R. H. and WHEELER, J. R., *Handbook of Greek Archaeology*, New York, 1909

FRAZER, SIR J. G., *Pausanias's Description of Greece*, 1913

GARDINER, E. N., *Olympia: Its History and Remains*, Oxford, 1925

GRINNELL, I. H., *Greek Temples*, Metropolitan Museum of Art, New York, 1943

GUTHRIE, W. K. C., *The Greeks and their Gods*, 1950

HEGE, W., and RODENWALDT, G., *Olympia*, 1936

MARCONI, P., *Agrigento*, Florence, 1929

MURRAY, A. S., *The Sculptures of the Parthenon*, 1903

MYLONAS, G. E., *Eleusis and the Eleusinian Mysteries*, 1961

NOACK, F., *Eleusis*, Berlin, 1927

PATON, J. M., *The Erechtheum*, Harvard University Press, 1927

POULSEN, F., *Delphi*, 1920

POWELL, B., *The Temple of Apollo at Corinth*, A.J.A., IX, 1905

RANDALL-MACIVER, D., *Greek Cities in Italy and Sicily*, Oxford, 1931

ROBERTSON, D. S., *Handbook of Greek and Roman Architecture*, Cambridge, 1943

SMITH, A. H., *The Sculptures of the Parthenon*, 1910

STEVENS, G. P., *The Erechtheum*, Cambridge, Mass., 1927

WALDSTEIN, C., *The Argive Heraeum*, New York, 1902

CHAPTER VIII

ALTHEIM, F., *A History of Roman Religion*, 1938

ANDERSON, W. J. and SPIERS, R. P., *The Architecture of Ancient Rome*, 1927

ANDREN, A., *Architectural Terracottas from Etruscan-Italic Temples*, Lund, 1940

BAILEY, C., *Phases in the Religion of Ancient Rome*, Oxford, 1932

BLAKE, M. E., *Ancient Roman Construction in Italy from the Prehistoric Period to Augustus*, Washington, 1947

CARTER, J. B., *The Religion of Numa*, 1906

DEMAN, E. VAN, *Atrium Vestae*, 1909

FOWLER, W. WARDE, *The Roman Festivals*, 1899; *Religious Experience of the Roman People*, 1911

FRANK, T., *Roman Buildings of the Republic*, Rome, 1924

FRAZER, J. G., *The Fasti of Ovid*, 5 vols, 1929

GRAILLOT, H., *La Culte de Cybèle*, Paris, 1912

GRENIER, A., *Les religions etrusques et romaines*, Paris, 1948

HÜLSEN, C. C. F., *The Roman Forum*, Rome, 1909; *Forum and the Palatine*, New York, 1928

JORDAN, H. *Topographie der Stadt Rom im Alterum*, 3 vols., Berlin, 1906

LANCIANI, R., *The Ruins and Excavations of Ancient Rome*, 1897; *L'Atrio di Vesta*, 1884; *Forma Urbis Romae*, 1893–1901

LUGLI, E., *Roma Antica II, Centro Monumentale*, Roma, 1946

PLATNER, S. B. and ASHBY, T., *A Topographical Dictionary of Ancient Rome*, Oxford, 1929

RIVOIRA, G. J., *Roman Architecture*, Oxford, 1925

ROBERTSON, D. S., *Greek and Roman Architecture*, Cambridge, 1943

RUGGIERO, E. DE, *Il Foro Romano*, Roma, 1913

VITRUVIUS, *The Ten Books on Architecture*, E.T. by M. H. Morgan, Harvard Press, 1914

WISSOWA, G., *Religion und Kultus der Römer*, Leipzig, 1912

WORSFOLD, SIR T. C., *A History of the Vestal Virgins of Rome*, 1932

CHAPTER IX

AGNELLUS, 'Liber pontificalis ecclesiae Ravennatis', Ed. O. Holder-Egger, *Monumenta Germaniae Historica*

BOVINI, G., *Ravenna*, Faenza, 1959

BURTON, R. F., *Personal Narrative of a pilgrimage to El-Medinah and Meccah*, 1855–56

BUTLER, H. C., *Architecture and other Arts* (Syria), 1903

CARRINTON, R. C., *Pompeii*, Oxford, 1936

CECCHELLI, C., *Mater Christi*, Rome, 1946

CRESSWELL, K. A. C., *Early Muslim Architecture*, 1958 (2 vols., 1932–40)

DAVIS, J. G., *The Origin and Development of Early Christian Church Architecture*, 1952

DUCHESNE, L., *Liber Pontificalis*, 2 vols., 1886–92; *Christian Worship: Its Origin and Evolution*. E.T. 4th. ed., 1912

FERRUA, A., and KIRSCHBAUM, J. E., *Explorazione sotto la confessioni di San Pietro in San Pietro in Vaticano, 1940–49*, 2 vols., 1951

HAMILTON, R. W., *The Structural History of the Aqsa Mosque*, Oxford, 1949

HÜLSEN, C. C. F., *The Roman Forum*, 1909

HUTTON, E., *Ravenna*, New ed., 1926

JORDAN, H., *Topographie der Stadt Rom im Altertum*, Berlin, 1912

KRAUTHEIMER, R., *Corpus Basilicarum Christanarum Romae*, Series 2, ii, 1937 ff.

LANCIANI, R., *The Ruins and Excavations of Ancient Rome*, Rome, 1897

LETHARBY, H. and SWAINSON, W. R., *The Church of Santa Sophia, Constantinople*, 1894

Masdjed (Mosques) in *Encyclopaedia of Islam*, vol. iii, New ed. by H. A. R. Gibb and J. H. Kramer, Leiden, 1953

MAU, A., *Pompeii, its Life and Art*, 1899, new ed., 1902

MULLOOLY, J., *St Clement Pope and Martyr and his Basilica in Rome*, 1873

NOLAN, *The Basilica of San Clemente in Rome*, 1910

NORDSTRÖM, C. O., *Ravennastudien*, Stockholm, 1953

RICE, D. J., and HIRMER, MAX, *The Art of Byzantium*, 1959

RICHMOND, E. T., *Moslem Architecture*, 1926

RIVOIRA, G. T., *Roman Architecture*, Oxford, 1925; *Lombardic Architecture*, Oxford, 1933; *Moslem Architecture*, Oxford, 1918

SIMSON, O. G. VON, *Sacred Fortress*, Chicago, 1948

TOYNBEE, J. and PERKINS, J. W., *The Shrine of Peter and the Vatican Excavations*, 1956

VALENTINI, A., *La Patriarcale Basilica Lateranense*, 1836

VITRUVIUS, *De Architectura*, vol. v, 1; vi, 3, 9

VOGUE, DE (Melchior), *Le Temple de Jérusalem*, Paris, 1864

ZIMMERMANN, F. X., *Die Kirchen Roms*, 1935

LIST OF ILLUSTRATIONS IN THE TEXT

CHAPTER IV   *Babylonian and Assyrian Temples*

CHAPTER V   *Sanctuaries in Palestine and the Temple in Jerusalem*

CHAPTER VI   *Indian Temples*

LIST OF PLATES

CHAPTER I *The Palaeolithic Cavern Sanctuaries*

Plate

1   Hand imprint, Castillo, Spain, after Breuil. Upper Palaeolithic.
2   Cave paintings, Lascaux.
3   Black bull, detail of cave painting, Lascaux.
4   Paintings from ceiling of Great Hall, Altamira, Spain. After Breuil.
5   Wounded bison, cave painting, Altamira, Spain.
6   Dying bison and claviform designs, Niaux, France.
7   Bisons modelled in clay. Grotto of Tuc d'Audoubert, France.
8   Clay model of bear. Montespan, France.
9   'The Sorcerer' engraved and painted in black. Les Trois Frères, France.
10 'The Sorcerer', after Breuil, Les Trois Frères, France.
11 The dead man from the Shaft of the Dead Man, Lascaux.
12 'The Venus of Laussel', from rock shelter. Limestone, Laussel, France.
13 Ivory figure from Lespugne, France. *Photo:* Courtesy, Musée des Antiquités Nationales, St Germain en Laye.
14 So-called 'Venus' from Dolni Vestoniče, Czechoslovakia.
15 Ivory head, Brassempouy, France. *Photo:* Courtesy, Musée des Antiquités Nationales, St Germain en Laye.
16 Stone figure, Aegina, Greece. *Photo:* Deutches Arch. Inst. Athens.
17 'Venus' from Grotte des Rideaux, Lespugne, France. *Photo:* Courtesy, Musée des Antiquités Nationales, St Germain en Laye.
18 Skull of Homo Neanderthalensis, La Chapelle aux Saintes. *Photo:* Courtesy, Musée de l'Homme, Paris.
19 Nest of skulls, Ofnet, Bavaria.

CHAPTER II *Neolithic and Bronze Age Sanctuaries*

20 Gold seal ring, Mycenae. National Museum, Athens.
21 Lower Natufian shrine, Jericho. *Photo:* British School of Archaeology, Jerusalem, Jordan.

Plate

CHAPTER III   *Egyptian Temples*

INDEX